THE GOLDEN MAILBOX

How To Get Rich Direct Marketing Your Product

Enterprise • Dearborn
a division of Dearborn Publishing Group, Inc.

While a great deal of care has been taken to provide accurate and current information, the ideas, suggestions, general principles and conclusions presented in this text are subject to local, state and federal laws and regulations, court cases and any revisions of same. The reader is thus urged to consult legal counsel regarding any points of law—this publication should not be used as a substitute for competent legal advice.

© 1992 by Dearborn Financial Publishing, Inc.
© 1988 by Ted Nicholas

Published by Enterprise • Dearborn
a division of Dearborn Publishing Group, Inc.

All rights reserved. The text of this publication, or any part thereof, may not be reproduced in any manner whatsoever without written permission from the publisher.

Printed in the United States of America

92 93 94 10 9 8 7 6 5 4 3 2 1

Library of Congress Cataloging-in-Publication Data

Nicholas, Ted, 1934-
    The golden mailbox / Ted Nicholas.—[Newly rev.]
      p. cm.
    Includes index.
    ISBN 0-79310-486-6 : $39.95
    1. Mail-order business. 2. Direct marketing. I. Title.
HF5466.N53 1992
658.8'4—dc20

92-31853
CIP

Books by Ted Nicholas

The Complete Book of Corporate Forms

The Complete Guide to Business Agreements

The Complete Guide to Consulting Success (coauthor, Howard Shenson)

The Executive's Business Letter Book

43 Proven Ways To Raise Capital for Your Small Business

The Golden Mailbox: How To Get Rich Direct Marketing Your Product

How To Form Your Own Corporation Without a Lawyer for Under $75.00

How To Get a Top Job in Tough Times (coauthor, Bethany Waller)

How To Get Your Own Trademark

Secrets of Entrepreneurial Leadership: Building Top Performance Through Trust and Teamwork

Contents

Preface xi
    Draw on Several Disciplines, xi
    Make Prospects Notice You, xi
    Many Steps Lead to the Finished Ad, xii
    Which Ads Will Work?, xii
    Learn How To Sell, xiii
    If It Works, Don't Fix It, xiii
    A Hard-Easy Job, xiii
    Make Choices, Not Guesses, xiv

Introduction: My Secrets for Direct Marketing Success xv
    Selling Is the Key, xv
    Taking the Plunge, xvi
    Sweet Taste of Success, xvi
    No Sour Grapes, xvii
    A New Challenge Emerges, xvii
    What Makes It Sell?, xvii
    Growing Pains, xix
    Stay True to Your Interests, xix
    Finding the Right Balance, xx
    No Easy Money in Sales, xxi
    Marketing Questionnaire, xxi

Chapter One: Direct Response Opportunities and Pitfalls 1
    Where the Action Is, 2
    Social Trends Helping Direct Sales, 2
    What's Behind It All?, 3
    Express Yourself, 4
    Your First List, 4
    Finding Copy That Sells, 5
    What Your Piece Should Do, 7

Chapter Two: How To Choose Products 9
    Uniqueness Is a Virtue, 9
    Confirm Ideas by Testing Them, 10
    Marketing Madness, 12
    To Market We Go, 12
    Discovering the Right Business Tools, 12
    Promotional Products, 13

Chapter Three: More Ways of Picking Products 16

    Triple Threat for Direct Marketers, 16
    A Quick Check, 17
    Innovative Products Work Well, 17
    How Others Got Started, 18
    Creating Consumer Products, 20
    A Calculated Success, 20

Chapter Four: Direct Marketing Products and Services for the Future 25

    Economic Forecasting, 25
    Profit from Changes, 25
    Create Your Own Future, 26
    Give People What They Want, 26
    Multiple Choice Society, 26
    Why They Buy, 26
    Retailers Also Mail, 26
    Growing Pains for Young Firms, 27
    Nontraditional Direct Mailers, 27
    Give Your Store a Promotion, 27
    Selling Stock, 28
    More Success Stories, 28
    Treasure Hunting, 29

Chapter Five: How To Make Offers That Sell 33

    One Chance To Make a Sale, 33
    Asking the Right Way, 33
    Knock on the Right Doors, 34
    Get Going!, 35
    "Make Me an Offer" Worksheet, 35
    Mix and Match, 37

Chapter Six: Creating a Direct Response Firm 40

    To Market We Go, 40
    Be a Mapmaker, 41
    Have It Your Way, 44
    Seeing Your Business at a Glance, 47
    Adding It Up, 49

Chapter Seven: Cutting and Counting Costs 51

    Little Changes Can Make a Big Difference, 51
    When Marketing, Think Small, 52
    Be King of the Mountain, 52
    Stay in Touch, 52
    Big Profits in Small Markets, 53
    Numbers Game, 53
    Save Money by Mailing Twice, 56
    Study Customer Buying Habits, 57

Chapter Eight: Ways To Help Your Direct Marketing Business Grow 58

Turning Up the Volume, 58
Listen to Your Records, 59
What's All the Promotion About?, 59
Slicing Up Your Business, 60
Markets Ripe for the Picking, 61
Finding Money for Others, 62
Tangible Results, 62
Natural Selling, 66
How To Find Low-Cost Mailing Lists, 66

Chapter Nine: Future Shock for Direct Marketing? 68

Liquid Profits, 68
Slow Path to Success, 68
Truth or Consequences, 70
Marketing To Win, 71
Finding Your Niche, 72
Sales Talk, 73
How To Avoid the Post Office, 74

Chapter Ten: Starting Your Campaign 75

When It Pays To Advertise, 76
Slicing Your Market, 77
Get on the Right Track, 81
Media Round-Up for Direct Sellers, 81

Chapter Eleven: Managing Your Customers 84

Listening to Yourself, 86
Magazine Ad Options, 89
Selling Electronically, 89
Getting the Electronic Order, 91

Chapter Twelve: Testing for Success 92

Marketing in Moderation, 93
What Can You Test?, 93
How Can You Be Sure?, 96
Play It Again, Sam, 97
Ads vs. Direct Mail, 98

Chapter Thirteen: How To Write Copy That Sells 100

Time for a Change, 100
How To Lose Money in Direct Marketing, 101
Keep It Fun, 101
It's All in Your Head, 101
Have I Got a Deal for You!, 102
Nicholas's Copy Mistake Checklist, 105
Strengthen Your Hand, 106

viii   Contents

    Why Did the Chicken Cross the Road?, 106
    What's the Pitch?, 107

Chapter Fourteen: Twelve Ways To Get Your Prospect's Attention 112
    Headline and Teaser Technique Checklist, 112

Chapter Fifteen: Writing Print Ads That Sell 121
    Rule Number One, 121
    Putting It Together, 121
    Will Anyone Remember You?, 122
    Smooth Selling, 123
    Starting To Sell, 124

Chapter Sixteen: Writing Direct Mail Letters That Sell 128
    The Cost of Freedom, 128
    Do It Right, 128
    Building Your Package, 130
    Putting It Together, 134

Chapter Seventeen: How To Get Noticed 146
    Setting the Mood, 146
    Dress Your Mailing Appropriately, 146
    Keeping Artists on Track, 151
    Cataloging Sales, 152

Chapter Eighteen: Managing Production Costs 153
    Cost-Cutting Guidelines, 153
    Picking a Face No One Will Forget, 156
    Spotting Printing Problems, 157
    Other Production Costs, 158

Chapter Nineteen: How To Fulfill Orders 161
    Keeping Things Orderly, 161
    New Methods Aid Cash Flow, 162
    Discovering Fulfillment, 162
    Fulfilling Your Goals, 163
    Letters Perfect, 164
    Test Yourself, 165
    Computerizing Your Business, 166
    Keep Those Cards and Letters Coming, 167

Chapter Twenty: Other Ways of Selling Directly 169
    Not Lonely at the Top, 169
    How To Find New Markets, 170
    Using Public Relations, 173

Chapter Twenty-One: Legal and Ethical Concerns **177**
    Check the Facts in Your Offer, 177
    Be Picture Perfect, 178
    Questionable Selling Tactics, 179
    Telling Customers How To Say "No," 179
    Look at the Picture You're Presenting, 180
    How New Is It?, 180
    Planning for the Impossible, 181

Appendix **185**
    Ted Nicholas Space Ad, 187
    Enterprise • Dearborn Catalog Page, 188
    JS&A Space Ads, 189
    Enterprise • Dearborn Direct Mail Outside Envelope, 191
    Typestyle Samples, 192
    Point Size Chart, 193
    Sample Imposition/Signature, 194
    Envelope Size Chart, 195
    Printer Checklist, 196
    Order Form, 197
    Sample Press Release, 198
    Sample Option Notice, 200
    Sample Renewed Option Notice, 201

Afterword **203**

Index **205**

About the Author **213**

How Ted Can Help You **215**

Preface

You can dramatically boost revenues in your company through effective direct marketing.

I've used the techniques presented in this book in various businesses ranging from candy and ice cream manufacturing and retailing to publishing. It doesn't matter if you are a retailer or a manufacturer. Nor does it matter if you are selling products or services. You don't need a huge marketing budget either. I started with one $90 ad.

My selling strategies, as outlined in this book, are tested and proven. While my ads are studied in college advertising classes, the students usually are not taught why the ads work. The techniques behind these ads are little known in the business world.

Business owners, copywriters, ad managers, teachers and students can profit from this book by being able, for the first time, to learn these techniques.

Draw on Several Disciplines

Results come from combining direct marketing with traditional advertising and marketing techniques; both are essential to a company's growth.

Direct response advertising can best be understood as being *measurable* advertising. First, you get immediate feedback from cash orders, which is especially important in a new business. And, you don't have to worry about guesswork. You'll know which ads are effective by the results.

Traditional advertising is different. Much of it is image-oriented. A company is trying to define the way you view it. IBM, for instance, won't urge you to rush out and buy a computer. Since they have retail distribution, they urge you to go talk to the salespeople in the computer store. IBM doesn't go for the order right away. Instead, they cast themselves as experts, so that when consumers are interested in buying computers, they'll naturally consider IBM.

By contrast, direct response advertising is advertising that can't wait. It can't wait for a consumer to get ready to buy something. If you put a coupon in a magazine and a reader doesn't tear it out right then, you probably don't have a sale. If your prospects later decide that they want what you're selling, they'll most likely go to the local mall to find the item. They probably won't recall when and where they saw your ad.

Make Prospects Notice You

When I had a roadside candy and ice cream store, I designed a billboard that got motorists to stop right away. I couldn't wait until they'd driven another two hours and were a little hungrier. Direct response advertising, to be effective, demands immediate attention.

Advertising agencies tend to sell image—attempting to get prospects to come to the company, and then relying on the firm's salesforce to close the sale. It's indirect selling, which is fine in those circumstances.

When I worked at McCann-Erickson in New York, I'd ask the owner, "Mr. Harper, how can you tell that the advertising we're doing for Buick is the reason people are buying the cars? Don't other factors—such as the economy and the styling of the car itself—enter into buying patterns?" I'd get a response something like this:

"Ted, our surveys aren't absolutely precise, but they indicate that readers are responding to our ads."

I would then ask naive questions such as, "Why don't you put an offer for a brochure into the Buick ads so that interested persons could obtain more information?"

Mr. Harper would respond, "Then the client would know how many people are interested as a result of the ad."

"Sure, isn't that good to know?"

"Well, not in all cases. Because our task as an advertising agency is primarily to sell the product. But we also have to please our client. And we don't want them to be upset if their response to the ads isn't as high as they think it should be."

I'd rather have advertising that you run and you pay for that provides an absolute measurable return on each ad.

Enterprise • Dearborn has advertisements and direct mail campaigns going constantly in different magazines and on various direct mail lists. We know exactly what every dollar spent on advertising produces in sales. We track it. Daily and weekly, a computer compiles the results so we know where our ads and mailings are appearing, and how much income each one is pulling. There's no other advertising that's measurable to that precise degree. It's a wonderful tool. You can compare what you've invested with the dollars returned.

Many Steps Lead to the Finished Ad

It's important that you understand how direct marketing works if you want it to work for you. In this book we'll cover everything from the psychology of selling to how to write and produce ads. Right now you might not realize that not every copywriter or ad agency can write direct response copy. This book contains tips for picking the right person or company to put your ads together.

If you're a small business owner, we'll show you how to use advertising to help plan for your firm's growth. Since direct response ads also track sales, you can find what products are moving. Then you can use that information as a tool for developing new products or services. Companies also grow by planning for the future. If you start a company with one product, you'll soon need to find other items to sell if you want the business to grow. Traditional advertising and marketing concepts will be useful as a business grows. Having a *campaign* approach and using strategic planning will be stressed. If you know where your business is trying to go, you'll get there more quickly.

We'll also look at ways to manage all of the elements of direct marketing to ensure that you're making money. If you're not profiting, you can quickly find out why not. List management, order fulfillment and inventory control will be examined here.

I've started 18 companies, so I know how adaptable these principles are to many different situations. Yet their profitable use depends heavily on your creativity. Give your mind freedom once you understand the basics.

One basic premise is that someone with a good product who can reach prospects can also sell directly to them. Advertising works. It's all around us. It's part of our way of life. It allows us to start a business if we have an idea. Then the people in the marketplace decide if they want our product or service at that price.

Which Ads Will Work?

Advertising doesn't automatically work. There's a lot of competition out there. You drive down the street and see store signs, billboards and bus placards. You turn on the radio and hear jingles, or well-known persons discussing the virtues of various products and services. The same thing occurs on TV, in magazines and in your mailbox.

Which ads will motivate you to spend money— ads that are entertaining, ads that meet your needs or ads featuring people you respect?

Consider the risks involved for the advertiser making the above decisions. There's a lot of money involved. It's expensive to write and produce the ads or mailings and to buy space or lists. But you can make advertising earn money for you. If you do it right, you don't have to risk a lot. In the next chapter, I'll share some personal experiences as an entrepreneur, copywriter and marketing consultant. You'll be able to learn from my actual experiences, most of which I've learned at heavy cost.

Have you ever noticed someone excited about the television show he watched last night? He will talk about it at work the next day, describing the parts that were enjoyable. Good advertising should also create excitement for your product or service. It's not hard to do. TV merely entertains; a good product actually helps people. Advertising informs the public about the important uses of your product. In plain, compelling language your product's benefits are described. Make a good offer, and ask for an order. If a TV show can move people to action, your ads should, too.

Can advertising force people to buy things they don't need? No. You can't force, but you can describe your product's benefits. Tell prospects how it can meet their needs. The market eventually decides your success. Don't let a poor ad or mail piece put you out of the running before you've had a chance to tell your story. Put yourself in a winning position to get a sale.

Learn How To Sell

Advertising is selling on a large scale. You should understand selling before trying to understand advertising. Salespersons like to see four characteristics in their potential customers. If these traits aren't present, a good salesperson will find someone else to talk to. The four characteristics of a good prospect are:

1. Having a need for the product or service
2. Being able to pay for it
3. Having an open mind when listening to the sales pitch
4. Showing a willingness to take action

Salespersons who talk to people who don't need their products are wasting time. For the direct marketer, buying the wrong direct mail list or putting an ad in the wrong publication means that you are wasting money in the same manner.

If you find that your product is considered too costly, refocus your marketing to find different prospects or rewrite the ad so that the product is perceived more valuable. You might try repricing your product. First, check to be sure that your competitors' prices justify the change.

Appeal to prospects who have an open mind and a willingness to take action. This means try to sell to persons who are known respondents to direct marketing. Make a list of your customers; they already know you, your company and your products. Or buy lists of persons who previously have bought by mail. With direct marketing you need to present yourself to many qualified prospects, show them that you meet their needs, put yourself in a good light and urge them to take action.

If It Works, Don't Fix It

A good ad is one that works. For instance, some consumers say they find Proctor and Gamble's "Don't Squeeze the Charmin" ads to be ridiculous. Yet these spots continue to run on television because the ads, starring "Mr. Whipple" as the storekeeper, have been effective in placing in consumers' minds the notion that Charmin is a soft bathroom tissue. Sometimes ads that are seen critically as being more creative or intellectually more clever cause viewers to remember the ad but not the product or company.

You don't have to be a creative genius to be an effective copywriter, but you do have to understand selling. The number of people who have learned to apply the techniques of effective copy are few. It's highly rewarding to the people who are able to do so, since literally millions of dollars worth of sales and profits are available to them.

Such profits also are open to you, the reader of this book, if you begin to apply the techniques of effective copy that we will be discussing here.

Good copy looks like it's very easy to produce. In other words, once it's completed, it looks as though almost anyone could do it because it's so simple. The words and the sentences are short. The thoughts presented in the copy speak directly to the point.

A Hard-Easy Job

It's deceptively simple, actually. That's one of the reasons why almost everyone thinks he or she can just sit down and write effective copy. Professional copywriters know their job is a very difficult skill to perform well. I can apply the same principal to copywriting that applies to selling in general: It's the lowest paid easy job in the world and the highest paid hard job. To do it well requires great effort, skill and much rewriting.

Does that mean that you can't learn the techniques of writing effective copy? No. A lot of people can learn to write effective copy if they choose to and if they spend the necessary time and energy refining their techniques. It isn't necessary to be an excellent writer as much as it helps to be a clear, cogent writer.

Effective copywriting is hardworking salesmanship in print. You have to be an effective salesperson before you can be an effective copywriter. When people ask me what they can do to become effective copywriters, I tell them to: "Learn how to be an effective salesperson first. Then you have a much better chance to write effective copy."

There are more than 220 million people in this country, and 60,000 to 70,000 books published annually. Yet only about 50 copywriters make their living writing direct mail and direct response copy. They make a tremendous living at it.

I know. Since I use direct mail and space ads all the time, I'm constantly looking for ad writing talent. Only about 50 copywriters in the country can consistently sell products through the mail and in space ads. There are also entrepreneurs who write copy for their own companies successfully. If you are going to market through direct response, you have a very limited group of writers from which to hire.

Even in ad agencies, there are very few people who can effectively write direct response copy that works and pulls. When I say that works, I mean that an ad or direct mail package has to bring in enough orders for the advertising to pay for itself, pay for the product and make a profit.

Three main types of material are covered in this book. First, there are the *techniques and theories*. You need to understand what makes direct marketing work before you can fit it to your needs and bring out the creativity your situation demands. Second, there are *true accounts of how direct selling has worked* for me and other businesspeople. Next will come *examples of ads*. You can use them to see what has worked in the past and what *typical* ads are used in different marketing situations.

Make Choices, Not Guesses

Why cover so much? As a writer or manager of advertising you are going to have to pay attention to the selling concept behind your ad as well as the actual words. You'll also be making art, production and media choices. If any one of these elements isn't as good as it could be, your response will suffer—and sales will drop.

If the call to action at the end of the ad or letter isn't right, your coupon response will be down. Plan your ad or letter so that it flows through the needs of your prospects, from your attention-grabbing headline into the lead that backs it up, and down to the offer.

Finally, there are worksheets that have been designed to help you apply what you've learned. What I've written here won't work if you can't apply it to your situation. These worksheets will help you make specific choices guided by what you'll learn in this book. Apply the worksheet results and use your understanding and creativity to mold a campaign that's right for you.

Good luck!

Ted Nicholas
September 1992

Introduction

My Secrets for Direct Marketing Success

At the age of 29 I was a guest at the White House. The year was 1963. I'd never visited the White House before, not even as a tourist. It was thrilling for me. I was there after having been voted one of the two most outstanding businessmen in Delaware by an advisory council to the Small Business Administration.

My trip to see the President really began at a small candy and ice cream store I'd started next to Delaware's Route 40. Advertising and marketing were what made my business noteworthy.

When I started at the age of 21, all I had was $800 in savings and a $5,000 personal loan. Yet because of creative, cost-effective advertising, Peterson's House of Fudge grew. At its peak I had a chain of 30 candy and ice cream parlors in six states. All this happened within six years after I started the first roadside stand.

Eight years later, it was an honor meeting with President Lyndon Johnson, along with representative businessmen from the other 49 states. I'll never forget how exciting it was for me to spend an entire day with the President and his chief advisors!

Little did I expect at the time that soon afterwards I would begin another career as a writer and publisher. I recently sold my publishing company, Enterprise Publishing, (now Enterprise • Dearborn), which at one time had annual sales exceeding $10 million.

Besides being successful, my career has brought me great satisfaction. In addition to starting 18 businesses personally, I've advised hundreds of thousands of other entrepreneurs through *How To Form Your Own Corporation Without a Lawyer for Under $75* and other books.

Selling Is the Key

One reason for my success involved the selection of topics for books and special reports that appeal to the small business market. However, that was only ten percent of the task. The main reason for my success can be attributed to the time and energy that I spent writing effective copy for ads and direct mail pieces after the books were published.

Selling has always intrigued me. That's probably why all of my businesses emphasize marketing as their base.

My interest in selling began in my teens. At that time—as far as I was concerned—the most interesting, financially successful and happy people I knew were salespeople.

I became fascinated with selling. I began working on developing sales skills. As my mastery grew, my confidence soared—especially in my dealings with businesspeople.

As I grew up, selling vacuum cleaners, delivering milk and working in restaurants were my main business activities. My parents owned a small restaurant in Bradley Beach, New Jersey. I was born there in 1934, and from the age of 11 I helped out in the restaurant. I worked behind the counter, waited on tables, washed dishes and did whatever else I could.

Even my schooling was interrupted by business duties. I went to Susquehanna University for one semester before going home when my father became very ill. He had phlebitis and some complications from which he never fully recovered. I felt a need to help out with the family business.

Growing up in a family that owned a small business had a great influence on me. My father had a small candy, confectionery and ice cream department in the restaurant. From the time I was a boy the machinery fascinated me. Making candy and ice cream on my own was something I always wanted to do.

An even greater inspiration to starting my own business came from my Uncle Frank, a successful restauranteur. But before I would be ready to open my own firm I needed to gain even more selling experience. That came while working for New York's McCann-Erickson advertising agency. I was interested in advertising because I knew that good ads were responsible for producing sales. Advertising was super salesmanship, as far as I was concerned, a way to present your firm before lots of potential buyers!

For me it was a big step up from selling vacuum cleaners door-to-door. At that time McCann-Erickson had the Coca-Cola and Buick accounts and was on its way to becoming the largest ad agency in the world. Later it went public as Interpublic. In the process President and Chairman Marion Harper, Jr., and his father, Marion Harper, Sr., made their fortunes.

I started as a clerk. However, both Mr. Harpers seemed to take an interest in me. And amazingly, while I was learning about advertising, I had the good fortune to be given the opportunity to realize one of my longstanding dreams.

Mr. Harper, Sr., and his son had formed quite a few side investments. Money they had made from the advertising agency funded these ventures. One of the investments happened to be a candy and ice cream company called Candy Industries. Because of my background in that business, they sent me to Elkton, Maryland, to become the assistant general manager of this business.

Taking the Plunge

At the age of 21 I was able to become the general manager of their confectionery division. I stayed there for about a year and a half, all the time becoming more fascinated with the idea of having my own roadside candy and ice cream shop.

Finally I found a location. I took my $800 in savings and got a loan for $5,000 to buy a building on Route 40 near a town called Bear, Delaware. At that time Route 40 was the main highway from Wilmington to Baltimore and on to Washington, D.C.

Actually I bought the $50,000 property for no money down, and I got a long-term mortgage. Evidently the owner didn't think it was that valuable a property, and with good reason. Although it seemed like a good location to me, the three previous tenants had gone bankrupt.

Undismayed, I convinced the owner that my enthusiasm made up for what I lacked in the bank. I promised him I would paint and refurbish the property, and if my business succeeded, I would be able to make the payments. If I didn't succeed, at least he would have an improved property, while at the moment all he had was an empty building. He agreed, and I got out my paintbrush.

Of course it takes more than a fresh coat of paint to make and sell candy. The strategy that had worked with the property owner was soon tested with equipment suppliers. I went to equipment companies and told them that since they had used confectionery equipment in their warehouses, they could put it to use in my new shop. If I succeeded, I could pay them every month for the equipment. But if their machinery stayed in storage, they wouldn't even have a chance of making money from it.

Many people turned me down, of course. Eventually I was able to find several equipment suppliers who helped me open my candy kitchens in my newly decorated building. Almost immediately I was making money.

Sweet Taste of Success

The key to the prosperity of that business was really the way that it was advertised. I developed a roadside billboard program featuring the first animated sign in Delaware.

I convinced a local business, The Hessler Sign Co., that if they were to work with me and develop this landmark it would be unique not only to my business, but to theirs as well. Together we made a sign that showed a big chef stirring a large kettle of fudge. It was a 75-foot long billboard that practically stopped traffic as soon as it went up. People had never seen anything like this animated advertisement.

Because of the quality of our candy and ice cream and our novel marketing approach, I was able to open an additional store in each of the next five years. Then I started franchising. I stopped with 24 franchises in addition to the 6 stores I owned. At this time I was also involved in other ventures, including a confectionery machinery company. This was quite a big step for someone who had to work a deal with suppliers to get the equipment for his first store!

No Sour Grapes

Around the time I was being honored at the White House, some circumstances I hadn't foreseen were about to bring the business down around me. But at the same time, that painful process helped me realize what my real talents were.

From its rapid expansion, my candy and ice cream business was highly leveraged. My monthly expenses were high because of the need to repay these borrowed funds. It all worked as long as business was stable or growing. But then a limited access highway bypassed my number one and number two stores. Almost overnight the volume of the chain was cut in half. Without people driving by the roadside stands there was no one to see the billboard and no one to stop at the stores.

I struggled with the situation for two years, and eventually an investor came in and bought me out. I wound up with very little money but was happy to see the business continue.

A New Challenge Emerges

During this time I had a lot of nervous energy, and writing helped me channel this energy in a positive way. Even during the time I was running the candy business I was a big *Letters to the Editor* writer. I sent many letters to editors that were published in some of the world's leading newspapers and magazines. I often thought, "Wouldn't it be wonderful if some day I could get paid for what I do for free?" It seemed like a distant dream.

Part of me always felt that I had some literary ability. I really wanted to combine my interests in psychology and sales with writing. But even after having worked at an advertising agency I wasn't sure that I had the very formidable skills needed to succeed as a writer.

Yet even as I struggled with the problems of my confectionery business by day, I spent evenings and weekends over a two year period writing *How To Form Your Own Corporation Without a Lawyer for Under $75*.

After finishing this book I went the route traveled by many writers. I tried to get a major publisher interested in the work—but I couldn't seem to get a favorable response. Publishers wouldn't buy the idea even after I pointed out to them that most entrepreneurs start with little or no capital, as I had done with Peterson's House of Fudge.

I'm not anti-lawyers, but I do believe that lawyers often overcharge for some services. For instance, I noticed as I formed my 18 companies that my lawyer's secretary just filed a simple form with the state while I was being charged hundreds of dollars for each filing. Tear-out forms in my book solved that problem. They made incorporating simple and inexpensive for new entrepreneurs.

I knew the market for the book was large because if there had been a book like it when I began incorporating my businesses, I certainly would have used it. When the New York publishers had finished turning down the project, I decided to form my own publishing company—Enterprise Publishing. At that time I began the task of getting the book printed, distributed and sold. I began developing and using the direct selling techniques that I used every day with Enterprise Publishing. The company was formed in 1972. In 1973 the first books were published. And, in 1991 I sold Enterprise Publishing to Dearborn Financial Publishing, Inc.

As far as we can determine, *How To Form Your Own Corporation Without a Lawyer for Under $75* has become the largest-selling business book ever promoted through direct mail. More than 900,000 copies are now in print, and the current price of the book is $39.95.

Our first ad appeared in March of 1973—in the classified section of *The Wall Street Journal's* eastern edition. It cost me $90 to run. Because the book was still at the printer, I sent respondents a blue brochure describing the features and benefits of the book. From the $90 ad I got $360 in paid orders. I knew then that I had a viable book and a viable business.

After running that first ad, I realized that every time I ran a slightly larger ad, I got more orders. For the money invested I got a greater return. Within a few months I was running full-page ads in magazines. I was operating out of the corner of my rec room in my home in Wilmington, Delaware, and I was spending $50,000 a month on advertising. Imagine—a national business being run out of a recreation room! Publications such as *U.S. News & World Report, Time, Fortune, Business Week, Dun's Review* and the airline magazines were running ads I'd written for the book.

What Makes It Sell?

I've written about 50 different full-page ads for *How To Form Your Own Corporation Without a Lawyer for Under $75,* 15 to 20 of which have been profitable. One of the ads, using the headline "The Ultimate Tax Shelter," has sold over 200,000 copies of that book. But one thing I soon learned in direct

CERTIFICATE OF INCORPORATION
of

_____

A CLOSE CORPORATION

FIRST. The name of this Corporation is _____

SECOND. Its registered office in the State of Delaware is to be located at _____ County of _____. The registered agent in charge thereof is _____ address "same as above".

THIRD. The nature of the business and, the objects and purposes proposed to be transacted, promoted and carried on, are to engage in any lawful act or activity for which corporations may be organized under the General Corporation Law of Delaware.

FOURTH. The amount of total authorized capital stock of the corporation is divided into _____ _____ shares of _____

FIFTH. The name and mailing address of the incorporator is as follows:

SIXTH. The powers of the incorporator are to terminate upon filing of the certificate of incorporation, and the name(s) and mailing address(es) of persons who are to serve as director(s) until the first annual meeting of stockholders or until their successors are elected and qualify are as follows:

_____
_____
_____
_____
_____

SEVENTH. All of the corporations issued stock, exclusive of treasury shares, shall be held of record by not more than thirty (30) persons.

EIGHTH. All of the issued stock of all classes shall be subject to the following restriction on transfer permitted by Section 202 of the General Corporation Law.
Each stockholder shall offer to the Corporation or to other stockholders of the corporation a thirty (30) day "first refusal" option to purchase their stock should they elect to sell their stock.

NINTH. The corporation shall make no offering of any of its stock of any class which would constitute a "public offering" within the meaning of the United States Security Act of 1933, as it may be amended from time to time.

TENTH. Directors of the corporation shall not be liable to either the corporation or its stockholders for monetary damages for a breach of fiduciary duties unless the breach involves: (1) a director's duty of loyalty to the corporation or of its stockholders; (2) acts or omissions not in good faith or which involve intentional misconduct or a knowing violation of law; (3) liability for unlawful payments of dividends or unlawful stock purchases or redemption by the corporation; or (4) a transaction from which the director derived an improper personal benefit.

I, THE UNDERSIGNED, for the purpose of forming a corporation under the laws of the State of Delaware do make, file and record this certificate, and do certify that the facts herein stated are true; and I have accordingly hereunto set my hand.

DATED AT:_____

_____

Usable forms such as the one pictured above gave my first book, *How To Form Your Own Corporation Without a Lawyer For Under $75*, its unique selling edge.

response marketing was that no matter how well the present *winning* ad is pulling, you need to continue working to beat it with an even better ad.

All ads have a finite life. Some you can run for a few months, some for a couple of years or even longer. In all cases there's a response drop in a successful ad each time it runs.

Approximately 90 percent of the ads for Enterprise Publishing were written by me. But we continued to hire outside copywriters to try to beat the *controls*—or the successful ads and direct mail packages currently being used.

Growing Pains

I've always admired the kind of people who fall in love with the piano at age four, and that's all they ever want to do. I've always enjoyed many different activities. Until I reached my mid-30s, it was difficult finding the time and energy to devote myself to all of my interests. I liked different kinds of businesses. I liked sports. I played a lot of competitive sports in school, and still do, for that matter. Currently I swim, run and play tennis. I've always enjoyed psychology and philosophy. In Wilmington I started several discussion groups on these subjects. I'm also interested in constitutional law.

Although it's nice having so many interests, it's also tough. We can't be experts at everything in life, and we can do only a certain number of things in our work. Part of the reason I went into so many businesses was really a search for what was suited to me.

However, during my mid-30s I had a friend who was an executive with a large chemical firm called ICI Americas. At that time he had just finished taking part in what he felt was the best, most useful career aid he'd ever seen. It was an aptitude test put together by a company called Human Engineering Laboratories. After a week of testing, my friend found out that he really wasn't cut out for the type of executive work he was doing. When you think about it, that's not surprising. I'm sure many people are in situations similar to my friend's.

Stay True to Your Interests

We actually spend less time picking careers in business than we do picking a new car. At least then we'll comparison shop, talk to people we trust and read reports on the autos we like. Often a relative or teacher unduly influences our career choice. I know that one of the reasons I went into the candy business was because both my uncle and father ran restaurants. Just following your interests usually helps you find what you're good at.

It works better than following the example of those around you. If you should be in marketing, you probably like to sell. And every sale you make now is teaching you sales concepts you can apply for the rest of your career.

Copywriters enjoy both writing and selling. You can learn the concepts of copywriting, but you'll never have the flair in your writing that will make your products stand out unless you have an understanding of selling. You have to truly enjoy salesmanship.

Learning and practice also help. No matter how rusty you are at any task when you first try it, you'll always get better through practice and by studying others whose work you respect. As I've said earlier, good copywriting is good salesmanship in print.

One way you can find unique appeals is by understanding what's going on in our world. Find out what other products your customers enjoy. Look at what is having an impact on them, and you'll have more of an understanding of how to sell to them. You'll be able to paint your product or service in an appealing light, as far as your prospects are concerned.

A decade ago many people were interested in living a simple life. They believed they'd find more happiness by forsaking some of what modern culture provides. Natural foods replaced processed meals. Backpacking took on more of an allure than cruises. Whether you agreed with the popular thinking then or not, as a marketer you would need to understand what was happening in many of your prospects' minds.

Today people usually are more interested in having a nice life-style, and they often need to have two paychecks in order to get what they want. You need to understand what is going on and what people are thinking. What's fashionable today? What trends are affecting our lives?

One way to learn these things is by reading. I like to read at least two newspapers daily. *The Washington Post* and *The New York Times* are essential, I think. Additionally, *The Wall Street Journal* offers business and financial news. *U.S. News & World Report* effectively covers trends. *Reader's Digest* provides an overview of the concerns of middle America. Popular books on topics of interest should also be read. A good course in speedreading can be a boon to you since you need time for this type of reading and your regular workload. A copywriter needs to be a generalist in understanding the world, and so does a salesperson.

Finding the Right Balance

All people are different, and their interests and aptitudes will pull them into different lines of work. I found through testing that I need a combination of business management and creative work to feel happy. I actually split my week now by having a place where I write ads and another spot from which I run my company. Since you are uniquely different from me, the work you enjoy will be different. But we can use similar techniques to discover what's best for us. We're all happiest when doing work that we're good at—work that interests us for which we have an aptitude.

To help you apply the techniques and ideas in this book I periodically have inserted worksheets to help you put the principles I'm talking about to work in your specific situation. The first set of worksheets is based on a technique attributed to Benjamin Franklin. I think you'll find them useful.

• • •

1. Draw a line vertically down the center of a piece of paper. On one side of your dividing line put a *plus* sign. On the other side, place a *minus* sign. Under the plus sign list all your positive skills. Beneath the minus sign write your weaknesses.

The idea behind this exercise is to identify your traits so that you can concentrate your daily efforts on your strong areas. If you're good at making sales projections, stick to that. Don't try to force yourself to be a hands-on people manager.

When a small person tries to pick up a sofa or other large object, observers consider that person foolish. It's obvious to all that he or she is taking on a job better left to someone stronger. Too often people make similar mistakes in their jobs. However, the contrast isn't as outwardly striking as when a weakling attempts to lift a large weight.

Others often applaud people trying to do what they can't, saying that it's great to try. Or they merely shake their heads and talk about the *Peter Principle*. You're wasting your time if you get caught in a similar situation. Build on your strengths. In business you can find others to take up the tasks you don't excel at. In Chapter 3 you'll even use this exercise to help choose products or services to bring to market.

Start by listing your skills. Be concrete. What are your demonstrated abilities? Are you a manager, an accountant or a salesperson?

In order to find the career best suited to you, try to go beyond a simple listing of skills. List your personal characteristics. Are you a person who likes to make decisions? Or would you prefer that your job emphasize helping others? Answers to these questions can hold the key to discovering your dream job. Soon we'll look at a method for turning your self-knowledge into a better understanding of where and how you should work.

2. Our next exercise emphasizes the fact that the path you've been on is probably going to help determine your next job. Start by listing what jobs you've held previously. Of course, this could look much like a resumé. The question you need to ask yourself while doing this exercise is: "What is all this leading to?" You're trying to find hints of what the next step is in your personal development.

Don't emphasize the resumé form. You'll get more out of this step by writing a biography than by listing past jobs. Try to get a sense of a current flowing through your life, expressing itself in the various positions you've held.

At the same time, jot down acquaintances or associates who might help you now. You need information to make decisions. Use the people and groups you know to get that information. You'll save time that way; you won't have to do all your research by yourself. Rely on others who are knowledgeable. They might know of some career twists you never thought of, or they might have an idea based on a currently available business opportunity.

Don't just call someone up and ask if they know of anyone who has a job. Instead, meet informally. Let your business associates know that you're looking to get into something else. Review your background with them and your reasons for wanting a change. Tell them the type of job you think you're looking for.

Naturally they'll respond within the context of their work. You'll then have a source within a specific field. With their help you can decide if what you're looking for is in that industry. Perhaps they'll even know of someone who is doing what you'd like to do, and can refer you to that person.

3. While you're gathering *realistic* information on career possibilities, don't forget to dream. In fact, aptitude test centers and career counselors agree that the best way to learn someone's preferred career is simply to ask them what they'd like to be doing for work.

This is a very powerful tool when combined with a knowledge of your past achievements and your character traits. Within that context, your dreams will probably be realistic.

Once you've stated a goal, you'll most likely find that the means of reaching it pops into your mind. If you want to do a certain kind of work, ways of making it happen will occur to you. All this comes up after you have specifically chosen a dream.

Direct marketing helps many dreams come true. Those who understand the power of direct marketing can be more successful than they ever imagined possible. You can operate a national firm while working out of your home. I did that for many years, although now I have two outside offices. With only five persons on our marketing staff, Enterprise Publishing has sales in the millions of dollars annually.

No Easy Money in Sales

Don't misunderstand me. Direct marketing isn't a get-rich-quick scheme. You have to know what you're doing. And you must do it right. Attention to detail is essential. Let me give you an example:

"Half-price!"

"50 percent off!"

"Buy one—get one free!"

Look carefully. Do you think these phrases all say the same thing? You won't think so if you're a direct marketer. You'll test responses to these offers to see which one pulls in the most orders. One might give you that little extra pull on readers that makes for a winning direct mail package.

Once you've got a good marketing piece, it becomes your *control*. Keep running your control. Successful direct marketers then take two more steps. First, they refine their control by testing other aspects of the piece. Your efforts are highly leveraged. If you're advertising in a publication with only 100,000 readers, a small response increase means a lot of money to you. Suppose you're selling a $20 item. If you can increase your response from one-half percent to one percent, you'll bring in an additional $10,000 on that one ad. Small improvements in response have big effects in direct selling.

Second, a good marketer will test new packages. Try to find packages that work even better than your control. Every marketing piece has a limited effective life. Constantly test new appeals and approaches.

Before paying for any ads or mailings, make sure that you can sell your product or service at a profit. For instance, I thought I could save entrepreneurs money by showing them how to form a corporation without paying legal fees. Still I went through a grid like the one below, to make sure my thinking was straight.

Marketing Questionnaire

1. What is my product or service?
2. What is my target market for sales?
3. How will I reach that market to sell to them?
4. Who are my competitors in that market? Describe their marketing plans. What is the price of their product or service?
5. What is the cost I'm charging for my product or service? Is it profitable for me to enter this market? Look at the competition, the size of the market and the strength of their need.

Make sure the business can be profitable for you. Start by listing the basic cost you pay for the product or personal service, the expected marketing costs, mailing and fulfillment costs and other expenses for running the business. Expect your marketing responses to be as follows: one percent for direct mail and one-half of one percent for space ads.

Now let's see if you're really making money on the $20 offer you hypothetically made. Let's say the ad costs $10,000 to run. Your product costs you $5 each, with another $3 apiece for mailing and overhead. If you have 1,000 responses, you'll bring in $20,000. Subtract $10,000 for the ad and $8,000 for your fixed costs. You have a profit of $2,000 before taxes. That's not bad, but not great, either.

In this book you'll find out how to improve those numbers by learning how to write better ads and direct mail pieces, by choosing mailing lists and media buys with stronger results and by saving money on inventory and mailing. But, first we'll take an overview of the industry to help you see where you fit in.

Chapter One

Direct Response Opportunities and Pitfalls

Direct response marketing is the most cost-effective means of selling anything to anyone. That's because direct response sells—period. Your purpose in direct response marketing is not to tell prospects about your company, nor to get people to come into your store.

What you want to get are orders, and you can test your product, your market and your offer at the same time. Ads or mailing pieces can be targeted to audiences you think are most likely to respond. Subsequent responses can be tracked so that you know where every order comes from. Keeping accurate response records lets you determine the profit or loss of any ad or mailing.

Direct response marketing looks simple. Although you don't need a big budget or a national name to start out, it takes an organized, creative mind to start bringing orders in quickly. If you can't generate immediate responses, you'll soon be out of business.

Direct response is market-driven. It teaches you not to be too stubborn about your own ideas. If something doesn't work, drop it and go on. In fact, you should test everything in the marketplace before making a business commitment to it.

Let me give you an example. Suppose you take a trip to Hong Kong and find a unique desk organizer manufactured there. Do you immediately order 1,000 and stock them in your basement? No. First find out the price. Then come home and put together a marketing campaign. Test ads in consumer magazines. Mail special offers to office supply wholesalers and to corporate purchasers. See what your response is. If the product has a market at a profitable price, order stock from Hong Kong.

You can't take this idea too far. One of my friends in the newsletter business tells me that when his firm comes up with a proposal for a new publication, the first thing they do is test it with a direct mail offer. If they get enough subscribers to make it worthwhile, they find an editor and start the newsletter.

Of course, there are legal limitations to this approach that must be observed. Under the Mail Order Rule, the Federal Trade Commission (FTC) has set guidelines for the shipment of mail order goods. When a shipping delay occurs, direct marketers are required to tell customers about the delay. In addition, customers must be given the option of either agreeing to the delayed shipment or canceling the order and promptly receiving a refund.

The FTC requires that when making your offer, you must have a "reasonable basis" for expecting to ship within the length of time stated in your marketing material. If you don't state when you'll ship, you must do so within 30 days of receiving a "properly completed" order—one containing payment and all the information needed to process the order. If you can't produce, an "option" notice must be sent to the customer.

Explain why there's a delay—such as a shipper's strike or not having enough goods in stock. Send the notice soon after you know there will be a delay. The FTC stipulates that you must notify customers of delays *prior* to the original shipment deadline. Other regulations cover what you must do if it appears you'll miss your revised shipping time. At that point, customers must write and tell you they agree to a second delay, or else their orders must be canceled by you and their money refunded by first class mail within seven days of cancellation.

All delay notices also must be sent by first class mail. You also must provide a prepaid post card or other means of letting your customers reply concerning their choice of options.

Additionally, keep records on how your firm responds to any shipping delays or customer complaints. If the FTC ever investigates your firm, you'll be able to show that you've complied with the Mail Order Rule. In Chapter 21 you can learn about other areas of potential regulatory concern to direct marketers. You'll also find samples of option notices provided by the FTC.

Where the Action Is

Direct marketing is big business. Just consider Sears, Roebuck & Co.'s estimated $1.8 billion in annual catalog sales. Can you find a niche in this market with a special product or service of your own? I believe so, since many others are doing it.

In fact, the mail order business is growing much faster than retailing. Revenues are increasing more for direct marketers than for retailers. And retailers have the overhead responsibilities of paying rent on a store and making payroll. Today many retailers are becoming direct marketers—and vice versa. These people have the best of both worlds.

Many forces account for the growth of direct response marketing. In looking at the reasons for this growth we can see that the upward trend should continue. Note the following trends:

1. *More women are working than ever before.* More than 50 percent of all married women are currently employed. After spending the day on the job, they don't want the hassle of fighting traffic in order to shop. They don't want to have to look for parking when they can order through the mail. Because they are working all day, they don't need the "social experience" of going shopping. Shopping has become a chore for many; it's no longer an excuse to get out of the house for awhile.

2. *Everyone has charge cards.* Although first established to help retailers, charge cards make shopping by mail easier. A customer doesn't have to write a check before ordering, and the merchant knows that payment will be received for the goods being shipped.

3. *Poor workmanship makes money-back guarantees more important.* Consumers have become more wary, and they will continue to be cautious. We live in a time when cars are recalled by Detroit. Buyers realize that going to the showroom and kicking the tires doesn't guarantee a car will work. Such a dilemma makes the money-back guarantee—offered by virtually all direct marketers—an important selling tool. When the buyer knows that an item can be sent back for any reason, he or she will have confidence in buying by mail, and be encouraged to do so.

4. *Retailing is expensive.* Often someone buying through the mail can save money, because the direct marketer has fewer expenses.

Successful retailers are generally in shopping malls. Impulse buying is encouraged in that setting. A customer can go shopping with the thought of only buying new shoes. In a mall the shopper might also buy some cologne, a record, batteries, pharmacy items, magazines or a meal before coming home.

The concept of mall shopping is an effective marketing formula. The cost of renting space in such an environment, however, is high for retailers, who then have to raise prices accordingly. Many of the items found in malls can be sold less expensively by direct marketing.

Social Trends Helping Direct Sales

Consumers can save time by ordering at home rather than traveling to a store. That convenience is important when both partners in a marriage are working. It's no wonder that direct mail selling is growing 50 percent faster than traditional retailing.

Other trends make direct marketing more cost-effective to the seller. These developments are expected to continue in the future:

1. *Special interest publications are growing in number and diversity.* In the 1960s most magazines appealed broadly. The *Saturday Evening Post, Life, Look* and *National Geographic* all had many readers with widely diverse backgrounds. A seller with a specialized product couldn't advertise effectively. Many of the readers wouldn't be good prospects to buy. However, today a direct marketer can target appropriate advertising more easily, choosing between *Runner's World* and *Bon Appetit*.

2. *A similar situation exists in the direct mail industry.* The growing use of computers has made the acquisition of information less expensive. In particular, finding names of prospects has become cheaper. Computers are ideal for storing names and making changes in mailing lists.

3. *Computers are becoming sales tools.* Consumers can shop with their computers now. Using the same technology as online databases, a computer user can order from an electronic catalog. Direct response marketing allows a small firm to offer good prices to prospects all across the country.

Local companies can gain entry to potential customer bases nationally. Although this is a relatively new trend, the effects will continue to grow, helping the direct marketing industry.

4. *Despite popular criticism, the United States Postal system has improved.* The establishment of the universal use of zip codes 20 years ago also helped the mailing list industry. List makers can target neighborhoods with average family incomes in any range a marketer wants.

Because of these trends, direct marketing is a good place to make money today. Even the retailers know this. Macy's-by-Mail, for instance, started off as a service to the department store's local customers. Over the years it grew into a profit center with loyal customers all over the country.

Businesses selling to other businesses are also using direct marketing as the cost of keeping a sales force rises. Telemarketing, for example, can reinforce mail campaigns to businesses. It's a lot cheaper than paying travel costs for a group of salespersons.

Computer equipment and office supplies are the strongest-selling business products by dollar volume for direct marketers, yet you can sell almost anything through the mail. Very successful direct marketing is done for products ranging from clothes to food to insurance to charitable and political fundraising.

What's Behind It All?

Officially, direct marketing is said to have begun when Montgomery Ward sent out its first mail order catalogs in 1872. I would say it started about 100 years earlier. At that time colonists nailed *broadsides* in public places to list their political beliefs. In the 1770s our ancestors used direct techniques to "sell" the idea of freedom.

Today marketers can choose to sell via phone, mail, print ads or electronic media. The idea is still the same—put your message before an *interested* audience. Be effective. Offer a specific plan of action. Make sure all of these elements are in place, and watch the results come in.

Mail order sales have increased 30 percent in the past five years according to Arnold Fishman of Marketing Logistics in Lincolnshire, Illinois. Current at-home consumer product mail order sales are estimated at $65 billion annually. Marketing Logistics publishes both *The Annual Guide to Mail Order Sales* ($525) and *The Annual Guide to Telemarketing* ($475). For further information about these publications, call (708) 634-4700.

Direct marketers understand that consumers are changing. Today consumers look for special products, and they expect to have their specific needs and desires met by merchants. The Coca-Cola Company is evidence of this broad-based consumer trend.

Originally *Coke* was one soft drink in a six-ounce bottle. Today there's also *New Coke, Diet Coke* and *Tab*. You can get all beverages with or without caffeine, in 6-ounce, 12-ounce, 16-ounce, 24-ounce or 48-ounce glass, plastic or aluminum containers. Why does Coca-Cola go to the expense of offering so many choices? Consumers expect them. What traditionally has been called the *mass market* is little more than a conglomeration of specialized markets, each with its own distinct product needs.

What does this trend mean for direct marketers? It means that you sell specialized products by finding the group to which your product appeals. You don't need traditional mass marketing backup to sell a product nationally.

Suppose you are selling holiday cookie cutters. You can try to get K mart or J.C. Penney's to stock them in their stores. You can put an ad in a magazine such as *Good Housekeeping*, or you can buy a mailing list of persons who previously purchased culinary items through the mail.

If you can make your customers remember you, you'll be successful. That's why direct marketing so often uses special offers and guarantees. You want the buyer to have confidence in both the product and the company behind it. You want them to feel as though they got a good deal. It's very important in direct marketing to cultivate a base of clients.

In fact, you won't make nearly as much money if you don't have repeat customers. Here's why: You pay for a mailing list. You pay to have your package printed. Finally you pay for postage. And what happens? One or two percent of those receiving the package buy.

Now I'm not knocking those results. You can make good money that way.

Once you've spent quite a bit of money finding customers, don't let them go. Sell them something else. Make them a good offer. Keep at them until you've convinced them to buy from you again. Your best prospects are always your current customers. That's true in any business, and in direct response, it's much cheaper to sell to customers who already know you and your products than it is to send blind letters to another mailing list.

Although that might seem obvious to you, almost everyone who starts in the mail order business realizes that fact only after a period of time elapses. You'd be amazed at how many successful direct marketers will tell you about their early days when they threw away the names of customers after orders were mailed out.

Express Yourself

Within direct marketing there's plenty of room for imagination. I'd say there's even a demand for it. You have to be able to respond to the needs of the marketplace. More than any other medium, direct marketing has few restrictions. That's especially true with direct mail. Television ads, for instance, are limited by their length. Space ads are limited by page size. Yet a direct mail package can be as long as you like. It can unfold to any size you want. You can choose it to be a simple letter or a full catalog.

Most of all, you can make a specific offer and give the prospect a simple means of ordering. You can get the money right away. That's an effective business tool. You can pay for your mailing or ad from sales revenues that come in right away.

Today direct marketers sell everything from tulips to cosmetics. Clothes, electronics, fruit and porcelain figures are also successfully marketed with direct response. It doesn't matter if you want to sell tools or lingerie, you can be a direct marketing hero.

Countless direct response success stories can be cited. More occur all the time. There's absolutely no reason why you—armed with the information in this book—can't make more money with direct marketing than you've dreamed possible.

Let's pause for a moment, and look at the downside. What are you risking as you go into direct marketing? How much could you lose if your plans went awry?

Suppose you've found a product you're sure is a winner. To get the jump on any competition you take out the biggest ad you can in a national publication. Of course, you borrow money to pay for the ad, expecting orders to come in that will more than cover your expenses. And then nothing happens. What do you do then?

Now that is a problem. Let's look at a way around it that direct marketers always use. First, you have to learn to test everything. You let the market make decisions for you, and you go with that wisdom. What that means is that you don't jump in with both feet.

Do a small ad or mailing to test your product. If it shows promise, then *roll out*, or increase your marketing to the groups that bought from you in the test.

Your First List

Persons just starting in direct marketing need a base. It's nice to begin with a group of customers you believe will buy from you. One way to acquire a base is to start with a small, hand-picked list. As you move along in direct marketing you'll have to use large lists purchased from a broker. For now try to come up with at least a few hundred names of people who either already know you or are qualified prospects. Here are some ways to form that *base* list:

1. Use the names of current customers, friends and relatives.
2. Go to your competitors. You'll be surprised how many of them will sell or even give names away that they aren't going to use.
3. Use a local telephone directory. With a reverse directory you can collect the names of all homes or businesses on any given street. If you think your product would appeal to persons or firms in a certain neighborhood, try this technique.
4. For business to business selling, go to a professional, trade or association directory. Credit bureau rating books and the *Yellow Pages* in your local phone directory can also steer you to target businesses.
5. For some products you might be able to find prospects by compiling names from official listings. Permits for new buildings and birth announcements are examples of target lists that are in the public domain.

Since response rates to mailings are often one percent or less, your lists must have more than 100 names in order to determine if you've located a useful group of prospects. Some of your hand-picked lists might be smaller, but try to keep the numbers as high as possible.

You can see that direct response takes a commitment. Putting together a list and a mailing is a big project. Either enter the names into a database management program on a personal computer, or put together a manual list on label masters. You can run the labels through a photocopier whenever you want to put out a mailing.

As orders come in, take the time to find out who your best customers are. Divide your list so that your favored clients are separated out. This is much easier to do if you have a computer, but you can still stay up-to-date with your list even if you use 3 x 5 filing cards. Get someone on your staff to code the cards. Coding is a means of collecting marketing data on your direct response customers.

Usually lists are coded by three criteria: recency, frequency and dollar amount of orders. Recency is simple. Mark on your card the date of the last order. Your most recent customers are your best prospects for another sale. Why? Your name and products are familiar to them, they like your product, feel a need for it and can afford what you're selling.

The frequency coding shows how often a customer has ordered over any time period—information which is meaningful to you. Dollar amounts are listed for the size of their orders over the same time period.

Generally your strategy will be to keep mailing to your most recent customers. As their orders become less frequent and dollar volumes grow smaller, make an extra special offer to encourage a fresh order from your customers.

Accurate coding is also a key. Your biggest single cost in direct response is the cost of finding customers and getting their first orders. Once you've found people who will buy from you, don't let them go. A list of 100 current customers is worth more than a list of 5,000 people who have never heard of you.

As you code your lists for recency, frequency and dollar amount, also make any address changes that come in with orders. If you are compiling lists from telephone or professional directories, update your lists every time a new directory comes out. You might think it's not worth the trouble for a few names, but your lists need to be as accurate as possible. You will be throwing money away if you mail to incorrect addresses. Mailing lists as a rule contain five percent wrong addresses, simply because people move so often that it's impossible to be totally accurate. Work to keep that figure as low as possible, since you're paying for the mailings.

Let the Postal Service help you here. Print on third-class mailings, "Address Correction Requested." The Post Office will charge a small fee, but they will give you new addresses or let you know why a letter was undeliverable. If your mailing piece weighs more than six ounces, also print on the envelope "Return Postage Guaranteed" with the first message.

After putting together a list, you have to decide on your offer and come up with a compelling way to present it. I don't necessarily mean that you have to spend a lot of money. Many successful direct marketing campaigns started with classified ads, but, mind you, they were compelling classified ads.

Finding Copy That Sells

I'm an entrepreneur who also does my own direct marketing work—writing almost all of my own ads. My advice to you then might seem a little strange. From my own experience and from talking with other direct response experts, I'd suggest finding a company or person who understands direct response to help you put together your package.

Even if you're very good at selling prospects one-on-one, you should have an experienced direct response person helping you. Ads and direct mail have their own special means of making customers buy.

Before you retain an ad agency or copywriter, make them prove to you that they have successful experience in direct response. If they don't, keep looking. Advertisers who are good at broadcast ads or company image ads might not be effective direct marketers. Resist the temptation to "save money" by hiring a Journalism or English major just out of school. All you'll be doing is paying them to make mistakes. It could be a great experience for the new graduate but won't generate much business for you. Mailings and ads are expensive. Protect your investment by hiring a pro to do the work. A good copywriter can present your merchandise so that people want to buy.

Reinforce the importance of copy within your organization. Talk to your financial people. Make sure they don't get upset because you're spending $5,000 to $25,000 or more for a four-page direct mail letter. The real test is the bottom line. If that letter pulls, just keep mailing it and bringing in orders.

Before you talk to ad agencies, understand the different people you'll be meeting. First is the Account Executive (AE), who is primarily a salesperson. He or she will be your contact with the agency and will do whatever is needed to keep you happy. AEs usually will advise on overall marketing. Sometimes they also will assist in writing your ads or direct mail pieces.

More often they will assign a copywriter and artist in their office to write and design your pieces. Make sure to give the AE and creative staff as much input as possible about your product and market. With that information they can better construct winning ads, letters and brochures.

An agency will save you time by coming up with your marketing plan, putting together the specific pieces, producing them and choosing the specific media to advertise in or recommending mailing lists. Of course, you'll pay for these services.

Agencies make money in three ways. First, they receive a 15 percent commission for placing ads. In other words, if you place a display ad in your local paper through an agency, the commission is subtracted from the space bill. Only ad agencies receive these commissions from the paper. If you placed the ad yourself, you would pay the full amount.

One reason agencies receive commissions is that they are responsible for paying for the ads. A retailer might not pay the newspaper quickly for an ad, but an agency will, since it works with local papers all the time. Also the paper wants to reward the agency for urging its client to put an ad in the newspaper. Finally, the paper recognizes that an ad put together by an agency will meet its product specifications, and should look better than an ad done by a nonprofessional.

If you place enough ads, the agency might get enough money from commissions for compensation. If your *billing*, or total amount of advertising purchased, isn't high enough, the agency might also charge a monthly retainer fee. Or, if you choose not to commit to the agency for any length of time, they can quote a project fee. Often you can get a good start in direct response with just a few mail pieces or ads to test. Finally, the agency will add about 17 percent onto their art production costs.

Ad agencies are set up to produce print and media ads. A single consultant who specializes in direct response often is the best choice for many firms. Again, make sure that the consultant or freelancer you pick has substantial direct marketing experience, preferably with products or services similar to yours.

You can look in several places for such a person. Find out if any copywriters from an ad agency or company that puts out direct response pieces will do free-lance work. Look in the *Yellow Pages* under "Advertising—Direct Mail" for direct response specialists. Or call the Direct Marketing Association (212) 768-7277 for a list of free-lance copywriters in your area. Look for writers with experience in your industry. Find them by asking other companies like yours for suggestions. Trade journals and industry directories are also sources for names of copywriters.

Once you have the names of copywriters, ask them for samples. Tell them about your product or service. Ask to see the ads or mailing pieces they've written on similar products that are now the *control* pieces for other companies. Control ads are the ones with the best responses. A firm uses its control pieces as benchmarks; other ads or mailings are compared in their effectiveness to the control.

Also ask for professional references. Find out from the copywriter's references if his or her work brought in orders. Before interviewing a copywriter, prepare a packet for the writer containing the following information:

- Specifications of the product, or a description of the service—Include pictures of the product or of persons using the service.
- A profile of the markets you're selling to now, and other markets you think are worth exploring
- A full description of your competition—What types of marketing do they use? Are there differences in price, quality, offer or distribution between you and your competition?
- A copy of your standard sales pitch—Include most common objections used by prospects, and how the salesperson overcomes them.
- Letters from product users that could serve as testimonials
- Current ads and brochures—Note which ones worked and which didn't.

When meeting with a free-lancer, watch reactions carefully. You're looking for excitement. If the writer doesn't get excited about your product, he or she probably won't get anyone else excited, either. You need excitement to get readers to buy.

Notice whether or not the writer asks you questions. If he or she is hungry for information, there's a good chance your market will benefit.

Make sure that your writer understands your prospects as well as he or she understands your product. One of the biggest mistakes you can make is writing with a *me* message. Your copy should always tout your product's benefits from *the customer's point of view*. Don't talk about how great your product, service or company is. Instead, tell how it can solve problems or meet needs faced by your prospects. If your writer doesn't know what those needs are, he or she probably won't develop an effective package for you.

Once you find a good writer, you'll probably need to pay him or her a retainer fee to start the project. The writer will need cash flow while taking the time to work for you. Usually you'll pay a flat fee plus 2.5 percent to 5 percent of gross sales for the work. Copy rates for a full-page ad or a direct mail package can run from $2,000 to $50,000, depending on the writer's experience.

Direct mail writers often prefer to receive a few cents commission for every letter you mail or every dollar you receive from a print ad. Such a deal gives the writer an incentive to put extra effort into the project. The better it is, the more you'll use the promotion, and the more money the writer will make. Always plan ahead. Anticipate your copy needs—the best writers are booked months in advance.

Retain control over the project by seeing it in draft form. Ask for a rewrite if you're not totally satisfied. The difference between good writing and great writing often comes from rewriting. Every word should be weighed for its contribution to selling your product or service.

In my opinion, some of the best examples of American writing in this century are found in good sales copy. It always amazes me when people talk about so-called "junk mail." Some of the work they disdain contains the premier examples of writing in our country today. I think deep down people realize that. When they're asked if they want to be removed from a mailing list, most people prefer to stay on. It may be that they just like getting mail and enjoy seeing the offers. But I still believe that the writing of ad copy is a unique art form.

No matter how successful you are with one writer, keep trying others. Someone else might have a new approach or a clearer benefit to offer. If you're in direct response, keep testing. Try to find a mailing package or ad that can top your best to date. If you want your company to grow, your efforts have to keep improving.

What Your Piece Should Do

You can start a national company without a large sales force or a big store by letting direct response sell for you. More and more companies are seeing the positive uses of direct response. Effective direct marketing offers the following advantages:

1. *A good marketing piece will clearly state your product's position in the marketplace.* You will be easily discernible from your competition. Everyone reading your material should understand what unique benefits your product or service offers. If the differences between yourself and your competitors aren't obvious, get a new copywriter.

2. *You can target specific audiences for your marketing material.* Media and mailing lists can be targeted by profession, geographic area, hobbies or income. You can show different appeals to different markets. Suppose you're selling electronic gear. A professional market might need a more technical approach than would a target of hobbyists.

You also can use direct marketing to test new markets. Don't allow yourself to think that any potential sale is closed to you. You can always reach someone through the mail, over the phone, or in a publication that they read.

3. *Direct response makes buying easy.* Ease of purchase encourages repeat purchases. Make sure your copy leads prospects to make orders. Also check that your coupon or ordering information is clear and easy to use. Do whatever you can to make sure your customers buy more than once from you.

4. *When done right, direct marketing is predictable.* You'll know at about what level your results should average out. With that information, you can manage your cash flow. Inventories also can be controlled when you can predict orders.

You'll anticipate your marketing costs, and you can easily test new products on your current customers. Enclose new product offers either in current bills to customers or in special mailings.

What if your first ad doesn't pull enough to meet your costs? Do you forget about direct response, figuring that you don't have what it takes? Do you run the ad again, and risk throwing good money after bad?

Many persons and companies face such a dilemma. Remember, however, that the greatest cost in mail order is getting that first order.

Of course you've seen the ads in catalogs and magazine classified sections offering address labels at a very low price. I doubt that those companies made money on their first sale—especially since they must individually prepare each new set of address labels. They can, however, have repeat label sales, and they can offer letter openers, personalized pencils and other items for sale to the same customers.

Have a plan when starting direct response marketing. Don't just randomly throw a bottle into the sea and hope it comes back. Commit to the process. If your first ad doesn't work out, start testing new ads to see what does work. Try different lists or media. Try new offers. And always keep going back to however many customers you have for subsequent sales.

Results hinge on your offer. If you can make a great offer, just announcing it to the right people in even a very small ad will bring back good results. In the next chapter we'll look more closely at which offers work—and why.

Before you begin marketing let's take a quick overview of the regulations and laws you'll have to understand. Probably the most important are postal regulations. Go to your local Post Office to check on rates and envelope sizes before doing a mailing. You also can request the weekly *Postal Bulletin* at no charge from the United States Postal Service. In it are described changes in mail service and rates. To get the full picture, buy the *United States Postal Service Manual* from the Superintendent of Documents, Government Printing Office, Washington, DC 20402.

In general, advertising and direct mail are protected by the First Amendment, which guarantees freedom of speech. You must make sure your product claims and descriptions are accurate. If not, you might be visited by the Federal Trade Commission. If your plan is to sell food through the mail, check Food and Drug Administration regulations first. Write the FDA at 5600 Fishers Ln., Rockville, MD 20857.

Find out whether a state sales tax or federal excise tax is required for your product. Also, check to see if your state has fair trade laws, which set minimum prices for goods. Most mail order products, however, aren't fair trade items.

Usually you won't need a permit or license to start a mail order business. You might have to register your company name, if you use one, with your city or state clerk. If you use a company name, you should check with your city or county to ensure that no zoning ordinance prohibits you from getting company mail at a home address. Register your company name at the Post Office so that your business mail will get delivered.

You can get around all of these possible restrictions by using just your personal name when starting a mail order business. You might find that your customers enjoy ordering from a person rather than a company. Try to use a real address, rather than a postal box number. You're trying to build a personal sales relationship with customers, and using a box number could make you seem less human to them.

I strongly advise that you incorporate yourself. The tax breaks and limited liability are just two of the many important reasons why even one-person mail order companies should incorporate.

One of the theories behind direct marketing is that most people enjoy getting mail. Make letters as personal as possible. Talk to people about their needs, and show them something you're selling that can help them. Remember, you're competing against the sales clerk in a local store. You have to get the attention and trust needed for a sale without being face-to-face.

Chapter Two

How To Choose Products

You can make lots of money in direct response, but first you need a product or service to sell. How do you discover a product with direct response potential?

Almost anything can be sold through direct response. However, the key is to find a product that suits you. That sounds easy, doesn't it? The exercise isn't as obvious as it seems.

Look at your background. Consider what you have going for you that others don't. How can you profit from your experiences? If you know foreign languages, perhaps you should look at importing items. Or, find an article that's useful to a certain trade or profession, if you have an understanding of that business.

A fine example to follow is Royal Silk, a company founded in 1978 by Pak Melwani who had contacts with silk clothing manufacturers in the Far East. With a source of products at a reasonable price, Pak looked at markets and chose the growing group of working women.

Finally, Pak picked a product to start out with. This is a real key. First you need a product with broad appeal; Pak chose a simple silk blouse. Secondly, you have to have something unique about the product or the offer to get people to buy it. Royal Silk's drawing card was price.

With these decisions made, Royal Silk bought a full-page, four-color ad in *Cosmopolitan* for its $22 silk blouse. Three thousand orders came in—$66,000 worth of business from one ad.

This wasn't an accident. Pak knew exactly what he was doing. Royal Silk continues to use space ads, but also has booming catalog sales and is opening retail outlets on the East Coast.

Start with a general idea of a product area you're familiar with. You have to be knowledgeable so you can decide on specific markets, products and offers. Let's say you collect coins and stamps. You read the trade publications, and you know the going prices. You can spot the good from the bad. You know how the market works and what your prospects are like.

Right there you have a mass of marketing information. Finding supplies isn't a problem. You put ads in the newspaper classifieds saying you want to buy old coins, or you talk to dealers, go to trade shows, auctions and estate sales.

If you're a collector, it sounds enjoyable, right? But you are also getting a sense of the market. Sooner or later, the one offer you can make to get your business started will come to mind. You're looking for a product that has broad appeal but is presented uniquely.

Uniqueness Is a Virtue

Don't let your direct response be advertising for local retailers. What do I mean? Every Christmas you probably get loads of catalogs. Like myself, you probably skim through them. Perhaps something catches your eye. "Here's a wool scarf," you might say. "It's the perfect gift for my Aunt Tillie."

Here's the catch, though. Will you buy from the catalog, or will you purchase a similar scarf from a local clothing store? You might buy from a local store as you do other holiday shopping, unless the offer in the catalog is exceptional. Is this a scarf so different no store could match it? Is the quality special? What about the price?

If your scarf, or gourmet cheese or mail photo finishing service isn't extraordinary in some way, your ads won't pull. They might just encourage readers to buy a similar item at a store they already know.

Because of the money you'll eventually make from it, finding a unique product is worth the time spent hunting. First, read all the publications concerning your general area of interest. From that you'll see what the hot new products are. You'll learn more about the needs of the market. You'll also see what other firms are offering, and at what price.

Search out both trade and consumer publications. Trade publications will help you keep up on suppliers. You need to know where to get products. Consumer publications can teach you about markets in your field. You can't sell to people unless you know what they want. Don't shirk this research. You need to be an expert before you'll feel comfortable choosing products and advising prospects on what they should buy.

Another set of publications you'll need are the catalogs competitors send out. From them you'll see what products and offers they're trying. Also try to read between the lines. Some companies make promotional offers just to get customers. You might try to make it your regular offer and find you can't make money from it. Use what others do as a guideline.

Don't disregard what you read, yet recognize that your business is unique. As such, you will be able to make different offers and profit in different ways than anyone else can. If not, what would be the point of having your own business?

Gerardo Joffe, founder and president of Haverhill's and Henniker's, relies on trade journals. His companies have focused on importing unique consumer products, and much of Joffe's time is spent looking at foreign trade journals. He doesn't stop there, however. Once he finds a unique item, Joffe changes it slightly. Usually he believes it needs modifications to be right for the United States market.

At the same time, making a modification ensures uniqueness. Joffe will ask the manufacturer to make modifications, or at times he will make them himself. In return he has one-of-a-kind products. He knows where to look for suppliers of unique products. He also knows how to add value to the items by slightly modifying them for his markets.

Trade shows are another product source. Vendors display a multitude of new products there. Even if you don't buy anything, you'll come back with lots of ideas. Walking through an exhibit hall packed with manufacturers gives you a good view of what's happening in your industry. Talking with people you meet is also very stimulating and can provide wonderful opportunities for working with others. Perhaps someone will share a product or merchandising idea that had never occurred to you. People are happy to talk with you at these shows and to tell you about their successes.

If you can't afford to go to a national show, at least attend a regional conference every year. Learn about upcoming conferences in trade publications or from the association allied with your industry. Before you go to one, talk with the sponsor or with someone who has attended previous shows. See if the material presented will meet your expectations.

When you attend trade shows, you'll find that manufacturers and suppliers are eager for your business card. Soon after the show, you'll be hearing from them through a direct mail piece or a call from their rep. You might not find a specific product from these contacts, but you can keep up on new products and find out what items are being discontinued. By cultivating industry contacts, you'll be on top of news that can help you plan and build your business. You'll hear what your competition is doing—what's working and not working for them. If you enjoy your field, being on top of what's happening in it will be fun—and profitable—for you.

If you are starting direct response on a small scale, you might not believe you can spare the time for all this input and still run your business. Up to a point, I agree. I started selling *How To Form Your Own Corporation Without a Lawyer for Under $75* from my basement. To revise the book, I needed to keep up with legal matters. I also had to find time to study the ads and catalogs of successful book marketers to small businesses, such as *Boardroom Reports* and *Commerce Clearing House*.

If I can find a little better price, or a more reliable supplier than I have now, my business makes more money. Time spent looking for such suppliers is not wasted. It can mean the difference between getting by and doing really well as a company.

Confirm Ideas by Testing Them

You should have similar confidence in your product and offer. Test your offer by comparing it to what your competition is doing. See what's selling at trade shows. Look at catalogs. Try an offer on a mailing list you formed from the principles outlined in the previous chapter. Test on small groups before marketing.

Try to determine if your market will buy your product at the price you've set. Researchers often use interviews to determine what the probable mass response will be to an offer. Just putting a group of your target audience into a room and asking what their response is to various offers can be revealing. Such research can be done informally, although be careful not to ask just your friends for their opinions!

Paying ten prospects to spend two hours in a monitored discussion is a good way to get information. Choose your prospects carefully. Generally both a demographic characteristic and a behavior are used to select the group. For instance, a hardware company might want "males ages 25-45 who spend two days or more each month on home repair or improvement projects."

When you've found ten prospects, you have a *focus group*. From them you will learn how your product appeals to them. Focus groups provide the quickest, easiest and least expensive form of consumer research for most direct marketers.

Consider hiring a professional monitor for your focus group. Teach your monitor about your product, and let him or her develop a written discussion guide. With a professional monitor you'll have a better chance of getting meaningful results. The monitor can ensure that the group stays on track and can help interpret responses.

Use a focus group early in your marketing. Its main benefit is to save you money by providing information about your prospects. Marketing people and copywriters should observe the focus group. They'll discover sales handles that will help them later.

Here are some guidelines for getting the most out of a focus group:

1. *Try to find out how the group views your company and product.* Usually focus groups are used before bringing out a new product. However, they're useful as well in markets that are changing quickly.

For instance, you might be pushing your products for their prestige appeal. You might find a focus group that says it's attracted by the choice of colors rather than the foreign craftsmanship. Armed with that information, your copywriters will know to emphasize in the future the varieties of colors offered by your product.

2. *Identify the prospects' needs that your product meets.* From this information you'll learn how to better hone your appeals. Essentially you're finding what motivates the focus group to buy. Should you emphasize price or ease of use? Does the group really care if your product is built to last for 25 years?

Also look for any negative attitudes towards your product. Is it too expensive now for the focus group? Does a competitor offer better service?

When faced with negative remarks, marketers sometimes realize they need to switch markets. Perhaps a different group will find your strong points more appealing.

In the 1980s, too many companies tried to sell "home computers." Businesses have more need for the capabilities of computers than do homeowners. I suspect consumers would rather spend money on entertainment products, such as VCRs. So the computer firms are refocusing their efforts on the business market. Home computers are being recast more as small business tools.

3. *Find out how your focus group talks.* Copywriters who talk with product development types will pick up their terms. However, the consumer could then misunderstand what's being said as the copywriters prepare an offer.

Miscommunication is terrible in a selling situation. Don't use words that bring up negative images in the minds of your prospects. Find the words and phrases that appeal to them positively. Use those terms as much as possible in your marketing.

4. *Don't test specific copy or offers.* Listen to a focus group. But recognize that with only ten people you have a small sample. From them you can detect general attitudes. Individual tastes might prevail if you ask them questions that are too specific. Use a focus group to get a general direction for your pitch.

Incorporate what they say into your marketing material, and then do test ads and mailings. Let the market as a whole tell you what works. Also realize that good copywriters are best left alone to work after sitting with a focus group. They know how to fashion winning marketing pieces. Don't try to get a focus group to tell them how to write.

If you have trouble assembling a group of prospects in a room, try door-to-door surveys in an area whose demographics fit your proposed market. Or, mail a questionnaire to your current customers. You could even try questioning customers as they come out of a competitor's store.

From talking with people you get an idea of the motives they have for buying goods. Such knowledge will help you find unique products. Royal Silk knew women liked the luxuriousness of silk blouses but that they needed practical clothes for everyday work. So Royal Silk started selling silk blouses at a low price to working women.

Discovering motives for buying means you are uncovering needs. When you are able to meet needs, you'll gain sales. Often you can take an existing product and improve on it. You'll then have an exclusive product that performs better than what your prospects are currently using.

Let's assume you have a market, a product and an offer in mind. Now it's time to change gears. You need to research your markets, suppliers and distribution channels to see if they can support your business.

Marketing Madness

When trying to sell consumer items, too many optimistic entrepreneurs fall into the same trap. They assume that "everyone will want to buy this. My market is everyone in the country." Now you might truly believe in your product. You might think that it can benefit every soul on the face of the earth. But you're not going to get everyone to buy.

As we noted before with the Coca-Cola Company, the mass market can be profitably seen as the combination of many segmented markets. Each segment expects special products, special treatment and special offers. Your role is to find a product and a market that match, and make them that special offer, again and again and again.

First, clearly state who comprises your market. Is it CPAs in offices with less than ten employees? Persons who like to knit? Tennis players? You have to be able to define your market. If you don't know who you're selling to, how can you pick the media to reach them? And how will you know which product benefits to stress in order to appeal to your market?

Find out how to approach these persons. You're looking for mailing lists, phone lists, publications they read and trade shows they attend. Determine if there are enough persons in the market for you to profitably sell to them. And don't count on capturing more than one percent of the prospects you approach.

To Market We Go

Learn as much as you can about your market's buying habits. Try to find out what an average dollar amount is for a direct response order from them. You can learn this from other direct marketers approaching the group. If that amount is too low for you, come up with strategies for increasing the order size.

Also find out when your market buys. Most direct response goes out in September and January. Don't waste your money mailing in July. People are at the beach or playing softball. Don't run an ad with a coupon in December—because of holiday shopping, people feel "poor" then. The new year brings optimism and a renewed capacity and vigor for spending.

Those are general rules. Your target group might be different. For instance, you might do a profitable mailing in June to hunters getting ready for the fall deer season.

Discovering the Right Business Tools

Let's leave the market and research the product side. Make a list of potential suppliers. Get prices from them. Ask how long they can guarantee that those prices will stay in effect. Find out what quantities they can supply and how long it will take them to ship to you. Finally, ask to be an exclusive representative of the product. Usually to get this right from a supplier you must guarantee sizable monthly purchases from them. Also get quality guarantees—especially if your product has any moving or electronic parts. If customers send back defective units within a year of purchase, the manufacturer should credit your account for the replacement.

Finally, consider how you will fulfill orders. You should avoid products that are difficult to store. Be wary of items that are heavy and require high mailing costs, which drive up your expenses. Also steer clear of fragile items that could be damaged in shipping.

When pricing items there are three main factors to consider. First, see what your competition is charging for similar goods. Next, determine what your specific market is willing to pay for this item. Finally, look at your fixed costs to see what you have to charge in order to make a profit.

If you can sell something for less than your competition does, consider doing so. Your item will look more attractive, especially if both products are basically the same.

If you sell your product for too little, some prospects might be concerned about its quality. You have to match your product to your market. Find out what offer has the best value to your prospects. You can do this by testing different offers in smaller mailings and seeing which one brings in the most orders.

Of course, a product must be priced so it can make a profit. A general rule for direct response is to charge at least twice what the item cost you. In this way you'll have enough to pay for marketing and shipping. With inexpensive items, add even more than 50 percent to your base cost.

Rules are made to be broken. Some direct response pros even plan on losing money on certain offers. Although I don't follow that philosophy, it has made a lot of money for others. A low-price offer is used to gain a list of happy, loyal customers. Basically the philosophy behind this selling scheme is similar to retailers touting *loss leaders*.

Promotional Products

Almost every grocery chain has its share of loss leaders. Grocers are willing to practically give away a few items if they can get customers in the store because of those special prices. Once inside the store, most customers will buy a whole cartful of food. Additional purchases make up for the money lost on the promotional products. Loss leaders keep customers coming back week after week.

Promotional products can have an even more dramatic effect on the profits of a mail order business than they do at the retail level. Marketers use the strategy to quickly gain a large group of customers who know and like their company. Profitable products are then sold to these customers

Offering promotional products carries risk. You will need to have enough capital to pay for the ad or mailing. You won't be able to count on orders paying your expenses when you're offering a product at a low price. You might not even get enough back to pay for the products themselves.

But, it's a fast way to grow a business. Earlier I mentioned that the most expensive part of direct response is getting a customer to order from you for the first time. On profitable mailings you will gain a few new customers each time. Each new customer can easily cost a few dollars—or more. Your business will grow in steps as you balance your marketing between finding new customers for business growth and going after old ones for profits.

Companies offering promos, however, get a quick burst of happy customers. Generally the money received from them only covers mailing costs. Marketing and product expenses have to be borne by the company making the offer. In a later chapter we'll look more closely at choosing a business strategy that best suits you. But since we're looking now at merchandise, let's examine guidelines for picking promo products. We'll also look at strategies for making promotional selling work.

All direct response sellers want lists of people who like their merchandise. When mailing to prospects, the sellers want to hear the customers saying, "Oh boy! I wonder what good offer I'm getting this time!" If you can get customers that excited, you'll measure the results in sales.

When you mail to people who don't know you, too often the response is more like this: "What? More junk mail? I don't want this! Why do these people waste their money mailing to me?" And you will be doing just that. For every person who reads your material and orders, dozens will throw it away. All direct marketers know that's part of the business. Marketers use promo products to cut through that initial reluctance and turn first-time prospects into customers.

In general there are two main guides for picking promotional products. First, make sure the product you choose fits your line of merchandise. If you are selling to sportsmen, don't offer them a desk organizer. Even more so, make sure your promotional products have the same value to customers as does everything else you sell. Strive to offer promotional products that are as unique as the rest of your line.

Secondly, make sure the promotional product truly promotes the firm. Two rules help you decide. First, is it good quality? An inferior product won't make your customers happy. Spend the extra money to get good workmanship.

Remember that customers will be ordering through the mail. They can't look a product over before buying. They can't pick it up to see if it's well-made. If your product leaves something to be desired, you probably won't get many follow-up orders.

Another way your product will promote you is if your customers use it often. Make certain your name is on the product, to remind users where they got it. In that way you'll have free advertising. That's another reason you want the item to last a long time. Small flashlights and tools, calendars and workshop, kitchen or desk organizers are examples of promotional items that have helped others.

When mailing the promo product, enclose a brochure. Encourage *bounce-back orders*. If your promo customer turns around and buys something through the catalog you send with the promo, that's a bounce-back. Usually marketers include another special offer or a coupon for one to five dollars off any order from the catalog. Try to get customers in the habit of ordering from a catalog. Make them look through the catalog and choose an item in order to take advantage of your offer.

Make Money with Promo Products

Promotional products also can add value to normal for-profit offers. Let's assume a hardware firm is going into direct response. They have three products to test. First is a set of wrenches, to be sold for $29.95. Originally they considered offering a set of screwdrivers as well, but wisely the direct response consultant they hired told them not to.

"Screwdrivers and wrenches are similar," he said. "Try a different sort of product to capture people who aren't in the market for a tool set." Instead they developed a portable worktable for $39.95. Finally, they have a miniature tape measure as a promotional item.

A worktable, a set of wrenches and a tape measure. How do they fit their offer together? Remember that different offers will bring different responses. It's an important decision, and their direct response consultant will suggest they test the following:

> 1. *Encourage buyers to purchase both the wrenches and the worktable by offering the tape measure as a bonus with the double order.* "If you order both, we'll send you absolutely free our miniature tape measure. Alone it's a $7.95 value."

To make that offer work, the hardware company will probably have to lower the price of the worktable to $29.95 as an added incentive. They will be gaining added revenue, but at a lower profit.

> 2. *Encourage business by offering the tape measure at a low cost with any order.* In this case you can add value to the offer without having to give the tape measure away. In effect you are making the deal on the worktable or the wrenches look better.

"If you order the wrenches or worktable within seven days, we'll also send you our miniature tape measure for just $1.95 more. By itself the tape measure sells for $7.95."

> 3. *Sell the tape measure as a separate item for enough money to make a profit on that sale alone.* Having a low-priced item should improve total response. If customers like the tape measure, they might buy the wrenches or worktable later.

With the added revenue from offering the tape measure at full price, there could be a reduction on the sales price of the other two items. With lower prices, their perceived values would be enhanced. That alone could boost orders for the higher-priced pieces.

Put all three offers in separate mailings. Keep careful track of responses. Analyze the returns. Which offer brought in the most dollar volume? Which one had the highest profit margin, or brought in the most new customers?

No one knows the answers to such questions until mailings are done and results tabulated. Then the direct marketer can decide which strategy looks best.

Finding Promo Items

How do you locate promotional products? Most consumer items sold through direct response come from the Orient, especially the lower-priced products used as promotions. Read trade publications to find products and manufacturers.

People often start importing businesses after returning from an overseas vacation. They may have found a unique item suitable for import while shopping in a foreign bazaar or boutique.

Selling foreign goods can be quite lucrative, but the paperwork required for our government, as well as the country you're importing from, can be strenuous until you get used to it. It will also take some effort to learn the rules of financing, communicating and shipping from overseas.

When looking for products to import, approach smaller overseas firms. Large companies usually don't deal in small orders. And stay on your toes. Political events, foreign currency fluctuations and even the weather can make your venture less profitable. At the very least you can expect late shipments at times.

Find out where goods are made and any potential trade problems by contacting embassies. Production statistics, tariffs, quotas and currency restrictions can be supplied by the Washington, D.C. embassies. The trade press for the industry you're interested in can give you a sense of the pricing situation. Finally, a freight company will help you figure transportation costs.

If you want to shop in Europe, look at *Made in Europe, General Merchandise,* a monthly import guide (text in English), published by Made in Europe Marketing Organization, GmbH Hahnstrasse 70, 6000 Frankfurt a.M. 71, Germany. United States subscribers can write to *Made in Europe,* 111 West 24th Street, New York, NY 10011. For domestic product information, check your library's copy of *Thomas Register of American Manufacturers,* or write to the Thomas Publishing Co., One Penn Plaza, New York, NY 10119.

Products are only one piece of the puzzle. Earlier in this chapter we discussed picking your market. You'll try to choose products that will appeal to that market. It's tough to get a perfect fit, but good marketers are like tailors. They can make prospects feel as though a product was made just for them.

How is that done? Often the marketer develops a *breakthrough* concept to bridge any gap between the product and the prospects. An alteration is made, and the product being sold seems to fit perfectly.

Many times breakthrough items emerge during brainstorming sessions. Brainstorming is a tool used by creative people to solve problems. In brainstorming a group tries to find a solution by getting a unique viewpoint on the problem.

No holds are barred in brainstorming. Before your session, decide what the problem is. Make sure that everyone who will be attending is thoroughly familiar with the issue. Don't waste any time at the meeting explaining the problem or its background. You need to spend your energy creatively when you're together. Try to meet away from an office. Don't allow phones or other interruptions. Once you've started, don't stop for anything.

Before you get going, though, elect a leader. He or she isn't there to dominate the meeting—far from it. Instead, the leader coordinates the brainstorming to ensure its effectiveness. Here are the main duties of a brainstorming group leader:

1. *Pose the problem.* Make sure the group stays on it. Avoid talking about anything not related to your central concern.

2. *Develop every idea.* Brainstorming builds on ideas. Treat each idea as the germ of an answer. Don't allow any thought to be dropped in favor of the next idea someone comes up with. Instead, the leader should ask group members to follow up on the ideas that came out earlier.

3. *Get everyone to contribute.* Within the group are product people, finance types and marketers. Each one has a different perspective. One of them might hold the key to a solution. For instance, a cash flow problem might inspire a marketer to develop a new offer that both excites prospects and changes the way money comes into the business.

4. *Don't allow criticism.* Nothing shuts down a brainstorming session faster than allowing someone to say, "That's the dumbest idea I've ever heard." When such statements are allowed, participants become reluctant to speak. No one likes being a sitting duck for negative comments.

5. *Take notes.* After the meeting the ideas need to be reviewed. Many will be thrown out as unworkable. But don't let any gems slip away by relying solely on memory to retain them.

Those of you who work alone can also do creative exercises to solve problems. For instance, if you don't have a group to brainstorm with, try making associations. Pick up a magazine. Choose topics or words at random, and try to relate them to your problem. As with brainstorming, the idea is to get out of the perspective you're now in. You're trying to get a solution with freewheeling, creative thought. Abandon logical processes for a moment, and see what happens.

Many times breakthrough concepts have helped marketers develop winning offers. In the next chapter you'll find out why different offers encourage prospects to buy.

Chapter Three

More Ways of Picking Products

Starting a direct marketing firm is deceptively easy. I put one ad in *The Wall Street Journal*, to sell a book that I'd written to help people incorporate their businesses without using lawyers.

If you look more closely at what I did—or what any direct marketer does—you'll find three distinct elements. If they don't all fit, your firm will have tough going. First, you must have a product. Second, you need to be able to reach your prospects. Third, you must have an offer that appeals to the prospects.

All three of these elements must be taken into account as you pick products, for it's no use having a good product if you can't effectively reach your target market with ads or mailings. Publications and lists targeted toward your market must be available.

There's no use bringing a product to the market if you can't make a better offer than your competition has already made. If you can't add value by improving the product or lowering the price, you probably won't get much business.

Triple Threat for Direct Marketers

Which of these three elements is the most important? None of them is. You must have a balance among the strengths in your product, marketing media and offer. Rather than seeing this balancing act as difficult, see it as opening up opportunities. You can start at any point in the direct selling process and find product opportunities there. Here are some examples of how to find products:

1. *Opportunities through looking at markets.* Suppose that from your background you've determined that tennis players are a good market for you to approach. You've played tennis all your life, and many of your friends also play. You know the mindset and needs of tennis players.

How do you find products for this market? Look at the needs of tennis players. Your list could include: staying in shape during the winter, keeping racquets from warping and finding a way to mark tennis balls so they don't get mixed up with those of other players.

Armed with just those three needs you can go to trade shows, manufacturers and inventors in search of products. You've identified needs, now you can find a product. Make sure that your product has direct marketing potential. Ask yourself if you can effectively reach your target audience and offer them a product so important that they'll pay you to sell it directly to them.

One of the fastest-growing and exciting marketplaces is the high-tech area. Some firms have done well in high-tech ventures; others haven't done as well. Due to constant change, it's a volatile field. Many high-tech products and services are expensive to develop and difficult to explain in marketing materials. Yet the high-tech arena creates a lot of interest on the part of would-be entrepreneurs.

Here are some strategies to help you spot high-tech opportunities:

First, consider targeting a specific area of the high-tech marketplace. Using this strategy you could sell a book on hardware or software to many different types of owners. You'd be showing them generically how to use their computers.

Also consider picking a smaller market and providing more complete service. Let's say you've had experience as an insurance agent. You know that agent offices are run pretty much the same all over the country. You also know that a computer could help them. In fact, most insurance agents have computers that they're using in some functions. These computers could do much more for insurance agents, yet the agents don't have the time to learn how they could apply their computers to other tasks.

What you could do is develop tools to help insurance agents get more from their computers—software written specifically to their needs, or a book telling them how to program their computers to perform functions important to their work.

Many such systems have been developed for different industries. Before abandoning this notion, look closely at the businesses you understand. Perhaps you could help make technology more usable to them, in a way they had never imagined.

A Quick Check

What specific need of the prospect are you meeting? Although some products become fashionable with little outward reason for their popularity, don't assume this will happen in your case. Accept that sort of success if it comes, but don't count on it.

Instead, define how your product or service appeals to prospects in your chosen market. Do you help them save time, be more efficient or make more money? Do you make them look more attractive, do their jobs better or enjoy their hobbies more than before?

Try to isolate both the outer need and the inner, or emotional need that your product or service meets. If you can't do these things, you might have trouble in sales. If you aren't helping anyone, why should they spend their money on your product or service?

> 2. *Opportunities through looking at products.* This is probably the most enjoyable way to find products. Simply put, you can focus your efforts on locating unique products and then determining if there's a market for them.

Most consumer direct marketers use this approach. Often they'll go on buying trips in the Orient or Europe, checking small shops for items that haven't appeared on the American market. They're covering the places that the large department store buyers don't have time to look at. If they find an item and can work a deal with the manufacturer, they might be able to get exclusive rights for the American market.

Patents are a good source for finding new products for some entrepreneurs. Be aware that most patents don't make money for their inventors. But if you're tenacious and know what you're looking for, you might spot a product that you can license, manufacture and sell profitably. Better yet, you might be able to find a patented product, see a way to improve it and then patent that improved version.

How do you find information on patents before they've been licensed to someone else? Order *The Official Gazette* from the United States Patent Office. It provides a weekly list of newly issued patents.

Additionally, patents available for licensing or sale are listed separately. To order, write to the Superintendent of Documents, U.S. Government Printing Office, Washington, DC 20402.

An even better deal comes from patents owned by the United States Government. Such patents can be licensed for free and used for commercial purposes. Even patents held by NASA are available for use by entrepreneurs. For more information on available patents, write to the U.S. Patent Office, Department of Commerce, Washington, DC 20231.

How does my product or service compete with others on the market? If you can't say that your product or service looks better, works faster or costs less, you have a problem. You must find a way to point out to prospects why they should buy from you and not from your competition.

Perhaps the only way you can make yourself seem different is by packaging yourself in a unique fashion, or marketing to a different group than is traditional for the business you're in. If so, that's fine.

In fact, one of the best ways to build a successful business comes from looking at profitable firms. Innovate on their success. Find markets they aren't reaching. Alter the product or service slightly so that it meets a need of that new market. Then you'll have the new market all to yourself.

Innovative Products Work Well

Innovation is easier than invention. Alter existing success stories rather than trying to create new industries. What you're trying to do is find new solutions to old needs. Don't try to "create a need" by convincing your market they have a problem or concern they weren't aware of. Find a need your market is aware of, and develop a product to fit that need.

> 3. *Opportunities through looking at the media.* Here you look at what other successful marketers are doing. Try to figure a way you can

deliver the same product at a greater value. If you can make a proven product better, selling it shouldn't be too tough.

A different tactic involves finding an already successful product. Develop another product or service that makes the established product more useful, something that protects it or makes it easier to use.

Supplies for the already-successful product are also needed. One company participated in the high-tech boom with a low risk by selling computer paper.

Your strategy is to find an established market that still has needs. For instance, sell instructional manuals to persons with computers who aren't using the machines to their full potential. They've already bought an expensive computer. Surely they'll pay you at least $20 to show them how to use it more effectively.

You can find successful direct marketers who use each of these three methods. Pick the approach that best suits you: looking at products, markets or media to find opportunities for direct selling. To get a look at 250 direct marketing firms, see *Inside the Leading Mail Order Houses* (Maxwell Sroge Publishing, Inc., 3rd Edition, 650 pages, 1987). In this volume you'll find short histories and projections on the companies. Product, marketing, financial statement and ownership information is given.

How Others Got Started

While reading the histories of the firms, you'll find that some are subsidiaries of large companies, such as Bloomingdale's or American Express. But many direct marketing firms began as mine did—in someone's home. Usually the founders spent some time researching or developing their products after discovering a need.

Brookstone sells hard-to-find tools and specialty housewares. It was started in 1965 by hobbyist and machinist Pierre de Beaumont. As a consultant for the United States Navy Bureau of Aeronautics, de Beaumont had found that many specialized tools were unknown outside of the industry that developed them. Yet these tools could be useful to other workers.

With his wife, Deland, Pierre spent months looking for such items. Forty-two such tools were put in their first catalog. Today Brookstone is owned by Quaker Oats.

You can see that the Beaumonts found a need in a field in which they had a background. Many workers were unaware of specialized tools that could help them at work or in the hobby shop. After locating the need they used their experience to hunt for products that filled it. Someone without their background in the tool field would have more trouble spotting the need and knowing how to find useful products.

Another way to find opportunities comes from reading. Looking at popular magazines helps you see trends. Take a trip to a newsstand or bookstore. Scan many publications, and see what ideas you pick up.

Some common themes are likely to emerge as you research. Like the Beaumonts did, you might be able to solve one group's problem by looking for the solution in another field. Many problems are solved by looking for solutions somewhere else.

Discover what problems others admit to having today. If someone isn't aware of a need, you'll have a harder time convincing him or her to buy. But if the magazines and books of the day are talking about weight loss, then perhaps you can find a weight reduction device that can be sold through the mail.

You don't need a huge market. No one would have considered the market for *specialty tools* to be overwhelming, but look what Brookstone's made of it. In addition, you'll probably encounter more competition in a large marketplace, such as the weight reduction field. Unless you have a truly revolutionary product, it will be hard to stand out against firms having bigger names, longer track records and larger marketing muscles.

In fact, you might be better off selling easy-to-assemble duck decoys to hunters. Although the market's smaller, it's probably large enough to support you. Also, there's less competition, which means your firm will stand out more.

If you want to go into the consumer market, you can be a bit more creative than when selling to businesses. You can focus on meeting internal needs rather than external ones. In other words, you can sell products that will make your customers feel more attractive, secure or dynamic. You don't have to prove that your product will make their business more productive.

Not that there aren't plenty of consumer needs, however. If you can make someone's home safer,

Proven Direct Marketing Product Categories

Clothing—Leisure wear, business clothes and special sizes

Collectibles—Porcelain figures, stamps, coins and artwork

Crafts—Needlecrafts, decorations, toy kits and supplies

Electronics—Audio equipment for home and car; computer supplies, software and some hardware

Financial products—Insurance and credit cards

Food—Fruit, meat, baked goods and seasonings

Gardening—Bulbs, seeds, plants and tools

Home furnishings—Kitchen utensils and accessories, wall coverings, draperies and bathroom accessories

Information and Entertainment—Records, tapes, newsletters and books

Office products—Furniture and supplies

Sporting goods—Golf clubs, tennis racquets and camping equipment

Tools—Hand and power tools

Other products successfully sold directly include toys, cosmetics, photographic equipment and personalized goods for consumers and companies. When choosing your product category, it's wise to pick one that has proven it can be sold directly.

garden grow faster or car last longer, you're on your way to sales. Other products meet mainly internal needs. You can come up with new, exciting products that will bring customers to you. Just as stores restock seasonally to keep customers interested, you can start a direct mail firm with unique products.

Creating Consumer Products

How do you develop products? One method is to combine different products to create one with a new appeal. Perhaps you can sell soaps or bubble bath with fragrances no one's thought of putting into such products before. I've heard of one entrepreneur who puts Zinfandel wine into bubble bath. If your combination can attract a following, you can have a nice start on a direct selling business.

Peter Drucker writes in *Innovation and Entrepreneurship* (HarperCollins) about the process of looking for opportunity. He states "... it is change that always provides the opportunity for the new and different." Drucker describes seven ways in which change can be seen and developed by business owners.

1. Drucker's first example is *"the unexpected."* He says to look for both unexpected success and failure within a business. When something happens that you aren't counting on, usually there's a business opportunity to be found—but only if you start doing something different to take advantage of that unexpected opportunity.
2. *"Incongruities"* offer opportunity as well. If you find that a firm is using a marketing appeal that isn't the primary benefit to most buyers, you can use the stronger appeal yourself and gain some of the established firm's business.
3. Finding a *"process need"* means looking for something that people do regularly and making it easier for them. As we said before, often you can find solutions from other fields.
4. Changes in *"industry and market structures"* bring opportunities. For instance, the growth of the personal computer industry has developed the need for many new products for businesses and consumers. Companies who saw those needs earliest were able to make money off the market changes.
5. *"Demographics"* is a powerful agent of change. Many direct marketing firms owe their growth to the rising number of working women who don't have time to shop outside their homes. My own firm has been helped by the growing number of people wanting to start their own businesses.
6. *"Changes in perception"* cause the buying habits of people to change, because they see new needs in themselves. For instance, the fitness movement is changing the way many of us eat and spend our leisure time. Lots of products have been—and will be—developed to cater to this change of perception about ourselves.
7. *"New knowledge"* is the force behind inventions and new technologies. New industries can be created, with new needs, but you need to get the right product out fast to benefit from innovations based on new knowledge.

Drucker's method gives an overview of where to look for change. It offers a discipline to those wanting to start a business. It's not the only method—many businesses start with a gut feeling or financial need.

A Calculated Success

Joseph Sugarman, president of JS&A, is a direct marketer who relies on innovative products. At the same time, he understands the selling and management that go into direct marketing. Joe knows he must make a unique offer. His firm's trademark is *Products That Think.*

Most of what Sugarman offers are high-tech and other new products geared to a "middle-upper income buying group." Successful JS&A products often help meet the entertainment, business and health needs of prospects.

In the high-tech field products often can be sold only for a short period. Sugarman says an average product lasts only three months before being replaced, but in that three months he can make a lot of money.

For instance, in February 1972 Sugarman ran the first ad for a pocket calculator. It was the Craig Mark II—priced at $179.95. Because of its uniqueness, the Mark II is reported to have brought in half a million dollars in sales within a year. In that ad Sugarman relied heavily on copy. Most of the ad, in fact, is copy, accompanied by two photos showing the calculator and its accessories. The ad ended with a coupon and the JS&A logo.

Other Sugarman ads selling calculators haven't even used a picture or an order form, but they've also been very successful. Joe believes that people enjoy reading his copy because he's selling to intelligent buyers. Most of his products are tested relatively inexpensively in the southwest edition of *The Wall Street Journal*.

Although he tells all the benefits of his products, Sugarman also writes with an entertaining style. Many of his ads and catalog entries seem more like short stories than sales copy. Joe uses the long copy to do a lot of selling, which his products often need. Besides being fairly expensive technical items, these products often are made by manufacturers who aren't household names. Because of that, the products require reinforcement in order to get prospects to buy something made by a firm they've never heard of before.

In a story setting Joe can tell why the product is so good and why the price is so low. For instance, in one catalog entry he describes a visit to the offices of Visual Technology, a computer manufacturer. He finds that all the secretaries are typing on "Amigos," instead of on Visual Technology computers. He goes on to tell how Visual had bought the manufacturer of the Amigos and a few hundred of them in stock. Unexpectedly the staff at Visual had come to enjoy using this computer, because it needs little desk space.

When Sugarman saw the Amigos features, so the story goes, he bought the remaining ones from Visual. Of course, he also got Visual to include some free software worth over $500. And he now is selling the entire hardware and software package for only $499.

Additionally, JS&A has sold a letter-quality printer with a suggested retail price of $1,795 for $499. Joe couldn't reveal the name of the manufacturer, in order to keep retailers happy.

Another ad has a headline stating: "Cast Your Vote Sale." A subhead reads: "It's hard to believe the value in the new line of Yorx stereo systems until you understand our scheme." Underneath that, the copy starts: "It's simple. Price them so low that the consumer won't believe the value. Sell a ton of them and make everybody happy. And finally, run for president. Not a bad goal."

Because of their long copy, Sugarman's space ads are one-third of a page or larger. He's used such ads to sell products ranging from a $250,000 airplane to quartz watches. Looking through past JS&A catalogs and ads provides a short history of high-tech product development.

Joe asks himself two questions when considering products. First, he finds out how big the market is for that product. Then he asks himself what's "novel or unique" concerning the merchandise. Often that uniqueness becomes part of his sales pitch. During the height of the consumer interest in Citizens Band radios, Sugarman found a pocket transmitter and receiver.

By chance, the unit happened to transmit on Citizens Band Channel 14. Joe sold 250,000 of the units starting in 1975 by using the CB tie-in. Headlines stated: "Pocket CB." In a subhead he wrote: "New integrated circuit technology and a major electronic breakthrough bring you the world's smallest citizens band transceiver." The price for that "PocketCom" was $39.95. Sugarman still finds average orders to be between $40-$60.

"My approach to advertising," he states, "literally destroys many of the myths and concepts that you've learned, and creates a greater understanding and awareness of what really works and what doesn't work."

Most of Sugarman's sales come from space ads. He was one of the top ten advertisers in *The Wall Street Journal* while still working out of his basement. In ads he piles on benefits and keeps improving the offer throughout the ads.

Not afraid to try innovations, Joe was the first to advertise a toll-free number for ordering. He did so in 1973, with a calculator offer. Another innovation Joe introduced was crediting postage charges toward future purchases on catalog orders.

Sugarman studied electrical engineering in college and admits that high-tech products got him interested in direct marketing. One reason for the personal touch in his ad copy is no doubt the genuine interest he has for those products. He tries the products out before writing his copy. Often personal experience will set the tone of the ad or catalog.

In one catalog entry for a Chinon Bellami camera, Sugarman relates his love of camera equipment. However, Joe adds that the Bellami is so exceptional that he's selling all his other cameras. His offer to readers is to write him for prices on his Nikons, Minoltas and other equipment. Or, they can simply buy a Bellami from him. To sweeten the deal he adds, "not only will

I send you the Bellami, but I'll also include the two silver oxide batteries (available at any camera store), a roll of film, lens tissue and a carrying case." Improving the offer at the end of the sales copy helps get prospects to act.

More health and investment advisory products now are appearing in JS&A's offerings. But no matter what he sells, Sugarman always checks out his supplier before making an offer to the public. Sometimes he inspects a manufacturer's plant before running any ads for those products. Dealing with honest people is important to him.

When examining products for possible sale, Sugarman also tries to spot trends. Demand for products is cyclical, he believes. One year expensive items move, but the next year, customers might want less costly goods. Specific products—whether printing calculators or phone answering machines—also can have cyclical sales over the years.

Sugarman tries to plan his promotions to take advantage of times when there's rising demand for an item. And so should you. In the next chapter, we'll look at some trends affecting direct marketers, to help you get in with the flow of the times.

Smithsonian Magazine (July 1992)

Advertiser/ Product	Offer	Appeal	Space
Nordic Sport	Free video/ brochure	30-day trial in-home	1/3 page b & w
Mary Laura's Native American jewelry	catalog for $2	gives story behind pieces	1/3 page 4-color
Metropolitan Museum of Art	$1 for full color catalog	unusual & distinctive gifts	1/4 page b & w
Lands' End/ clothing	free catalog	100% guarantee	1 page b & w
Franklin Mint	Monopoly game	Collector's edition /easy payments	1 page full color
Nordic Track	free video/ brochure	30-day trial in-home	1 page b & w
Audio Forum/ language tapes	free catalog	children/adult various levels of learning	1/6 page b & w
Camera Man	free video/ brochure	improved videos	1/3 page b & w
Blue Ribbon Beef/ filet mignons	6 for $29.95/ free brochure	order by phone overnight delivery	1/3 page b & w
Back Technologies/ The Back Machine	free video/ brochure	60-day free home trial	1/6 page b & w
Clipper/ Antarctica	call toll-free for info	expedition ship/adventure	1/6 page b & w
Prairie Edge/ Indian arts & crafts	$3 for catalog	unique gifts	1/2 page b & w
Old West Outfitters/ hats, boots, clothing	free catalog	call toll-free	1/2 page b & w
Fine Art Prints, Ltd./ framing	free catalog	custom framing	1/12 page b & w
Franklin Mint	die-cast antique car models	return guarantee easy installments	1 page full color

Here's a partial listing of the direct marketing advertisers in the July 1992 issue of *Smithsonian* magazine. Before buying space, make a list such as this one covering several issues. You can see from it what products are sold through the publication. You'll also see how much space they buy, if they use color and what their offers are. Look for ads that are repeated. Most likely they are successful direct selling tools.

Product / Prospect / Offer

Here is how a direct marketer would divide up potential markets and develop different offers for each.

Product: Pencils

Prospects:

1. Schools
2. Businesses
3. Office Supply Stores
4. Individuals

Offers:

1. *Schools would use your pencils in bulk. Teachers, office staff and the bookstore would need your pencils.*

    In your promotional material you'd stress the quality of the product. No school wants to have poor pencils, since for many a pencil is a symbol of education.

    To make your offer stand out more, you might want to offer personalizing the pencils with the school's name and colors. Doing so could also open up another market—pencils as a fundraiser for the PTA or other school organization. You'd sell the personalized pencils in bulk at a good price, and the school would resell them to community members at a profit for themselves.

2. *Businesses would also buy in bulk. Your offer can stand out in two ways. First, you can sell to office managers or other buyers in bulk. You might want to sell the pencils at a very small profit in order to introduce buyers to your other office supply products.*

    In that way you'll make the pencils a promotional item and follow up their purchase with a catalog. You'll get your company noticed and encourage more profitable orders. Try to establish yourself as a firm that can save prospects money in comparison to what they'll pay at the local office supply store.

    Another way you can get your offer noticed is by personalizing the pencil. With businesses you'll need to be able to print a longer message than just a name. Most companies would want to add their address and possibly a slogan.

3. *Office Supply Stores will order from you if you can help them sell the pencils. Do so by offering point-of-purchase displays to hold the pencils.*

    You'll also gain with retailers by giving them good margins and letting them know how your product is different from the competition. Show them how easy selling your pencils will be.

4. *Individuals will buy in smaller quantities, so your prices will be higher. To get their purchase, you'll push the enjoyment and novelty of owning personalized pencils in a variety of colors.*

Chapter Four

Direct Marketing Products and Services for the Future

Today thousands of companies produce catalogs. Looking through catalogs gives an idea of successful direct marketing product categories.

Everything from Biobottoms—wool felt diaper covers designed to prevent rashes—to Asian women looking for American husbands is available through mail order. You can buy a Ticonderoga yellow pencil that is almost six feet tall for $90 from Think Big, or purchase a peacock for $100 from Stromberg's. Send your favorite snacker a chocolate bar made in his or her likeness. You can order a package of 12 for about $22.50.

In this chapter we're going to take a stab at seeing some trends in the mail order business. Being able to pick products that will be in demand for years to come is a great attribute for any marketer. To do so, you must walk a fine line: Be unique, not faddish, and have a target market large enough to supply you with a steady stream of business.

Economic Forecasting

No one can predict the future down to the letter. Be aware of the many forces acting on our economy and society. Everything from international events to the weather can affect your business.

With so many variables influencing the future, it's impossible to sort through all the possibilities. A drought in the Farm Belt affects the federal budget due to increased subsidy payments. In turn that growing deficit might influence Congress as it passes tax or budget legislation. Seemingly unrelated factors can then work for or against your business.

Profit from Changes

I believe it is possible to see the general approaching effect of powerful forces. Align yourself and your work with these forces, so that you won't be swimming against the tide of the times. Be flexible. Your view of the future might be wrong. If changes occur that you aren't expecting, don't fight them. Instead, welcome the opportunities afforded by such changes.

For instance, every time Congress changes laws concerning corporations, many of the books published by my firm are instantly out-of-date. Instead of becoming upset at a warehouse full of unsellable products, I try to quickly develop new books reflecting the legislative changes. I see the opportunity in the situation—every business owner needs to have an explanation of the new laws. Instead of losing sales, I try to gain them because of what happened—even if it was unexpected.

Let's start our search for business opportunities by looking at the economy in general. What forces are acting on it now? Which current trends will continue in the future?

One force that is helping business is the growth of what I call *positive skeptics*. People today are less trusting of government, big business, religions and professionals. Instead of blindly following the lead of these groups, they are looking inside themselves. Conformity is giving way to free thinking.

This trend toward nonconformity has been going on for more than 20 years and the expression of nonconformity is starting to have profound effects on society. One example of this is entrepreneurism.

When people start their own businesses, they take control of their lives. Entrepreneurism shows a willingness to make decisions and to take responsibility for actions. Entrepreneurs aren't afraid of trying new ideas, yet they're willing to abide by how the marketplace judges their efforts.

Direct mail is a good place for entrepreneurs to work. In direct selling, new products can be developed and tested. Results come quickly. Failure or success is straightforward—either a promotion works or it doesn't.

Entrepreneurs can run with their direct mail successes, using them to build a company. They learn from their mistakes. If a product or marketing approach isn't effective, the direct marketing entrepreneur either drops or alters it.

Create Your Own Future

Many young people today are living by this work ethic. Instead of working for someone else, they want to be in charge of their own futures. In colleges, the notion of entrepreneurism is now bolstered by complementary ideas. The study of Austrian economics is coming back into vogue.

Austrian economics teaches that the best markets are open and free. Everyone with ideas for a product or service should be able to expose their business to the marketplace of their choice. And that marketplace should be as unhindered as possible by laws and regulations that could inhibit trade.

Additionally, students are learning more humanistic forms of management. New businesses are trying to avoid the bureaucratic structures many older firms have. Managers today are recognizing that all workers have something to offer. Ideas that can help a company will just as likely come from the production line as they will from the president's office.

Many businesses managed in the older style are seeing themselves become noncompetitive. Markets they thought were dominated by their company are being taken over by more entrepreneurial firms. Look at the automobile industry, for example. Japanese, European and Korean companies have been able to gain market share by producing cars consumers want, at prices they can handle.

Give People What They Want

Entrepreneurism means responding to markets and, instead of building a big company, building an efficient one. Today many American corporations are becoming more entrepreneurial. People are being given the chance within lots of firms to take responsibility for their daily work. As a result, businesses are finding that they can do more with fewer layers of middle management.

Although American companies have been challenged by global competition, they are responding and getting stronger. Out of this challenge will come an American economic boom during the next 20 years that I think will rival any we've ever had. Much of the responsibility for our prosperity will go to the workers at all levels who have rolled up their sleeves and been productive every day at their jobs.

As we return to the work ethic of this nation's founders, we can see other traditional values reappearing. In fact, many free thinkers today have concluded that hard work, a close family structure, good educational institutions and quality workmanship are to be valued and sought after.

Many aspects of life today are different from the past. For instance, families are still important, yet many families are finding that they need two paychecks in order to have the life-style they want.

Multiple Choice Society

More choices are available to us today. My first business choices were shaped by what my relatives did. Young people today won't automatically go into the same business their parents were in. Instead there is a recognition that the whole world is open to us now. Freedom also means that today's buyers won't necessarily buy from a store just because it's close to where they live. In fact, a mail order business might be able to give customers exactly the product they're looking for—at a lower price, while also providing the convenience of at-home shopping.

Why They Buy

Consider the sheer volume of advertising messages striking buyers through radio, billboards, TV, print and direct mail. Research shows that despite the number of available outlets to buy from, consumers might not be as fickle as one might imagine. Studies reveal that buyers shop at businesses they know. Confidence is the number one factor behind buying decisions. Quality is next, followed by selection, service and price.

Retailers Also Mail

You can see the problem for direct marketers. An unknown firm sending out a mailing has a hard time inspiring confidence. People who might prefer the convenience of shopping at home will turn to known direct marketing names, such as Bloomingdale's or L.L. Bean.

Bloomingdale's By Mail is an example of a large firm that went into direct marketing out of a retail base. Having a well-known name, existing customers to sell to and plenty of money to spend helped Bloomingdale's establish itself as a direct marketing force. L.L. Bean is an example of a small direct marketer that has grown over the last 20 years and made a national name for itself.

Both companies have benefited from the growth of direct mail over the last two decades. Customers can buy from Bloomingdale's and Bean's with complete confidence. Buyers also enjoy the range of product choices, low prices and shopping convenience direct marketing provides.

Too many people are tired of driving long distances to shop in stores where the sales personnel don't know what fabric a dress is made of and don't have their size or the color they want. Direct marketing cuts through those problems. Additionally, direct marketing appeals to the entrepreneurial desire to put a needed product on the market, which can be sold immediately.

Growing Pains for Young Firms

Entrepreneurs will have more difficulty starting a direct marketing firm now, simply because of the existence of firms like Bean's and Bloomingdale's. Due to the growth of direct marketing, founding a company totally devoted to that function is tougher now than ever before.

Because of direct marketing's growth, it's getting harder to find new lists that pull. So many lists are rented out so frequently, the poor consumers barely have time to open all of their mail! For instance, 10 or 15 years ago, direct marketing buyers would get a few Christmas catalogs, and customers would spend hours poring over them, enjoying the unique offerings.

Today a known direct mail buyer gets dozens of holiday catalogs. Most of today's catalogs are much more slickly produced than their predecessors. The volume of catalogs received makes it hard for consumers to notice them. More and more money is spent on art and design, and more lists must be rented by the direct marketer. In the future, I see more firms using direct marketing as part of an overall marketing mix.

I'm not saying that direct mail is ineffective; I'm just saying it's more competitive. Marketers must use it wisely—from the products and sales offers they choose to how carefully they segment their markets to find the best lists and publications to sell through.

Nontraditional Direct Mailers

More direct marketers are becoming creative. Instead of relying solely on sales through the mail, they're opening up local retail outlets. In that way they can get more sales without losing anything from the direct marketing side. Additionally, firms can test new products and appeals more cheaply in stores than they can through the mail. All they have to do to test a different price or product is put it in the store. If it doesn't work, the owners know not to put that offer or product into the next mailing.

What's more, the store provides a wonderful mailing list. Having a core group of customers can help make a direct marketing business. People coming into the retail business provide that core. You can reach them through the mail for special promotions open to regular customers first. Or, write a newsletter—tell your customers about the latest styles or the newest products.

Give Your Store a Promotion

Stay in touch with your customers, and you'll be remembered. By communicating with them you'll also show that you're an expert in fashion, arts and crafts, gourmet foods or whatever you're selling. You'll let them know you think they're special. With that combination of special attention, expert advice and unique promotions, you'll find the customers on your mailing lists coming back to you again and again. Give them the options of ordering over the phone, through the mail or by coming into the store.

A customer list can give you lots of repeat sales. In fact, your customers are your best prospects to begin with, so they're worth lavishing some attention on. If you do a good job following up on them, you should get the time and money you spend on them back in sales.

A retail outlet actually can increase the effectiveness of your direct marketing efforts. How? It's simple. Your customers are aware that you have a retail outlet. You let the mail customers know that because they've bought from you before, they're getting better deals than you're offering to the public. For instance, announce a "Private Sale" to your direct buyers. In that way you're making them feel special since they're part of a select group. You're rewarding their membership in that group by making them a very nice offer.

Of course, all they did to *join* was be on your customer file. By making this offer you're making that initial buying decision momentous. Here are some other ideas to make your retail/direct mail campaign a success:

1. *Make your sale seem more special by offering it for a limited time.* This encourages customers to order quickly.

2. *Choose products that are distinctive.* You want your offer to express your firm's individuality. If you simply offer low prices to your previous customers, you're just a discounter. Instead, make a special offer on a hard-to-get item that establishes the unique identity of your business.

3. *Make sure you can repeat the offer.* If your promotion works, you'll want to do it again. Many stores pick easily remembered holidays to base their promotions around. You'll probably want to do a Christmas promotion. Depending on your merchandise, you might find back-to-school, Valentine's Day or other holidays good times to make offers to your customer lists. Holidays are good shopping days, since your customers won't be at work.

Promotions can also be planned around events as simple as the times during the year when you want to clean out your inventory because new models or fashions are arriving.

People will remember your promotions no matter when you do them. One quality men's shoe store always reduces prices by half in January and July. Most likely the managers are aware that men might tend to put off a fairly expensive purchase of shoes. By having promotions at the same times every year, buyers plan to purchase at those times.

4. *Give your customers something extra to make them come back again.* A small gift when they buy, or a coupon for the next purchase makes your customers feel good about buying from you. The gift or coupon will be in their homes or offices reminding your customers of the good values you've given them. Try to make retail shopping fun and value-packed for your customers. Of course, during promotions you should take orders over the phone, through the mail or in person at your store.

Keep going back to your customers; you might be surprised at what will happen. L.L. Bean increased its annual sales from $10 million to $127 million over a ten-year period. One reason cited for the increase was a decision to mail catalogs 13 times a year—or 11 times more each year than in the past.

Even service companies, such as accounting firms, find that keeping in touch with their clients leads to repeat business. Direct mail is an important part of their marketing. It helps establish such firms as experts who are interested in meeting the continuing needs of their customers in a professional way.

Since your customer list is compiled from persons coming into the store, they might not be on the direct mail lists that you can rent. In other words, they might not be subjected to the amount of direct marketing promotions that list prospects are. For that reason, they'll be even more receptive to your message.

A store opens up more possibilities for promotional activities with other businesses and through public relations. In fact, a retail side gives your whole business credibility. Direct sales firms, such as L.L. Bean and Royal Silk, have retail stores in addition to their direct sales. Gaining credibility along with another revenue source are the primary reasons for opening a retail outlet.

Selling Stock

A store can also help get rid of inventory that doesn't move through the mail. Although you hope that will never happen, every direct marketer eventually stocks up on a product that doesn't sell.

Small businesses are using direct marketing and retail combinations to help locate their markets and stay in close touch with them. Direct marketing can encourage prospects near the retail outlet to come in for the next special promotion or urge customers further away to phone or mail in their orders. The firm's goal is to have a customer base who will produce steady income through the mail and in a store.

More Success Stories

Edgar B Furniture Plantation is an example of a direct marketing firm that opened a retail store to gain credibility with its customers and prospects. However, Edgar B's main marketing is through direct selling. Although it's a $15 million firm, Edgar B knew it wouldn't be totally accepted without a storefront. Edgar B's niche is its ability to sell quality furniture at low prices. By not having a lot of showrooms, Edgar B can sell at lower prices than retailers.

A salesperson only needs a desk, a copy of Edgar B's catalog and a phone. Most sales are over the phone or through the mail. Furniture salespeople at Edgar B's keep file cards on clients to remind themselves of the styles preferred by their customers. In that way they can give good service over the phone, while saving clients money.

More dramatic is the success of Systems Center Inc., a manufacturer of software for IBM computers that relies on targeted marketing methods—direct mail letters, seminars and telephone solicitation to sell its products. "We can sell a $75,000 software package and install it without ever seeing our customer," says Richard Moore, vice president of corporate communications. He estimates that Systems Center saves millions each year by not having the usual field sales staff and regional offices for servicing clients.

Instead, the sales reps provide constant support from their Virginia offices. Seminars are held around the country, giving customers a chance to talk with employees of Systems Center. Based on this formula, Systems Center saw revenues jump from $1.8 million in 1982 to $18 million in 1985 and $123 million in 1991.

The company found that it can lower the costs of sales by using direct marketing tools. Traditionally, much of a field rep's time would be spent traveling. With phone contact, reps can sell all day, answering questions and handling problems and objections.

In fact, direct marketing lends itself to sophisticated products. Direct mail and telemarketing give the seller the time and space necessary to explain complicated merchandise.

Often a business will have a specific marketing concern. Anything from "Who are my best prospects?" to "How can I keep wholesalers up-to-date on applications for our technical products?" can be a problem for marketers. Once the problem is formulated, direct mail can generally be used to quickly, inexpensively and accurately provide an answer. Below is a list of marketing functions direct marketing can perform. See if direct marketing could do these faster and at less cost than methods you're currently using.

1. *Identify prospects* through the use of a reply device on an ad or mailing.
2. *Contact prospects* at a minimal expense with direct mail or telemarketing.
3. *Service customers* by answering questions about orders or product use.
4. *Solicit follow-up sales.* While the rest of the marketing plan is looking for new customers, direct mail can ask for additional orders from existing accounts.
5. *Identify new markets* by test ads and mailings to those markets.
6. *Differentiate products from the competition* by having uniquely designed ads or mailings that also explain how your merchandise and company philosophy differ from your competition.
7. *Keep market share.* Don't let sales slip through neglect. Direct marketing can remind both prospects and previous clients that you exist and have useful products or services for them.
8. *Service your marginal accounts inexpensively* by getting them to order over the phone or through the mail. If you have a sales force, let it call on the bigger accounts.
9. *Provide product or application updates* on your merchandise. Your goods will be most useful to clients when you show them how to best use what they've bought.
10. *Coordinate the introduction of new products to different markets* simply by timing the mailing of your promotional material.

Since you know the results of a direct marketing campaign quickly, you should be able to have the answers you need soon. Good answers to the above questions help companies run more smoothly. With direct marketing you can better predict how much inventory you'll need, because you know the response to previous ads and mailings.

Treasure Hunting

One question often asked of creative people is, "Where do you get your ideas?" Most creative thinkers have a system for uncovering potential. A combination of study, talking with experts and consumers, and thought helps them to come up with solutions to problems.

Remember that you're not looking for a product that will be a sure-fire seller. Instead, you're looking for a solution. Having a solution gives you something worth selling, if enough people are aware that they have the problem you're helping to solve.

To help you look into specific areas for products, consider these sources:

1. *Trade shows and journals.* To find them, go to your library for *Successful Meetings*

magazine's semiannual "Exhibits Schedule." Also see *Trade Shows and Professional Exhibits Directory* (Gale Research).

Additionally, take a look at the appropriate trade journal for the industry, or contact the professional or trade association. Your library should have a copy of *National Trade and Professional Associations of the United States*.

> 2. *Newsletters Newsletter Yearbook Directory, Ayer Directory of Publications* and the *Oxbridge Directory of Newsletters* should be in your library.

> 3. *Government sources.* For a look at available government publications, contact the Superintendent of Documents, U.S. Government Printing Office, Washington, DC 20402. Catalogs are free. *Price List 36* lists publications by government agency and subject. *Subject Bibliography Index* covers publications by topics. You can also ask for *New Books*, a bimonthly catalog of new releases by subject.

Another approach to finding new products is the National Technical Information Service/Center for the Utilization of Federal Technology, 5285 Port Royal Road, Springfield, VA 22161. NTIS is the body that licenses federal patents for commercial use.

If you want to protect your own development, get in touch with the Patent and Trademark Office, Washington, DC 20231.

> 4. *Databases.* Computer databases are started up all the time. Ask your reference librarian for the latest guidebook to databases. Many industry periodicals can be found on specialized databases that are updated for timeliness.

Your local library is the natural place to start researching. A few hours there can shed light on whether you've got an exclusive product for a market with a need.

Product development becomes more complex if you are going to manufacture the goods yourself. You'll then be dealing with suppliers and production facilities.

With a new product you'll want to start by making a prototype to see if the product works, if it can be made economically and to set up a test market. If your prospects look good, you'll need to write a business plan describing how you'll put together a firm that can make and sell this product.

In *Building a Mail Order Business* (John Wiley & Sons: Third edition, 1991), William Cohen offers guidelines to entrepreneurs choosing mail order products. First, he says you should choose a product you can control. By that he means you must make sure no one else can sell the product. For instance, don't try to sell something that can be copied or bought at stores, or someone else will get sales as a result of your marketing efforts.

Other ways of controlling your products include having patents on inventions or processes you've developed. However, you'll probably have to pay thousands of dollars to obtain a patent. One reason patent fees are so high is that you will usually need to use an attorney experienced in patent law. A patent gives you the right to sue anyone copying your innovation. You need to be careful in a legal sense about how the document represents your invention. Once patented, a product is protected from imitations for 17 years. It's up to you to make sure your patent isn't being violated; no one in the government will enforce your patent unless you first file a claim.

Patents have other limitations. Someone may copy your basic design, alter it somewhat and then use it for their own gain. At best, patent protection lasts only 17 years. If you don't think anyone can figure out how your product works, you're probably better off not patenting it. In order to protect your product or process, you must describe it in the patent file. Don't educate others, keep your secrets to yourself.

At the same office you can file for trademarks. Distinctive logos, company names and product names can be trademarked to give you exclusive rights to use them. You can't, however, claim a trademark on words in general use. Suppose your firm is called "Best Direct Mail, Inc." If someone else starts "Best Gardening Products," you can't claim they've taken your name. You can't have exclusive rights to the word "Best."

As with patents, searches are made before granting trademarks to make sure no one else has already registered a similar trademark. To start the process, contact the Patent and Trademark Office, Washington, DC 20231. You also might want a patent attorney to assist in the filing. If an attorney can help you fill out the forms correctly the first time, that can make up for their cost.

Your intellectual creations, such as books and software, should be copyrighted. Doing so costs only $20. Write to the Register of Copyrights, Copyright

Office, Library of Congress, Washington, DC 20559. Copyrighting gives you exclusive use of your product for 50 years.

Direct marketers also can retain control by getting an exclusive agreement from a manufacturer. Such an agreement gives you the right to be the sole marketer of that product within a set geographic area. Of course, you'll have to convince the manufacturer you can move large numbers of product before you'll get an exclusive agreement.

William Cohen also suggests staying away from fad items. You can't plan a business when you don't know how long your product will be a good seller. He adds that "you can lose as much money as you can make."

Your product needn't be of the finest quality, but make sure it isn't cheap. Poor quality will encourage costly returns and could give you a poor reputation. Stay away from products that are regulated by the government, such as medical goods. Only those who are familiar with that business should sell such items.

Cohen adds that how you communicate what you have to offer is just as important as what you're selling. In fact, by using good marketing techniques you can be very successful with products that are readily available. You don't have to invent something.

Approach local manufacturers. See if they have any discontinued products, something that they couldn't sell through their existing marketing channels. If it's discontinued, you'll probably be able to buy enough to test the product at a low price. If your test is successful, offer to buy the tooling for the discontinued product. You should also be able to purchase it at a good price. Then you can do the manufacturing yourself.

Also consider contacting corporations that have research and development departments. If such a corporation has patented a product that it doesn't want to sell, you might be able to get a license to market it. An example would be a useful product that doesn't fit a company's marketing needs.

In the same way, you can contact inventors who have a product that either hasn't been marketed or is selling poorly. Expired patents are another source of products. Ask the patent office in large cities for the number of patents covering product areas you're interested in. You can then look these patents up by number. If you find one that you think you can help sell, get in touch with the individual or firm that owns the patent.

William Cohen also has a "product evaluation form" that weighs the importance of different factors to determine the probable success of a direct marketing product. It's reproduced on the following page for your use.

Once you've found a product, you still must convince people to buy it. In the next chapter, we'll look at how to put together offers that will entice your target market to buy.

Mail Order Product Evaluation Form

Instructions: Give each evaluation item—

    4 points for an evaluation of excellent
    3 points for an evaluation of very good
    2 points for an evaluation of good
    1 point for an evaluation of fair
    0 points for an evaluation of poor

Multiply the evaluation points times the importance weighting. Pick only new products that have a high point total.

I. Marketability

1. How large is the potential market?   0.03 X____ = ____
2. How important is the need that the product fills?   0.08 X____ = ____
3. Can the customer buy the product easily in a store?   0.03 X____ = ____

II. Profitability

1. What is the total and yearly profitability estimate?   0.08 X____ = ____
2. Can the item be sold at 3 to 4 times your cost?   0.08 X____ = ____
3. Does the product lend itself to repeat business?   0.07 X____ = ____
4. What is the ratio of the total profit to total investment?   0.03 X____ = ____

III. Investment

1. How much investment will the project require?   0.05 X____ = ____
2. How many units must be sold until the investment is recouped?   0.04 X____ = ____

IV. Legal Consideration

1. Is the product strictly legal?   0.15 X____ = ____
2. Is the product completely safe?   0.09 X____ = ____
3. Can there be any legal repercussion through use or misuse of the product?   0.08 X____ = ____

V. Mailing

1. Can the product be shipped and mailed easily?   0.06 X____ = ____
2. Is the product breakable?   0.06 X____ = ____
3. Can the product be shipped at low cost?   0.0? X____ = ____

Grand Total   = ____

Use this chart to evaluate products you are considering for your direct marketing program.

Chapter Five

How To Make Offers That Sell

Direct response marketing is competitive. Go one week without throwing away any of your mail, and you'll see what I mean. You'll probably receive direct mail offers from a charity, a local department store, a national catalog and perhaps a politician.

One Chance To Make a Sale

All this mail puts a lot of demands on your attention—and attempts to drain your wallet. You can't respond to all of these offers. Which ones will you choose? What makes a direct response campaign stand out?

This is not an academic point for direct marketers. Their letters and ads are the only way they can generate income. As we pointed out before, direct marketers can't be content with generating interest. They don't want inquiries; they need sales. If there aren't enough orders, the direct marketer is out of business. It's as simple as that.

A good offer is what brings in sales. Unfortunately, many direct marketers don't understand how to make an offer. Often they'll run into problems by just giving their prospects information.

Very few people act on information alone. Here's an example. Let's say your neighbor just returned from a vacation to the Far East. While in Taiwan, he saw in a gift store a paper stapler that never jams. He bought a carton of them and wants to see if they'll sell in this country.

Your neighbor doesn't want to spend too much money before making sure there's a good market for the staplers. Instead of hiring a professional copywriter he says, "I've written lots of business letters. I can handle this by myself." So he writes a letter describing the product and giving the price. He gets very few responses. "I guess there's just not enough demand for this stapler," he concludes.

He actually didn't give the product a fair chance. He just gave the facts. He communicated and probably created some curiosity. But he didn't sell. That's what makes direct marketing different. The funny thing is, according to the Direct Marketing Association, only seven percent of the direct mail sent out is done by professionals.

Asking the Right Way

When marketers make offers, they really are making requests. A direct response offer asks the prospect to do something. If the prospect doesn't do what you ask, your effort has been wasted. Direct response is a success only when it brings in orders. Because of that, your "offer" has to be a planned sales piece. In it you will anticipate what salespeople refer to as *objections*, or common reasons that prospects give for not buying.

Each product has its own set of customer objections. A salesperson needs to have an answer ready for all the objections and a countering argument for why the prospect needs to buy right now. When selling through the mail or in ads there are no salespeople involved. Objections must be anticipated and answered in the copy. A knowledge of selling must be applied to the offer.

An exercise that helps discover objections is simply to practice selling your product one-on-one. Do this before putting your offer down on paper. Captured below is a sample conversation between a merchant (M) selling photocopier paper and his or her prospect (P). Watch how the merchant handles the prospect's objections and gets the sale:

M: "Since I know you have a photocopier, I'd like to make you a special offer on paper for your machine."

P: "I get all my paper from the photocopier's manufacturer. The sales rep's a real nice guy."

M: "But I can offer you a savings of 20 percent or more on his prices." (*Offer*)

P: "I really don't use the machine all that much. It's probably not worth switching accounts, even if I would save a little money." (*Objection #1*)

M: "If you just make 20 copies a day, you can save $100 a year. Would you like it if someone gave you a $100 check at the end of the year?" (*Overcoming Objection #1*)

P: "Well, I've tried other brands before, and they just don't seem to have the quality of the manufacturer's paper. Having nice-looking copies is important in my work." (*Objection #2*)

M: "Let me show you an independent study that proves there's no difference between the quality of our paper and the product you're using now." (*Overcoming Objection #2*)

P: "This is all pretty technical to me. I can't really understand what they're saying here." (*Objection #3*)

M: "I certainly understand that. Let me show you some testimonials from business owners like yourself who are glad they switched to our product." (*Overcoming Objection #3*)

P: "This looks good, but I've heard horror stories from other people. Some say their paper turns yellow after a few months." (*Objection #4*)

M: "We stand behind our product. If you're unsatisfied for any reason, at any time after your purchase, just send us back the paper you didn't use. We'll give you a full refund on your entire purchase—no questions asked." (*Overcoming Objection #4*)

P: "The rep I use always delivers on time. How can I be sure I won't run out if I switch to you?" (*Objection #5*)

M: "Here's our toll-free number. We ship all orders within 24 hours of receiving them." (*Overcoming Objection #5*)

P: "I'm still not sure."

M: "If you order right now, I'll also send you two bottles of toner for your copying machine. You can keep the toner even if you aren't satisfied with the paper." (*Call to Action*)

P: "I just did my payroll. I can't write you a check for an order now. Try me later." (*Objection #6*)

M: "We accept credit cards." (*Overcoming Objection #6*)

P: "What can I lose? Okay, I'll try your product once." (*Sale closed*)

Any type of selling is complicated. It's much more than making an offer and waiting for responses. Prospects have objections that must be met before they will give you any money. You must anticipate those objections when selling directly because you won't be there to answer them in person. One reason direct response offers have a lot of copy is that they have to overcome objections. Start with a general offer, and then add material to persuade your prospects to buy.

Knock on the Right Doors

Make sure that your offer matches the needs and covers the objections of your target market. Here's where your choices begin, for the same product could have very different offers to separate markets. Some of your prospects are interested only in price. Others prefer hearing about quality. You would approach those markets through different media, and sell at different prices.

Perhaps you are a supplier of personalized pencils. Your market could be to sell in bulk to businesses. To reach them you might advertise in trade journals. Or you could sell in much smaller quantities to individuals. Space ads could be put in general interest magazines, and the price to consumers would be higher than the bulk rate to businesses.

A direct response offer must take into account the product, market, price and advertising medium or mailing list. Everything must fit together if the offer is to be effective.

Start by studying effective campaigns. Look at ads that appear regularly in publications. Study mailings you receive more than once. Chances are if someone repeats an ad or mailing, it's working.

If you're interested in starting a business, you might consider trying to get into a market where other companies have succeeded. Try to find a similar product that is better than the competition's. Always be aware of the fact that you can improve on a product by meeting your market's needs better than your competition.

For instance, some markets might respond to a similar product at a lower price. However, other groups might be price-resistant. Their response could be worse to a low price because they might fear the quality is lower. Understand your market before making an offer to any prospects. Finding a unique way to appeal to part of an established market is a good way to start.

Get Going!

Start with one product. Repeat your winning ads for that first product as long as they're working. Run those winning ads in similar publications, or mail to similar lists.

Next test different offers to new markets. Change the ad and offer to fit the new prospects. At the same time look for similar products to try on your original market. Come up with new offers for these items. This is the way a direct response firm grows—by moving into both new products and new markets.

My publishing company's expansion mirrors this pattern. In fact, it is the rule for most direct marketers—from Royal Silk to Sears. Start direct marketing with one product. Learn selling techniques with one item. Eventually you can develop a whole catalog.

A direct response *offer* could more accurately be termed a request. You're asking prospects to order something. Build your offer so that it makes responding easy. Your customer should see the benefits of a positive response.

Let me give you a simple example. A man doesn't want to cut his lawn. He will try to get someone else to do it by making them offers. Each offer is different, depending upon whom he talks to. First, he goes to his son, and says, "I have to weed the garden and mow the lawn today. If you mow the lawn, I think we can get through with both jobs in time to go to the movies."

However, if the man goes to the neighbor's boy, his offer is much different. In that case he would probably just offer money as an inducement for the boy to cut his lawn. Each offer could be successful, but if he tried the offer he made to his son on the neighbor's child, he probably would have been turned down.

When making offers, consider what response you want. Here are two possibilities:

1. *If you want your marketing to stand on its own, go for good profits with your offer. High prices mean higher profit.* Would lower prices bring in more volume?

Here you need to understand pricing theories. Demand for necessities, like food, stay the same no matter what the price. People must pay the going rate.

When you offer nonessential items, people buy more when prices drop. Such items are more affordable then. However, when prices get out of line with your prospects' expectations, they're not sure what value they're getting for their money. Generally your prices shouldn't be too high or too low.

2. *If you prefer building a mailing list for follow-up sales, make a low-priced promotional offer.* We looked at the philosophy behind promotional offers in Chapter 3.

Many other elements besides pricing go into making an offer. Fill in the following worksheet as the first step toward putting together an offer. It will help orient you to the main points of offers.

"Make Me an Offer" Worksheet

1. *Price.* First list the following: your cost for the product, projected selling costs per order and minimum markup needed to make a profit.

Now consider your competitors' prices. Ask yourself how long you can go without making a profit as you attempt to make a name for yourself in your market. Finally, ask yourself if your price reflects the *value* your product has in the eyes of your prospects.

It's not as hard as it sounds. Most direct marketers need to make money immediately. Because of that, they avoid promotional items that might not bring back enough immediate orders. Not that promotional items don't work—some wonderful success stories have begun with the use of a unique promotional effort.

Firms that have been successful with promotional items tend to be large. They can afford to take a loss on one item in order to gain names to send their full catalog to. Because of the size of these companies, they buy promotional and regular merchandise at large quantity discounts. Getting many items at a low cost helps them to sell cheaply. It also encourages a low-margin, high-volume strategy.

Most direct marketers generally estimate expenses, see what their competition is charging, determine their needed markup and price accordingly. However, it's important to accurately estimate all costs. If you don't, profits will directly suffer.

2. *Number of items offered.* Here you are trying to maximize your sales and profit. Do you sell a complete set or single items? First, consider what your market will respond to, and then make sure your offer fits your product. It

makes more sense to offer screwdrivers in sets, but usually you wouldn't sell six calendars at once.

In many ways your decisions will go hand-in-hand with pricing choices. Usually if you offer sets instead of single items your total response will be lower. Some people won't have the money or the inclination to start off buying more than one item. Dollar volume will be higher when selling multiple units, because you charge more for the bigger sale.

When starting you generally will offer one product at one price. As we will see later, this strategy makes it easiest to test and refine your offer. You will get the most responses with a single item, which is what a beginner needs. After you have one offer, you can go back for another sale. So you really aren't losing anything.

> 3. *Optional choices.* Let the customer personalize the item, especially if doing so doesn't raise your costs by much. Optional choices include color, style and monogramming.

Some direct marketers have carved out a niche for themselves by specializing in options. Personalized pencils and address labels are examples. You don't have to go that far, but you can give a product added value by offering choices to your prospect.

Choices give prospects one less reason to say "No." Offer a range of color choices. Then your prospects can't think, "This is nice, I'd buy one if it came in red."

If offering options markedly increases your costs, pass those expenses on to your customers. Include a profit in the extra you're asking for the option.

An option that is desired by your customers is one they'll pay for. Offering it makes your product stand out. Your customers will remember you and will tend to give you repeat orders.

> 4. *Shipping and fulfillment costs.* Decide how to put these in your pricing formula. Most direct marketers don't include shipping, handling and tax costs in their basic offer. This makes your prospects feel as though they are getting a good deal when they first read the ad.

However, some sales can be lost when the prospect realizes that shipping charges are tacked onto this nice offer. Be aware of this problem. Keep shipping and fulfillment costs as low as possible while also offering fast service to your customers. As a general rule, shipping and handling charges should be no more than ten percent of an item's price.

Also understand that adding operational costs can at times boost your business. Having a toll-free 800 number for ordering may strengthen sales. Shipping and fulfillment costs aren't bad per se; however, the customer is ultimately paying for them. If these added costs aren't adding value in your prospects' eyes, your offer may be spurned.

> 5. *Credit options.* Your costs go up when offering credit options beyond cash or check with each order. Many direct response firms start by shipping only after receiving payment. With growth it's usually necessary to add options that make ordering easier for the customers. More options mean more work for you, but they also increase the response.

Once again you're giving prospects one less reason to say "No" to the offer. Accepting credit cards allows customers to order when they have little money in the bank. *Bill me* options are good for items that people order for their work. Sending a bill makes it easy for a company to write the check, especially if the person receiving the item has to get someone else in the company to cut the check.

Most direct marketers stay away from offering their own installment plans. You don't want to have long distance collection difficulties.

Don't attempt to offer all services at once, and make sure you won't encounter collection problems because of your credit options. Remember that much of the growth of direct response is due to the international proliferation of credit cards. Offering them as an option is fairly easy and safe. Direct marketers find that offering credit card orders increases their average order more than enough to offset the costs involved in honoring cards. Honoring major credit cards should increase your response rate by 10 percent to 20 percent.

> 6. *Extra incentives to buy.* Gifts, discounts and contests give prospects more reasons to buy.

You can enhance the perceived value of your product by offering extras. For instance, offer a gardening tool for $14.95. To encourage orders, tell prospects that for a limited time you'll sell it for $8.95. People can't resist a bargain.

Contests and sweepstakes also attract interest. You can get some people to buy just so they have a chance to win your sweepstakes. Obviously, the problem is that if you try to sell again to such customers without offering an incentive, they might not buy. In this case, make sure you're making money on the current order.

Always check the legal ramifications of your offers. Advertised prizes must be given. Discounts of more than 50 percent off your original price can cause revocation of your second class mailing permit. Don't use the word *free* if a purchase must be made to get the free item.

7. *Continuing offers.* Subscriptions and food clubs are examples of how direct marketers can ensure regular annual cash flow. By getting customers to sign up for *Fruit of the Month* or *Book of the Month* you are receiving commitments to future purchases.

Several positive factors are behind this strategy. First, you are identifying a stable group of customers. You know they are interested in your product and have the money to spend. A good direct marketer should be able to keep most of these customers buying regularly for years. You also are obligating them to a nice-sized purchase right off the bat.

Getting this sort of commitment from customers can take more marketing work up front. That's simply because fewer people are interested in promising that they'll buy regularly from you. To overcome this reluctance, many marketers make the initial cash commitment small. Book clubs advertise "Any four books for $1!" if you agree to buy six more at full price over the next year. Between marketing costs and inexpensive initial orders, you will be lucky to break even at first. The steady flow of full-priced orders that follows is what brings in your profit. Don't try this strategy unless you are willing to wait for your money.

You also can have tax advantages with these sales. Let's suppose you are selling subscriptions to a newsletter. You will receive payment up front for 12 issues, yet on your tax form that income is offset by your liability to fulfill that subscription.

8. *Time limits.* Here you are playing on psychology. While you might think limiting the time in which your prospects can place an order will reduce sales, it does the opposite. Having a time limit gives a sense of urgency.

Do this to avoid your prospects' tendency to put away your offer in order to "think about it." You want them to order immediately. If they put your offer down, it probably will get shuffled among other papers on their desk. If they ever find it later, it's very easy for them to say, "I haven't missed anything by not ordering. I guess I don't need this product."

9. *Quantity limits.* Use such limits to enhance an item's perceived value. Prospects will see the product as being in great demand. If your prospects think supplies are short, they'll tend to order immediately—and they'll tend to order extra.

Some marketers increase sales by limiting the number of items that can be ordered. By doing so, many customers automatically purchase the maximum amount. Without the limit, they actually would buy fewer items!

10. *Money-back guarantee.* When selling by direct response, always offer complete refunds for any reason. Customers are wary. They might be unsure of your reputation. When buying by mail, they can't come into the store to complain.

Nothing's wrong with that. Many retailers have liberal exchange policies. You should, too. Without that you will be cutting off sales. You'll be giving your prospects a reason not to order from you.

Mix and Match

When making an offer you should combine many of the following ten elements. You need a lot of different appeals to meet and overcome the objections your prospects can raise. For instance, suppose your basic offer is a pound of cheddar cheese for $4. Add a cheese cutter at a special price as a promotional item to cheese buyers for a limited time only. Honor credit cards. Offer a money-back guarantee if your buyers are not fully satisfied.

Passing the Test

How do you know if you have the right offer? You can tell to a certain extent by the orders you receive. If your orders are disappointing, it's hard to pinpoint the problem. Because offers are complex, you don't know what customers like and what puts them off.

Your only way to understand the problem is to test the offer. Make one change in your offer and present it to identical markets. For instance, have the exact same ad in similar magazines, but have different prices in each one. See which price brings in more profit and which one brings in more responses. By knowing how your customers react you can change your offer to get the results you want.

Later we'll look more closely at testing. The most important aspect to remember about copy testing is to change only one element at a time. It sounds self-evident, but you'd be surprised how many marketers think they can save money by testing several things at once. When someone does that, they're never sure which copy change affected the response.

Choosing Winning Strategies

Success will come easier when your offer fits your product and market. Take the principles outlined here, and use them to fit your needs. Make alterations as necessary. Let's suppose you want to offer discounts as an incentive to order. You can do so in several ways.

A relatively high-priced item can take a straight discount on single orders. Everyone likes to buy food, clothes or hardware and save a few dollars.

If you are selling low-priced items, give the discount as an incentive for bulk sales. Don't lower the price for small orders. If you are selling personalized pencils, offer a discount once a customer's order reaches a certain dollar amount.

Money isn't everything. Also test gifts and add-ons. Would your pencil buyers prefer a discount, or would they like a free desk organizer with a bulk order? At times a gift offer will bring back more responses than will a discount.

On items that have potential repeat sales, offer the cash discount up front. *Introductory offers* are used in selling magazine subscriptions, for instance. If the product is good, many who purchase because of the special offer will continue buying at full price when the first offer runs out.

Sometimes your special offer can be a more expensive item! Let's assume you're selling a calculator. Your special offer could be the same calculator at a higher price but with an extra feature added. In effect the lower-priced model establishes a base price. Customers will pay more and consider it a bargain if your higher-priced calculator is perceived as being much more valuable.

Many direct response offers include a free gift for an order. It doesn't have to be a gift. Free information, free trial subscriptions and free samples of other products are ways you can encourage increased response.

Making an offer is important, but remember that your primary concern is selling your product at a profit. When too much emphasis is placed on the free gift or the no-risk trial, too many of your respondents will be interested only in the free offer. Use the offer as an enticement, making sure customers know they are obligating themselves to buy something. Always sell your primary product, and use other techniques as incentives.

If you get customers with free gifts, some of them will expect free gifts with subsequent offers.

Remember what we said earlier about your main profits coming from repeat sales to stable customers. Your profits will be eroded if you must keep giving something away in order to get orders.

Here are two rules of thumb on free offers:

1. *Have a suitable margin of profit even with the special offer*. Don't rely on repeat sales to bail you out. Don't give away more than you need to get that first sale.
2. *Make sure your product stands on its own without a special offer*. If your offer outshines your product, people will respond just for the offer. For instance, creating a sweepstakes offer to help sell personalized pencils would be overkill.

Most sweepstakes are undertaken by large companies seeking to build a large mailing list. Sweepstakes are subject to legal restrictions. To justify grandiose prizes you have to market them on a large scale. Publisher's Clearing House, for instance, backs up its sweepstakes with both direct mail and national television ads. Most direct marketers should leave sweepstakes to large companies.

A tougher decision is deciding whether to offer a free gift or a cash discount as an incentive. Generally, cash discounts work best when the item you're selling has an acknowledged value. If I know that a suede coat costs more than $70, receiving an offer for one at $60 will make me take notice.

However, an item such as a coffee mug can vary in price. Its appeal is in the design more than price. So when selling mugs you would do better offering a free sample of a special blend of coffee with each order.

Consider combining price discounts and free gifts. Magazine publishers offer discounts to subscribers. In that way they give someone a logical reason to subscribe, rather than continuing to buy off the newsstand. To get the prospect to act now, the publisher will offer a gift as a premium. Since the prospects obviously are readers, the gift is often a reference book, such as an atlas.

You can see that many elements go into choosing an offer, but don't get overwhelmed. Remember that the purpose of your offer is to convince prospects to order. A gift, a discount or a guarantee is offered as a means of saying, "I'm sure you will love this product. In fact, I'm so sure that I'm offering you something extra just to get you to try my product."

You can't go too far in reassuring prospects that you're certain they'll love your product. An offer should make sense, but it should also be appealing and human. Strive to come across in your marketing as a person who is interested in the needs of your prospects. You should want to help your prospects by showing them how your product will improve their lives and solve their problems.

You probably know a store near you where the salespeople are concerned and helpful. I bet you shop there as much as possible—even if you might be able to get a better price elsewhere. A helpful salesperson will make sure you're not making a mistake. People are most ready to buy when they trust the person who's selling to them. As we said at the start of this chapter, just announcing your product and price won't do it.

Here's a summary of the attributes of successful offers:

1. Make sure you have a concrete offer.
2. Give your prospects all the information needed to make a decision.
3. Have a personal tone in your ad or mailing.
4. Appeal to the prospect's mind and emotions.
5. Ask for the order, and offer an incentive for that action.
6. Provide a device that makes responding easy.

Get It in Writing

In the chapters on writing copy we'll look specifically at putting together the elements of your mailing pieces and ads. But now I'll introduce some concepts you'll use when making offers.

One of the most important concepts is your reply device. Don't just give your prospects your address; enclose an order form. Give them an addressed, postage-paid envelope. Make ordering as easy as possible.

Is your reply card easy to read? Is there enough space for the customer to fill in his or her address? You'd be surprised at how irritated some people get when there's not enough room on the order form. Using a professional graphic designer is a good idea. An artist can make your response card both more functional and more exciting. Use every element in your package to attract attention to your offer. An experienced artist will also know some tricks here, such as putting dashes around a coupon rather than dots. People tend to connect dots, not cut them out.

Many packages try to get the prospect involved. Response rates improve when you ask customers to do more than just send in orders. Give them a sticker to attach to the order form, or a token to put in a slot. Let customers peel off their address labels and put them on the form. Although these gimmicks cost more to produce, at times they're worth it.

A cheaper way to get prospects involved comes from putting a coupon in a direct mail package. Make it stand out. Put an elaborate border around it so your prospects will notice the coupon. Ask them to send it back with their order to claim the discount. What you are doing then is making sure your prospects notice your offer of a savings in price.

Prospects who don't understand the ideas behind direct marketing complain that mailings are packed with different pieces of paper. Direct response ads are often too full of text, others say.

But the direct marketer isn't interested in the people who are bored with the offer. No matter what the marketing piece looked like, those prospects would ignore it. A direct marketer knows that the longer the prospect reads, the better the chances of closing a sale. Keep repeating the benefits of the product. Persist in overcoming any objections the prospect might have.

Don't Give Up

The longer you can keep a reader's attention, the greater your prospects are for getting an order. Many direct mail packages include a folded piece of paper that says something like, "Read this if you don't plan on ordering." Inside, the letter-writer says he or she can't believe the reader is turning down the offer. There again is a chance to repeat the offer—another chance to list all the benefits and encourage readers to change their minds and order immediately.

Creating offers that sell is demanding, exciting work. In the next chapter, where we'll cover everything from cash flow to meeting personal goals, you'll see how the right offer contributes to the orderly growth of a direct response firm.

Chapter Six

Creating a Direct Response Firm

Direct marketing is a wide-open creative field. You are limited only by your imagination as you develop offers and promotional pieces. At the same time successful marketers must stay under control. A marketing misstep can be costly. Starting an expensive campaign without doing enough advance research can be a big mistake.

One purpose of this book is to show you how to be very creative in your thinking, while avoiding huge risks because of your creative decisions. It's not impossible. Making the correct creative and business choices is the only way you can ensure your success.

Direct marketing is a heady sort of business in which everything is up to you. Remember my story about Peterson's House of Fudge? I could do little to help my business when the Highway Department bypassed my top two outlets. To a large degree, it was out of my control.

As a direct marketer I am now master of my business destiny. I choose the products, write my own ads and mailing pieces, decide the publications in which we advertise and pick which mailing lists my letters are sent to. If a product bombs, who's responsible? If a mailing doesn't work, whom do I point my finger at?

I can blame no one but myself. I like that. My decisions are made carefully. My business grows out of my unique traits and the strengths of my organization. That's what this chapter's about—not to tell you what to do, but to give you a model for developing your own direct marketing firm. Since you'll be making all the specific choices, your company will be only as strong as those decisions.

To Market We Go

As we saw in Chapter 5, any product can have several potential markets. Each market likes the product for different reasons. Consequently each market needs different offers.

Sometimes a beginning marketer believes he or she can approach all markets, but almost always that doesn't work. Selling is tough. You really need to focus on one group. If you spread yourself too thin, you won't effectively appeal to anyone. You'll be changing gears too quickly to convince anyone to buy from you.

You might believe that your product has wide appeal, and it might. However, it is unlikely you can reach everyone. Your organization should be geared up and committed to reaching a target, or you'll probably go nowhere.

Build your company so that it will meet your goals. Even your fulfillment and mailing departments have to be designed to meet the specific needs of your target market. Educate your personnel. Let them know whether your customers should get special attention, or if fast and efficient order-processing is the highest priority.

Choosing your market involves several other factors we haven't considered yet. Look at the resources and backgrounds of yourself and your firm. Which market segments are natural for you to go after? If you don't know a market, don't try to approach it, no matter how much opportunity you think is there. Taking advantage of an opportunity is a process. Unless you have the training to keep up with the needs of a market over time, leave it alone.

When I started Enterprise Ventures I wasn't a publishing professional, but I wasn't approaching publishing in the traditional sense of selling through bookstores. My market was entrepreneurs, and having started 18 businesses on my own, I knew that market.

I understood the people I was selling to, so I was able to come up with offers that appealed to their specific needs. Direct response pros must be able to do the same with their chosen markets.

Gerardo Joffe specializes in finding European products that he introduces on an exclusive basis to this country. His Haverhill's and Henniker's firms have marketed wind-up shavers, automatic wine cork removers and folding scissors—all of which were previously unavailable here. He found a niche with American consumers by drawing on his European roots.

Build your company on your strengths. In that way you'll be closer to your market. Solutions will come naturally to your problems. Your firm's growth and development of new products will also evolve naturally.

Allow these changes to happen. You and your firm will change—so will your market. You'll find that your product, your ads and the publications and mailing lists you rely upon have their own finite lives.

As a direct marketer you need to anticipate change. Being in tune with your market through having a natural affinity with it will help some. But you also need to have some business forecasting skills. Don't rely on crystal balls or intuition. If you do, you might have some successes, but you'll eventually make whopping errors as well.

Be a Mapmaker

By forecasting I mean that you must know where you're going. Your goal is to help your direct marketing business effectively serve your market.

Start by keeping basic records. From these you'll be able to see where you are right now. Over time you'll see trends in your market and your own firm. You'll know where you're going. You'll see new needs in the market that you can serve.

Keeping good records gives your creative decisions some basis. Most people in business acknowledge the need for records. At the same time, many of those people don't keep them. "Me keep records?" they say. "I'm too busy selling. I don't have time."

Starting up is the hardest part. Once you get a reporting format set, the work's half over. Then you just need to get into the habit of keeping the records. Acknowledge that recordkeeping is important work, and set a time to do it. It's not hard. But remember to use the data while making decisions about how to grow your business.

It's true that recordkeeping takes time, but it's essential. Set up some basic systems. Here are the most basic elements you need to record:

1. *Revenue.* How much money is coming in?
2. *Expenses.* How much are you spending?
3. *Your market.* How is it changing?

The first two elements look at your business, since your primary concern is to ensure its health. The third element requires you to look outside your own firm. Determine how your market is changing. Alter your business to meet its new needs.

This doesn't mean that your business should be constantly changing directions. Your response to changes in your market will come out of what you're currently doing. The emphasis should be on refining what you do instead of altering it. Any opportunity you see must fit the resources of your firm. If it doesn't, don't get involved.

Let me give you an example of how a company should change itself by taking small steps. Several years ago many persons—including myself—started looking carefully at what they were eating. Today many Americans are enjoying a more healthful diet than ever before. We recognize that we can choose from among many foods, but our choices can affect our health and our moods.

Sugar has been targeted by many as a food best avoided. This development was, of course, noted by the candy companies. Consider a firm such as Mars, Inc., which has factories and employees geared up to make candy while every day the world is turning more and more against sugar.

Mars could hope that this was a passing fad. The company could gamble by putting less emphasis on candy. It could try to get into new lines of business by acquiring companies or developing new products. Mars did something different. The company altered the perception of a candy bar. It's not *candy* anymore.

Look at the wrapper of a Three Musketeers or a Milky Way bar. These are products that have been around for decades. Everyone knows they're candy bars, right? Wrong. Today they're *snack bars*. It says so right on the wrapper.

Look at the Mars ads. The emphasis is now on the peanuts or almonds that are in the candy, or, snack bars. People in the ads talk about getting hungry midmorning or midafternoon and needing a snack bar to help them get through their busy schedules.

What Mars has done is reposition candy bars in light of a changing market. It's simple but profound. Candy is no longer a treat. It's portrayed as a tool for busy people with a lot of responsibility. Eating *candy* is now made socially acceptable.

Customer Profile for Consumer Products

Age: ❑ Under 19 ❑ 19-24 ❑ 25-29 ❑ 30-35 ❑ 36-45 ❑ 46-55 ❑ 56-65 ❑ over 65

Sex: Percentage M/F _____

Address: List any geographic tendencies. Region of country; urban/suburban/rural; single-family home, townhouse or apartment dwellers. _____
_____

Annual Household Income: _____

Marital Status: ❑ Single ❑ Married ❑ Divorced

Type of Job: ❑ Professional ❑ Laborer ❑ Clerical

Education: ❑ High school ❑ College ❑ Graduate Degree

What Media Exposed to Regularly: List magazines read, TV shows watched. _____
_____

What Owned: List typical possessions, such as: home, car, TV, audio equipment, boat, stocks, money market fund, vacation home. _____
_____

Leisure Activities: List sports, religious activities, volunteer work, hobbies and vacation preferences. _____
_____

Buying Habits: List any important characteristics, such as: where your customers shop, how often, what they buy and how much they spend. _____
_____

Organizations: List social, charitable, religious, educational, professional, hobby and sports groups they belong to. _____
_____

Important Attitudes: Write a few sentences describing the attitudes held by your target market. Describe their values, goals and dreams. _____
_____
_____

*Use this chart to summarize who your target consumer market is.
When possible, quantify the data.*

Customer Profile for Professional Products

Age: ❑ 19-25 ❑ 26-30 ❑ 31-35 ❑ 36-45 ❑ 46-55 ❑ over 55

Sex: Percentage M/F _____

Education: ❑ High school; ❑ College; ❑ Graduate Degree

Type of Company: ❑ High-tech; ❑ manufacturing; ❑ service

Size of Company: Annual sales _____

Position: Company title held by prospect group _____

Job Description: What is your prospect responsible for on the job? _____
_____

Address: What region of country or other geographic characteristics apply? _____
_____

Authority: Is this person able to make a buying decision concerning your product, or will he or she submit a request to someone else? _____
_____

Length of Time in Job: How long has your prospect been with the company? How long has he or she had his or her present title? _____
_____

Attitudes Held by Prospect: Here you'll list attitudes important to your prospect professionally and personally. However, place more emphasis on professional attitudes. What are the values, goals and dreams held by the company? _____
_____
_____

Use this chart to summarize who your target professional market is. When possible, quantify the data. For instance, tell the length of the vacations taken by your target group. How many hours a week do they spend on certain leisure activities?

I might add that this campaign wasn't dreamed up by a bunch of sociologists. It was put together by very practical marketing pros, and it works. Mars responded to a changing market. The company didn't need to get out of a business it knew. Proper marketing positioned Mars closer to the needs of its customers. Busy people learned how candy could be a part of their lives—without causing them guilt because of their dietary pledges to themselves.

Have It Your Way

Always stay tuned to your target market, and then communicate your product to them in terms of their most pressing need. If you can't do that, you either need a different product, a different target market or a different marketing strategy.

Selling is difficult. Competition is steep. No matter how good your product is, no matter what size your marketing budget is, you still have to appeal to the needs of your market. If you don't, your prospects will spend their money somewhere else. If they don't quickly and easily grasp how you will help them, you've lost their attention. When you've lost their attention, you've lost any possibility of a sale.

Once you've grasped that concept, everything can be quite simple. That's the beauty of direct selling. *I know what you want. Send me a check. I'll mail your product to you.*

Keep your appeals simple. Marketers have a theory they call *positioning*. Basically it says that the brain files information. Every product creates a file for itself in your prospect's mind. Here's an example. In your mind, the "Sears Diehard battery" file probably contains a message like "lasts a long time." That's the message the marketers have given you. It's on the basis of that one appeal that Sears successfully sells Diehard batteries.

The positioning theory also tells us that a product can occupy only one position in prospects' minds. Sears doesn't try to tell us that its battery lasts a long time and comes in seven colors.

Giving your product, as well as your company, the right position is crucial to selling success. Unless you have the first product of its type, you should adopt your position in a way that differentiates your item from that of your competition. Appeal to other needs. If the Diehard is seen as lasting a long time, contrast your product to that.

Sell your product as being less expensive, or easier to maintain. Of course, if you can prove that your battery actually does last longer than the Diehard, establish that fact.

Does your product have the strongest possible position in the minds of your market? You're paying for the marketing. Make sure you're receiving all the business you can.

That's where creative marketing comes in. Consider light beer. It was available before Miller Lite started putting ex-athletes in ads. But before Lite, light beer was marketed unenthusiastically. People sold it in a condescending manner, "for persons who like a lighter taste." Its position was negative in the minds of most beer drinkers. "Less full-bodied taste" was what it meant to most of them. No one mentioned that it also had less calories. No one had the creativity to connect that attribute to the needs of beer drinkers.

Until Miller Lite. Miller let weight-conscious men know that they could have their beer taste and less calories to worry about. Lite was marketed to meet a unique need. Customers responded by making Lite Beer a great success story. Lite Beer wasn't as much of a unique product as it was the result of unique marketing. Instead of just selling a product, Miller sold an idea.

As we mentioned earlier, you must collect data before unleashing your creative forces on the market. Assess your current situation by filling in the following worksheet steps:

1. *Name of target market.*
2. *Describe your target market.* First, get an overview. What is the overall size of the market? Figures should be available from the appropriate trade association. Is it growing or shrinking in size? If it's not a growing market, what strategy do you have for increasing your sales over time?

Look more specifically at the market. Categorize your prospects as follows:

- Age
- Sex
- Income
- Education
- Marital Status
- Family Size
- Place of Residence
- Job
- Hobbies

Knowing the above characteristics serves two marketing functions. First, you can identify the market clearly for advertising purchases. You'll know which publications to advertise in. Mailing lists can be easily identified, and you'll better understand the needs of your prospects when you visualize them.

Let's look further. Describe the attitudes of your market toward subjects relating to your product. For instance, if you are selling to businesspeople, don't just look at how they view your product. You need to understand your prospects' approach to business in general if you want to be able to appeal to them.

Talk to current customers, your competition, industry experts or focus groups for the information you need. Find out about the buying behavior of your target market. Do they buy through the mail? Do they use credit cards? How often do they buy the type of product you're offering? What other products do they regularly purchase?

Don't shirk this work. If you can't answer these questions, your sales will be off. You'll end up using your ad campaigns to do market research instead of selling. Try to get the answers you need before making sales calls. You'll save a lot of money that way.

In your market research you've identified your target market as specifically as possible. You've then determined that you can reach them through the mail or in publications. You've noted the size of the market, and you've looked closely at the individuals that make up your group. You've uncovered their buying habits, attitudes and problems. You also know what overall social or economic forces are causing changes within the group. In short, you've spotted your market, and you know how to appeal to them.

One way to organize your information is by constructing a grid similar to the sample on the next page. In this manner you'll be able to see the whole picture at once. Perhaps some new ideas will then develop.

Write at the top left of your grid *Very Important*. Number down the left side from ten to zero. At the zero mark at the bottom left write *Unimportant*. Across the bottom of the page, write phrases representing prospect attitudes that relate to your product. Samples might be: *Price, Durability* and *Easy To Clean*. You also can write down the more general traits of your prospects that don't directly relate to your product. Rate your prospects on each attitudinal point on the zero to ten scale. When finished, you'll have a fairly complete picture of your market.

Analyze the results. See how your product matches the needs and wants of your prospects. Determine also how well your competition lines up. As you position your product you will often position it in opposition to your competitors' products.

Point out unique areas in which your product alone shines. First, make sure that your prospects deem important the features you are highlighting in your marketing. In that way you can match your product benefits and your uniqueness to the needs of your market.

As you go through this exercise you might find that some of your original ideas are off-base. If that happens, just be glad you made this discovery before spending a lot of money marketing your product. Perhaps you'll find that your prospects are different than you assumed—or that there are too few of them. Maybe your product needs more features in order to be unique and compelling in your market's eyes.

Don't expect to come up with all the answers immediately. Juggle your strengths, the strengths of your firm, the needs of your market and the features of your product until they mesh. You might find some market segments where your product fits in comfortably.

Look for a strong need held by a part of your market that matches what you can deliver. If your product appeals to that subsection more than to the overall market, you might want to concentrate on that segment. See if there are ways to identify and reach that smaller group through ads and the mail. If you can market to them in large enough numbers, you might find a niche for your product.

> 3. Let's go back to a more technical analysis. *Write down the mailing lists or publications you'll use for advertising*. Enter their costs per thousand prospects reached (CPM).

Let's assume that one percent of the people you reach through direct mail respond with an order. Half of one percent of the persons who read your magazine ads should buy from you. Multiply the number of orders by your product's price to get your gross revenue. Out of this come your marketing and fulfillment costs. What remains is your profit.

Later in this book we'll look specifically at the math of direct marketing. Right now I just want to give you an overview, and stress the need to keep accurate records. If you don't, you'll make poor decisions. Direct marketing is measurable. If your measurements are incorrect, you will be in for a big surprise at the end of the month.

I'll agree that a business goes nowhere if no one sells. But, a firm also needs to know how much its sales are costing. Without that knowledge the owner won't know if the new ad agency's work is making the firm more profitable, or which mailing lists need to be used more often and which ones should be forgotten.

46 The Golden Mailbox

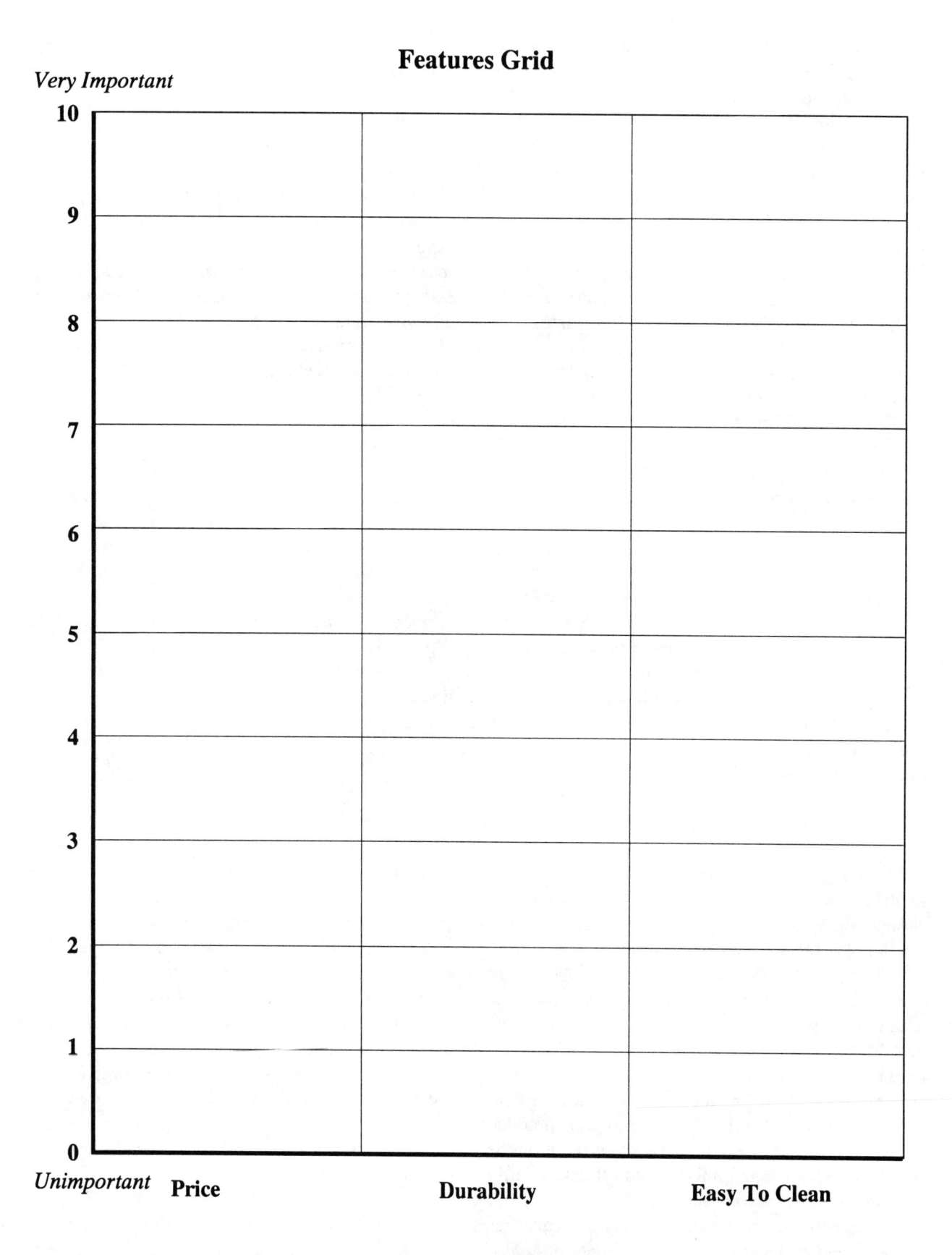

Features Grid

Very Important
10
9
8
7
6
5
4
3
2
1
0
Unimportant   Price   Durability   Easy To Clean

Use this grid to help visualize the position you occupy in your prospects' minds and how your position compares to your competition's.

Keeping records of how much you spend and where your sales come from isn't easy—especially not at first. You have to go to the trouble of deciding what information's important. What do you need to know about your business to help it grow?

Next, develop a system for recording that information, and make sure someone stays on top of it. You don't want your records to be wrong any more than a pilot wants an incorrect map.

Creativity can blossom after you've come up with an accurate picture of your firm. Problems can be identified and solved. Too many businesses fail because of poor records. Perhaps the president has a great idea, but if he can't manage cash flow, his ideas won't have much of a chance. Every business is hard. There's no easy money out there. Use every tool you can to ensure success.

Making extra cash in a part-time direct response business is fine, but your goal should be to have a continuously growing firm. People wanting salaries should work on an hourly basis. Those who want to grow a money machine start a business. By letting your business grow in a controlled fashion, it takes on a life of its own. Its value goes beyond the amount of time and effort you've put into it.

You help a business grow by making good choices. Should you borrow from the bank to finance growth? Would it be more prudent to stay out of debt and use only your firm's earnings to grow on?

Such questions can be very important, and there are no right answers. Business owners look hard at their projected earnings and expenses when making such a decision. Relying solely on intuition could lead to a catastrophe.

When choosing among offers, an owner can run tests to predict outcomes. Other business decisions are harder to test before they are implemented.

What you should attempt to do is to simulate on paper the effects of any decisions. In that way you can try out choices without risking any money.

Behind the idea of testing offers and simulating business growth are similar philosophies. There is one big difference. When testing offers, you only look at a single variable at a time. You try to isolate elements of the offer to see what differences in your profits would result from changing your offer.

When looking at business growth, however, it can be a mistake to isolate variables. You are trying to recreate the entire environment. If you stare too intently at one variable, you can lose sight of other forces acting on your business. You can fall prey in those circumstances to thinking you see a single *permanent trend*. Don't lose sight of the many other forces you're working with. By concentrating on one variable, you can get caught off guard by another.

Seeing Your Business at a Glance

Below I'll introduce you to a model that helps you see your business at a glance. Although simple, it's not simplistic. To use this tool you need to know your overhead, or fixed expenses. In addition, you have to have your total expenses and sales for the current month and an estimate of your firm's maximum potential sales.

When drawn together to form a break-even chart, you get a picture of where you are. From that you can estimate the effect of running another ad or hiring more staff. You'll be able to visualize how such moves would alter sales and profits. Here's how to put together your break-even chart:

1. Draw a vertical line down the left side of your page. On this axis you'll record both sales and expense figures. Label it from "$0" to the maximum dollar volume you could bring in during a month without drastically altering your business.

2. Now mark a horizontal line across the bottom of your page. Label it from zero to 100 percent. On this line you'll show how close you are to reaching all potential sales.

3. By charting expenses and sales together you can see how each affects the other. Start showing this relationship by drawing a diagonal line splitting your graph in half. Label it *Sales*.

4. Draw a horizontal line from the left axis representing fixed expenses. Any cost that you have no month-to-month control over is fixed. Rent and insurance are examples. Payroll is usually seen as a variable expense, since you can quickly raise or reduce your number of employees if necessary. In the example that follows, fixed expenses are $2,500 a month.

5. Find where current sales (bottom axis) and total expenses (left axis) intersect. In the example, current sales were $8,000, or 80 percent of the firm's potential.

Go up from the 80 percent point on the bottom line until you intersect total monthly expenses. For this

48   The Golden Mailbox

Break-Even Chart

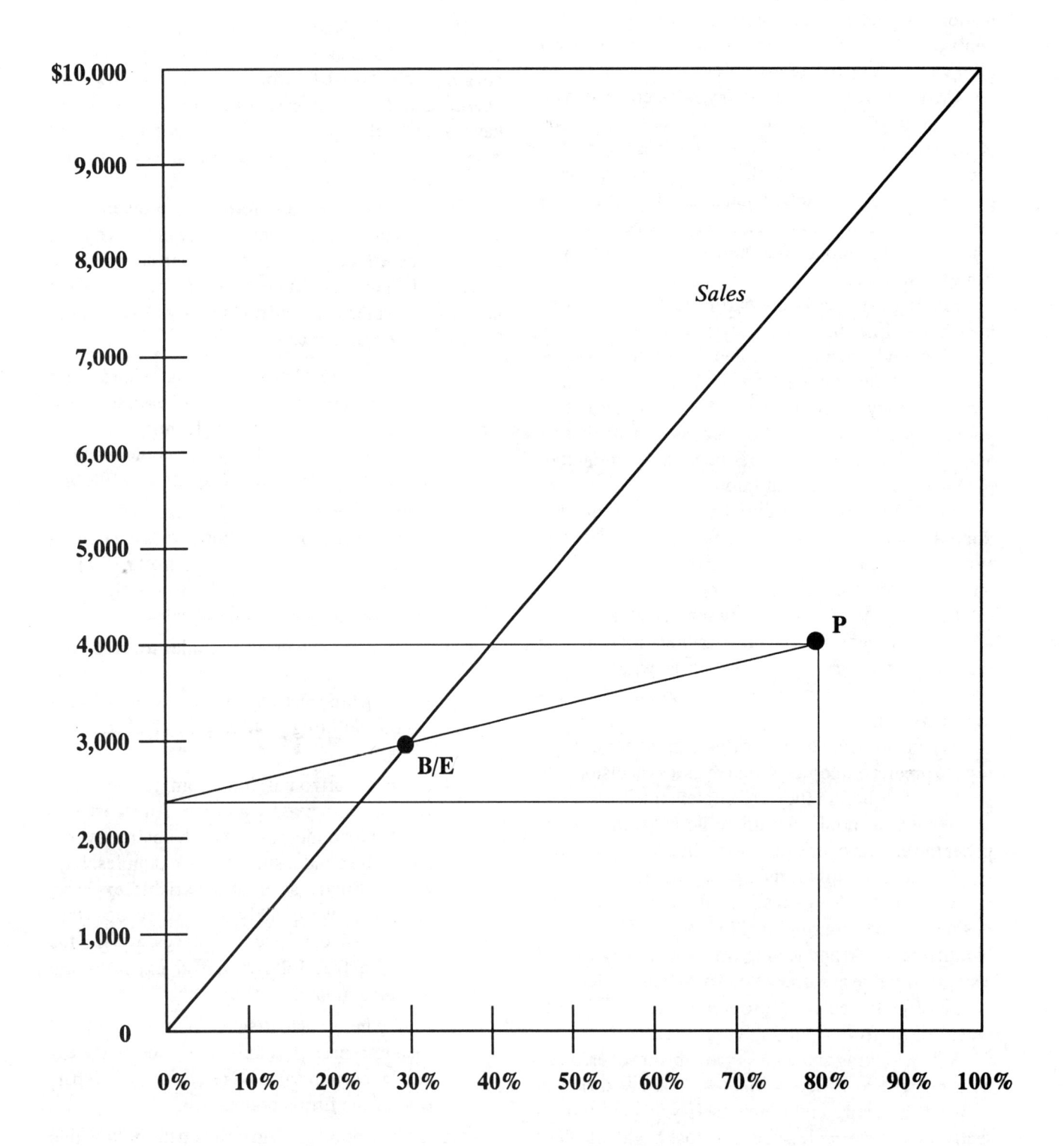

firm, total expenses run $4,000 a month. Find the $4,000 point on the vertical axis. Move horizontally from that point until you intersect the $8,000 in sales at point "P."

Now look at the diagonal Sales line. It represents break-even points—places where sales cover expenses. You can see the profit in this example because the distance point P is below the Sales line. If P were above that line, it would show that expenses were higher than sales. The company would be losing money.

> 6. Find your specific break-even point by drawing a line from fixed expenses to total expenses, or point "P." Where that line crosses the "Sales" line is your current break-even point. In this example we see the break-even point is about $3000. Monthly sales could drop to that level before the company loses money.

What you have is a spreadsheet—a flexible tool that can let you see how different elements affect each other. Let's suppose you're considering buying an ad in a new publication. From your break-even chart you can tell if you'll cover expenses if the ad's unsuccessful and brings in no responses.

Or you can assume the ad will be about as successful as other ads you've run. Your chart will show if your firm will become more profitable with such an ad. Also compare the ad's expected return to the results you could get from doing another mailing. Again, which expense will result in more profits? In this way you can really get down to how much money you keep, rather than looking strictly at revenue.

Be creative with the break-even chart. You can figure how many units you would have to sell to break even if you raised prices. Break-even charts are good tools for people who don't have the time or background to put together complicated spreadsheets. You can easily get a picture of where your company is and what would happen if you made changes in the future.

Often it's wise to change more than one element at a time when you're encouraging business growth. Let's suppose you've decided to lower prices. You'll have at the same time the expense of new ads and mailing pieces to tell your market about the great new opportunity for savings. You might need to add more staff to help process the greater number of orders that will come with lower prices. A break-even chart will help you see if all the expenses can be offset by a reasonable amount of increased business.

A break-even chart isn't an exact forecasting tool, but it can quickly show whether or not your thinking is realistic. It's just one method. Other factors also will leave their mark on your decisions. For instance, any price changes you're considering will be affected by the finances of the people you're selling to, as well as by what the competition's offering.

Adding It Up

Often the need to use break-even charts and other tools arises after you've been successful with one product. How do you help your business grow? Why do some businesses falter and stagnate, while others keep moving forward?

Unless you're working in a strong economic cycle or within a growing segment of the market, you eventually will need to find ways to help your business grow. You basically can choose to find either new people to sell to or new products to sell.

Remember that as you go into new areas you must continue selling your original product, and continue going back to your previous customers. How does all this mesh together without throwing your business off track? Start by having a plan that meets your objectives but presents the fewest risks. Here are four strategies to consider:

> 1. *Acquire new customers.* Here you must decide how much you are willing to spend for a new customer. Do this by figuring how much profit you make on current customers each year.

Some direct mail businesses will lose money in order to get a first-time order, but they know they'll get enough repeat business to offset that initial loss. Magazines are an example. A good subscriber might buy for years, so a first offer might not even cover all marketing expenses.

> 2. *Find new markets for your original product.* Try a different offer to smaller, secondary markets, but make sure you aren't competing against yourself. If you are making vastly different offers, don't let yourself be in a position where your primary customers know you are selling at better terms to others.

In essence you are giving your company two different positions for two markets. Each market should be independent of the other one. If each market needs your product at a price at which you can profitably sell it, then this strategy makes sense. Be sure to do test mailings to your new markets before plunging in.

> 3. *Develop a new product.* Start by selling to your current mailing list. Market to

customers who have already purchased another product from you.

Here's an example that demonstrates natural and progressive company growth. Don't try developing a new product unless you know your customers want something similar to what they've already bought from you.

Our personalized pencil company, for instance, could easily go back to its customers with an offer for personalized pens or stationery.

This company probably shouldn't try to sell calculators. A pencil company just doesn't have a high-tech image. When picking new products, remember how you've positioned your firm in the minds of your customers. Even if the pencil company could offer a good deal on calculators, it's probably not a wise move—unless it wanted to get out of the pencil business and reposition itself as a calculator company.

Also consider the capital risks involved with new products. Inventory and promotional costs are the main expenses. Before launching a big campaign, be sure to test parts of your current customer lists. If you have a winner your company will grow from sales to old customers, and you might be able to profitably sell to new markets with the new product.

4. *Sell more to your old customers.* Basically this strategy means going back to your customers more often for new orders. If you think your customers have a need to buy more often and the money to spend, it's easy to try to get more sales from existing customers. Just go back to your current list more frequently.

My own firm grew by helping others. Researching *How To Form Your Own Corporation Without a Lawyer for Under $75* revealed to me that about half of the companies listed on the New York and American stock exchanges are incorporated in the state of Delaware. The main reason is that there are no state taxes on corporations in Delaware.

Any firm wishing to incorporate in Delaware must have an agent. So I formed The Company Corporation to assist the readers of my book wishing to incorporate in Delaware. By providing a legal address, The Company Corporation has enabled tens of thousands of firms to enjoy the Delaware advantages.

But I didn't stop there. Since I'm in contact with many small firms, I published other works to help their businesses grow. Everything from advertising to legal agreements was covered in the books and special reports sold by Enterprise Publishing.

With hindsight, it all sounds very natural. But it takes daily discipline to stay on a certain course, especially for entrepreneurs who often spot opportunities in diverse areas. It's essential to stay with the market you know if you're going to be a direct marketing success story. In the next chapter I'll give you some tips on squeezing more profit out of your efforts.

Chapter Seven

Cutting and Counting Costs

You can be successful in direct marketing without following a set formula. Numerous paths lead to direct response success. Once you've started selling your product, many of the pieces we've talked about earlier fall into place.

The key will be staying on top of business developments and responding to them. Let's assume that you did some mailings and got consistent results, however they were consistently lower than you expected. Revenue and profits aren't where they should be. What can you do? First of all, don't ignore the problem. If your response rate is disappointing, don't tell yourself that the "next list" you mail to will be better.

Realize that a small direct response firm is fluid. You can change quickly to meet the market. That's one of the positive benefits of starting small. You'll be able to make changes as you explore your market. Offers, product, prices and media can all be changed.

Make sure any changes you make are calculated. It's very easy for a small businessperson to say, "This market is tougher to crack than I thought it would be. Maybe I could do better selling something different." Don't make wholesale changes lightly. If you know your market, stick with it. Refine your operation until you're successful.

Little Changes Can Make a Big Difference

Let's face it. You probably don't have a revolutionary product that everyone wants. You probably can't undercut the competition by 25 percent and still make money.

That doesn't mean you can't be wildly successful in direct response. My point is that the subtle differences between you and your competition will make you successful over time. In business it's very rare to be given an obvious advantage for very long. Don't count on finding a benefit that will put your firm head and shoulders above the rest.

Pay attention to the little matters. Perhaps you can improve your response rate one-half of one percent with a better-designed package. If you do that, your profits will soar as you continue marketing with that slight advantage. Over time, small differences add up.

First let's make sure you're on track in an overall sense. Then we'll look at ways of refining your operation to become more successful. You shouldn't be in direct marketing, though, unless you can pass this Uniqueness Test:

1. *Can your product be bought through other channels, such as retail stores?* If so, you are losing sales unless you have an advantage such as a better guarantee, a lower price or an easier ordering process.

2. *Do your prospects have an identifiable and definable characteristic?* If not, you will have a hard time buying lists or ad space profitably. When your target market is vague, you can't hone in on it. You'll be spending money reaching people who aren't good prospects.

Make sure your product and offer are positioned for a market uniquely suited to them. As we've seen in previous chapters, this is where your creativity comes into play. Try to position your product to satisfy the emotional needs of prospects in your target market. Make it very difficult for a prospect to say "no."

Take a piece of paper. You should be able to quickly describe your market and the offer you're putting before it. Now look over what you've written. Is it strong and concrete; or is it vague? Don't, for instance, say your market is "Homeowners." Make it more specifically fit your product or service. You should say "Homeowners with dogs," or "Homeowners in areas that receive lots of rain."

By doing this you'll save money by paying to reach only the best prospects. You'll also be able to focus clearly on the best prospects, and make them offers that specifically suit them.

When Marketing, Think Small

Think SMALL? Yes. Think as small as you can. And then try to think smaller.

Find a niche that's so small you can dominate it. Your prospects will have to come to you. If you pick a larger target market, your competition increases. All of a sudden the prospect has several choices. Maybe you get the sale. Maybe you don't.

Small firms do better in small niches. Once you're in a larger market you're competing against firms with more experience and resources. Instead, find a spot too small for them to be interested in.

It happens all the time in the computer industry. No one wants to take on IBM, yet many smaller firms are finding niches that are making them rich. Designing software for a specific industry is an example. Such businesses can target the product to the exact needs of their prospects, and they can target the marketing effort. Fortunes are being made selling software not to the masses but to small groups such as engineers or accountants.

You can apply the same principle to your firm. Even if you believe your product has broad appeal, target your marketing. If others outside your market buy, that's fine.

By focusing your market your customers will identify with your firm. They'll know you provide goods or services "just for them." And that will make them feel good about buying from you, because you'll be seen as understanding their needs.

Look at L.L. Bean. Are they a clothing store? Of course not. They specialize in shoes and clothes for the outdoors. And that's one reason people buy from them. L.L. Bean has a special niche. If they get too far away from it, they'll lose their special identity, and sales would probably drop. Clothes you can buy anywhere. But if you want something specific, you'll look at L.L. Bean and other specialty marketers.

L.L. Bean has gradually expanded its catalog to include items that don't belong in the woods, yet they still wisely hold onto their original image. If someone at L.L. Bean were to suggest selling all types of clothing, the company would be competing against thousands of other stores. No longer would it be unique, and it might not have the resources to take on Sears and J.C. Penney.

Be King of the Mountain

Having a specialized market suits small companies. You can respond quickly to competitive threats and to opportunities. Larger firms have layers of staff that separate decision makers from the salespeople. The executives often don't know what their prospects want. Since they have an established distribution chain, they don't have to be totally in touch with their market.

As a direct response marketer, you can carve out your niche and change with it. You'll be in sync. Right choices will come naturally as you pick products and make offers to your target market.

Stay in Touch

From time to time a direct marketer should take an afternoon to call recent customers. Pick out the names of a few customers from the orders that came in the day's mail. Use directory assistance to find their number. Usually they'll be pleasantly pleased—if not shocked—to receive a call from a company they just gave an order to.

Ask your customers why they bought your product. What appealed to them? What needs did your product meet? What competing products did your customers consider before ordering from you? Why did they go with your product rather than another firm's? After talking with a few customers you'll start seeing patterns.

Perhaps you'll find your marketing's on target. On the other hand, you might discover that features you think are secondary are the primary reasons your customers are purchasing. If that's the case you'll want to change your offer to emphasize the benefits that are most appealing to your target market.

Find a niche by picking out a segment of a larger market. Here are four techniques used by direct marketers for finding niches:

1. *Quality.* Coming out with the best example of any product is a niche. Usually you try to establish yourself in this position by making your product expensive.

Many marketers would prefer to lower prices and go for higher volume, yet every product has potential for the quality niche. People intent on buying the best will then come to you. Since the number of such persons is relatively small, pick your product carefully. If someone else is already in the "quality" position, you should go somewhere else. Usually a market isn't big enough to support two high-priced models.

 2. *Demographics.* Take a product and alter it so that it's uniquely suited to a specific part of the population. Consider Virginia Slims cigarettes. Many people would say that a cigarette is a cigarette. If you design one for women, aren't you alienating half of your potential market?

Yet Virginia Slims have been a resounding success. In a market dominated by the Marlboro Man, there indeed was room for a cigarette aimed narrowly at women.

Here you also see the power of marketing. A product can be designed narrowly and must be directed exclusively to that market. Virginia Slims wouldn't be seen as a women's product if it had a different name and marketing campaign behind it. Just as it takes courage to market to the high-priced niche, it takes courage to appeal to a small segment of the market.

You can base some brainstorming sessions on this concept. Take a common product. Try to find a way to make it appeal to one market segment. Consider clothing, for instance. A few years ago, clothes manufacturers developed fabrics that would reveal hidden designs after the cloth got cold or wet. Different manufacturers applied the technology to specific markets. Children's gloves and women's bathing suits are very different products that found new life after this development.

Tools for left-handers and recipes for people with allergies are other examples of everyday products that were altered to fit the needs of specific groups.

 3. *Industries.* Look at ways of appealing to specific professions rather than to demographic segments. As we noted before, many computer companies meet the need for specialized software within different industries.

 4. *Geography.* A product can be seen as unique when it's from a specific area. In fact, many direct marketers get their start by offering the goods of one region to a larger market.

Food, clothes and art items make common geographic products. If you can get authentic pralines, serapes or scrimshaw, you have the makings of a successful direct marketing program.

When choosing lists or media for selling such items, don't look at demographics. What you want are prospects who have bought items similar to what you're selling. If you're selling scrimshaw, find a list of art buyers.

 5. *Product.* Creating a unique product can give you a niche. Direct marketers who sell miniature busts of the presidents and other collectibles follow this strategy.

Developing products with limited appeal means that you will have little competition. If you are successful at identifying buyers, you can develop a profitable niche business.

Big Profits in Small Markets

Part of the reason for the existence of today's many entrepreneurs is the need for firms that can quickly respond to the demands of unique, small markets.

We noted before how consumers want specialized products. Direct marketers are able to find specialized markets through publications and mailing lists. Small markets can be reached effectively through direct response. Your firm will grow naturally, and you won't get stretched too thin, if you only have a small market to reach and you work effectively.

Numbers Game

Direct response certainly is a numbers game. It provides another example of how small changes can mean the difference between success and breaking even. We've already noted that many direct marketers fail by not focusing on the smallest possible market.

I think that comes from a lack of self-confidence. People tend to believe their odds for success are greater when they're in a big market. Some business should come their way practically by accident, they reason, if the market's large enough. Rather than trusting in their ability to individually attract a following, they follow the crowd.

Another reason marketers try to sell to large groups is that most people hold out the largest companies they can find as examples for themselves. Too many entrepreneurs dream of starting the next IBM just because IBM is big and well-known. Because of its preeminence, outside observers see IBM as a model. That's not necessarily appropriate. In fact, most business founders would be happier heading up a small, profitable firm.

Other problems develop from that same lack of confidence. Marketers often believe they will lose sales by charging too much. Undercutting is the way to wealth, they assert. But nothing could be further from the truth. Discounting prices just means you'll make less money, and usually your customers would be happy to pay more than what you're asking. That's assuming, of course, that you have a unique product and a well-defined market. If you don't, keep looking for them.

People rarely buy through the mail to save money. Discount merchants can't afford the expense of marketing and delivering through the mail. Kmart doesn't sell through the mail; but Neiman-Marcus and Bloomingdale's do. People shop through catalogs for convenience and to buy unique merchandise—not just because they can save money.

At times direct marketers charge less than they should simply because they haven't accurately figured their revenue needs. Make sure that all costs are built into your pricing formula. Even a one-person, part-time direct marketing firm would have the following costs: product, marketing, shipping, overhead, returns and no-pays.

You should know your product cost. Marketing expenses can be estimated. Remember to include all marketing costs—from the artist pasting up your mailer to buying lists to paying for stuffing the envelopes. Marketing costs for direct mail usually run about 30 percent to 35 percent of gross sales.

Count all of your overhead costs. Legal and bookkeeping services, administrative time, order processing, rent, insurance, utilities and association fees should all be included in overhead, or fixed expenses.

Refunds and damaged goods can add up to ten percent to your total costs. Another five percent should be added for uncollectible bills. Subtract all costs from your selling price. What's left is your profit. As you sell your product, you should keep track of all sources of income and expense. It's essential to know how you're spending and making money. If your assumptions are incorrect, you need to know that as soon as possible.

Perhaps your lists won't pull as well as you hoped, or unexpected costs might appear as you fulfill orders. To keep your profits up, you must either cut costs somewhere in your business or raise prices.

Later in this chapter we'll consider ways of improving your response. But, as suggested before, a direct response program often can tolerate a price increase. Here are some specific pricing strategies useful for various products and types of firms:

1. *Loss leaders.* Previously we discussed the advantages of forming a large list of customers by offering premiums. Some direct marketers offer an item at an unbelievably low price, and send respondents their current catalog. Perhaps they'll even throw in a gift certificate for a few dollars off the new customer's first purchase from the catalog.

Behind this practice is the knowledge that having a large customer list provides a base for every successive marketing step the firm takes. If you introduce a new product and are sure enough regular customers will buy so that it will at least break even, your decisions are easier. You can try new mailings and products with the assurance that your steady customer base will keep any promotion from totally failing.

Lists of people who have previously bought by direct response provide the best responses. Sometimes it's easier to create your own list by offering a premium than to rent lists. Not only that, but the marketing efforts you put behind the premium will make your company's name known to your market.

You must have some cash reserves, however, to make a premium offer. Since you're counting on future orders after building a list, you realize that your first mailing will make little or no money. Premiums are used generally by companies that have many items to sell. If that weren't the case, they couldn't count on many future purchases.

Although building lists through premiums can be successful, it is usually attempted by larger firms with some capital and a full catalog of products to sell.

2. *Buy-outs.* Premium sales correspond to loss leaders used by retailers. Buy-outs correspond to retailers who use liquidation sales. This is done by looking for a firm that has products they want to get rid of quickly. You then buy the products at a low price, and sell them cheaply through direct response.

Keep your eyes open. Buy-outs are special situations that won't occur again. Look for companies going out of business. Offer to purchase their office supplies and resell them. Check local papers or national trade journals from industries you know.

Here's an example of an opportunity for direct marketers. Recently the Federal Communications Commission (FCC) opened more frequencies for cordless phones. Manufacturers rushed onto the scene with new cordless phones that offered better performance. The pipeline from manufacturer to retailer was full of the old phones. Retailers quickly discounted the old phones to get rid of them. There was no reason to take up store space when higher-priced, new and exciting models were on the way!

Wholesalers and manufacturers couldn't get rid of the old models they had. No retailer wanted them. So they turned to direct response firms. Perhaps you saw some of their ads in *The Wall Street Journal*. Special prices on closeouts of cordless phones were made possible through direct marketing. You can find similar opportunities if you have the sort of mind and eye needed to spot them.

> 3. *Skimming*. This is the opposite of the buy-out technique. If you have a new product, consider selling it at a very high price. Remember when calculators cost hundreds of dollars? Now they're less than 20 bucks.

If the need for your product is there, you can charge a lot. Since it's new, there's really no other price to compare it with. You can use high profits to recoup any product development costs. When competition shows up, you can always lower prices.

> 4. *Revitalizing and milking*. Perhaps you sell a product that has been around awhile. Its heyday is over. Each year sales drop a little.

Two strategies are possible in these circumstances. You can revitalize the product by coming out with a *New and Improved* version. Make sure it *is* an improved product. Combine it with the trusted name of the older product, and market aggressively.

Or you can choose to "milk" the older product by encouraging sales only from loyal customers. Don't spend any money approaching new lists. Instead keep going back to the same customers until demand for the product falls too low and the product is retired. You can increase profitability for the moment by reducing marketing costs. Rely on sales to loyal customers, and enjoy the high margins.

• • •

Because of the many direct mail variables, there are numerous ways to increase profits. Perhaps black-and-white ads would pull almost as well as four-color ads at a great savings to you. Maybe you should mail at bulk rates rather than second-class postage. Or increase response with a better offer.

Below are some profit strategies to consider.

> 1. *Increase the number of orders you get from an ad or a mailing*. Even a slight improvement in response rate can help your profits quite a bit. Let's say you increase responses by ten percent. Your total sales go from $10,000 to $11,000. At the same time your product, marketing and shipping and handling expenses might only rise from $8,000 to $8,500.

While sales increased by ten percent, profits went up twenty percent in this hypothetical example. Because no matter what the response rate is, the cost of marketing is set. You pay for the ad or mailing no matter what response you get. If you can improve the response, it doesn't cost any more. You'll pay a little extra for merchandise and shipping as you sell more, but as you can see from the example, at least half of the increased sales will be profit. Increasing responses generally come from choosing better lists or media, making better offers and improving the writing in your ad or mailer.

> 2. *Raise prices*. As we noted before, this is probably the easiest way to increase your bank account. Before doing this, compare your new price to what your competition charges. Test to make sure the price fits your market. Divide 5,000 or more names from a mailing list into two groups. Mail each group the same promotional piece, except use different prices. Track the results. You might be surprised at how raising the price changes responses and profits.
>
> 3. *Increase the size of orders*. You can raise your revenues by encouraging respondents to spend more. Several methods can help increase average dollar amounts without lowering overall response rates.

You can offer attractive discounts for quantity orders, of course, or raise the minimum order required from customers. If you offer several items, consider dropping those that are either low-priced or low in profit.

If you have one primary product, look at making a *good-better-best* offer. Here's how it works. Feature your flagship product, but offer higher-priced and lower-priced options to attract more buyers. Suppose you sell hand-knit sweaters. You have one basic model. In your ad or mailing this sweater would be featured as your *better* product. Prospects should see it as a good value.

Also offer a lighter-weight sweater at a lower price. This is your *good* offer. Because it resembles the *better* offer, most prospects will also regard it as a good value. Prospects not wanting to spend as much as the *better* sweater costs can still get a *good* deal.

You are gaining a sale that you probably wouldn't have if you only offered the one sweater.

On the other hand, offer leather buttons or monogramming as your *best* offer. In this way you are letting selective buyers get something really special—at an extra cost. Best offers can personalize the better product, make it easier to use or provide the buyer help with storing or moving it.

After trying this strategy, look at the results of your good-better-best offer. Most of your orders should be for the better product. If that's not true, then something is wrong with your offer.

Starting a campaign has other benefits besides increasing your sales revenue. Giving your prospects choices among products and options helps you observe their buying habits. What are they willing to pay extra for? What products get them excited?

For companies offering only one item for sale, a good-better-best campaign is also a logical step toward offering more products. It provides a means of experimenting with *add-on* products. Add-ons complement a featured product. In this manner they can complete a best offer, yet an add-on product could probably stand on its own. You could do a mailing for your add-on product alone and get a good response.

You are actually selling a second item with an add-on offer. It's more than just an option on the featured product, like leather buttons for a sweater. If you were to use a bonafide add-on product in that good-better-best offer, you might sell cedar blocks to keep sweaters smelling nice. Using the good-better-best format to introduce the new add-on product lets you use existing, proven products as support while selling a new item at the same time.

You probably won't lose financially, since you know from experience how your better sweater will pull. If you gain more sales with the add-on, that's even better.

Save Money by Mailing Twice

I know it sounds strange to claim you can save money by sending out two mailings. But two-step mailings work for some products. Behind the strategy, in fact, is the desire to save money. Your first mailing or ad is done to large numbers. Your goal is to get as many inquiries as possible.

When the inquiries come back, you will have a much smaller list. But you should be able to *convert* over ten percent of them. Conversion is a direct mail term that means getting prospects to take full-price orders.

You save money by mailing your expensive catalog or direct mail package only to persons requesting one after your first ad or mailing. Obviously these are hot prospects. They've gone to the trouble of sending a card to you requesting information on your products.

In order to convert them while they're hot, send the information back by first-class mail. Your postage costs will rise, but these are important names. You want to reach them before they decide to purchase something else.

You'll save money by having an inexpensive means for getting inquiries. Small space ads, card decks and self-mailers can generate requests. We'll look more closely at these tools in Chapter 10.

Two-step selling can be similar to offering promotional products. In both cases your primary objective is to gain a list of interested parties. However, when making promotional offers you ask the respondent to send in at least a nominal amount of money to get the promotion item.

There are big differences in the use of promotional items and inquiry solicitation. Promotional products generally back up lines of inexpensive consumer items. Requests for information, however, more often represent business goods.

You don't have to offer a promotion to get business inquiries. If prospects think your products can help their work, they will ask for more information. A gimmick won't bring in any more responses. Asking for inquiries is also best suited for technical and expensive goods. Prospects will want more information. Receiving inquiries makes it easier to send a large amount of information to prospects. Since you know they're interested, you can afford to follow up intensively.

When marketing a product with potential future sales, try a different strategy. Offer the product at a discount on an introductory basis. After your customers come to rely on the product, convert them to paying full price for it. Subscription sales are an example of this.

Conversion rates from an introductory offer can be anywhere from less than 25 percent to 75 percent. To be safe, assume that less than half of those accepting the cut-rate offer will pay for a full-price subscription when the introductory offer's over.

Many times two-step sales take more than two steps. Although you should get many orders from your mailing after the initial inquiry, remember that these are all good prospects. Additional mailings should be sent to those on your list who don't order at first.

Keep track of the results. Continue subsequent mailings until the number of orders you get back doesn't cover the costs of the mailing.

When I advise follow-up mailings, I don't mean just sending the same piece out over and over. Have several packages. Try different copy. Use varied appeals. Have more than one arrow in your quiver. If the first offer fails, try another. Show your prospects a different side to the product. Explain other benefits, and keep track of which mailings pull best.

You can see that starting a direct marketing campaign takes planning and commitment if you want your efforts to reach their highest potential.

Study Customer Buying Habits

Industry outsiders see the large amounts of mail generated by direct marketing firms, and they assume it's all a numbers game. Pick a list, do a mailing and wait for the orders to come back. But when such persons try to start a direct response campaign, they soon see how limited that viewpoint is.

Sure, direct marketing involves reaching many people, yet most direct marketers probably can recall a mailing they did that failed miserably. The product wasn't unique, or the offer wasn't compelling enough. The mailing list had the right demographics, but the prospects weren't proven users of direct response marketing.

Direct response purchases are not just the result of large mailings. They are individual buying decisions. Good direct marketers don't view lists as groups of people. Customer lists represent future purchases—income to a direct marketing firm. To maximize income, customer lists must be managed.

List managers find which customers are most loyal, and keep going back to them. As mentioned earlier, lists are segmented by time of last purchase, dollar amount of last purchase and number of purchases over a set time period.

Every market is different. You need to analyze your customers' buying habits to see which traits are most profitable to your firm. If you sell seasonal merchandise, then dollar amount of the last purchase probably will be more important to you than the time of that purchase.

Keep studying the buying habits of your customers. You'll learn how to weed out nonproductive names. You'll discover how often to mail and how many mailings to attempt before giving up on the list.

Most marketers come up with a point system to help rate customers. Points for recency would be awarded depending on the time of the last purchase. An example would be 12 points for buying within the last 3 months, 6 points for buying within the past 6 months, 3 points for purchasing within 9 months and 1 1/2 points for buying within the last year.

Frequency points would be given for purchases over the last year. The number of actual purchases multiplied by two probably would make the frequency points compatible with the recency rating. Of course, the dollar amount of purchases over time would be discounted to fit in the point scheme. Awarding points based on five percent of actual dollars spent would be appropriate for many marketers.

Once a system has been set up and computerized, you can manage your lists so that you are soliciting prospects in a manner corresponding to their individual buying habits.

Such a system is worth its weight in gold. Your main asset in direct marketing is your creative mind. The next most important ingredient is your customer list. Use your list effectively. Don't waste opportunities. Direct marketing is intended to be a very personal way of selling. You won't get your message across as well, however, if you don't start out by managing your list with the idea that all of your customers are different.

Chapter Eight

Ways To Help Your Direct Marketing Business Grow

Direct marketers may be unsure of how to expand their businesses after initial success. Such firms may have used a classified ad to bring in some extra income. They mastered the direct marketing formula by finding a successful offer for a product that can be sold through ads in specific publications. Or perhaps they've put together a small mailing list to which they're selling.

Such firms want their businesses to grow, but they aren't sure how to make that happen. They know they don't have enough money coming in to be able to make many mistakes. A wrong choice of product, offer or media could set their businesses back.

Such decisions can be made fairly easily by looking at the options. In this chapter we'll explore both traditional and unorthodox methods for making direct marketing firms larger and stronger.

Turning Up the Volume

One concern could be simply how to increase the amount of sales. For instance, a successful classified ad could be very profitable. Advertising and fulfillment in a national magazine could run only $150 a month while bringing in $250. Yet despite an 80 percent profit, the company still earns only $100 a month. You won't get rich soon that way.

Often the volume can be raised by increasing the marketing costs. You can plow money back into the company, reaping it later through increased sales. Here's how to do it. Run a bigger classified ad. If that works, try a display ad, and run it more often than you have in the past. Also try different ads to see which one pulls in the most orders.

Or find similar publications in which you can place your ad. With more ads and bigger ads, you'll attract more attention. Your goal is to keep your profit about the same while increasing the overall size of your business. You want more orders, knowing that you'll make money on each one.

However, at some point you'll discover the law of diminishing returns. You can't find any more publications or mailing lists containing good prospects. Increasing the size of your ads doesn't bring in more orders. Running more ads also doesn't help. Although your first product and offer might become the backbone of your business, you're now getting all the business out of it that you can. If your firm is going to get any larger, you'll have to look at other strategies.

To recap, here are four ways to turn up sales volume:

1. *Run bigger ads* in publications that are now working for you.
2. *Run ads or do mailings more often* in the same publications and to the same lists.
3. *Try other publications or lists* that are similar to the ones you're now using.
4. *Try different ads* for the same product. Feature different product benefits in your ads or mailings. Also see if you get more response with different offers.

Whenever doing something new, ease into it. If you want to try a new publication, use a classified or small display ad. Recognize that you're taking a gamble the first time you try something. Unless you can afford to lose the money invested in marketing, be able to cut your losses. Run a small ad. You can try a bigger one the next month if the small effort works.

Have a tracking system set up before placing the ad. When orders begin arriving, you won't have time to figure who's going to record where they came from. You might ask, "Why should I keep track of everything? I can tell without doing that whether an ad's profitable or not—and that's all I care about."

If you're interested in helping your business grow as much as possible, you'll care about more than that. Analyzing sales results can help you find opportunities and avoid making mistakes.

Suppose that you run two ads in new publications. Both ads appeal to groups similar to your target prospect. In fact, the only difference is that one publication's readers are a little older than most of your current customers.

Both ads might be successful, yet one might not be quite as profitable as most other ads you run. The other could actually be more profitable than any ad you've ever done before. Knowing these results will help you see new markets—and avoid losers before wading in too deeply. Or you might find the group you've been selling to isn't as natural a market for your product as another one is.

Listen to Your Records

Keeping good records will give you more insight into why a market works well for you. Let's say you've found that the younger group was more profitable—a much higher percentage of them bought. When compared to older buyers, however, their average order size was actually lower.

From this information you can conclude that you've got good merchandise for the younger prospects, but they don't have as much to spend as the older shoppers. Go back to these younger buyers with merchandise that is slightly less expensive. Doing so might be a strong opportunity for you.

In that way you'll see a key to more ways of growing a direct marketing business. Below are four more traditional growth methods. The methods that suit you best will depend upon your professional background and the dynamics of your market. By presenting them all together, you can decide which ones can be used most profitably in your situation:

1. *Find new products to sell.* Use this approach if you know your market well and can reach it. Don't stray from a niche if you understand it.

2. *Discover new markets for your current products.* If you're a marketer with broad experience, consider ways to expand your sales to new groups. Repackaging your product and refocusing your sales pitch are methods you can use so that your current products will meet the needs of other markets.

3. *Grow along with your market.* If you're selling to a growing market, you might not have to do anything but fill orders. Your sales volume will go up naturally, and your profits can increase as you develop economies of scale.

4. *Combine several of the strategies listed above.* For instance, you might be in a growing market but find competitors are taking some of your business. You then will need to go to new markets, or develop other products.

Let's look at some examples of how sales volume can be increased by properly applying these principles. Recently I received a promotion from a seller of fishing equipment. Evidently someone at the company wanted to raise sales volume. Perhaps they were trying some new lists.

The basic offer was a collapsible rod and reel for $5. Persons who ordered within 11 days could also receive another reel for $2. Those who wanted both and ordered within a week would receive a free knife. Shipping and handling charges were $3 on each order.

You can see what's happening. Let's say I wanted the rod and reel. However, if I'm willing to make that decision, the seller wants to go for more. So if I think a rod and reel at $5 is worth buying, I might think a reel by itself at $2 is also a good deal. And to push me a little harder, there's the *free* knife thrown in. Many customers will buy the whole package.

All of a sudden the basic order has doubled! What I first considered was a $5 rod and reel. With add-on orders and shipping charges, I'm actually sending in a check for $10. It all happens quite naturally in the direct mail package. But the process probably began with a direct marketer who wanted to increase the dollar amount of an average order.

Finally, this marketer also talks about how he can only allow each household to buy five of the collapsible rods and reels from him. Doing so makes the idea of buying additional sets for other family members more attractive to many potential purchasers.

In the section of this book on writing ads and direct mail packages we'll look at more ways direct marketers increase order size by adding product features and new items to their original offer.

What's All the Promotion About?

Another way to increase a direct marketing firm's size is to add onto its customer list. Making promotional offers, which we looked at earlier, is the primary method here. At times you'll receive direct mail solicitations in which the company even states that they're making a special offer just to find more people who like their products. Once you've chosen the promotional products, you're ready to implement the strategy.

Even if you're in a very competitive situation, a well-planned promotion can push your firm well out in front of the others.

As the term implies, a promotion doesn't do its job unless it really does *promote* your firm. Afterwards your firm should be better off than before in terms of business activity. A promotion is one direct marketing technique that is hard to test. You can run a few smaller ads or do test mailings if you like. But if you're in a competitive environment you run the risk of someone else rolling out with a similar offer before you've thoroughly approached the market.

A promotion can resemble a splash. You're trying to get the attention of your market with a compelling offer. Be as sure as possible that your product and offer are going to be irresistible to many who will see your promotion. Before you make that promotional offer, here are the principles you need to know:

1. *Stand out.* If you try to gain market share by lowering your prices slightly, you're inviting the competition to do the same. A good promotion puts the price so low that your competition will be hard-pressed to respond competitively. Why not? Mainly because your promotion is planned.

You've ordered a larger quantity than normal, so your cost is less than theirs. Additionally, you have bouncebacks and other offers designed to get secondary sales after fulfilling the promotional offer.

For instance, suppose a direct marketing firm that specializes in craft items has a promotion on yarn. If the firm moves a lot of yarn, it can expect to sell plenty of patterns and other accessories in the near future.

2. *Sell out.* Have a product and offer that will make the splash you need. Your promotion must work well in order to get new customers, get rid of the promotional product you've bought in bulk and make secondary sales.

3. *Get a good price.* Even though you're making a good offer, you should make enough to at least break even on the promotion itself. Make sure you get a good price on the product. Due to your large order from the supplier you should be able to sell very inexpensively and still make a little. Your main profit will come from follow-up sales to the new customers you've found with the promotion.

Add-on offers and promotional offers are different tools. My point is that you can build a business in different ways, but you'll do so by focusing on product, offer or marketing. The element that is your strongest suit will probably become the guiding force in your company's growth.

Slicing Up Your Business

Another method for growth comes through identifying business segments and choosing which ones to pursue. Consider a direct seller who makes and markets cheese—selling gourmet cheese through the mail to individuals. But many other groups also buy cheese. Our direct seller should make a list of all the cheese buyers that are potential markets for his firm:
- Restaurants
- Grocery Stores
- Airlines
- Gift Shops
- Food Processors and Packagers

Now our seller has to decide which of these market segments to approach. He might not have the capacity to make, package or sell wholesale to restaurants, airlines or grocery stores. But he might help his business grow by calling on local gift shops and delis.

By thinking further about segmenting, he might decide to venture into segments where cheese isn't a traditional choice. For instance he might work at getting orders from businesses at Christmas, suggesting they use cheese as a gift for employees and clients.

His choice of market segments to sell to would be based on several factors. Next to each potential segment listed on a chart, he should describe his current ability to meet the needs of each new segment. He should then write in how he'd have to alter his business from the way it is now to effectively find and retain customers in a new segment. A chart could look something like this:

Market Segment: Gourmet Restaurants
Administrative Requirements: Field salespeople would have to be managed.
Production Requirements: The company must be able to manufacture and package cheese in bulk.
Marketing Requirements: Salespeople would need to be found, and ads and direct mail pieces would have to be put together.
Fulfillment Requirements: The shipping process would remain the same.

Competition: Local suppliers might be able to sell at a better price. I'd probably have to sell only hard-to-find cheeses in smaller quantities.

Such an analysis of each market segment you're considering can show you if going into a market offers a growth opportunity for your firm.

You can also approach segmenting by looking at a market group rather than a product. Instead of asking "Who buys the product I'm selling?", ask about the needs of a specific market you're familiar with.

Obviously, this approach works best with direct marketers who are more familiar with a market than they are with a product. Let's say you're concerned about the needs of working women. You can list their needs and use research and thinking to see which of those needs you can competitively meet. Such a list could look like this:

- Child Care
- Shopping Help
- Office Clothes
- Easy-To-Prepare Meals
- Transportation to Work
- Career Opportunities and Strategies
- Health and Stress Information
- Time-Budgeting Tools
- Recreation and Relaxation Products
- Beauty Products
- Tips on Handling Family and Career

You can see from this partial list that the needs of working women are varied. Each need represents a market segment. Before deciding to try to sell to a certain segment, find out how large the segment is. Also think about how you'll reach that group. Your analysis could look something like this:

Market Segment: Working women who need time-budgeting tools.

Possible products: Consider calendars and appointment books designed for working women. When designing, consider materials and colors that will look good both at home and at work. Sizes should take into account: the average size of a woman's hand, the need to fit into purses and briefcases and also how the product will fit on desks and nighttables. Consider coming out with sets—one for work and one for home. Inner design should have room for an entire day of activities, not just for business hours.

Research what is important to women besides a calendar. Do they want pictures, a pen, a calculator, an address book, metric conversion tables, an area code directory or other accessories? What choices of materials, sizes and colors do they prefer? How much similarity should the product have with other time budgeting products? In what ways should it be different?

Market Size: In the millions

Marketing Techniques: Take out ads in publications such as *Savvy* and *Working Woman*. Find lists of single, affluent women between the ages of 24 and 35 who live in urban areas.

Competition: Office supply stores and firms such as Daytimers sell traditional appointment books and calendars through retail outlets and by direct marketing. Some direct marketing catalogs offer appointment books, but often these are more decorative than useful. Our product should be somewhere in between. Have a design that will appeal to women but also fit into a male-dominated career world and be practical.

Course of Action: Do market research on what working women want in time budgeting tools. Get quotes from manufacturers and rates on ads and mailing lists. If things still look good, design and manufacture the product and start marketing.

Once you've started selling appointment books, you could expand into other items for working women. Consider selling *feminine* designs of: calculators, artwork for offices, lamps and furniture.

With your knowledge of the market, you might later choose to go into an entirely different market segment. For instance, you might discover that working women are willing to pay more of a markup on food that is easily prepared than they will pay on office supplies. At that time you could work up some ready-to-fix meals that are directly salable.

Markets Ripe for the Picking

One firm that expanded by understanding its market is J.E. Miller Nurseries, Incorporated in Canandaigua, New York. It started when a German immigrant named John Miller settled in the New York State wine-growing region in the late 1800s.

Neighbors started buying Miller's grapevine stock for their vineyards. Miller then expanded by selling through the mail with the help of a simple fact sheet. By World War II the company was mailing color catalogs and had expanded beyond grapes.

Fruit trees, berry bushes and ornamental shrubs are now available through J.E. Miller Nurseries, Incorporated. The company also offers products such as soil testing equipment.

Finding Money for Others

Fundraising is currently one of direct marketing's most competitive fields. It hasn't always been that way. "It used to be like shooting fish in a barrel," says Jeremy Squire of The Viguerie Company, a 21-year-old direct response firm outside of Washington, D.C. "The fundraising dollar is getting harder and harder to go after," he adds. "Even the Salvation Army's street collections are down."

Squire recalls when Viguerie could get an average of $2 to $3 back on every letter mailed—and they prospected by the millions. Over the last three years, in fact, Viguerie has mailed over 200 million letters. Many of them have gone to help raise funds for conservative groups.

In those earlier heady years "people left and started their own agencies," Squire notes. One reason was the strong response mailings were receiving at the time, encouraging those in the field to go out on their own. A direct marketer could mail two to three million letters prospecting for donations. Total mailing costs would be about 35 cents a letter. With a 1.5 percent response rate, the mailing would break even.

If you didn't get your initial investment back, it was "no big deal" according to Squire. In four weeks you could mail again to those who responded to the first package. You could get ten percent of them to give again—and donate higher amounts.

But Squire reports that such a scenario "no longer works." Viguerie now works more on commercial accounts. The lessons the company learned while struggling to maintain its traditional results on fundraiser mailings provides a gold mine of information to direct sellers of all types.

Tangible Results

One problem fundraisers have is finding something tangible to give back to their donors. "A letter states the problem—a need for money," says Squire. "Someone responds, and writes a check. And then nothing happens."

One solution to this concern has been the "adopted child" program. Donors receive a letter each month from the poverty-stricken child they're helping.

Below are other methods Squire asserts help to increase response to their mailings. Many of these ideas can be used to help sell other types of products and services. In general, these techniques try to get the prospect to open the package by using gifts and gimmicks to get their attention. "Eighty percent of the problem is getting people to open the envelope," Squire asserts. Here are some of his ideas on attacking that problem:

1. *Make the letter look like a personal letter.* Use a personal computer to produce mail that looks like your Aunt Tillie sent it. Add a regular first-class stamp for the finishing touch.

2. *Make your letter seem more urgent.* At times Squire has used Federal Express to get the attention of his prospects. At other times he has used envelopes designed to look like they're from an overnight mail service.

In order to be effective with these techniques, you have to know what the people on your lists will respond to. For instance, many donors to charities are older people. Overnight mail isn't perceived as overly important by retirees, but they *are* used to sending and receiving packages by United Parcel Service (UPS). To get the attention of such prospects, Squire would consider sending something by UPS.

You might as well continue with that idea, and enclose a gift in your UPS package. Political buttons, framed pictures of the President and books are examples developed by The Viguerie Company.

Make your gift fit your purpose. For instance, a fundraiser might print 100,000 paperback copies of a 150-page book for 20 to 25 cents apiece. After paying for a letter and postage, the packages will cost about 40 cents each to mail. In that example, using a book can easily pay for the additional cost in terms of the "substantially higher response," says Squire.

In this case the book would be part of a *front-end promotion*. Circulating a book helps educate people about a cause. As they read the book they'll remember the group that sent it to them.

You would use a different method when using a book as a *back-end promotion*. In that case you'd print 1,000 copies of a hardcover book and have them autographed by the author or a noteworthy person allied with the group seeking money. Then you'd offer the books to people sending contributions above, say, $250. Such a strategy can "help tip them if they're leaning toward making big donations," Squire adds.

3. *Try to find a natural attention-getter you can use on your envelopes.* One of Viguerie's clients sent letters airmail from Guatemala. Of course, the plea concerned Central American issues. Squire claims that 99 percent of the prospects opened that letter. An added benefit was that airmail from Guatemala was

8 / *Ways To Help Your Direct Marketing Business Grow* 63

This envelope is designed to show the urgency of its contents.

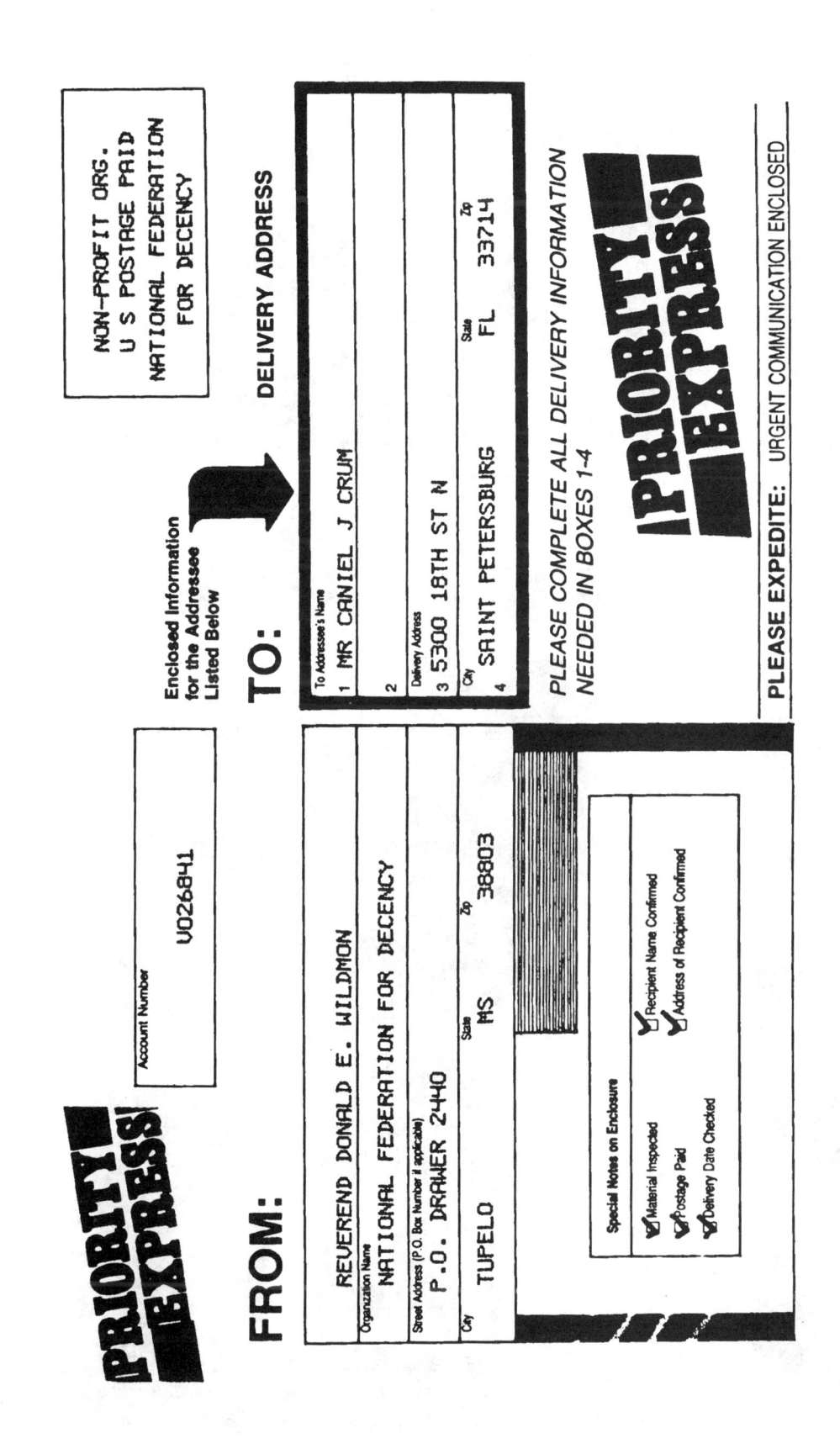

64 The Golden Mailbox

PRIORITY EXPRESS
EXTREMELY URGENT LETTER

8 / *Ways To Help Your Direct Marketing Business Grow* **65**

less expensive than United States postage would have been!

4. *Let something interesting peep through the pane of a window envelope.* For instance, Viguerie has used currency from Argentina. One of the firm's clients also put a .357 cartridge case in a mailing. When going to the right prospects, such gimmicks increase the likelihood that your envelopes will be opened.

Make your direct mail letter seem more like a package. If you put something in there, prospects will be more curious about the contents, and it won't seem like just another unsolicited letter.

Natural Selling

Despite the innovations the Viguerie Company has introduced in direct marketing, Squire sees it as an easy field to enter, even for business owners without any background in direct selling. "Direct marketing's simple. An entrepreneur can fall into it," he says. "You just write a personal letter to an interested friend, asking them to buy another pair of socks."

After starting on his own, Squire adds that an entrepreneur might want to get "a fresh look" later on from an outside consultant or agency. He notes that Viguerie has helped a seller of log homes by suggesting they use direct marketing to sell dealerships as well as individual houses. However, Squire cautions against using advertising agencies as direct marketing consultants. Although they can make "beautiful and expensive" brochures, they're "not response-oriented."

The Viguerie Company hopes to have 60 percent of its clients coming from commercial businesses within the next five years. One advantage to the for-profit area is that it's "easy to figure out your competition," Squire says.

Squire suggests that direct marketing entrepreneurs send away for about 50 catalogs advertised in publications full of direct marketing offers, such as *Yankee Trader*. Doing so will give you an idea of what successful direct marketers are doing. You might be surprised how similar many of the catalogs are. If that's the case, you'd better be different if you want to break into the market.

For instance, Squire notes that L.L. Bean and Lands' End's catalogs are quite similar. Although they're both making money, a new firm might have trouble competing against several established companies. Banana Republic is the only recent breakthrough in direct clothing sales, Squire says.

When doing your research, Squire adds that you should give a slightly different name to each catalog you send for. In that way you also can see how often your name gets rented and to whom. By looking at the labels on unsolicited mailings you later receive, you can tell which firm initially rented your name to other catalog sellers.

How To Find Low-Cost Mailing Lists

One way to boost profits is simply to lower your costs. If you can find mailing lists, for instance, at less cost than you generally pay a list broker, you might be able to lower your prices and still make a larger profit!

Such lists can be found, although they take some hunting and salesmanship to get. What you're looking for is an opportunity for a cross promotion.

In a cross promotion you make an offer to a list belonging to someone else. Rather than renting the list as you would from a broker, you give them something else of value—a discount on merchandise, perhaps.

A direct seller of gourmet foods might go to a local import car dealership. "I have a terrific idea for a promotion that will help you sell cars," the direct marketer might begin.

"Really? How could you know anything about selling cars?"

"I know that most of your customers come here because they enjoy the finer things in life. Right?"

"Of course," replies the car dealer.

"You can tell them that they'll get discounts on my fine gourmet foods as a bonus for buying a car from you during the next month."

At this point the direct marketer explains the marketing benefits of such a promotion. "A 25 percent discount on my merchandise is a real value. In years to come your customers will appreciate and remember you because of this promotion. We'll kick it off with a gourmet cheese party in your showroom, and that's bound to get media coverage."

You can see how the direct marketer is selling the car dealership owner on the idea by showing how his plan will help sell cars. But actually, a cross promotion works only when both parties benefit. Here the direct seller can attract customers to the car dealership. In doing so, however, he gains new prospects for his own food business.

Endless variations are possible. Rather than doing a sales promotion together, the direct marketer might offer to rent or buy the names of recent car buyers. Since he doesn't compete with the car dealer directly, he can probably get the names cheaper than from a list broker. Or he might suggest that the dealer give him the names in exchange for a percentage of the gourmet food sales he gets from the first mailing.

Other cross promotions might involve going to a professional association. Tell them you'll give their members a discount on your products. You'll supply the association with a mail stuffer touting this as a benefit to the members. All the association has to do is add the stuffer to a regularly scheduled mailing to give its membership that benefit.

You actually can't get something for nothing. Instead of paying for a list, you'll probably end up spending quite a bit of time talking with people in order to convince them to do a cross promotion with you. Most businesses and associations are wary of a new idea. But if your firm is short on cash, you might be happy to spend your time finding a cross promotion candidate and saving money on mailing costs.

Cross promotions are good ways to build mailing lists. But make sure you heed the following rules before proceeding:

1. *Pick appropriate candidates for cross promotions.* Will a cross promotion truly help both parties? Does such a promotion fit in with the way both firms do business? It's hard to ask a company to do something that's out of character.

In fact, make sure the promotion helps establish your firm's uniqueness. Gourmet foods and imported cars go together well, for instance. Doing such a promotion could elevate and enhance the image of both businesses.

2. *Raise the idea only with someone who can make a decision at the other company or association.* Lots of people there might like your idea, and you can waste lots of time talking with them. Make sure you're dealing with a decision maker. If you can't quickly get through to such a person, you probably don't have enough clout with the group to convince them of your notion anyway.

A good way to find possible cross promotion candidates, in fact, is by looking at your own *centers of influence*. Business associates and groups you belong to are prime targets. You'll get a more receptive audience with someone who knows you than you will with a stranger.

Finding a cross promotion partner is an exercise in selling—but you're probably a good salesperson or you wouldn't be in direct marketing. In fact, after approaching prospects through the mail or via space ads, it might be fun to do a little one-on-one selling for a change.

In the next chapter we'll look at more ways to save and make money in direct marketing. By understanding some current trends you'll be able to benefit as you let those forces build and strengthen your direct marketing company.

Chapter Nine

Future Shock for Direct Marketing?

Smaller direct marketers must work smarter now. Large corporations are flooding the scene with high-budget mailings, ads and telemarketing campaigns.

Entrepreneurial direct marketers can't compete directly with big bucks. They must use tools such as classified ads, direct delivery and trade shows to lower costs of finding prospects and selling to them.

Many new entrepreneurs think their work is done after finding a product. What they're actually doing is searching for the Holy Grail or some similar object they know will be in universal demand if they can only find it.

Successful direct marketers don't look for the Holy Grail. As far as they're concerned, it doesn't exist. Many products have potential if they are marketed correctly. To get into direct marketing you'll choose a product or service you know well. Most likely you'll take an existing successful product and enhance its value. Personalize it, offer it in more colors or sizes, give better terms or price, improve it or alter it to make the product just right for a specific market.

You'll do some research to see if the market needs what you're offering and if it's willing to pay for your product or service in sufficient amounts to support your firm.

Liquid Profits

One recent product success story is the growth of the wine cooler industry. Stuart Bewley and Michael Crete started the boom in 1981 when they first bottled California Cooler by hand. All that year they shipped only 700 cases of their wine and fruit juice concoction, but three years later they sold nine million cases. At that point large firms such as Gallo and Anheuser-Busch saw the potential and got into the market.

It's easy to have 20-20 hindsight and say that Bewley and Crete saw a great opportunity in a product that fit what Americans wanted at the time. But, before a product is on the market, it's hard to predict accurately how it will sell. For instance, few thought zippers were that much of an improvement over buttons. After all, they had an embarrassing tendency to jam.

Your success depends more on how you market a product than on the product itself. I'm not saying you can over-hype a poor product and do well. More frequently, a needed product or service never reaches its full sales potential.

Slow Path to Success

"Zillions of great ideas are out there," says Stuart Bewley, chairman of California Cooler. "We had a great cooler recipe." But his challenge came from deciding how to produce and distribute the product for the public.

Most people "overestimate the brilliance" of entrepreneurs, he adds. "It's logic. You think something through, break it down and do it."

Bewley spent a year working full-time developing his firm before he put the cooler on the market. Much of that time was spent doing market research at nearby Chico State.

"We took a card table, two chairs, a case of coolers, cups and ice." Bewley gave out free samples and then asked the students to fill out a questionnaire. On it he'd ask if they liked the cooler. What did they normally drink? Would they drink this new product instead? Should it come in four-packs or six-packs?

How much would they pay for it? Which of the names listed did they prefer for the new product? "You learn a lot," Bewley says.

Many of the same principles can be applied to direct marketers. Careful development of product presentation, marketing and fulfillment are the essence of starting a direct marketing firm.

Below is a checklist developed by Sunset House's Len Carlson. Originally this list appeared in an *Advertising Age* article written by Bob Stone, president of Stone and Adler in Chicago. Use it to evaluate the marketability of your product idea. Also use it to develop a list of things you need to find out, as California Cooler's Stuart Bewley did, before going into production and marketing.

- ✓ Is there a perceived need for the product or service?
- ✓ Is it practical?
- ✓ Is it unique?
- ✓ Is the price right for your customers or prospects?
- ✓ Is it a good value?
- ✓ Is the markup sufficient to assure a profit?
- ✓ Is the market large enough? Does the product or service have broad appeal?
- ✓ Are there specific smaller segments of your list that have a strong desire for your product or service?
- ✓ Is it new? Will your customers perceive it as being new?
- ✓ Can it be photographed or illustrated interestingly?
- ✓ Are there sufficient unusual selling features to make your copy sizzle?
- ✓ Is it economical to ship? Is it fragile? Odd-shaped? Heavy? Bulky?
- ✓ Can it be personalized?
- ✓ Are there any legal problems to overcome?
- ✓ Is it safe to use?
- ✓ Is the supplier reputable?
- ✓ Will back-up merchandise be available for fast shipment on reorders?
- ✓ Might returns be too huge?
- ✓ Will refurbishing of returned merchandise be practical?
- ✓ Is it, or can it be, packaged attractively?
- ✓ Are usage instructions clear?
- ✓ How does it compare to competitive products or services?
- ✓ Will it have exclusivity?
- ✓ Will it lend itself to repeat business?
- ✓ Is it consumable, so that there will be repeat orders?
- ✓ Is it faddish? Too short-lived?
- ✓ Is it too seasonal for direct mail selling?
- ✓ Can an add-on to the product make it more distinctive and salable?
- ✓ Will the number of stock-keeping units—various sizes and colors—create problems?
- ✓ Does it lend itself to multiple pricing?
- ✓ Is it too readily available in stores?
- ✓ Is it like an old, hot item, so that its success is guaranteed?
- ✓ Is it doomed because similar items have failed?
- ✓ Does your mother, wife, brother, husband, girlfriend, boyfriend, sister or kid like it?
- ✓ Is direct mail the way to go with it?
- ✓ Does it fill an open niche in the marketplace?

• • •

One thing to remember about any product you develop is that it must be sold. No matter how good it is, no matter what need it fills and no matter what a great value you're offering, you still must go through a sales cycle in order to get orders. Don't let your enthusiasm blind you to this business fact. You must have a marketing process in place to sell your product.

Selling is the name of the game. Direct marketing consultant Gary Halbert says that "selling encyclopedias door-to-door" helped him develop the skills he'd later hone in direct selling.

In fact, he still sees himself as a door-to-door salesperson when writing successful sales packages. Most marketers with poor results "don't need a better copywriter," he says. "They need a better salesperson."

Halbert explains that if the seller already has chosen a product and offer, most any writer then can turn out a letter or ad following that lead. What can result is "a control package that's working but poorly conceived," and that's the situation Halbert enjoys working in.

Generally he will start by changing the envelope. Gary wants the package to "look personal." He affirms that "the people of America sort their mail while standing over a wastebasket." Halbert doesn't believe that most people enjoy reading advertising material. To counter that bias, he makes the envelope appear to be a personal letter.

A bulk-rate stamp rather than an indicia is used by Halbert. He also believes that most direct marketers should at least try first-class mail. Besides making the letter more personal, it also bypasses the problem of nondelivery of bulk mail by the United States Postal Service. Some direct sellers claim that at times the USPS never gets around to processing their letters.

Addresses are put on through direct impression, such as by use of a laser printer, rather than with labels. Inside the letter Halbert continues using a personal tone. Brochures and order forms are sealed in a white envelope inside the main package. In that way the reader doesn't open the personal-looking envelope and say, "Oh, Yuck!" when seeing brochures. Instead there's a personal letter and an envelope marked, "Open this after you've read the letter."

To improve responses Halbert often suggests using a double-your-money-back guarantee. Such an offer is contingent upon the customer trying the product for a period of time and using it correctly. He contends that "people don't buy goods to return them." If customers use the merchandise properly, the product should work. Promised benefits should be received and returns shouldn't rise.

Halbert admits that his thinking isn't revolutionary. After writing successful campaigns, "people think you're a genius," he says. "But the bigger reason is that you'll do the work necessary."

Because of the list industry's sophistication, weak offers can still make money when sent to the right prospects. "Lazy people get by," Halbert says, noting that increased competition will make life harder for those direct sellers. For instance, 15 to 20 years ago computer-generated letters could triple the results of a direct marketer, he says. "And everyone did it wrong." Now direct sellers use the technology correctly, "but it increases their results only marginally."

Halbert relies on the basics. When his first direct marketing venture—selling family crests and name histories—wasn't going well, he actually went door-to-door to research the problem.

Today Halbert might spend five weeks putting together one mail package—including 23 drafts of the first page. Lots of time is spent analyzing the "market, product, price levels, offer—and how to dramatize the offer." For his efforts Halbert usually takes a percentage of gross sales.

"It's a wide-open field now," he says. "to anyone willing to work."

Yet direct marketing sales techniques are changing. Perhaps with tongue in cheek, Chuck Sussman gave the following mail-order history lesson in an *Inc.* magazine interview. Sussman founded Pretty Neat Industries, Inc., a leading mail order firm:

INC.: "You say 'the old days.' Has the mail order business changed?"

SUSSMAN: "Changed? It's like night and day. In the real old days, before my time, a guy would run a tiny classified ad in the back of do-it-yourself magazines or newspapers: 'How to make a fortune in mail order. Send $1 for mail order secrets.' You'd send in your buck, and the guy would send back a copy of the ad you just answered, telling you to place it in classified ad sections of magazines. That was a classic.

"Then you had the guaranteed bug killer. 'No pesticide, no chemicals, perfectly safe to use around babies.' You'd send in your dollar, and they'd send you two pieces of wood. One had an x on it, and the instructions said, 'Place bug on x and hit with other piece of wood.' That ad ran for years.

"Another one was, 'A genuine copper engraving of Abraham Lincoln that you can hang in your home.' You'd send in a dollar, they send you a penny. That one was dynamite.

"Of course, you couldn't get away with that stuff today."

Truth or Consequences

Sussman goes on in the interview to describe how big businesses and the government have legitimatized mail order selling. Some of that change is good. No one wants to be in an industry that abuses customers.

Companies such as Bloomingdale's, Time-Life, Quaker Oats and The National Geographic Society are now in direct marketing. For such firms, producing a slick, four-color catalog and mailing it to millions is the way business is done.

Of course, your budget might not allow for mailings in the millions. But that doesn't mean you can't learn from what larger companies are doing. In fact, you should. They've put considerable amounts of money and energy into defining what works in direct marketing.

"Editing the merchandise," is how Bill Williams, senior vice president of marketing at Neiman-Marcus, describes what is chosen for their catalog. Some items that go into Neiman-Marcus stores aren't put into the catalogs. Williams explains that goods must fit the delivery schedules needed for the direct marketers and photograph well. Additionally, he doesn't want to put clothes in the Neiman-Marcus catalog that need to be tried on before purchasing.

"Knowing who we're editing it for includes knowing what customers want in terms of quality, workmanship and styling—and what they expect to pay for it," he adds.

Williams notes that "we try to liven it up somewhat by mixing in our assortment of unusual offerings. All the way from his-and-her gifts to travel offerings." For instance, recent Neiman-Marcus Christmas catalogs have featured trips to Africa or Australia. For a mere $80,000, you could take your own trip in a Bubble Boat. Neiman-Marcus tries "to be very sensitive to the peculiarities of the mail order distribution channel," Bill Williams says.

You can buy food from the Neiman-Marcus Epicure Shop, delivered on a monthly basis. Want videos of Fred Astaire and Ginger Rogers? You can find them in the Neiman-Marcus catalog. And there's also a maintenance-free aquarium, a collection of regional American foods and a paper airplane book.

In fact, you can find items ranging from two dozen personalized pencils in a monogrammed wooden box for $22 to a white Russian fox fur coat for $7,500. All of these items are chosen with the Neiman-Marcus customer in mind—especially, perhaps, the California Spangled Cat. One of these spotted kittens can be personally delivered for $1,400.

Neiman-Marcus has found its direct marketing business to be growing "faster than the industry average," Bill Williams says. "We're primarily a traditional retailer," he affirms. However, "mail order's been a very integral part of our merchandising focus." Neiman-Marcus concentrates its mail order efforts in geographic areas without N-M retail stores.

Names come from several different sources, according to Bill Williams. Retail customers, responses to ads and rented lists all supply prospects for "N-M By Post."

Once someone has made a purchase, they might receive a specialty catalog showing only one type of merchandise. To decide who receives these mailings Neiman-Marcus looks at variables such as: category of previous purchases, amount of purchases and recency of last purchase.

Finding methods of coding purchases and segmenting Neiman-Marcus lists "continues to evolve," Williams says. "We're not where we want to be." He adds that levels of expertise differ throughout the direct marketing industry. "By no means are we the most sophisticated," says Williams.

"Everything's becoming much more focused and segmented," he adds. "Efficiency of your circulation" is what he describes as being "the major issue of our day." More traditional issues—such as merchandising exclusivity and pricing—are constant themes, he adds. "It doesn't mean that they're less valid as points to compete on, but the newest competitive arena is definitely segmentation and target marketing."

In the future Williams can see more use of cable and regular television for selling. He notes that Home Shopping Network currently is bringing in sales of $2 million daily. Right now it's selling mainly low-priced items. Other channels are starting to present items in a catalog format, rather than in Home Shopping Network's auction style of selling. However, sales results for those higher-priced items have been unexceptional to date.

Entrepreneurial direct sellers are finding it harder to compete against such well-financed competition. "The direct marketing industry isn't the mom-and-pop, kitchen table industry it was," Williams notes. "It's increasingly difficult to be a small business in it." For instance, Neiman-Marcus spends $200,000 on every catalog—before counting any inventory costs.

Even if your merchandise is unique, it's getting harder to be noticed. Because of the growth of direct mail, it seems like everyone's doing it—from local retailers to Fortune 500 companies.

Oddly enough, many direct marketers got into the business so that their message could stand out. Wishing to avoid the "noise" from other advertising messages in media such as radio and TV, they turned to direct marketing. Now that more businesses are selling directly, many entrepreneurial marketers might be wondering, "Is the party finally over?"

Marketing To Win

After all, beating a leader is hard. In 1923 Campbell's Soup, Coca-Cola and Ivory Soap were the top brands. And they still are today. In fact, in 20 out of 25 categories the leading brands in 1923 are still favored today. Of the five who slipped out of first place, four are now in second place. And the other one is fifth in its product group.

RCA spent a quarter of a billion dollars trying to take on IBM in the computer business 15 years ago. After losing $250 million, RCA got out of the race. On the other hand, IBM tried to get into the photocopying machine business and could hardly dent the market share held by Xerox.

From the beginning these firms fell into a trap. They believed that putting out a good product was enough to bring in customers. Obviously, it wasn't. When customers could choose between RCA and

IBM with computers, they picked IBM—not because RCA had poor products, but because consumers saw IBM as a computer firm. And, RCA is in communications, not computers.

In effect, RCA was playing against a stacked deck. IBM already had a solid reputation. By going against them head-on, RCA chose the wrong strategy. Having the best technology or price isn't enough. You also have to know how to position yourself against your competitors.

Unfortunately, many entrepreneurs don't admit they have competitors. "We're the best. If we could get people to try our company, I know they'd switch." All too often, that doesn't happen.

And what's true for RCA also holds for smaller firms, says Al Ries in *Marketing Warfare* (McGraw-Hill: 1986). Ries and co-author Jack Trout run their own advertising agency and marketing consulting firm in New York City.

Don't go head-on against your competitors. Use strategy, Ries suggests. In military history, he notes, the bigger army usually wins. That's the reason, as noted earlier, 80 percent of the number one brands of 1923 are still tops in their categories.

If you want to survive, don't imitate the leaders in your field. They're dug in at the top of the marketing mountain; you aren't. Ries looks at four basic strategies for marketing warfare: defensive, offensive, flanking and guerrilla. Most entrepreneurs should engage in guerrilla warfare, he says.

For instance, Ries advises small firms to "concentrate on one product. In that area you can have a superior force." He adds that successful competitors to IBM in computers have chosen to be experts in a narrow market, such as scientific workstations.

A good product for guerrillas is one that has a market too small for large companies to be concerned about. For instance, a Palo Alto woman sells recipes for persons with food allergies.

"Find a segment of the market small enough to defend," urge Ries and Trout in their book. Don't encourage competition from firms larger than yours. They have more resources, and will probably win any marketing confrontation. Stay strong in a market that suits your size.

Finding Your Niche

As we've noted before, many direct marketing firms start with entrepreneurs running classified ads. They don't have to spend much, yet they get results. Classifieds help newcomers to direct marketing learn quickly which products, offers and media work.

Specialized magazines help you find your target audience. If you were selling mass market consumer goods, however, you might try putting ads in daily newspapers in various cities around the country.

Starting with the classified ads, direct marketers can look to any of three principal strategies to help their companies grow.

1. *Use classified ads as a springboard.* In that case you'll use ads to prove the viability of your product and offer. Even with the small size of classifieds, you can test different headlines and appeals. If you're selling gourmet cheeses, for instance, find out which classified ad lead-in gets the most orders:

   Real blue cheese at $3 a lb.! (Price benefit)

   Blue cheese direct from the farm to you. (Quality benefit)

   Make your parties memorable with real blue cheese. (Emotional benefit)

Classifieds can help you find products, offers and media that work—without requiring much investment on your part. Once you have a winning combination, you can spring for larger display ads and develop some mailing pieces. At the same time, your classifieds should bring in some profit and help you start building a customer list.

2. *Well-established direct marketers also use classifieds to test new products and offers.* Direct marketing can be expensive. A classified ad can give you quick results at a much lower cost. Our cheese seller could run all three types of headlines in classified ads and compare results before buying larger space.

3. *Other direct marketers use classifieds to bring in extra income.* Usually these people have one product they can sell successfully through classifieds. Instead of trying to grow a business, they simply keep selling one product and pocketing the profits each month.

Don't underestimate this work. Some ads can keep pulling for years. Once the product is developed, an effective ad is written and proper publications found. Such activity almost runs itself. Often the seller hires a fulfillment house to receive orders and mail the product. Checks sent to the seller are coded to show how well each ad worked. After enough customers order, the list of names can be rented out to other direct marketers in order to generate additional income.

No matter how you plan on using classifieds, here are some specific ways to make money with them:

1. *Compare your product, price and offer with other classifieds in the publication you're considering using.* If your ad won't fit in with what's already being done successfully, your idea might not be right for that publication.

2. *Be a little different.* You don't want to be too much like the other ads. Strive to be similar, but stand out. That's where your creative selling ability comes into play.

3. *Start your ad with words that capture the interest of your readers.* Grab their attention with a phrase that points out the need your product meets or the target group you're after. Here are some examples:

   Want to make money at home? No experience or investment necessary.

   Fishermen! My Glo-Go Worms are guaranteed to help you catch more bass than you ever have.

Notice that the headline, or first statement, captures reader attention. Try to keep that interest up while supplying more facts about your product in the next sentence. Keep doing this as long as is needed to explain your product. Then tell your readers how to order.

Sales Talk

Your writing style should be conversational. Don't try to save a few dollars by using clipped sentences, as do many classified ad writers. You can stand out just by writing the ad as though you're talking to your prospect. Make sure that what you say is understandable. Try the ad out on friends. If only a few aren't sure what your product and offer is, that same percentage of readers won't understand once the ad is published. You can't afford to lose sales due to misunderstanding.

If you need more space, you might try using a classified display ad. Although they appear in the classified section, these ads are larger and have a ruled box around them. You pay more for them, but the ad gets noticed. They still cost a lot less than regular display ads.

Sometimes classifieds even outperform more expensive display ads. Why? Most likely it's because display ads compete with the magazine articles for a reader's attention. Consequently, many readers skip over the ads and keep reading the article. Classified readers see the ads as opportunities. Many of them are looking for something specific. You can see this in the number of local publications sold in convenience stores that are made up entirely of classifieds.

You can sell things through classifieds. People know bargains and interesting offers will be there. The ads will be read even though they aren't beautiful—just as hard-to-read grocery store ads in newspapers are read. People are willing to work to find out what you're offering. In no other medium will you find such eager prospects. Just make sure your ad makes readers want to buy.

See which ads you notice, and model yours after them. When buying classified space, remember that you can get discounts for agreeing to several ad insertions in the publication. Also think carefully about which classified section you advertise under. Because of the number of classified ads, most readers look mainly in the section they think is most likely to have an offer that interests them.

In fact, you might want to try ads in different classified sections of the same publication. You then can see which section works best for you.

You might find that classified ads can provide you with an opportunity. However, they're not the only interesting method open to direct marketers. New technologies are developing that are probably more exciting than classified ads. Videotext and computer databases raise the possibility of selling over people's TVs and PCs. Such technologies currently aren't very accessible to most direct marketers, simply because they're too expensive.

Another development that direct mailers should be aware of is the use of private delivery firms. Companies are finding they can save money by hiring someone besides the United States Postal Service to deliver their mail. Billions of pieces of direct marketing material will come into people's homes this year without going through the Postal Service. In my own firm I've switched from using the Postal Service almost exclusively and rely mainly on UPS.

One reason for this growing use of private delivery firms is the rise in mailing costs. Second-class, third-class and special fourth-class rates have doubled several times since 1970. Direct mailers are finding their profits shrinking as the Postal Service continues asking for more money. With those costs rising so dramatically, direct marketers are trying to find other ways to get their materials out.

How To Avoid the Post Office

Some firms are using newspaper inserts. Many newspapers now accept ad inserts, ranging from one-page stuffers to glossy four-color catalogs. With an insert, your message will be delivered to the newspaper readership at a low cost. The wide range of publications accepting inserts increases your chances of finding one going to your prospects. Both local publications and metropolitan dailies accept inserts.

Other firms, such as many magazine and catalog mailers, use private delivery companies. Costs are less at such firms because they have lower labor costs and handling techniques set up to help mass mailers. Due to this competition, the Postal Service is trying to become more effective. Before automatically taking your mailings to the post office, though, check out what private delivery firms can offer.

You might be able to save more than you'd think. Let's suppose, for example, that you have a mailing planned to specific zip codes. You picked those codes to ensure that your promotion would go to communities whose residents fit the demographics of your prospects. If you decide not to mail, contact the private delivery firms in those communities.

Try to piggyback your mailing onto another mailing or perhaps a product sampling they'll be doing to the same zip code. Your mailing could be delivered at the same time as a sample of a new toothpaste or detergent from Procter & Gamble, which is being given to the people living in that zip code.

Another way to sell directly without licking any stamps is to do one-on-one selling. Admittedly most direct marketers would find such a technique too time-consuming. If you can get a big order, however, it's worthwhile.

A good place to find prospects is at trade shows. Recognize that many attendees come to the show mainly to find out what's going on in their industry, meet friends and make deals. You want to find those attendees who are ready to talk, tell you about their needs and spend money.

Look through the *Tradeshow/Convention Guide* (Budd Publications) to find shows that might be helpful to you. If you're sure you can sell at the show, sign up for booth space in their exhibit hall. If you're not sure, *walk* the convention. You might find someone with a complementary product who will let you share a portion of his or her booth.

But even without a booth you can gain a lot—and sell some, as well. Talk to people. Find out what merchandise others have, and what price they're selling it for. What unmet needs can you reach with your product?

In the following chapters, we'll look at the creative side of direct marketing. You'll learn how to put the principles already outlined into forms that will sell—such as direct mail packages and space ads. Whether you write your own marketing material or job it out, you need to know some of the elements that separate profitable direct selling tools from ones that fail to make money.

Chapter Ten

Starting Your Campaign

You've chosen a product. You know exactly who your market is. You've prepared an enticing offer. And, you've tested that offer on focus groups to make certain it will be effective.

Now you're ready to sell. What that actually means is that you're ready to spend money buying mailing lists and ad space. Don't fall into the trap we mentioned earlier of believing mail order is just a numbers game. "If you throw enough mud against the wall, some of it has to stick," say many salespeople.

Perhaps they can hold that belief and be successful in one-on-one selling. But the direct seller leverages the sales pitch by putting it before thousands of prospects. If you don't choose your prospects carefully, you will waste money on a grand scale. Our first rule for picking media, then, seems to be obvious:

Choose media that can reach your chosen market.

Many marketers bend this rule. As a result their response rates are often lower than they should be. Remember what we said earlier about the difference between success and failure often being based on small habits practiced over time.

One habit you should cultivate is spending time on every media buying decision. I can't tell you how disappointing it is to spend money on an ad or mailing and get almost no orders. That happens at some time to every direct marketer.

By thinking through your media choices you can minimize the number of times your marketing is ineffective. Let's look at mailing lists first. You can rent names from many different places. Some associations rent out their member lists. Magazines might let you approach their subscribers. Call the magazines or associations you're interested in. Find out what their policy is on letting outsiders rent names. You might even find that your competitors will rent names that no longer work for them.

Most of your lists will probably come from list brokers. You can find them by looking in the *Yellow Pages* under "Advertising—Direct Mail." A more complete listing is in *Standard Rate and Data Service* (SRDS). SRDS regularly updates the prices of space in magazines and newspapers and also contains information about list brokers. You should be able to find SRDS in the reference section of a business library. No matter where you find it, there are some things you should know before renting a list:

1. *Who are the people on the list?* This seems obvious, but remember the need to have your market defined as clearly as possible.

I'm sure you've received direct mail solicitations for items you had no interest in at all. You might have wondered how you got on a mailing list for which you would receive such a solicitation.

When you're paying for the list and the mailing, you want to avoid mistakes like that. Do so by having very specific characteristics for the names you want. Instead of saying you're interested in *business owners* or in *computer owners*, state exactly what you want. Your desired list should be as specific as: "Owners of retail businesses with less than $1 million in annual sales who have a business computer." Such a list would be ideal for a direct marketer of inventory software designed for small retail businesses. But if the business owners or computer owners lists had been chosen, our marketer would be renting the names of many persons.

2. *Where did the list come from?* By finding the answer to this question you can learn about the habits of the persons on the list. They had to

75

have done something in the past to get on the mailing list.

For direct marketers the best habit for a prospect to have is a tendency to order products through the mail. Any list of previous direct mail buyers is worth its weight in gold.

Most direct marketers don't believe that until they find out for themselves. Because they believe in their product, they think everyone will want it. They forget that not everyone will see things in the same light. This is especially true when approaching the consumer market. Always look for names of persons who have a habit of ordering through the mail.

Business people will usually be open to good offers through the mail. They'll consider anything that looks as if it could help their firm. But consumers are more fickle. Many simply don't buy through the mail. Many others love to order from direct marketers.

Suppose you're starting a newsletter on cats. You can choose either a list of cat owners or a list of previous subscribers to other cat publications. Which do you pick? Without a moment's hesitation, get the list of *expires* from the other cat magazines and newsletters. It's full of persons who have shown a willingness to buy information on cats through the mail. For your purposes it would be about the best list you could find.

When selling to consumers, another technique is to make demographic choices. It can work if you know that most buyers of your product have consistent age, sex or income characteristics. List brokers use zip codes to *segment* a list into demographic sections. From Census Bureau data they learn about the income levels of various neighborhoods.

In fact, any meaningful demographic characteristic shared by your prospects can be a key to choosing lists. Go over a diagram of your customers when renting lists. You might find some traits to which rentable lists correspond.

Beware of *compiled* lists. Such lists are made by taking names out of a professional directory, or even out of the phone book. With a compiled list you can reach all the stockbrokers in town, or all the pig farmers west of the Mississippi.

Ask your list broker where the names came from. If you find that they're compiled from a directory, think twice. Usually such names don't pull very well. Because they're compiled from lists, the names haven't done anything to indicate that they like to buy directly.

Ask how old the list is that you're considering renting. As a general rule, don't use any lists over one year old. Too many people on that list will move in a 12-month period, and once they've moved, your letter is undeliverable.

Even the best, most-recent mailing lists will have five percent of the letters returned as undeliverable. Using an older mailing list with more undeliverable addresses will bring down your overall response rate.

If you are renting lists of previous direct response buyers, find out the recency and frequency of their orders. Generally such lists are segmented to indicate the best prospects. It's worth paying more to get a list of people who've made recent, multiple direct response purchases. Also make sure that the dollar amount of your prospects' past purchases isn't less than what you're asking them to spend.

Another general rule for list renters is to try to mail to persons over age 35. Lists of country dwellers also outpull lists of city dwellers.

Take these generalities, and apply them to your product and company. Some might not apply to your situation; others could be lifesavers.

When It Pays To Advertise

If you can't find a list to your liking, consider the publications available to you. Space ads in magazines and newspapers have some strong selling points for direct marketers:

1. *Preparing an ad is easier and less expensive than developing a direct mail package and printing, addressing and mailing thousands of letters.* Even experienced direct mailers save money with space ads. For instance, testing marginal lists is expensive. Thousands of packages must be mailed out just to test. For the same amount of money a marketer can run an ad in a publication known to reach the target market.

2. *You can save even more money when starting out by placing classified ads instead of display ads in publications.*

3. *Editorial material in well-respected publications can enhance your ad.* An atmosphere is created that adds value to your product or service. None of this happens by itself, but the potential is there.

You can also misuse this potential. Editorial copy can work against your ad, providing competition for the reader's attention.

With both advertising and direct mail you work with the elements available to you. Understanding their use helps you be more effective in selling. For example, some ads make you want to turn the page and read the next article. But others stand out. You linger over them. You think about what they say. You give more attention to some ads than you do the articles in the publication.

The same is true with direct mail. Some packages you receive seem destined to be thrown out without being opened. Others get opened before any other mail. In a later chapter, we'll look at how to make your ads and mailings irresistible.

You'll find which ad size is most profitable for you. A large ad attracts the reader and can help you hold the prospect's attention longer and do more selling. But if the ads are larger than they need to be, part of your profits are going to the magazine running your ads.

Mailing lists are usually more effective than ads. With lists you can target who receives your offer. Mailings are also more expensive than ads. Often both techniques are used together: an ad can be used to generate inquiries; direct mail then follows up those inquiries.

Or you can go for the order directly with both ads and mailings, knowing that you'll be reaching different groups. Even if there is overlap in persons receiving your letters and reading your ads, that's good. Each one will serve to reinforce the other. In that way you have more chances to reach into a prospect's mind and make a sale.

Start with mailing lists if you have good ones, such as lists of existing customers. Look more to space ads when effective lists become hard to find. New customers brought in by ads can help form better lists for you.

If you're starting without lists, consider using classified ads to get customers. Because of their small size, classifieds can be used either for getting leads or for getting orders for items costing less than $5. Usually you'll find that classifieds in magazines bring more responses than they do in newspapers. Magazines today cater to select groups. You can shop there for audiences much as you can with mailing lists.

Newspapers, however, go to the general population in a region. Most newspaper advertisers are merchants in the area. Grocery stores are prime newspaper advertisers, but newspapers have little appeal for most direct marketers.

Publications can give you a good understanding of the inner characteristics of your target groups. Just reading the articles will let you see the attitudes, motivations and concerns of the readers. You can build more emotional appeal into your offers once you understand the inner values held by your prospects. Often these values are called the psychographics of your target group.

Mailing lists offer a closer look at demographics: age, sex, geographic location, income and buying habits. When making space and list purchases, understand the limits involved in the selection process. If you see your market as a distinct demographic group, you'll probably want to emphasize direct mail. If you're selling to people holding specific attitudes, you'll have an easier time finding suitable publications than you will finding mailing lists.

Another method for determining which mailing lists and publications to use involves researching your present customers. Isolate variables on the customer information you keep. Ask your computer to search for those variables to see if one or more is held by many of your customers. Some of the results might surprise you.

Find out if your customers are mainly men or women. Look at the zip codes to see if any geographic areas seem to work better for you. If you find that most of your sales are to women who live in urban areas, use that information when choosing media and lists.

You also can build prospect mailing lists by asking your current customers for the names of friends who would be interested in receiving information about your firm. As an incentive you can offer your customers and their friends discounts on their next orders. But usually that's not necessary. If customers like your merchandise, many of them will be happy to give you the names of friends with similar needs.

What you are doing is continuing to break down, or segment, your target market. You're trying to find which identifiable group responds best to your product offer. This strategy is in keeping with the philosophy of pitching your company on as narrow a plane as possible. You want to target your marketing. You want to know exactly who your best prospects are, and put your offer before them.

You're avoiding the common pitfall of looking for a huge market and wanting to take a very small percentage of it. In approaching a huge market you will find an unbelievable amount of competition.

Slicing Your Market

Several tools can be used when analyzing your customer list to see which segments are most fruitful for you. Once you're aware of the best zip codes for you, see what types of people live in those areas. After all, you're selling to people, not addresses. Get

Census Bureau data to complete the picture. If you're selling home workshop tools, find out if most of your buyers are homeowners instead of renters.

If you're selling electronic equipment, see if most of your customers own several phones. You can get such information by contacting the Census Bureau at (301) 763-7662. Once you've collected some information on your customers, you can analyze it. By getting a better picture of who's buying, you can readily find lists of good prospects. Listed below are three ways to analyze your customer lists.

> 1. *Get various pieces of information on your customers, and see if most of them share more than one element.* For instance, the marketer we discussed who sells to women living in urban areas would want to know if the women are generally married or not. If marital status is a constant factor, the marketer can specify more clearly what type of prospects he or she wants, quickly culling out names that probably won't pull in sales.

Looking at groups of variables is known as *factor analysis*. Although it can be a disciplined statistical exercise, any computer or file card system can do the same thing.

Let's consider the direct response seller of electronic goods who discovers that most of his or her customers own more than one phone. With Census Bureau data other significant factors can also be examined. Do most customers have a college education? Do they buy expensive cars? After answering these questions a composite picture of the customers can be compiled.

New lists can then be seen. If most customers buy expensive cars, a list of recent Mercedes buyers can be tried. Since there's no competition involved, a local dealership might be willing to rent names inexpensively so the marketer can run a test.

Dividing your market into segments through factoring helps you find more prospects by letting you view the life-style of your customers. Start with a vague understanding of your customers. By doing Census research, you can find out traits common to your customers. Their zip code is the key to getting to know them better.

> 2. *Once you have determined factors that are important to you, put them together to approach the best prospects. Cluster analysis* lets you pick out sections from, say, a larger zip code file to tailor a list to your needs.

For instance, the marketer looking for married women in urban areas could tell a list broker to look at zip codes within urban areas and pick names of married women from those geographic areas.

If you aren't using a list broker, you can still perform cluster analysis. Do it by learning how to *merge and purge*. Suppose the marketer had access to a list of city dwellers and also a list of married women. The two lists could be compared. Names appearing on both lists would be sent the mailings.

Merging and purging can be performed either manually or by a computer. It can really save expenses when you weed out ineffective names. You can also merge and purge in order to eliminate names found on two lists. In that way you won't mail duplicate packages to the same address.

> 3. *A good list consultant should be able to take the above information and come up with new lists you've never approached.* A mathematical technique—*regression analysis*—helps predict how effective lists should be when they are similar to your current mailings.

You should be able to do the same thing yourself by carefully looking at your current lists and comparing them to lists or publications you're considering. Remember that all customers aren't created alike. When looking for names, try to find ones whose characteristics match those of your best customers. Most direct marketers use the rating system discussed earlier to cull superior clients based on recency, frequency and dollar amount of purchases. After compiling these names they'll make up your *hot list*.

In the search for the perfect prospect, direct marketing decisions come down to costs. The Profit Worksheet on the next page will help you make marketing choices.

Part of the reason for keeping records on worksheets is so you'll be able to compare results of different efforts and relate results to costs. You'll notice this worksheet is divided into three sections: Costs, Results and Follow-up. Information gathered at different times is represented by the three categories.

Code the names in your computer so you can find how many later orders come from the new customers generated by this promotion. Every quarter search through your active customer list. Find out how your best customers came to you. If you advertise in *The Wall Street Journal*, code all the names of new customers with "WSJ." Compare the follow-up buys your "WSJ" customers make to the purchases made by customers obtained from other publications.

Profit Worksheet

1. Costs

   a. *Price of space or mailing list*
   b. *Creative and production costs to put together ad or mailing*
   c. *Cost of mailing (direct mail only)*
   d. *Add a, b, and c to get Sum of Costs*
   e. *Divide Sum by number of persons reached. Express as Cost per Thousand.*
   f. *(Not to be filled in until results are in.) Divide Sum of Costs by number of responses to get Cost per Response.*

2. Results

   a. *Date of mailing or ad*
   b. *Sum of costs*
   c. *Gross margin in dollars of item being promoted* Subtract shipping and overhead costs from sales price to get Gross Margin. Shipping and overhead can be referred to as internal costs.
   d. *Number of items this ad or mailing must sell in order to break-even* Divide the Sum of Costs of this promo by the Gross Margin for the product to get the break-even number.
   e. *Number sold* Also put this figure in "f" in the Costs section above.
   f. *Gross revenue after internal costs* Multiply Gross Margin (c) by number of items sold (e).
   g. *Profitability of ad or mailing* Express your gross revenue after internal costs as a percentage of the sum of your marketing expenses (b).

Let's say your Gross Margin is $10 per item. Your ad cost $100. It brought in 15 orders, or $150 in Gross Revenue. Obviously this is a successful ad. Its profitability is 50 percent, because the revenue was 50 percent over the cost of the ad. If the ad had brought in 10 orders you would have earned only $100, and just broken even. Your profit would be zero.

3. Follow-up

   a. *Number of returns*
   b. *Returns as a percentage of order* If you had ten orders originally, and one person returned the item, you would have ten percent returns on this ad or mailing.
   c. *Adjusted profit* Consider the case above where we needed ten orders to break even. One return off ten original orders would take us from breaking even on the promo to losing ten percent on it
   d. *Dollar Amount of Subsequent Purchases made by customers developed through this promotion* Fill this item in later. After fulfilling the orders from this promotion you will place the names in your active customer mailing list, and you'll continue following up these customers with new offers.

We've talked before about how the most expensive part of direct marketing is getting a customer to make the first order. Profit is achieved more from subsequent orders. And we've also noted that customers aren't created equally.

Analyze your results over time. Looking at the cost per response is a good indicator. It's recorded in the first part of your Profit Worksheet. Cost per response divides the total price of your marketing effort by the number of responses it brings in.

Yet you should go further than that. That's why we've put the *follow-up* section in the worksheet. Your real profits will come from those later orders. You might be able to segment your customers to find out which ones tend to keep buying from you.

On the flip side, you might find that some lists or publications bring in customers who return merchandise in greater numbers than average. Obviously you will look beyond initial results in such cases. Keep marketing in the avenues bringing few returns and more subsequent sales. Even if the initial cost per response is high, you might simply be paying more for better customers.

Making comparisons is an important part of direct marketing. You need to know which list is better and which product is better. You can then make the right choices to maximize your profits.

Much of your recordkeeping will be used to make comparisons, and your efforts should be structured to help you make valid comparisons. For instance, whenever you do a mailing to a new list, you should do the same mailing to part of your in-house list of current customers.

In that way you can see how the new mailing list stacks up against your current customers. If responses to an offer are low for both lists, you probably have a bad offer. In that case you might want to try another offer on the new list. If the in-house list drastically outperforms the new list, drop the new list—even if response is pretty good. You know that by comparing responses with your current list you can get better results with other lists.

Make comparisons in any way you can in order to see what circumstances are the best for your marketing efforts. For instance, see if results differ depending on the time of year your ad or mailing appears. Most direct marketers say January and September are the best months. Test that with your own situation.

More money-making comparisons can be compiled from your Profit Worksheets. Suppose you're selling three items separately to two mailing lists and in two magazines. What efforts are bringing in the most dollars? Find out by analyzing each item and media separately for profitability. Since each item has a different margin, and each promotion has different costs, you must make sure that you're comparing apples to apples.

Do this by looking at the profit figures on your worksheet. You want to make as much as possible for every marketing dollar spent. Label a sheet of paper *Item A*. For that product see how much profit it has produced in each marketing effort. You might decide that its profit across the board is weaker than the return from the other two products. In that case, you should drop the item.

You might find that it's profitable to one market segment but not to others. Or that it sells well through the mail but does less well in space ads.

Do the same analysis for each item and on each marketing medium. If for each of the products an ad in *Forbes* is more profitable than an ad in *The Wall Street Journal*, drop the *Journal* and spend more money in *Forbes*.

But always compare profit. If you were just to look at revenue, for instance, you could be misled. You should know the return you get as you spend money on different items and in various media. Once you start keeping accurate records, you'll have that information at your fingertips.

In order to be able to make necessary decisions, you need to keep track of sales. As each order comes in, put the names in your master filing system. Code them for recency, frequency and amount of purchase.

Mail more often to customers who are rated high on those three criteria. Decide at what point mailing to someone is no longer profitable to you. If there are no additional orders after five mailings, you should consider taking them off your active list.

The right number of unsuccessful mailings you can tolerate depends on your specific finances. You don't want to lose sales, but you also don't want to waste money.

Although direct mail costs are rising less than rates for newspaper, magazine and television ads, your profits will be determined by how well you spend marketing dollars. You aren't a retailer who can rely on a great location to bring in customers. You aren't a franchisee who markets off a national firm's name.

As a direct marketer your sales depend solely on reaching individual prospects and offering a product of value to them. Your direct response success will depend on how effectively you do this.

Get on the Right Track

Two methods are available for helping you make effective decisions. We've already looked at segmenting, the first money-saving method. Segmenting markets helps you buy lists or space with little *fat* in them. Strive to have as many strong prospects as possible reached with your marketing. Clearly define your company, product, offer and market.

Our next tool is simply choosing the right medium and method of approach. Here you must make judgments on how to spend wisely. Saving money isn't always the key.

Remember the marketer who tried to write his own direct mail letter when he didn't have any experience selling that way? He wasted money on that mailing, simply because he wouldn't spend enough to put together a working package. In direct response, if you're off target with your choice of medium or message, you'll suffer in sales.

To help you make the right decisions, a brief summary of the media you'll be considering is below. Use it to see what your product and customers need in order to be sold. Go back to your own specifics, and plug in your numbers to find out which method will most likely work for you.

Media Round-Up for Direct Sellers

1. *Direct mail letters.* A typical direct mail package contains several elements. The letter itself can range in size from one undersized page to a dozen pages. Two to four pages would be average, although you should feel free to use whatever amount of space you need to sell effectively.

One of the appeals of direct mail is that your format isn't preset. You can use almost any size envelope. Put in an oversized, fold-out brochure if you like. Make your letter as long or short as you please. Every element in the package is designed to make an individualized appeal to the recipient, one which encourages action on the part of the reader.

To do that the mailer includes a coupon or reply card and a business reply envelope to make ordering easy. Often a second, smaller letter is put in and marked "Read this only if you've decided not to order." In it the president of the firm expresses disbelief that such a valuable, no-risk offer is being passed up by the reader. And then the benefits of the product are repeated, and the offer is made again. Tests show that having such a letter increases the selling power in a package.

2. *Self-mailers.* A one-page announcement or a brochure that can be folded and have an address label affixed is called a self-mailer. Firms use them because they can save lots of money when compared to a direct mail package. Postage, printing and assembling costs are all lower when a self-mailer is employed.

Self-mailers usually should be overlooked by direct marketers. They're useful for making announcements, but they aren't sophisticated enough to sell successfully. Few people will order from you if you just send a self-mailer. Additional elements found in a direct mail package are needed to get prospects to buy.

Merchants use self-mailers to announce sales. Other companies send out information about themselves in self-mailing brochures. You can cover a lot of territory with self-mailers because of their low cost, but your money won't come back to you in sales. Most firms use them to entice interest in their company by providing news or information.

3. *Card decks.* Each card in the deck offers one product for sale. Prospects receive the entire deck through the mail. Customers order by putting their address on the card, signing it and sticking it in the mail. In a credit offer, billing comes later. Business-to-business selling is generally the place for card decks. Businesspersons who know what they want can leaf through a card deck and quickly make decisions. Ordering is very easy. Card decks are quite inexpensive, and they can be very effective. Make sure the card deck is going to good prospects.

4. *Catalogs.* If card decks are meant more for professionals, then catalogs are preferred by consumers. A nice catalog makes shopping fun with breezy descriptions, fetching photos and slick art design.

Make sure you have a good stable of products before putting together a catalog. Do they all fit together logically in your catalog? Will most of the persons you mail to be prospects for most of the merchandise?

Catalogs pose a risk because of their expense. Design, production and postage costs are high. If you are selling to businesses, resist the temptation to make

82 The Golden Mailbox

What Will You Do When Your Personal Assets Are Seized to Satisfy a Judgement Against Your Corporation?

Every single one of the many tax benefits you receive from owning a corporation could be wiped out overnight. How? The IRS could visit and claim you have not kept proper corporate records.

And banks, insurance companies and various government agencies require notarized authorizations to grant loans, enter into leases and even sell assets.

In a small, one person business, it seems silly to keep records. Isn't it just a waste of time? NO! Recordkeeping is part of the price you pay to receive all the advantages of incorporation.

You could hire a lawyer to keep your records — just like the big corporations do. And to have one form prepared, you'll pay $100 or more, even though your lawyer's secretary may complete the standard forms.

There is now a way for you to solve your corporate recordkeeping problems. Without a lawyer. Without the high fees. And without spending a lot of your valuable time. It's THE COMPLETE BOOK OF CORPORATE FORMS by Ted Nicholas, author of the bestselling book, HOW TO FORM YOUR OWN CORPORATION WITHOUT A LAWYER FOR UNDER $75.

➡ SEE OTHER SIDE FOR MORE DETAILS

Virtually every form your corporation will ever need is prepared for you, and there are simple easy to follow instructions for each document. Each form can be completed in minutes. And you have permission to reproduce any form in the book.

Here is just a sampling of what you'll receive:

- Minutes of Stockholders' and Director's meetings.
- Minutes of Special Meetings.
- Forms authorizing your expenses and salary. And much more.

Even if you are behind in keeping accurate corporate records, this book will help you catch up. Just complete a few blanks to document your companies' activities. It's legal and it works. And best of all, if you use just one of the forms in the next year, you will more than justify your modest investment in it.

K-1043

©1992 ENTERPRISE • DEARBORN

Please rush me _____ copy(s) of THE COMPLETE BOOK OF CORPORATE FORMS by Ted Nicholas at $69.95 plus $6.00 for shipping and handling. I understand my purchase is covered under the **Enterprise • Dearborn** 30-Day Money-Back Guarantee if not satisfied.
☐ Check enclosed.
☐ Visa ☐ MasterCard ☐ American Express

_____
Account No.   Exp. Date Initials
_____
Name
_____
Company
_____
Address
_____
City   State   Zip

Daytime phone (in case we have a question about your order)
Mail to: **Enterprise • Dearborn**
          520 North Dearborn Street
          Chicago, IL 60610-4354
          1-800-554-4379

This is a sample of a card from a cooperative advertising deck.

up a catalog unless your clients will regularly order from it, as is the case with office supplies. Most businesspeople aren't interested in shopping. They won't look through your catalog just to see what you have. Rather, they'll come to you when they have a specific need, and see if you have what they want. Let your business clients know about your special offers, but usually it's unprofitable to go to the trouble of sending them a catalog.

> 5. *Bill inserts.* If you are going to send someone a bill through the mail, why not see if you can't get another order at the same time? That's the idea behind bill inserts.

Because of their light weight, these *stuffers* won't add to your postage costs. Try them on your own customers first, since they already know you.

Some credit card companies sell other firms the right to put inserts in their bills. Your primary concern here is to make sure that the people receiving the bill are good prospects for you.

> 6. *Radio and television.* Although you don't think of television as a direct selling medium, products ranging from *Time* magazine to records to Japanese knives have been sold directly on TV. Generally you need a toll-free number to get viewers to order. If they can't call, you'll lose most potential sales. TV viewers usually won't bother taking down your address and writing you for more information.

Some direct marketers use television to support telemarketing or direct mail campaigns. Broadcast ads are used to create name identification, in the hopes that prospects will be a bit more likely to listen to the telemarketing or read the direct mail package when it reaches them.

Use this medium with caution. Broadcast time is expensive and generally suited to reaching a mass audience, not market segments.

> 7. *Telemarketing.* Having salespersons work the phones is expensive. You pay for both the phone time and the seller's time. Yet prospects are approached only one at a time.

More people can be reached more quickly and less expensively with direct mail. Telemarketing works best when you are selling an expensive product that demands lengthy explanations and personal selling skills. Often telemarketers talk to an interested prospect several times before all objections are met and a sale is closed.

> 8. *Videotext and electronic databases.* New technologies allow consumers to shop at home. Merchandise is shown or described on their TV screen or computer monitor. Orders can be placed automatically in the system.

Right now it's still growing. But in a few years shopping with electronic catalogs could be widespread, at which time costs for getting your merchandise in such a service should also drop. For now, most direct marketers should probably learn about the new technologies but not get involved with them.

> 9. *Magazines.* As we mentioned earlier, magazine ads can allow you to approach market segments. At times you can be surer of whom you're reaching through a magazine than you can with a mailing list.
>
> 10. *Newspapers.* Because of their general audience, newspapers are poor tools for direct marketers. However, the classified ad section can be used for direct sales in both newspapers and magazines. Remember that people are usually scanning these ads looking for something specific. Make sure you can describe your product in a few words, so you can catch the *scanners* who want what you're selling. Just add a price and a phone number or an address after the catch phrase.

Classifieds are also used in two-step selling. Offer free information on a subject in order to get inquiries. Send your brochure to respondents, and then follow up with a direct mail package.

Actually buying space, time or lists is your next task after deciding which media you'll use. We'll look at media buying tips in the next chapter.

Chapter Eleven

Managing Your Customers

As a direct marketer your most expensive and valuable asset is your customer list. Your list is as important to you as assembly lines are to General Motors. You'll need to look after your customers as carefully as IBM protects its microchips.

You'll need to know what these names are worth. Just as any other company compiles the value of its capital assets, you'll want to know what your names cost and how much money you can expect back from them. The value of your lists will change—even as factories depreciate in value, so will your customer names.

How do you maximize the income you'll receive from a depreciating asset? How can you tell—before paying for a mailing—if the list is still able to work hard and bring you more money than you spent on it?

Before, we mentioned the Recency-Frequency-Dollar Amount (RFD) model. Now I'll show you how to construct one to suit your specific situation.

You have to understand that customers go to merchants out of habit—although I'm not saying that they don't have good reasons for those habits. Perhaps the seller's location is convenient, or the goods are exactly what the consumer needs and the price is probably right for the value perceived by the buyer.

But you're not a retailer. You can't wait for buyers of habit to walk into your store the next time they need your products. Instead, you must identify those buyers who are willing and able to make a habit of purchasing from you, and keep making them offers through the mail.

As you construct your RFD model, put most of the emphasis on the most recent buyers. Lists age rapidly. If prospects don't become repeat buyers, many of them will never purchase from you again. Another section of the list will move away, and their addresses will become worthless.

Most direct marketers find that customer lists over one year old are, at best, only marginally profitable. Talk about rapid depreciation! If you want to make money from your lists, you can't waste time.

You probably spent quite a bit to acquire those names through a list broker, ad or previous mailing. Don't let that money go to waste.

When constructing an RFD model, many marketers put 50 percent of the coding values on recency. Another 35 percent goes to frequency, and the final 15 percent makes up the dollar amount category. This is just a guideline to help you start coding your lists. If it is accurate in your situation, most of your sales can be predicted. You can segment your lists to pull out the best prospects. Put most of your marketing follow-up into those lists, and most of your sales should come from those efforts.

If you see lots of sales coming from a different list, try to discover the important distinctions of that winning list. Perhaps they have different demographic attributes. Or you might find that the 50-35-15 percent weighting is not appropriate for your situation.

Here's how it works. Let's say you can be profitable by receiving one order a year for $15 from each person on your customer mailing list. Now you want to look at actual buying habits to isolate customers who can make you profit and those who can't. In the Customer Rating Grid on the next page you'll see that we've given recency, frequency and dollar amount ratings for this example. Of course, the parameters of the grid will be different for every firm.

Rating numerals represent different customer performance levels. For instance, customers scoring *four*, or the highest possible, in the recency category are those who ordered within the last three months.

Next, determine where each customer fits into the one through four rating grid within each category, and then multiply by the weighting index. The recency score of a customer who bought in the last quarter is multiplied by 50. Frequency scores are multiplied by 35, and dollar amount ratings by 15. The highest possible *Customer Rating Score* is 400 in this model.

In this example we'll consider the score of someone who spent $15 on a first-time buy eight months ago. In the recency category the 8 months rates a 2. Multiply that *2* times 50 (the recency weighting factor), to get 100. Now look at frequency. Since the customer just bought once, she scores *1* in this category. Multiply *1* by 35. Add that to 100 from the recency category to get 135. Finally, let's consider dollar amount. A $15 purchase scores *2* in this grid. Multiply that by 15 to get 30. Add that onto 135 to find the total of 165 for this average but profitable customer.

That total means nothing by itself. Once you get all your customers rated, you can compare them. You can pull out lists of, say, everyone who scores over 250 in your rating system. In all probability those would be very good prospects for a mailing.

Despite the emphasis on recent buyers, factors in the other two categories can be very important. You might even want to put high scorers in frequency and dollar amount into separate lists. For instance, mailing to a list of habitual big spenders can be very profitable. Conversely, you might find a list of multiple buyers much stronger than one of first-time purchasers simply because they are in the habit of buying from you, and it's easy to keep getting them to purchase.

Still, you should find that, in general, your most recent buyers are the easiest to get subsequent sales from. But that's not the only way to make money in direct mail.

Often the key to profitability comes from renting lists to other direct marketers. You need to know which lists to rent in order to avoid hurting your direct mail business by renting out your best names.

Do that by offering for rent only names of nonactive customers. That is, customers who haven't responded to a certain number of mailings, or who have gone a set amount of time without placing an order. Again, you fill in the specific guidelines that suit the economics of your firm.

Even though such lists are no longer profitable to you, they might work for someone else for they are proven mail order buyers. A different firm with a new offer or product might be able to get them to buy again.

Any direct response company that rents a list from you will want to know how the names were generated. Were they actual orders or just inquiries? If they were orders, how do their recency, frequency and dollar amount figures look?

Instead of renting lists, you might be able to work a trade with another firm—your nonactive buyers in exchange for theirs. Often you can work such a deal through a list broker. You'll have to pay a commission to the broker, though. If you are in a tightly knit industry and know your competitors, you can save money by approaching them directly to exchange lists. Commissions to list brokers run at 20 percent of a list's normal rental cost. Most lists will rent for about $35 for a thousand names, and up.

Obviously the more selective the list, the more it will cost. Renting a list of "previous mail order buyers of flower seeds" is cheaper than going after "previous mail order buyers of imported tulip bulbs." However, if you're selling imported tulip bulbs, renting the

Customer Rating Grid

Recency (last purchase date)	*Frequency* (purchases per year)	*Dollar Amount* (last purchase)
Score		Score
1— 9 to 12 months ago	1	1—$2.95-$9.95
2— 6 to 9 months ago	2	2—$10.00-$19.95
3— 3 to 6 months ago	3	3—$20.00-$29.95
4— 1 to 3 months ago	4	4—$30.00-$39.95

second list would probably bring in more sales. It would most likely be a more profitable choice for you, since more of the prospects would be past buyers of products similar to yours.

When renting out one of your lists through a broker, you'll receive the rental price minus commission. You'll also have to pay for the clerical and computer time needed to print labels of the list. That might take another ten percent out of your profit. If you are going to rent out your lists frequently, you might consider retaining a list broker who will attempt to rent your list on a regular basis.

A good list broker will help you put in decoy names to make sure the renter only uses your list once. A decoy is a person paid to keep track of mailings they receive. If a renter uses a list more often than they've contracted to, the decoy will alert the list owner or broker. Because of the use of decoys, no reputable company tries such a cheap trick. If they did, they would be blackballed by list brokers and would have a hard time getting the lists they want in the future.

Unless you currently have large lists, you'll probably use a broker to help you find lists to rent more than for renting out your own lists. In many ways good list brokers are like direct mail consultants. Before choosing one, find out what services they can provide besides supplying names. They earn their commission by understanding your needs and suggesting lists you can profitably mail to.

When choosing a list broker, find one who is experienced in the type of lists you need. Check the firm's reputation with other direct marketers, and learn what their resources are. Can they help you find a list giving the exact market segment you need? Do they know the *history* of their lists? That is, can they tell you if a list you're considering has worked well with firms similar to yours?

Make sure they have the physical resources you need. Can they merge and purge lists? Are delivery dates for labels guaranteed? You don't want to miss a mailing date because your labels didn't show up.

Many brokers help prepare the offer for mailings, and analyze their effectiveness—at no extra charge. It's in their best interest. They know they'll get repeat business if mailings they supervise turn out well.

Demographic data should be available with most lists, in addition to the usual information about where the list came from. At times a list broker can provide very specific information on a list, such as which company last used the list, what their offer was and perhaps even resulting sales figures. If you use a list, keep track of your sales to see if the results you hoped for actually occurred. In that way you'll know whether you should continue mailing to that list.

Usually you'll rent a gross number of names. However, if you are renting a million or more names, you can pay only for the ones you use. By merging and purging the rented list with your current customer list, or lists rented from other sources, you avoid duplication. If you were mailing to a list of a million names and got rid of 15 percent duplication, you would avoid needlessly spending $25,000, or more.

List compilers usually don't provide services as thoroughly as brokers do. Compilers represent only the lists owned by the company that employs them. Brokers try to be knowledgeable of all lists that are available for rent. You can expect more objectivity from brokers. If a compiler has lists that could be valuable to your firm, though, consider using them.

Listening to Yourself

A direct response key is fitting together all the elements of your campaign. Your product, offer and market must all mesh. If not, sales will suffer. Good marketers develop an intuitive sense of these three elements. From working with their specific market they come to understand their needs. Of course, they test their intuition before committing lots of money.

Good marketers are salespeople who rely on their sales instincts more than on research. Many of them, like myself, have built their businesses and large mailing lists from scratch. They started with a single ad or small mailing to a list they'd compiled. Selling had to be effective from the start.

I don't consider such beginnings to be a handicap. If you're wise you'll always retain those salesperson's instincts. When using list brokers you'll listen and learn, but make the decisions yourself. If for whatever reason you don't feel comfortable with a list or a selling approach your broker suggests, then don't ignore those feelings. After all, it's your money.

For instance, most list brokers tend to think in categories. If you're selling household items to consumers, they'll be able to tell you other lists that have done well for marketers of similar goods. For most marketers list brokers provide an awareness of previous results from various lists. Also, they can help you track your results from mailing to those lists.

If you're interested in buying lists without using a broker, here's where to find them:

Direct Mail Lists Rates & Data
Standard Rate & Data Service, Inc.
3004 Glenview Road
Wilmette, IL 60091
(708) 256-6067

You'll find over 20,000 lists to choose from in SRDS. Each list will have the following information:

- name of list
- who to contact about renting
- description of the list names
- how the list was put together
- total number of names on list
- rental costs and credit terms
- formats in which the list can be delivered
- time of delivery
- restrictions on the use of the list

Before ordering lists, look carefully at how the names were obtained. Here you'll see whether it's a compiled list, names of previous buyers or inquiries. Ask for more segmented information, such as recency, frequency and dollar amount figures on the buyers.

When ordering, you will be asked the following:

1. *A sample of your mailing package* will be requested by the list owner.
2. *Date of your mailing.* Most lists take two or three weeks to arrive. Make your order in plenty of time so that your mailing schedule won't get thrown off.
3. *List segment you want.* Examples would be most recent buyers, certain zip codes and requesting mail order inquiries rather than previous buyers.
4. *Name any special information you want on the list segments*, such as average size of last order or geographic areas covered. You could use such information when analyzing your results. You must ask for this information at the time you order the lists.
5. *Specify the format in which you want to receive the lists.* Cheshire labels are the easiest to affix. If you want to merge and purge the list with your own files, you must request a magnetic tape for your computer operator or list manager to use.
6. *Make additional orders if you are planning more mailings from this list.* You probably can get a discount for using the list more than once.

After you get the list, take a look at it to make sure it's complete and represents your selection. Mistakes do happen, and you might not get what you asked for. One way to inspect the list is to look for any specific requests you made, such as specific zip codes.

List selection can be a technical process. For that reason I rely on good list brokers. I frankly don't know much about many of the tools they use for choosing lists. As I mentioned before, however, be sure that your own sales judgment is comfortable with a list before you commit to using it for a mailing.

When buying space ads in magazines you also can rely on both your instincts and good advice. Begin the process by imagining your ad in the publication's pages. Would it make sense there? Will the people reading the magazine be interested in your product? Will they notice your ad and respond to your offer?

Make a list of potential markets for ads. Write to these magazines, and ask for their rate card. You'll receive information on the cost of ad space in the publication. In addition, the magazine will usually supply demographic information and audited circulation figures on its readership. Look over this material carefully before buying space in the magazine. Be certain that the magazine's readers are good prospects for ordering your product.

Often you'll find what you need to know from the information the magazine sends you. How many hours a week do their readers spend playing tennis? Do most of them own a microwave oven? Answers to such questions should be available. If the publication doesn't offer the facts you want, then call or write them. Identify yourself as a potential advertiser, and you'll probably get an answer to your questions.

Prices for space in magazines are expressed in *Cost per Thousand (CPM)*. You should pay less than $10 per thousand readers. Obviously this is much less than paying more than $30 per thousand for mailing lists. And you don't have to pay the additional costs of printing and postage that mailings demand. Yet space ads pull only about 10 percent of the orders compared to direct mail.

With space ads you're competing for the reader's attention with every other ad and article in the magazine. And you're limited by the size of ad you've ordered. Mailings, on the other hand, can contain as much information as you want to send.

Magazines are often trusted because of their editorial content. Since they're read at a leisurely pace, many times an ad will get more attention than will a direct mail piece.

Enterprise • Dearborn Book Buyers

(This is a paid duplicate of the listing under classification No. 532.)

Media Code 3 045 4773 0.00   Mid 019155-000

Member: D.M.A.
Enterprise • Dearborn
520 North Dearborn Street
Chicago, IL 60610
Phone (312) 836-4400

1. PERSONNEL
List manager—Jeff Kessler.
List Assistant—LaWanda Miller.

2. DESCRIPTION
Buyers of or inquiries about business related how-to offers on incorporating, tax shelters, raising capital, etc. Includes bookbuyers of How To Form Your Own Corporation Without A Lawyer For Under 75.00 and The Complete Book of Corporate Forms. ZIP Coded in numerical sequence 100%.

3. LIST SOURCE
Direct mail and space ads.

4. QUANTITY AND RENTAL RATES
Rec'd Jan. 15, 1992

	Total Number	Price per/M
Total list	170,923	70.00
Hotline (3rd qtr. '91)	13,205	80.00
Last 12 months book buyers	26,400	75.00
How To Form Your Own Corporation Without A Lawyer For Under 75.00	16,779	85.00
Complete Book of Corporate Forms (1987-92)	40,406	85.00
Business Agreements (1987-92)	24,818	85.00

Selections: business address 6.00/M extra; state, SCF, ZIP Code, hotline, 10.00/M extra; keying, 2.00/M extra; hotline, split run, 25.00 extra; telephone numbers, 25.00/M extra.
Minimum order 5,000.

5. COMMISSION, CREDIT POLICY
20% commission to all recognized brokers

6. METHOD OF ADDRESSING
4-up Cheshire labels. Pressure sensitive labels, 9.00/M extra. Magnetic tape (9T 1600 BPI), 25.00 nonreturnable fee.

7. DELIVERY SCHEDULE
Two to three weeks.

8. RESTRICTIONS
Sample mailing piece required for approval. Mail date must be reserved. List owner must have option to rent mailer's list on a reciprocal basis. Cancellations beyond mail date charged full rate.

9. TEST ARRANGEMENT
Minimum 5,000. Nth name selection.

10. MAINTENANCE
Updated quarterly.

*This is an entry in SRDS for Enterprise • Dearborn mailing list.
Note the types of information given about the list, including which "Selections" may be specified.*

Before deciding if ads are suited for your product or not, let's look at some other space-buying tips. For specific space costs, Standard Rate and Data Service provides magazine ad costs and circulation figures in its publications.

Magazine Ad Options

1. *When to place ads.* High returns in magazine ads come the same months considered best for direct mail campaigns. After summer vacations and after the Christmas holidays are favored by direct marketers. Your best bets are August to October and January through March for all direct response marketing, that is, unless you're selling a seasonal product.

2. *How often to repeat ads.* Every situation is individual. Your budget and desire to grow will play large roles in the decision. One simple rule of thumb is to place an ad, and see how well it pulls.

If orders bring back less than your break-even point plus 20 percent, wait a year to run another ad in that publication. Run one in six months if you hit that 20 percent mark. If your gross sales are more than 20 percent above expenses, run the ad in that magazine again in three to four months.

3. *Position of the ad.* Talk with your ad rep before placing an order. Get a commitment in writing for where your ad will be run, both as to the page number and whether there will be other ads or articles around your ad.

Many magazines won't ensure ahead of time that you'll get everything you want in terms of placement. Editors and artists need leeway for moving material around as the magazine gets ready for printing. Try to get as much assurance as you can, because what's around your ad can determine your response.

Unless you're buying cover space, you'll get better results the closer your ad is to the front of the magazine. Ads on right-hand pages pull better, and it's better to be opposite editorial material than next to another ad. Get your space rep to agree to as many of these terms as possible. You probably won't be able to tie them down to a specific page, but work for a good position within guidelines agreeable to you and the magazine. Your sales will reflect those efforts.

4. *Space, color and bleeds.* With magazine advertising you buy more exposure with larger ads, the use of color and *bleeds*, or ads that are printed to the edge of the page. Each of these effects costs extra, but will tend to give your ad more impact. Obviously a full-page color ad will stand out more than a small classified.

Listen to your copywriters and artists as you make these decisions. Try to find out how much space is needed to sell your product. Generally, the more expensive the item you're marketing, the more space you need. For instance, car ads are often one or two pages.

Test a publication with a small ad, if it works well you can hit the market harder with a larger ad next time or use a color ad if it will show off your product well. Obviously you need to get enough extra sales to justify the added expense of more space or color.

Many direct marketers have found their responses improved by adding a coupon to the bottom of their ad. It's a device that helps make ordering easier. To include a coupon, you'll need at least a one-column space.

If you want to try a smaller ad, ask if the magazine has a classified or mail order section where the rates are usually less. Readers who like to order by mail can quickly scan these ads when they are grouped together in the magazine.

5. *Special deals.* When you're low on cash, see if a publication will accept a trade-out of your merchandise for their space. Some magazines will even take a commission based on the sales or inquiries generated by the ad, rather than a fixed payment.

6. *Insertion cards.* Reply cards can be bound into magazines alongside one-page ads. Although they can triple your total cost, reply cards also can boost responses by an even greater amount. Use them only if you have the money to spend and when you know a publication works for you.

Selling Electronically

Radio, TV, phones and new media such as videotext are too pervasive in our society to be ignored by the direct marketer. There are more than two radios for every person in this country, and 98 percent of all households have a television, which is usually on for more than six hours a day.

Much of the information and ads that Americans receive come through wires or over airwaves.

Remember that you are trying to position your product favorably in your prospects' minds. At the same time, many other commercials are trying to do the same thing. If you don't consider selling over the electronic media, you will automatically lose a lot of exposure that other advertisers gain. Today direct marketers are finding they can use electronic media to get their message across and still make money. As long as your marketing is profitable, don't be concerned about spreading your efforts too thin. If you can use direct mail, print ads and electronic media, then do it.

In fact there are several advantages to using different methods. First you can reach different prospects effectively. Think about people you know. Some read a lot of magazines. For these persons, information is gotten through print. Maybe they even look down on others who rely on TV or radio for information and entertainment.

You can reach such prospects through print ads and direct mail campaigns. What about the people you know who wake up to their clock radio and don't get out of earshot of a radio or TV all day? Electronic media are the best way to reach them.

For the majority of people who are exposed to a mix of electronic and print media, advertising in both reinforces your message. In fact it often takes several messages to get a person motivated to buy from you.

Since each medium is different, your ads will also be varied. People who read your print ad and hear a radio spot should find them complementary. Although each ad will have a different perspective, they'll make the same point.

Electronic media aren't for all direct marketers. If you write them off without first exploring the possibilities, however, you could be missing something. Don't leave some selling avenues totally open to your competition, especially if your firm needs to find new markets in which to grow. Electronic media could provide the key to tapping prospects you haven't reached before now. Prices for electronic media time also are available through Standard Rate and Data Service, Inc.

After you start analyzing radio and TV, you'll soon find that they can be segmented to reach different audiences. This tendency is more apparent with radio than with TV.

Radio stations develop programing to reach chosen demographic groups. Listeners are loyal to the format of the station. It can be all-news, Big Band, rock or oldies. Each station has its own demographics. Research shows that most listeners regularly tune in to no more than three radio stations.

Look deeper into a radio station's schedule. You'll see more audience segmentation. You might find special programs for opera lovers, jazz fans and persons who like talk shows on various subjects. All of those special interest shows could be part of the format for a radio station appealing to middle-aged persons.

Look at these segments carefully. One of them might fit your product perfectly. For instance, a marketer of a news magazine might advertise on a radio all-news show.

Buying time on radio and television is somewhat different than buying mailing lists. A station has a more or less set number of minutes of time it can sell to advertisers in every broadcasting hour. If that time doesn't get sold, it's lost forever as far as the station's concerned. When that happens there's no way they can reclaim the time and make money on it.

Ad reps for radio and television stations are consequently more likely to make deals in order to sell time. Rate card costs are generally disregarded. Payment based on the number of inquiries or orders received by an advertiser is common. Barter is also a frequently used way of buying time. Explore any of these opportunities when negotiating with a media time rep.

Four main strategies are available to direct marketers who like radio and TV. Look at each one below.

1. *Go for the order.* You're used to this idea, of course. But remember that you must pay for the time used for selling your product.

One hallmark of direct mail is being able to keep adding on to your sales letter until you've covered all possible objections. Repeat your offer several times. Remember that print and electronic media are more limited by space and time, respectively.

If you have a simple offer, you might try selling directly on the air. If your offer or product needs some explaining, you should consider an ad that would generate inquiries.

Spend more money on advertising time. TV commercials that sell directly are usually two minutes long, while commercials designed to generate inquiries or support other marketing activities can be just 30 seconds to 60 seconds in length.

2. *Ask for inquiries.* As is true with print ads, this strategy is used less than is going for the order. Consider the inquiry method mainly when approaching a business client—someone who is making a potentially costly decision that must be justified. You'll rely on direct mail, telemarketing or personal sales calls to close sales.

3. *Sell promotional products.* This is an alternative when selling consumer products with complicated offers. Use promotional products to build a mailing list. Then sell your more expensive product through direct mail.

4. *Support other marketing efforts.* Results of print ads or direct mail campaigns can be improved by using the electronic media. Basically you are telling viewers or listeners that they'll be seeing your other ad or mailing soon. Make them feel they'll be making a mistake if they don't pay attention to it. More people will then open and read the direct mail offer, and more replies will come back.

To make this a worthwhile strategy, you must do two things. First, time your air time and mailings so that people see them at the same time. Without that reinforcement, your strategy won't work. Next, see if the extra responses from the direct mail or print ads make up for the expense of air time.

Generally direct marketers test electronic media by trying radio first. It's less expensive than TV. You can more easily find the market segment you want because of the many specialized radio shows. Results from radio ads and TV ads should be about the same, so it's a fair test.

TV allows you to use visuals. With an announcer you can provide what appears to be a very personal message. A good radio personality can do the same thing, but radio is more of a background medium than TV. People usually listen to the radio while performing other tasks, and tend to give TV more attention.

Getting the Electronic Order

Marketing costs per order or inquiry should be the same for electronic media as they are for print or direct mail. What you lack with the electronic media are easy ways to get prospects to respond. You can't include a coupon or a business reply envelope in a radio or TV spot.

Having a toll-free number is the primary way to provide for responses to electronic advertising. When a number *and* an address are offered, 20 percent to 40 percent of all orders will come in through the mail.

If you use a toll-free number, make sure that your operators are good salespeople. They should, of course, know the product. Provide them with plenty of information. Also give them written scripts on overcoming objections raised by callers. Teach them how to try to upgrade orders by making callers a special offer if they buy extra items, take a longer subscription or otherwise enlarge their order.

Newer technologies allow prospects to order through their TVs, computers or fax machines. Some of these systems are limited to certain geographic areas. If you use these services, such as videotext or online databases, make sure to continue changing the offer you put on the service. Some marketers forget to do this. If you don't, it's like continuing to mail the exact same piece over and over.

Currently the best new technology for reaching prospects is *electronic mail*, which is offered by companies such as CompuServe. CompuServe subscribers from all over the country can order from any merchant in the electronic mail. This is one way for smaller firms to present themselves to prospects nationally. However, consumers aren't rushing to use the technology.

Whatever you decide to put into your media mix, make certain that you are reasonably committed. Don't make excuses for a losing ad or mailing and keep using it. On the other hand, don't run a single ad and give up if the results aren't what you want. Generally you need to commit to at least a nominal campaign before having conclusive results. In the next chapter we'll look at ways to save money and improve results by careful testing of offers before spending lots on space, mailings or media time.

Chapter Twelve

Testing for Success

After your product has been developed, your offer chosen and the media picked, you're probably raring to go. Yet some caution is needed at this point. This is when you begin signing checks. Copywriters, list houses, artists and magazine space aren't cheap.

The smart direct marketer doesn't jump in with both feet. Even after doing all the preliminaries outlined so far in this book, success is far from being assured. You still must discipline your enthusiasm for your firm and product by testing your decisions before putting a lot of money behind those choices. You have too much to lose if you don't.

In general my advice on testing is to rely on your judgment and experience when picking mailing lists or magazines to advertise in. Start cautiously, and see what results you get back from your marketing efforts. You will have some failures—even the best list brokers will be wrong more than right.

By that I mean that most lists you think will work actually won't. Testing helps you predict what will work in direct marketing. List broker Max Bartko, Direct Media, Inc., says that a typical direct marketing test would involve ten lists. Two of those would be profitable, two others would lose money and the remaining six lists would come "close to breaking even," Bartko notes.

Some direct sellers find success coming easier with experience. As they get to know their market, they can find products that will be accepted by lists they're already familiar with. If the lists are large enough they might be able to go back to them with new products and not have to test new lists.

Most marketers find testing a part of their business. New products, markets and offers tantalize the direct seller looking for a combination that clicks. If you can locate a group with plenty of names and can sell to them, you can move a lot of product.

Here's a situation in which a little knowledge can steer you wrong. Bartko says that it's better not to have "preconceived notions about a market." You have to recognize that "the marketplace is brighter than you are. You must be willing to be humbled." Marketers with open minds are more likely to cut their losses quickly, as well as spot unexpected successes and continue mailing to those lists.

List brokers can assist in this process by bringing their perspective into your marketing. Whereas sellers tend to concentrate on product, list brokers look at the promotion itself, Bartko says. Quality of the promotional material often will help decide which lists respond to the offer. For this reason, quality clothing sellers such as L.L. Bean and Neiman-Marcus will use four-color photos and glossy paper to help appeal to the people on their lists.

Price breaks are another point list brokers look at when advising direct marketers. Certain market groups respond to items within set price ranges. A list broker can tell you from experience which lists buy items for the amount of money you're asking. Price breaks reflect points where response falls off. If you try to sell to a group at the wrong price, your sales could be disappointing.

"A list broker is almost a commodities broker," Bartko asserts. From his vantage point, a good list broker knows which lists are working for certain types of products. He suggests looking for a broker by getting listings from the Direct Marketing Association or by looking at ads in *Direct Marketing News*.

You'll want to get background information about the list broker you're considering. You want someone who knows the business. For instance, a broker might tell a newcomer that an $8 item can't be sold through direct mail. Because of the cost of the medium, there is no list that can generate enough numbers to turn a profit.

On the other hand, a broker might remind someone trying to sell an investment newsletter that a subscription price of more than $100 annually is hard to get. A good broker also is "willing to do a lot of work for nothing" in order to get your order, Bartko says. Such work would consist of finding lists used in similar offers made successfully by other firms.

Bartko adds that when testing you should test at least 5,000 names per list. He says that tests can be done to determine the effectiveness of list choices, product price and the offer.

Testing, in its most basic form, means going into a proposed medium slowly. If the results don't satisfy you, then move onto another option. Cut your losses quickly. Do it before you've committed a large portion of your marketing budget to an unfruitful pick.

Marketing in Moderation

Now the problem is deciding how much is enough. When have you mailed enough names to a list to see if that list will work? Since you believe it's a good list for you, you want to give it a fair chance. On the other hand, you don't want to spend a nickel more than you have to if it's a poor choice.

Many rules of thumb exist: *You must mail to at least ten percent of the list. You can't compare results of two mailings unless you got at least 100 orders from each mailing. Five thousand names are usually enough to test a list.*

None of these rules should be followed blindly. As I've emphasized throughout this book, you need to understand marketing concepts and apply the economics of your firm to the situation.

I emphasize marketing concepts with good reason. Testing is actually an application of statistics, a mathematical discipline. You need to know some of the bottom-line marketing consequences of statistics. But you don't need to base every testing decision on statistical analysis. In fact, I think that would be impossible—at least it would be for me.

We can learn a lot from statistics, but most businesspeople don't have the time or resources to let statistics guide their decisions. Let me give you an example. Statistical tables, based on the laws of probability, can tell how large sample mailings need to be to ensure that the list is useful. Let's say I need a one percent response rate from the list. I can't tolerate an error of more than .02 percent. In other words, for my mailing to work the response rate must be between .98 and 1.02 percent. I need to know the results of the test are 99 percent correct.

According to statistics, I'd need to mail over 1.6 million letters to a single list before I could be sure that list would meet my specifications. Obviously that's ridiculous.

Now if I could tolerate a 0.3 percent error rate, my test mailing could be just over 7,000. In other words, a mailing works when the response rate is anywhere between 0.7 and 1.3 percent.

Don't get too caught up in the math. What this exercise shows is that a direct marketer with tight response demands needs to be more cautious. If a list is barely profitable in a sample mailing, the marketer should consider other choices before using more names. Statistically it's hard to say that later responses will stay at the same level the test sample did.

What Can You Test?

Testing is useful in more ways than choosing lists. One rule to remember, though, is to test important items. Don't try to find if responses are greater when your return address is on the front of the envelope rather than the back.

A good direct marketer will choose to test: the product or service, marketing media, the offer, formats of advertising material, copy approaches and timing of marketing efforts. Significant response differences will be found when these elements are altered. Let's look at each subject specifically:

1. *Product or service.* Previously we've explored ways to test products and services. For meaningful testing, look at both your current customers and noncustomers. Study your customers to determine who buys and why. But also look at why others in your target market didn't make a purchase in order to have a complete picture of your product's image.

You'll probably want to start by testing your current customers. You can learn their attitudes through telephone or mail surveys. Usually you'll get at least a 20 percent response without having to offer anything in return for responding. One key to getting good response rates to surveys is by letting your customers feel that you're really interested in hearing their needs. I know that sounds obvious. Too often, however, surveys are made by insecure business owners who want to be reassured that everyone loves their product.

Let customers know their responses are valued. Tell them you're looking for customer input to help you in marketing, in refining old products and introducing new ones.

Don't focus on your specific brand in the survey. Let's say you sell popcorn makers. What you want to know are the features customers find important in popcorn makers. A sample of a survey you could develop appears on the next page.

From such a survey you can learn what features are important to persons buying your product. You learn how often they use the product. And you learn what they are willing to pay in order to get the features they want.

If you don't get many survey responses you might want to include a dollar bill or a coupon for popping corn to make prospects feel obliged to respond. You probably won't need anything like that, unless you're shooting for a 50 percent response rate on the survey.

Use the survey information to compare your product to your competitors'. Does the other product have more of the features that appeal to your market? Direct marketers need to be aware of their competition. Even if you aren't, your prospects are. If your offer isn't exactly what they want, they'll look elsewhere.

You can stay ahead of the competition by finding out what your prospects want and giving it to them. Perhaps you can add a few features and raise your price. Looking at survey results should give you an idea of what will work.

Survey noncustomers by using focus groups or random surveys in shopping malls or through the mail. In addition to finding out their thoughts on product features, find out how these noncustomers differ from customers. Perhaps you can discover a new market or find out why persons in your current market aren't buying your product or service.

> 2. *Media*. Earlier in this chapter we saw how media testing can become a very technical subject. One idea should make it fairly simple for you. I'm assuming you've already figured your costs and know the minimum profit you need. Begin testing media by taking small bites. If the mailing or ad is profitable, take a bigger bite.

You'll need to continue monitoring results to see if the customers you develop bring in repeat sales, or if they turn around and ask for their money back. As long as you're keeping accurate records, you'll know what's making money. Keep doing what's successful, and you'll get more ideas of other media to try.

Don't be afraid to follow your instincts. Try a list or a publication very different from any you've ever used if you think it might work, especially if you're in a highly competitive direct mail field. Many lists get rented to others in the industry. A buyer is often swamped with other offers soon after purchasing through the mail. Find a group of prospects that hasn't been already deluged by your competition.

> 3. *Offers*. If you're new to direct marketing, you've hopefully done some focus group or other form of market testing. From that research you can put together some appealing offers. But generally it's not useful to pretest offers on focus groups.

Such groups can give you an idea of attitudes held by target markets toward your product. You can't accurately ask someone if they would respond more to specific offer *A* or specific offer *B*. Only their buying behavior can tell you that for sure.

If you have an existing mail order business, you can test new offers on your most recent customers. Unless, of course, you sell only one product that lasts a long time.

> 4. *Different ads and direct mail packages can be tested*. Since the cost of each one will be different, use profitability measures as a comparison. You want to go with formats that bring in the most sales per marketing dollar.
>
> 5. *Copy approach*. Here you are looking for the appeal that will bring in the most orders. Typical copy approaches include emphasizing unique features, price or a guarantee. Once you have a successful ad or mail package it becomes your *control*.

At that point you test other ads or packages against the control. See if you can beat the control by mailing a new package and the control to identical lists.

In addition, keep trying to improve the control package. Try to make your appeals stronger. More to the point. When you think you have a stronger control package, test it against the original. When you're planning a new mailing, split the list and mail each package to half the names. Track the results. If your new package pulls better with most lists, you have a new control.

> 6. *Timing*. Mail the same package to the same list, or run the same ad in the same publication—but at different times of the year. Track the results to see if there are seasonal differences in your customers' buying habits.

Sample Customer Survey

Dear Popcorn Lover:

Your (Brand Name) popcorn maker should give you and your family great popcorn for years. To help us in product development, please take a few moments to answer the following survey. Your responses will be used as we design new popcorn makers.

Thanks for your time.

Sincerely,

John Doe, President

1. Rank the features listed below that are most important to you in a popcorn maker. Rank them by writing numbers from one to nine next to the features, with one being most important and nine being least important.
   - _____ Built-in serving bowl
   - _____ Able to pop corn quickly
   - _____ Ease of cleaning
   - _____ Able to pop all kernels
   - _____ Automatic butter warmer
   - _____ Built-in measuring cup
   - _____ Use of air heat rather than oil
   - _____ Lightweight design
   - _____ Popcorn recipes or seasoning mixes

2. How much would you pay for a popcorn maker that has the top three features you listed above? Please check the appropriate range.
   - ❏ $10.95-$14.95
   - ❏ $15.00-$19.95
   - ❏ $20.00-$24.95
   - ❏ Over $25

3. Write below any other comments that could be incorporated in new popcorn makers.
   _____
   _____

4. How often do you use your popcorn maker?
   - _____ More than once a week
   - _____ Once a week
   - _____ Once every two weeks
   - _____ Once a month
   - _____ Less than once a month

Would you like more information on new kitchen products? If so, write your name and address below. Note: You can send in this survey even if you choose not to sign it. Just place it in the enclosed envelope and mail it. No postage is needed.

Name:_____
Street:_____
City, State, Zip:_____

Generally direct marketing does best when people are back from summer vacations, in September and October, and right after New Year's. Marketers suspect that the new year and recent holidays leave prospects feeling happy, prosperous and ready to spend. Also, most people are at home during the prime marketing months of September and January, ready to read the mail and ads coming their way.

When testing, direct marketers should also be aware of outside events beyond seasonal differences. Test results can be skewed by weather or world events. For instance, Christmas catalogs work best when the weather is bad and people prefer shopping through the mail rather than going to malls. When the stock market is flat or down, marketers selling investment newsletters are usually disappointed.

Try to anticipate such events as much as possible. Recognize that these factors can affect your responses.

You'll notice that in the above discussion several techniques were suggested. Each is appropriate at different times. A common question among direct marketers is whether to do test ads and mailings or basic consumer research. They note that successful packaged goods manufacturers rely heavily on consumer research.

If Procter and Gamble is thinking about a new soap product, it tests the product and packaging on consumer groups before starting to manufacture. Even then Procter and Gamble will usually start test marketing in only a few cities before making the product a part of its line.

For them, consumer research is a way of buying information. Direct marketers know that they won't make a sale while conducting consumer research. It's spending money without any hope for a direct return. Direct marketers don't like to do that. I know I don't.

At times it's better to spend a little money on research than a lot on an ad that might not work. Procter and Gamble does its research because it does not want to go to the expense of manufacturing a new product and getting it to their sales force, only to find that the product's concept or packaging is flawed.

Although they are unscientific, focus groups offer the best means of market research. However, some marketers find that groups are generally more productive when they're presented with products they're familiar with. Innovative products will often get downplayed in a group, say some researchers.

You must rely on your instincts. Once you have enough knowledge of your market to make a reasonable assumption about your product's appeal, ease into selling by purchasing lists or ads. As long as you make money on your marketing, keep it up.

Testing becomes easier the smaller your market is. Sampling a market of 10,000 is simpler than finding out how a market in the millions will respond.

If you know your market well to begin with, you can probably skip the stage of basic research. You then just have to make sure that lists and publications are available, which reach your market—at costs you can afford.

How Can You Be Sure?

At times even well-thought-out tests leave you unsure as to what the results mean. There are two main reasons behind this phenomenon, and there are solutions you can use to get better answers.

One way to avoid test problems is to avoid giving your copywriters too much free rein. When writers know that you want responses from a mailing, they go all out to get them. And that's good, as long as they stay within reason.

At times a copywriter will promise too much. Your product will be cast in terms it can't live up to, and that causes problems. First, it's unethical and potentially illegal to misrepresent products.

Second, you might get lots of orders—which are promptly followed by demands for refunds on up to half of those orders. So your high test response rate would ultimately be misleading in terms of how many orders you end up with.

Copywriters can also put too much emphasis on the "what have you got to lose?" angle of your offer. You should always have a money-back guarantee, but at the same time you want to encourage orders, not *lookers*. You don't want to have too many people ordering while thinking "If I don't like it, I'll send it right back."

Check your copy for these excesses before it is approved. Run the writing by your product experts to see if too much is being claimed in the offer.

Be especially aware of the possibility of misleading initial results if you make certain types of offers. Marketers who use two-step selling are examples. If you're trying to get names of interested prospects and then send them a catalog, you might do well in getting names. Actual orders after the catalogs are sent, however, could be disappointing. Similar situations can occur with marketers offering promotional items.

Play It Again, Sam

Any marketing plan depending on future sales can fall flat after receiving good initial results. Magazine subscriptions and book clubs are good examples. You can more readily rely on test results if you are selling one item and taking cash with orders. Your returns and bad debts then shouldn't be extraordinary.

Another testing problem occurs when you don't have enough money to do a large test. Many firms are in this situation. Most companies start out with little or no money. You want to avoid mistakes, but you don't have much of a budget for testing.

Suppose you test four lists by mailing to 2,500 names on each. Once you find the best list, you'll do a mailing of 20,000 to start bringing in orders. You want to get your company going, yet because of your small samples of the four lists, the differences between response rates might be just a few orders per list. This is especially true if you're selling a high-priced item that encourages low response rates.

So which list is best? Can you project low results onto a mailing of 20,000? Remember, that mailing will be a very important event for your firm. You can't do the big mailing to the wrong list.

What's your choice of action? One you should consider is retesting to confirm the results of the first test. If some of the lists you tested were profitable, retest them. You'll make more sales. And you'll have more information to help you decide which list to focus on.

Another problem that can skew test results is getting a poor sample of the list. When ordering a list you want a representation of the entire set of names. To do this, you'll ask for every *nth* name. If the list has 500,000 names and you want to test 5,000, you'll ask for every 100th name.

Lists are segmented by most recent respondents, by geography or any other means by which the list owner wants to separate names.

If the list is maintained on several reels of computer tape, the operator might not go through the whole list giving you every *nth* name. In other words, they might just give you the number of names you want off the first reel. But the first reel could hold segments of the list that don't adequately represent the entire list. Always specify when ordering that you want an *nth* name sampling over the entire list. If you don't get a good sample of the list, your test of that list won't be worth much.

Lists also might not be what you think they are. Remember the cases of good initial direct mail results that sour from excessive returns? Some direct marketers with lists such as that one might try to rent them to you, claiming they're names of people who've recently ordered through the mail. That may be true, but it's still not a good list. Always get as much information as you can about a list before renting it.

To control such problems, specify the segments of a list that you want. Good segmenting will let you separate poor names from good prospects. List owners segment their lists to suit the needs of their business. Proper segmentation for another firm will probably be wrong for you.

Demographics, life-style and buying habits can all be possible segments. Segmentation becomes more effective as it's layered. For instance, you might ask for "Male homeowners who have purchased audio tapes by mail during the last six months."

One note of caution, however. Specifying segments makes list rental more expensive. Don't ask for more than you need, or you'll be paying extra while skipping over useful names on a larger list.

Use segmenting to find matches with your current customers. Try to find others with similar buying habits and needs. When you can find segments you want, your testing becomes more reliable. Your overall marketing results should also improve. When you don't segment, you probably will have to work harder to make a sale. More letters must be mailed, because your list isn't full of exactly the prospects you want.

Segmenting allows you to tailor a large list to your needs. You can pull names out of the list that you think would be good prospects. Buying habits and demographics are the most common ways for lists to be segmented. Recency, frequency and dollar amount are common segment criteria. You can also specify type of product purchased and method of payment. Ask to look at recent mailings sent to the people on the list and find out what the response was. Use zip code analysis to segment different types of neighborhoods.

Although segmented lists cost more to rent than nonsegmented lists, remember that you're building your customer list. You hope to sell to good customers several times. If you can increase your response rates by just a small amount, the rewards can add up with time. Direct marketing demands care both as you rent names and manage your customer list.

But what if you're using advertising instead of, or in addition to, direct mail? Your segments are mostly defined by the makeup of the magazine's readers. Some additional segmenting is also possible. For instance, many national magazines allow advertisers to buy space in copies that will be shipped only to a certain region of the country. If you are selling winter clothes, you could advertise only to readers in the northern areas of the country.

Advertising testing involves testing approaches to the readers of various magazines. Which appeal works best? Should you describe the product in practical terms, or will more people respond if you goad their emotions? Is it better to have a celebrity touting your product or testimonials from everyday types?

There are no right answers to these questions. It helps, of course, to use talented, experienced professionals to write and produce your ads. But even then, each case is different. Keep testing different ways of motivating people to order.

Ads vs. Direct Mail

As we look at the economics of direct selling, you can conclude generally that it's wiser to start out with space ads before going into direct mail. In fact, that's the way my firm has grown. Let's look specifically at the advantages of advertising in the early days of a direct marketing business:

>   1. *Ads are less expensive to produce.* From both creative and production aspects, ads mean you pay less to start selling to your target market. Ads are generally smaller than direct mail packages are. Less copy means your creative fees will be smaller.

We've already noted that direct mail packages generally have a long letter, a short note and a coupon. All of these elements must be written. Unless you do it yourself, as I did for Enterprise Publishing, you'll have to pay quite a bit for good creative talent. In addition, the letter, note, coupon, reply envelope and mailing envelope all must be printed. Paper and printing aren't cheap, especially when you are printing in the tens of thousands.

If you run an ad instead, your production costs drop dramatically. You don't have to print thousands of letters and envelopes, and pay postage costs. You just have to prepare an art flat of your ad. Send a copy of that to the magazine, and they'll print it.

>   2. *Ads are less expensive to test.* When testing a direct mail package, you'll print just a few thousand to test against a control package. But printing in small quantities is expensive.

You can actually lose money on a test mailing that would have been profitable if you had mailed more letters. Your cost per order can drop in half just by increasing the size of your mailing several-fold.

Below is an example provided by Pierre Passavant in the Direct Marketing Association's Manual. In addition to making a point about costs, the format of this table might be useful for you when testing direct mail offers.

In Passavant's example you can see that test package *B* actually had a better response rate than did the control (C). Because fewer *B* test packages were mailed, though, they actually lost money. However, Passavant goes on to project that if package *B* were the control, its cost per thousand (CPM) would drop to $270/M. With the 4.2 percent response rate staying the same, cost per order (CPO) would fall to $6.43 if 100,000 packages were mailed.

Although both tests lost money, it's obvious that package *B* should become a big moneymaker. Now the marketer will *roll out*, by renting 100,000 names from the list with which he got the 4.2 percent test response. The marketer should make money when package *B* is mailed to those 100,000 prospects.

>   3. *Direct mail becomes cost-effective once you've built a large, dedicated mailing list.* Because of the high expenses connected with it, direct mail is costly as a prospecting tool. It's most useful when approaching current customers. You can afford to spend the extra money on people who know you and have ordered from you before.

Use low-cost ads to build your mailing list, and then approach them with direct mail packages. Just mailing blindly to people who have never heard of you can be costly.

Many catalog marketers use space ads to sell products and also to acquire names of people interested in their catalog. Selling through catalogs is usually the costliest form of direct mail marketing. For that reason many marketers mail catalogs mainly to current customers.

Space ads can do some selling and also give you names for a catalog mailing. Some marketers have formed catalogs after running space ads. Your top-selling merchandise in ads should produce a good catalog when brought together.

If you plan to mail a catalog to names received from print ads, first come up with a list of publications that reach your target market. From that list, choose one magazine that you think best reaches them.

Control vs. Test Promotion Costs

Pkg.	Quantity	Actual CPM	$ Cost	% Resp.	CPO	Profit
C	100M	$270/M	27,000	.5%	7.71	+12%
A	10M	$350/M	3,500	2.8%	12.5	-4%
B	10M	$600/M	6,000	4.2%	14.29	-10%
Combined	120M		36,500	3.5%	8.69	+9%

Develop several ads with different appeals. Split-run the ads in the publication you picked. A split run allows you to have several ads in one publication. Since each one reaches the same number of readers, you have an accurate test. Count results to the ads. Send your catalog to everyone who responds.

Keep counting the results after you've sent the catalog. Some ads will pull lots of response for that specific offer, but you won't get any follow-up catalog sales. Other ads will attract only a small portion of the magazine's readers. Maybe over 20 percent of the ones who do respond will order from your catalog.

If your primary offer is an item from your catalog, many persons might order that item. However, only a small percentage of prospects might later buy from the catalog you send them.

Often the best catalog customers will come from ads that just offer the catalog. Such two-step selling can be risky. You're paying for an ad to get inquiries for your catalog—you won't make your money back to pay for the ad until you get some catalog orders.

This can also be a very rewarding strategy. Although you're paying for inquiries, all your catalogs will then be going to good prospects. Eventual orders should compensate for the ad costs. Inquiries for a consumer catalog can cost as little as $2 per inquiry brought in through a space ad.

Such a strategy generally is more effective than mailing your expensive catalog to rented names although many catalog merchants do just that. If you've ever gotten on mailing lists as a catalog buyer, you can easily receive 20 catalogs during the next Christmas shopping season. By using ads to generate inquiries, you can find new names that aren't on the overused lists. You're hoping to find people who normally don't purchase through the mail.

Of course, you'll want to look at the overall profit open to you before doing any testing. One way of projecting profits is by using a standard Profit and Loss statement. The statement to the right resembles the P & L of a successful direct marketer.

Good testing techniques will help you find where your money is spent most profitably. You'll learn to combine your sixth sense about your prospects with hard analysis to make wise decisions.

Before placing any ads or renting any names, be certain you can make money. Look closely at your product, market and offer. Be sure you have the creative talent available to get prospects to order after reading your ads or mailings.

Finally, make realistic projections. Then double your expenses, and see if you would still make money. Often, the projections of people starting their own businesses are off by as much as one-half.

As a direct marketer you should be able to foresee costs better than most other entrepreneurs. You should be able to predict what your sales will cost. If a promotion doesn't work, you'll be able to cut your losses quickly. But first we'll look at more ways to avoid losing money. In the next chapter we'll start to examine how to write ads that work hard for your company.

Direct Marketing P&L Statement

Selling Price	$ 95	
+ Shipping & Handling Charge	5	
Gross Sales		$100
Less Returns		- 10
Net Sales		90
Cost of Goods Sold	22	
Promotion	25	
Fulfillment	16	
Overhead	11	
Premium	3	
Bad Debts	2	
Total Expenses		79
Profit per Order		$ 11
Profit as % of Net Sales	12.2%	

Chapter Thirteen

How To Write Copy That Sells

By now you see that it's possible to sell your product or service nationally without leaving your office. Direct response ads and mailings can make your selling efforts enormously successful. Your offers can reach thousands of good prospects every month.

Enterprise Publishing grew to sell millions of dollars worth of publications each year with only five people on our marketing staff. Most of our books and newsletters have been sold through the mail and space ads, and we've made money from the very first ad.

You have to know what you're doing. Being off target only slightly can ruin your efforts. Look at the actual ads I've reprinted in this chapter. In some of them little was changed from one to the other. But those small changes can cause an ad to go from making money to costing me money.

I can't afford that, and neither can you. At times, however, successful copy is so dramatic that some magazines ask you to change it. In 1974 *The New York Times* asked me to change three words in the body copy of one of my ads for *How To Form Your Own Corporation Without a Lawyer for Under $75*. We were running a full-page ad every other Sunday in their book review section.

We were asked to change three words concerning the advantages of incorporating in Delaware. Changes were made, and we ran the ad two weeks later. All that had been altered were three words—and the response fell off 50 percent. The *Times* legal staff thought the changes would make the ad clearer to readers. But changing the words actually caused confusion.

We hadn't thought the ad was confusing to begin with. And our customers seemed to agree. Although we had a money-back guarantee, almost no books were returned from customers responding to our original ad. Since the changed ad didn't pull, and the *Times* wouldn't go back to our original ad after making the change, we lost a good means of selling books.

We learned a lesson from that experience. Today when a magazine asks us to change successful copy I reply that we'll do it on one condition. Namely that they'll reimburse us for any loss of sales based on the change they propose. To date no one has taken us up on that offer. Generally the magazine reconsiders, and we run the ad as we want it.

Time for a Change

Never change successful copy—not for a magazine, not because your sales manager wants to try something new and not because your advertising agency says it's time to come up with a new approach.

Change copy only when it's no longer profitable. Your job in direct marketing is to develop successful copy and run it as long as you can. Of course, at the same time you'll test other approaches as you look for a more profitable ad.

Don't change your ads simply because the seasons are changing. You'd be surprised how many firms do that, often at the misguided suggestion of their ad agency. The fact is, you can run some ads profitably for years without altering a single word.

You might get tired of that ad; on an emotional level, you might want to change it. You might want to try something new and exciting. Don't do it. Good advertisers recognize that they are going to get tired of their ads, simply because they see them every day. They also understand that many of their prospects haven't even seen the ads yet, or haven't noticed them.

How often will you skip over an ad that appears every issue in a publication you read? After six or eight months of glancing at the ad you may take the time to read it. Your customers are the same. With so much competition for their attention, many will miss your ad. But if it's successful, keep running the ad. Give those who haven't looked at it a chance to respond.

How To Lose Money in Direct Marketing

Perhaps the easiest way to miss sales is by having poorly written ads and direct mail letters. Nothing is more important than the actual ad or mail package. In them you're presenting prospects with your product. In them you're also making choices on how you will motivate these prospects to buy.

If you make a mistake, you'll lose money.

In this chapter I'll give you some guidelines that have helped me successfully write almost all of the copy that sells Enterprise Publishing's products. I'll show you what has and hasn't worked for me.

Writing good copy isn't easy. As I take you through the process that I and other pros use, you'll see that it isn't always a straightforward process. Advertising is a complex way of communicating. You're simultaneously appealing to both the logic and emotions of your prospects.

As I write I go through a process of integrating elements into the copy: different appeal, finding the right headline, making sure the coupon works and paying attention to the visual impact of the ad.

Since these elements must complement each other, writing involves putting one brick in place and then making sure all the others fit snugly around it.

Keep It Fun

Although copywriting is important to my business, I always try to write with a light touch. If you don't have a sense of fun in your copy, no reader will stick with your ad. They'll turn to the next page of the magazine, or throw away your letter.

Capture the reader's imagination and attention. Strive to be engaging. One way to do this is to remind yourself that you're writing a very personal message. Some writers do this by pretending they're writing to a friend or relative. You might even want to put a picture representing your prospect on your bulletin board. Write as you would talk to that person. Tell him or her about your product.

First you must decide what to say to them. What can you say that will encourage prospects to buy? Two proven methods involve looking at your product's *Unique Selling Proposition* (USP) and finding out what customer needs it meets. We'll consider these two techniques at length below.

1. *Find your product's Unique Selling Proposition* (USP). Remember "Where's the Beef?" Your job is to uncover the *beef* in your product or service. Then make sure your prospects know about it.

The USP concept was formulated by adman Rosser Reeves in his book *Reality in Advertising*. Reeves describes an ad's USP as the claim it makes that cannot be made by the competition.

If your ad has a USP, you're on your way to creating winning copy. A USP can be a product feature, such as a light bulb that lasts 25 percent longer yet costs no more than normal bulbs. Also, a USP can be a benefit, such as special financing terms.

Whatever your USP is, write it down. Then work on coming up with a headline emphasizing the USP. If you're writing direct mail copy, you'll be looking for a teaser to go on the outside envelope.

It's All in Your Head

The importance of having a strong headline or teaser can't be overemphasized. In that way you can hook your prospects by conveying your product in a compelling way. Your choices for both the broad appeal and the specific words are very important. If your headline doesn't grab readers, few will bother reading the body copy.

Your headline or teaser should accomplish three tasks. First, it needs to emphasize the USP. Tell readers what your product has that they can find nowhere else.

Next, your head needs to qualify prospects. By that I mean that someone should be able to tell just by reading the headline or teaser if this is a product that can help them.

Third, you must grab the attention of the prospect to get them to want to find out more. In order to convince your prospects to buy, they'll usually have to read more than just the headline. But if your head or tease line isn't compelling, they might not care enough to go on. Even if your prospects recognize the product could be helpful to them, you have to give them a good reason to keep reading.

Don't be concerned about the length of your headline. Try whatever you think will work. Great headlines can run anywhere from one to seventeen words in length.

Let's look at an example from a direct response ad you've probably seen in *Parade*, the Sunday newspaper supplement—"My Feet Were Killing Me, Until I Discovered the Miracle in Germany."

What does this headline do to you? First, the USP is that this product can help aching feet. Uniqueness is claimed by suggesting the author searched all over the world for help. Finally relief came in Germany. But it was more than just relief. What the copywriter encountered was—a *miracle*. Now that's a unique claim.

Prospects are qualified simply by stating the problem the writer had—feet that were killing her. Anyone with hurting feet will know that this ad was written with them in mind.

Finally, the prospects are led to read on to discover the solution suggested in the headline. What is the *miracle in Germany*? If your feet ache, and you want to find out more about this product with the unique claim, you have to read on.

What's more, the writer of this ad does it in a narrative style to weave a story. As we dissect the head here, we do so in dry terms. But the copy itself is lively. Remember what I said about keeping a light touch. You want to keep your readers interested in what you're writing about.

It's worthwhile to spend time looking for a Unique Selling Proposition for your product. As you can see from the above example, having a USP makes the rest of the copywriting job simpler. A USP gives you direction and solidity while writing an ad or a mail package.

However, some products don't have a USP. Although it's much easier to sell unique goods, you might be marketing products that aren't head and shoulders above the competition.

Then there are writing strategies that you can use. If you don't have a USP, try to find a *Point of Difference* between yourself and your competitors. Perhaps you're selling address labels. It's hardly possible to find a Unique Selling Proposition with a product such as address labels—all the competitors are too much alike.

You might be able to offer typefaces, colors or seasonal designs. Those would be points of difference separating you from your competition. Promoting those differences would make you stand out.

If your point of difference is important, consider using it in your headline. If your point of difference isn't earthshaking, you should just put it in the body copy as another selling point.

Even if you don't have a point of difference or a USP, you can make your product stand out.

2. *Do so by focusing on the prospect needs you can satisfy.* People will buy your product for its uses, not for its features. You don't have to compare yourself to the competition.

What are the needs of your prospects? They can be very practical. If you are selling toolboxes, you are meeting a need to keep tools organized. A real need is being met for a weekend handyman who doesn't want to search for his tools.

A product can also meet inner needs. Ask yourself if your prospects have emotional needs that your product satisfies. Does your product make people feel more attractive? You might base your marketing on that attribute.

Advertisers call these needs *suffering points*. Inner needs cause your prospects to suffer, and you can show how your product relieves their anguish. Point out how you can help your prospects raise happy children, lose weight or save money. Keep asking yourself what your prospects' most important concerns are, and how your product addresses them.

Look at Sears's approach with its Diehard battery. Some Sears ads tell how long the Diehard lasts. Others tout its low price. Both of those ads promote product features.

Some ads appeal to the inner needs of customers by saying, "We Install Confidence." Sears recognizes that many people are concerned that auto mechanics won't do a good job. They suggest that their automotive products relieve such worries.

Have I Got a Deal for You!

To be successful in direct marketing you have to avoid talking about yourself. Even when you are promoting your product's USP, do it in terms of how valuable your product could become to the reader. You won't get many sales until you convince lots of people that their lives will be improved if they order your product.

Your prospects don't care about your company, or you or your product. What they do care about is their own aching feet or other problem. Make sure your writing is composed of *You* messages.

Even the ad we mentioned in which the writer described finding foot relief in Europe was a *You* message. In fact, the whole ad is like a personal letter. In it a lady tells her friends how the marvelous discovery she made can help them, too. You need to get your prospects to trust you.

These people haven't met you and might never have seen or heard of your product before. Yet, you're trying to get them to write you a check after spending a few minutes reading an ad or letter! It's not an impossible task if you know what you're doing. One technique is to engender trust by making the message seem like a personal letter.

The truth is that people often buy from salespersons whom they trust.

Let's say you go to a new restaurant. If the waiter is cool and indifferent, you'll make your choice based on the menu. Maybe you'll order something that you enjoyed at another restaurant.

But if the waiter is warm and likable, you'll listen to his suggestions. In fact, you'll probably ask him what he thinks of the different dishes on the menu.

In a direct response ad or letter you're trying to establish the same rapport the friendly waiter did. You have to do it with the words you put down on paper. Strive to come across as caring, yet authoritative.

Use anecdotes and testimonials from previous customers to weave in human interest and to establish credibility. No one can refute the experience of another person. Quote a user of your product as saying, "This is the best (product name) I've ever tried."

Be specific while maintaining a personal writing style. Use precise names, figures and documented facts. Back up your claims, and your writing will have authority. Your personal writing style will get readers to relax, to trust you. Your use of specifics will provide the reasons needed for logical minds to allow prospects to make a purchase.

What you're trying to do is keep the personal tone of the ad or letter while working in reasons for the prospect to buy. Don't just launch into superlatives about your product. Use specifics to back up your promises and claims. Tell how many satisfied customers you have. Let prospects know they have a money-back guarantee.

You'll notice in my ads that I'll mention how, for instance, a specific law has made the corporation a great tax shelter. Then I'll tell readers how my book can help them incorporate without using a lawyer. In that situation, the *Revenue Act of 1978* becomes a selling tool. It gives my prospects reasons to buy my product. My USP is that my product can show readers how to save legal fees while gaining this legal tax shelter.

Do your research. Learn all you can about the product you're promoting before you start writing. In that way you can write with authority. You'll have the facts you need to back up your product claims. Your copy should then become more convincing, and your sales will reflect that.

Following is a questionnaire that you should fill out before writing copy. Using questionnaires in copywriting was pioneered by Don Hauptman and later developed by Dennis S. LeBarron. However, this particular questionnaire originally was published in the *"Who's Mailing What!"* newsletter based in Stamford, Connecticut. It asks questions about the product and your marketing strategy that must be answered before actually putting pen to paper.

Learn all you can. It will make your sales job easier. After finishing the research, you're ready to start writing. Below are four rules I follow when I start to prepare copy.

1. *Clear your mind.* For some persons, this might mean lying down for a few minutes before going to work. For others, it could mean jumping in the pool or jogging around a track. Frolic, spend time with someone you love or go dancing. Do whatever comes naturally to you in order to have a clear mind for creative purposes.
2. *Never write when you're tired.* You're not going to try to drive or operate machinery when you're tired. Don't try to write if you're fatigued.
3. *Never write when you're busy.* If there are other demands pressing on you, tend to them first. I don't think anyone can write well when they are watching the clock. Don't try to write if you have appointments later in the day or errands to run.
4. *Don't write in bits and pieces.* Once you've turned on your creative energy, you need to keep it flowing. I don't stop until I complete a draft. I try not to stop even for meals.

Perhaps those rules sound idealistic to you, but for me and other direct response writers, they're essential. These guidelines have been key to my success.

That success allows me to have the kind of working conditions I prefer. I like to be away from an office atmosphere when writing. I think you need to have the right atmosphere to write well. Turn on music you like, if that helps you. Make sure the surroundings help you to create. Perhaps being around nature enables your creativity to emerge.

You might want to brainstorm with a colleague before you start writing. The actual writing, however, needs to be done by you. I don't think a committee can write effective direct response copy. It's too personal a form of communication. Strive to write as you would talk to a friend.

Copywriter's Questionnaire

1. Contact person at company offering product or service.
   Name of company.
   Company address and phone number.
2. Description of the product or service. In 50 words or less, write down what it is that you're offering.
3. Purpose of the product or service.
   What does it do?
   How does it work?
   How is it used?
4. Price. How much does it cost?
5. What is the offer? Is there a special introductory savings? A premium? Limited-time offer? 2 for 1 sale? Free information? Free bonus? Any other offer?
6. What are the features of the product? Write down all the facts and specifications.
7. What are the main benefits of the product? What will it do for customers? What specific problem does it solve? How will it make or save money for customers? How will it save customers time or work? Or make their life easier or better?
8. Other copy points? What information or service will it give customers that they can't get anywhere else? How and why is it newer, better or different than what's already available? Is it unique or exclusive?
9. What is the marketing assignment? Is it an ad, direct mail package, brochure or a complete campaign?
10. What is the objective of the project? Do I want to get inquiries or leads, direct sales, make announcements, build the company's image or perform any other task?
11. What's the budget I'm working with?
12. What's the schedule? When does the work need to be done by?
13. Who is the main prospect? If it's a businessperson, what's his title or responsibility? What are their biggest concerns, fears, attitudes and possible objections to my product? How will he use my product to get ahead or keep from falling behind?
    For consumers, what main interest, desire or fear does my product appeal to?
    Who are my secondary prospects? Are there enough of them to make another version of the copy so that the offer appeals more directly to them?
14. What lists or media will I use? What have I used in the past with this product or similar ones? What worked and what didn't? What is the past performance of these media by source?
15. Do I have a sample of the product?
16. Do I have samples of previous promotions for this product? Are they labeled as "winners" and "losers"?
17. Do I have any testimonials and endorsements? Any letters from happy users? Or media coverage? Any celebrity endorsements?
18. Do I have any complaints? Any letters from unhappy customers?
19. Will I be conducting any tests? Will I be testing copy, price, offer, media or any other elements of the promotion?
20. What copy points must be included?
21. What taboos do I have? Is there anything that must never be said or promised?
22. What about outside competition? Why am I better? Is it the product? Price? Service? Can my prospect make price comparisons with other products, or is my product exclusive?
23. Is there any in-house competition which might affect the positioning, copy approach or other aspect of this promotion?
24. Are there any operational restrictions on how the mailing or ad is prepared? How large can my brochure be? How long can my letter be? What about using 4-color?
25. In the offer, what is the method of payment? Cash with order, bill me, Visa/MC/American Express?
26. What about telephone orders? What percentage of business comes in by phone? Is there an 800 number? Are collect calls accepted?
27. What's the guarantee? One hundred percent money-back anytime? 30-day-free trial offer? Other?
28. What about the company? Is there anything special in its history, the background or personality of the owner, authority of the firm, its achievements or any other matter which could have sales importance?
29. Anything else? All research and background information is helpful. Go through it to look for other points, and to familiarize yourself with all aspects of the product.
30. Is there any recommended background reading or people you should talk to before starting the project?

Using questionnaires in copywriting was pioneered by New York free-lancer Don Hauptman and later developed by Dennis S. LeBarron of Clear Communications of Wilton, CT. This LeBarron version of the questionnaire was published in the "Who's Mailing What!" newsletter based in Stamford, CT and is reprinted by permission.

Show enthusiasm for your product. Many copy promotions that I've seen have little excitement, involvement, drama or passion. If the copy is flat and lifeless, you can't expect your readers to reach for their checkbooks. Most good copywriters use and enjoy the products they write about. In addition copywriters tend to be positive, upbeat people who enjoy telling the world through words what's great about the products or services they represent.

Don't ever write in a business office, and don't allow phone calls or other interruptions. Just knowing that the phone could ring at any time creates a certain amount of tension. That may rob your work of a little bit of vitality. It could take off the extra edge that would make your ad or mailer a winner.

Let your thoughts flow freely before you start writing. Go over the copywriter's questionnaire. Start making a list of the elements you want to include in the package. Write down the benefits and features you want to emphasize. Put on paper any ideas for headlines. Allow your ideas to come out. Collect them on paper. Start seeing how they fit together.

Before you get too organized, write the first draft of your copy. Again, you want the ideas to flow. Let them come out naturally. Later you'll impose more discipline on your work, tying all the elements together. Now you're trying to spark your creativity.

You are approaching readers on both emotional and logical levels. To get both of these appeals in, I suggest you write two drafts. You might even want to move back and forth between the two as ideas come. Use two different word processors for this, or two typewriters and a swivel chair or two notepads, if you prefer.

Work fast and furiously. Don't bother correcting anything. Just get your thoughts on paper as they come. Don't refer to your research at all in your first draft. Make your product or service as appealing as possible.

Use product data and your research when writing the second draft. As you've probably guessed by now, your first draft contains the emotional appeal. Your second brings out the facts that present your product as what it is.

Put both drafts away for a week after you're finished. At the end of the week compare both drafts. Rewrite and blend them together. Now you'll start to see how everything in your package will fit together.

Let that *blended draft* sit for a week, and then rework it again. Don't let a committee rewrite your work. Direct marketing is a personal approach to selling. A joint effort will only water down your work.

Do the rewriting yourself to keep alive the approach you started. Strive for shorter sentences as you rework your words. Add punch to your letter or ad by making your selling points clearer.

At the same time you might want to go over the following points as you reread your copy. From my experience as a writer and consultant these are the most common copy problems.

Nicholas's Copy Mistake Checklist

1. *Not doing enough research.* Have I looked at the competition carefully enough? Have I looked at the needs that my customers or clients really have and determined that the product meets their needs?

2. *Not beginning the sales letter or ad with the biggest benefit the product offers the prospect.* Instead writers sometimes try to make the lead an argument for why the prospect needs the product or service being offered. Meet needs that your prospects know they have. Don't try to "create" needs by trying to convince prospects they have needs they aren't aware of.

    Another problem is beginning the ad or letter with a *me* message. No one cares about your company. People will read your material only when you tell how you can meet their needs.

3. *Not ending the ad or letter by requesting a specific action.* You want your prospect to make an order or inquiry. You need to specifically ask for what you want, and give your prospect instructions on how to fulfill your request.

    Don't be modest. If your prospects have read the ad or letter to the end, they must be interested. Tell them what to do about it.

4. *Taking too long to introduce the product or service.* Let people know within the first eight to ten lines what you're selling. You don't have to detail the offer at that time, but you'll lose people if you don't tell them quickly what product you're talking about.

You're on your way to success if you remember to have a compelling headline or teaser. Many writers spend 70 percent to 90 percent of their time on the body copy and the rest on the headline or teaser. The reverse should be the case. You'd get a lot more sales by doing that.

Add personal touches to your writing. For instance, never send prospects a brochure without including a letter. Pile on the benefits in your ad or letter. Don't worry about how long-winded you are. If you're telling people how you can help them, they'll be happy to read it all. Finally, give your prospects a way to respond. Always ask for action.

Strengthen Your Hand

Keep looking for new ways to turn your prospects into customers. What can you add to make your product a little more desirable? How can you better emphasize the features of your product?

One way to acquire an edge is to have a good name for your product or company, a name that encourages your prospects to identify with you. Such identification means the prospects will tend to trust you, your product and your promotional material.

Consider Geico Insurance. Geico stands for Government Employees Insurance Company. It's a private company that sells life and auto insurance policies through the mail. Geico is based in the nation's capital, where there are many federal employees.

If you're a government employee, it's hard for you to ignore a letter from the Government Employees Insurance Company. You'll be receptive to their products because of the power of their name. A good name for a company or product positions it accurately. In other words, just from hearing your name, your prospects will think favorably of you.

At Enterprise Publishing, we chose with care the name of every book or report we put out. You want a name that describes the product. At the same time you'd like the name to convey the main feature of the product, or tell prospects how it will help them.

How do you come up with names that aren't silly or simplistic? Begin by looking closely at your prospects. Ask yourself why they would buy your product instead of anyone else's. What will be going through their minds when they purchase your product?

Let your name suggest the reason for buying. Is it the most technically advanced product in its field? If so, come up with a scientific-sounding name. Likewise, a discount product and an expensive, luxury item need different names to reflect their features and appeals.

Why Did the Chicken Cross the Road?

A simple question can have several answers, and all of them can be right. When you ask yourself why people will buy your product, you can come up with several answers.

As you write an ad you feature in your headline what the major benefit is. But some very different benefits might be just as compelling to your prospects. Write several ads or mailing pieces. Let each one assume that prospects are buying for a different reason. Each ad or letter will come out differently.

You can test them to see which one pulls best. Let's look at how it works. Suppose you're selling gourmet mustards and relishes by mail. From focus group and current customer research you develop four different reasons why people would buy your relishes. We'll consider them below. Note how each ad has a different copy approach and a different offer.

1. *Prospects will buy your relishes for gifts.* You would show in the ad how grateful friends, relatives or business associates are after receiving a gift of gourmet mustard. You're suggesting that your mustard is a wise choice.

    Additionally you would offer a special gift box at no extra charge. If you were selling through a direct mail letter, you'd tell prospects they had to order within ten days to get the special offer. In that way you'd encourage action.

2. *Prospects will buy your mustard because they see it as being exclusive.* You would describe how your product is lovingly made in small batches to ensure freshness and good flavor. In addition you could tell the romantic story of the recipe's background, to increase the allure of the product.

    Your offer would stress that supplies of the mustard are limited.

3. *Prospects will buy the mustard because it makes foods taste uniquely better.* In these ads you could point out what a hit you will be at parties when fixing appetizers containing the mustard. Add how it also improves the flavor of foods eaten every day.

    Your offer in these promotions will include recipes featuring the mustard.

4. *Prospects will buy because of the ingredients used.* If your mustard has no preservatives, or contains ingredients not found in other relishes, emphasize those features. In ads, describe the ingredients. Tell where they come from and why you spend so much money on pure, fresh or exotic ingredients.

Let your prospects know what a difference these ingredients make in their enjoyment of the relishes. With this promotion you could also include an offer of recipes as a premium with orders.

What's the Pitch?

Now you can see how direct marketing pros get their sales angles. Consider why your prospects will buy, and then develop ads giving your prospects reasons to buy.

You're assuming your prospects have sophisticated needs that your product will meet. Why will someone buy expensive mail order relishes? Because they like knowing their relishes are made of pure, fresh ingredients. They want to fix new and different dishes for their family or parties. They like knowing they use the best, most exclusive relish money can buy. They may also think a unique relish will make a wonderful gift.

You can look at any product this way. Get a picture of your prospects. Try to understand why they would buy, and then come up with an ad that helps make that buying decision easy. Describe how your product meets real needs.

Next we'll look at how to go from these broader decisions to actually creating copy. We'll begin in the next chapter by looking at how to create headlines and teaser lines.

The remaining pages in this chapter are dedicated to samples of successful space ads I have written.

108   The Golden Mailbox

Do You Hate to Spend Hours Writing Letters?

Slash Your Letter-Writing Time by 80%... and write better letters!

Give It Up! Quit wasting hours searching for the perfect words. Discover the *Two-Minute Letter!*

Tired of seeing correspondence chew up your schedule and force your work into overtime? Take heart! Now, you can produce letters with astonishing speed.

Instead of knocking yourself out day after day, in the endless quest for just the right phrase, now you can take the easy way out. You can create a hard-to-write, brain-bending business letter in about two easy minutes.

Use the **Executive's Business Letter Book.** You'll find useful letters on every common business subject. Over 150 letters in all—*plus countless variations when you use the optional paragraphs.*

Most of the Letters You'll Need to Write in the Year Ahead Are Already Written for You!

These easy-to-find letters are grouped by chapter:

- **Hiring Employees.** Don't get sued after you fire! Use these letters when you hire!
- **Building Employee Morale.** Show your staff you care about them and hold them in high esteem!
- **Building Careers.** Sell large groups of prospects on your unique talents.
- **Enhancing Shareholder Relations.** Loyal stockholders are made, not born! Build a warm relationship with them.
- **Writing to VIPS.** Make every letter to lenders or officials "letter-perfect"!
- **Creating the Sale.** Back your sales crew up with high-toned letters!
- **Turning Inquiries into Sales.** Turn questions and complaints into sales.
- **Following Up the Sales Pitch.** Now, it's easy to do that vital but commonly-delayed follow-up.
- **Building Customer Loyalty.** It's ten times easier to hold on to an old customer than to find a new one. These letters will do the trick. Use them!
- **Making the Most of the Media.** Handle the media like a pro! You can get priceless free publicity!
- **Building Personal and Community Goodwill.** Your competitors often fail to use these kinds of letters because they're so hard to compose. Use them, and you'll tower over everyone, especially in the profit department!
- **Dealing with Suppliers.** Stay out of lawsuits with your suppliers!
- **Requesting Credit.** Guard your credit—no one else will!
- **Granting Credit.** Don't let the world bleed you dry! Beef up your collections with this airtight battery of letters.
- **Dealing with Finances.** Keep banks and investors on your side.

Do Yourself 7 Favors

When you get the **Executive's Business Letter Book,** you'll be giving yourself seven big presents. The book will...

1. Cover everything, including all the normal, proper, legal points, greatly reducing your chance of lawsuits.
2. Save thousands of dollars. The average business letter today costs $11.71 plus postage. If you state something wrong, it could cost you far more!
3. Help prevent foul-ups, misunderstandings, and mistakes.
4. Increase productivity. The less time you waste on correspondence, the more time you have to do the jobs you really need to do.
5. Cut stress. No more stomach-churning decisions on "how to say it". No more "permanent backlog" of unwritten letters.
6. Let you enjoy life. We guarantee it: life will look a little brighter after you've removed a few hours of misery from your weekly schedule!
7. Boost your profits. Want your business to make more money? Hire a pro to write your letters! Get the **Executive's Business Letter Book.**

Don't let your correspondence run your life. Take charge of it today. Buy yourself hundreds of hours of free time!

No Risk 30 Day Guarantee

To order your copy of **Executive's Business Letter Book** at $69.95, call now toll free.

1-(800)-322-8621

or complete coupon below.

Also Available On Computer Diskette— save $40.00 when you buy the set.

© 1992 Enterprise • Dearborn

E10104

YES! ☐ I want to free myself from the drudgery of drafting letters from scratch. I also want the protection of thorough, legally-approved letters. Send me the *Executive's Business Letter Book* for $69.95 plus $6.00 shipping and handling.

☐ Send me the book and computer diskette set for $99.00 plus $6.00 shipping. IBM and compatibles ☐ 5 1/4" ☐ 3 1/2" ☐ Macintosh 3 1/2"

☐ Send me the diskettes only for $69.95 plus $6.00 shipping. IBM and compatibles ☐ 5 1/4" ☐ 3 1/2" ☐ Macintosh 3 1/2"

☐ Check enclosed payable to Enterprise • Dearborn   Charge my: ☐ MasterCard ☐ Visa

Account #_____ Signature_____ Exp. Date_____
(All charge orders must be signed.)

Name_____
Firm_____
Address_____
City_____ State_____ Zip_____
Daytime Phone (   )_____

Mail to: Enterprise • Dearborn, 520 North Dearborn Street, Dept. E10104, Chicago, IL 60610

What Will You Do When Your Personal Assets Are Seized to Satisfy A Judgment Against Your Corporation?

All your many tax benefits of owning a corporation could be wiped out overnight. How? The I.R.S. could visit you and claim you have not kept proper corporate minutes. You could lose the very tax benefits to which the law entitles you.

Here are some recent "horror stories" direct from actual court cases:

Joseph P. obtained a loan from his corporation without the proper loan documents and corporate minutes. As a result, the court required him to pay additional taxes of $27,111.60. He narrowly escaped a penalty of $13,555.80.

B.W.C., Inc. was forced to pay $106,358.61 of accumulated earnings tax because its corporate minutes were incomplete. They expressed "no specific, definite, or feasible plans" to justify accumulating earnings, according to the court.

Keeping records has always been a bother, and an expensive one, especially for small companies. Most entrepreneurs do not like to spend time keeping records. Probably because no one ever became rich by keeping records. And in a small, one-person business, it seems downright silly to keep records of stockholder meetings and board of directors meetings...keeping minutes...taking votes...adopting resolutions...isn't it all just a waste of time?

Not if you ask any of the thousands of entrepreneurs who have lost fortunes because they failed to keep records. You should look at corporate recordkeeping chores this way: *It's part of the price you pay to get the tax benefits and personal protection from having a corporation.*

A corporation does not exist except on paper, through its charter, by-laws, stock certificates, resolutions, etc. Anything you do as an officer or director has to be duly authorized and evidenced by a resolution of the stockholders or the board, or by both in some cases. It makes no difference if there is only one stockholder or one million stockholders. The rules are basically the same.

You can hire a lawyer, like the big companies do, and pay $100 or more just to prepare one form. But you may need, at minimum, a dozen or more documents to keep your corporation alive and functioning for just one year. This type of work is the bread and butter for many corporation lawyers. Most of the work can be done by their secretaries, yet they will charge you enormous sums because they know how important these forms are.

©1992 Enterprise • Dearborn

There is now a way for you to solve your corporate recordkeeping problems. Without a lawyer, without paying big fees, and without spending a lot of time. Virtually all the forms you will ever need are already compiled in **The Complete Book of Corporate Forms** by Ted Nicholas. Nicholas also publishes the highly popular special report, *How an "S" Corporation Can Save You Tax*. Written by Joseph Oliver, CPA, this report details how an "S" Corporation—one of the most underused tax avoidance methods—can save you literally thousands of tax dollars each year.

But forming a corporation is only the first step toward building "the ultimate tax shelter." Through carelessness or neglect, many people are denied their rightful benefits from owning their own corporation. Ted Nicholas saw that many business owners needed more help *after* they incorporated.

And so, he prepared **The Complete Book of Corporate Forms**. Everything is simplified. Either you or your secretary can complete any form in minutes. All you do is fill in a few blanks and insert the completed form in your record book. When you own this book, you are granted permission to reproduce every form. If you are behind on keeping your corporate records, now you can catch up in no time. Just complete a few blanks for the things you've already done in the company. It's legal and it works. Best of all, the price is less than you would pay a lawyer for one hour of counseling.

Here is just a sample of what you'll receive:
Minutes of Stockholders Meetings
Minutes of Directors Meetings
Minutes of Special Meetings
(Any of these can be used if you are the only stockholder and director.)
Amendments to Articles of Incorporation
Amendments to By-Laws

You will also receive all the stockholder and directors resolutions you will need including:
• Negotiations of contracts • Authorizing loans to corporation • Approval of corporate loans to you • Designation of purchasing agent *(some suppliers may want to know who is authorized to buy from them)* • Setting your salary • Directors fees • Authorizing your expense account • Mergers • Sale of corporate assets • Dissolution • Bankruptcy • Declaring dividends • Appointment of attorney or accountant

Plus, you'll receive the forms needed to authorize any of these tax-saving fringe benefits:
• Pension or profit-sharing plans • Medical and dental reimbursement plans • Sick pay plans • Split dollar life insurance • Educational loan program • Scholarship aid program • Stock options • Group life insurance • Financial counseling plan • Group legal services • Christmas bonus, special bonuses

Just one of the above forms can cost you hundreds of dollars in legal fees...

This entire loose-leaf collection of simplified forms (over 150 pages of forms), with clear instructions for their use, as well as samples of completed forms, sells for only $69.95.

And, as with all Enterprise • Dearborn products, it sells under an iron-clad 30-day money-back guarantee. Examine the collection, and if for any reason you are not pleased, return it for a prompt refund. Take a moment to place your order now, and immediately begin saving time and money. Complete the coupon below and mail.

E10101

For fastest service, call toll-free:
1-800-322-8621
or complete coupon and mail at once.

☐ Please rush me a copy of **The Complete Book of Corporate Forms** at $69.95 + $6.00 shipping, under your 30-day money-back guarantee. Also Available on Computer Disket—save $40.00 when you buy the set.
☐ Send me the book and computer diskette set for $99.00 plus $6.00 shipping   IBM & compatibles ☐ 5 1/4" ☐ 3 1/2" ☐ Macintosh 3 1/2"
☐ Send me the diskettes only for $69.95 plus $6.00 shipping and handling   ☐ IBM 5 1/4" ☐ IBM 3 1/2" ☐ Macintosh 3 1/2"
☐ Check enclosed. Charge to: ☐ MasterCard ☐ Visa

Account Number_____ Exp. Date_____
Signature_____
(All charge orders must be signed)
Name_____
Company_____
Street Address_____
City/State/Zip_____ Business Phone (   )_____

Orders shipped to the following states must include applicable sales tax: CA, FL, IL, NY.
Enterprise • Dearborn, Dept. E10101 / 520 North Dearborn Street, Chicago, IL 60610

What Makes a Consultant Successful?

America has been called "The Land of Consultants." Over 400,000 are engaged in that profession. Yet only 11% of the consultants in this country earn more than $50,000 per year, according to IRS figures. And unfortunately, most consultants struggle just to get by.

By contrast, the really successful earn well over $100,000 per year. And earnings of $250,000 per year and even more are not uncommon. Four skills set apart the super successful:
1. **Identifying** your clients' key needs.
2. **Solving** problems your clients can't solve themselves.
3. **Profiting** from your efforts.

And the skill every consultant needs most:
4. **Marketing** your services effectively.

You undoubtedly have the expertise in your field. But *unless you are able to effectively market yourself, you will never achieve the income you deserve.*

Whether new or established, you can be a highly paid, successful consultant in your own field by knowing how to do these four things. And if you don't master these skills, the increasing competition in your field will kill you.

Properly done, consulting can be the ideal profession. The highly successful can earn well into six figures, even on a part-time basis.

A new book, the *Complete Guide to Consulting Success* will show you how. You'll discover the best way to approach the four critical consulting principles of success. It need not be difficult. Once you master these skills with the help of this book, it's remarkably easy.

The author, the late Howard Shenson, was America's most recognized authority on consulting. In his seminars and books, he helped over 52,000 consultants improve their practice. He and his work have been featured in more than 400 newspaper and magazine articles and on more than 225 radio and TV news and talk shows.

The *Complete Guide to Consulting Success* is a remarkable book. You simply must have it if you are a consultant . . . or plan to become one. Not only is it filled with useful information, you also get ready-to-use forms, agreements and worksheets. Worksheet forms will help you determine your best strategies, and the contract and agreement forms will help protect you legally.

This book brings you the basic strategies you need to gain larger contracts from both existing and new clients. And it provides ways to increase profits on the work you get.

The Book Shows How To:
- Find the ten profit-producing situations that create a need for your service.
- Identify six danger signals telling you when not to take a client.
- Gain more work by applying your skills to a broader market.
- Increase your billings while you serve specific client needs.
- Go after 39 new markets for consulting services.
- Structure your consulting practice for maximum profit.
- Gain profitable consulting contracts with the government.

Selling Your Service
- Market your services using the nine most effective no cost/low cost methods.
- Develop a direct marketing campaign proven to get new business.
- Compete with larger consulting firms and win.
- Use an effective brochure that will have clients calling you for your services.

Getting the Contract
- Create sales through successful presentations that keep you in control.
- Prepare reliable cost estimates with one easy-to-use form.
- Write sharp proposals that will get you the job.
- Set the most profitable fees for your service.
- Learn why you should never "lowball" (low-estimate) an assignment– even if you really need the work.
- Decide what type of contract you should use with each client.

You get seven types of ready-to-use contracts and a description on how to use each. There is even a chapter for complete beginners on how to start your business. Plus a complete 25-page, annotated bibliography that serves as an in-depth reference source for you.

"Shenson's clients are the consultants themselves. He teaches them how to market themselves, tap their experience and expertise to find useable knowledge they can sell."
— *Los Angeles Times*

Free Bonus
Act now and you will also receive *How to Gain Financial Freedom as an Independent Contractor* absolutely free. Normally $19.95, this exclusive report shows how to increase your take home pay by up to 34% or more. As a full or part-time employee, this report shows how to convert your position to "consultant" on an independent contractor status. As an employer, the report shows how to work with independent contractors instead of employees—thereby eliminating employee record-keeping and saving thousands of tax dollars each year. This special report comes complete with all the ready-to-use contracts, letters and forms you need.

Unprecedented Money-Back Guarantee
Enterprise • Dearborn is confident this book will help make you at least 100 times its nominal cost. Take up to 30 days to use these techniques and if you are dissatisfied in any way, simply return the book and we'll refund the full amount you spent for it including postage.

We are confident this book will help you increase your profits by at least $7,000 and up to $100,000 or more in the next twelve months. Why not start today?

For easy ordering, call toll-free: 1-800-854-7466. Or complete coupon and mail at once.

Please rush me the *Complete Guide to Consulting Success*, by Howard Shenson. Also send my FREE Bonus, *How To Gain Financial Freedom as an Independent Contractor* (normally $19.95), which is mine to keep regardless. Here's my tax-deductible $69.95 plus $6.00 for shipping and handling. Orders for CA, FL, IL, NY please add applicable sales tax.

☐ Enclosed is my check payable to Enterprise • Dearborn.
Charge my ☐ MasterCard ☐ VISA
☐ AmEx

Acct. # _____ Exp. Date _____
Signature _____
Name (please print) _____
Company _____
Address _____
City _____ State _____ Zip _____
Telephone Number (if we have a question on your order) _____

Mail to: Enterprise • Dearborn
520 North Dearborn Street
Chicago, IL 60610-4354
Phone orders: 1-800-854-7466
©1992 Enterprise • Dearborn   E10107

*World Famous Entrepreneur Offers For The First Time Ever To Share The
Insider Information He's Used To Make Over $20,000,000.00 In Direct Marketing*

How To Get Rich By Learning These Jealously Guarded Secrets Of *Direct Marketing Success

Dear Friend,

A lot of marketing people claim to know how to make money using certain techniques, but the truth is most of these "so called experts" would never dig into their own pockets and lay their own money on the line to prove their non-tested theories.

Ted Nicholas, on the other hand, is different. He's invested millions of his own dollars in direct marketing campaigns that have been huge successes. Are there secrets to his success?

Yes. Ted knows what he's talking about. He's sold over $200,000,000.00 (yes, $200-million) worth of products and services using proven direct marketing systems he's perfected over the past 20 years.

By the time he was 35 years old, Ted founded 18 different businesses and sold 16 successfully.

Next, he went on to create another company, The Company Corporation, that has helped 89,274 people form their own corporation. (He's helped more people form their own corporation than all the lawyers on Wall Street put together.)

At the same time he created Enterprise Publishing, a successful publishing company selling two and a half million copies of his own 13 business books, as well as other books by numerous authors. His number one best seller, "How To Form Your Own Corporation Without A Lawyer For Less Than $75," has sold nearly one million copies.

Now, Ted has sold all of his companies and has started his new career — helping people just like you to be more successful selling your product or service using his proven direct marketing techniques.

Ted has spent the past 20 years honing his craft and he's the best in the world at selling products or services using direct marketing to get sales. Ted's 2-Day and 5-Day Direct Marketing Seminars will help you profit like you never dreamed possible. Plus, it's guaranteed. (To get the details, send the coupon for Ted's "FREE Direct Marketing Seminar Packet".)

Warning:

This is *not* a fluff and puff motivational seminar designed to make you walk away with a nice warm feeling in your gut.

It *is* an intensive seminar, often starting early in the morning and ending late at night, jam-packed with more real world direct marketing knowledge than you could ever get from any college.

Here Are What Attendees From Around The World Have To Say About Ted's Direct Marketing Seminars.

"Your seminar is the best I've ever attended. You really share all your practical experience with the participants: test results, successful headlines, best selling words, best magazines, etc. The value of the information presented is worth more than 10 times the cost of the seminar. Only one month after attending, I earned $15,000.00 using your advice."
*Francis Blot, Copywriter
Chantilly, France*

"The topics were exactly what we needed to learn and in the discussions you took your years of experience and passed it on to us with pin point precision. If I am wise enough to put into use 10% of what I learned from you I should be able to double our

Ted Nicholas

"If you want to learn more about successful direct marketing and proven ways you can boost your profits, read this and send for my <u>Free offer below</u>."

profits in the next 12 months."
*Dennis Blitz, Senior Vice-President
Dearborn Financial Publishing
Chicago, Illinois*

"Stimulating, great seminar...great investment. I woke up during the night of the last day with the urge to write an ad. In two hours I was finished. This ad now produces the best results I've ever had-without one cent of investment - thanks to your wonderful techniques."
*Christian H. Godfrey, Publisher
Chesiere, Switzerland*

"As a veteran direct-mail marketer, I was profoundly impressed with the depth and range of material covered at the Nicholas Direct Seminar. Not only did I gain several major new ideas for marketing my own products, I picked up literally hundreds of smaller ideas and tips for increasing the efficiency of both my current marketing pieces and my general business.

It is said that one learns more from mistakes than from successes. Your willingness to share your failures as well as your achievements has steered me away from repeating those errors, and was itself worth the time and expense of the seminar. Both the money and the time invested are already paying off!"
*John A. Pugsley, President
John Pugsley's Journal
Escondido, California*

"Value of information was worth 12 times the cost of attending. I especially recommend this seminar to those who want better results and lower cost from space advertising. I also recommend it to those who want to improve direct mail and catalogue results. The first day alone will help anyone, such as a retailer reducing advertising costs in newspaper and magazines by up to 75%. I thought I knew all the secrets, but you opened my eyes to cost saving ideas that I hadn't even considered before." *Richard E. Cremer, President
Richard E. Cremer & Associates
Kerrville, Texas*

"Ted Nicholas inspired me to get into publishing. I eventually gave up a busy law practice to be a self-publisher. His seminar and techniques helped me write a full page ad for the first time. Best marketing ideas I've heard and the contacts were as valuable as the information." *Mark Warda, President
Sphinx Publishing
Clearwater, Florida*

Here's A <u>Small</u> Sampling Of What You Will Learn When You Attend Ted's Direct Marketing Seminar:

- How to buy print advertising up to 80% off the "rate-card." Yes! How you buy your space is just as important as your offer and the copy elements.
- How to write headlines and envelope teaser copy that are so powerful they attract buyers like a magnet. Ted's proven that a successful headline can be 18 times more effective than a weak one.
- How to prepare both ongoing advertising in magazines, newspapers, and direct mail, as well as one-shot, cash-up-front offers in low-cost card decks and package inserts.
- How to create your Unique Selling Proposition (U.S.P.) to open the floodgates of sales.
- How to double the effectiveness of your ads and sales letters with the proper use of the telephone.
- How to run ads without any risk on your part whatsoever.
- How to use a checklist of 13 Important Points to multiply the effective success of your advertising.
- Learn all the rules of success, and when to break them when the "time is right."

And this is only just the beginning. Since there's not enough room on this page to tell you everything taught at Ted's Direct Marketing Seminar, you'll need to get his **FREE Direct Marketing Seminar Packet. Call Ted's office now at (813) 596-4966,** and he will send you by first class mail your FREE Direct Marketing Seminar Packet. Or, fill out the coupon below and mail it to Ted's office, or you can **fax this page to Ted's office at (813) 596-6900.**

Ted will send you everything you need to know about his incredible 2-Day and 5-Day Direct Marketing Seminars. The dates for Ted's next 2-Day Seminar is November 4th & 5th. The 5-Day Seminar is November 4th - 8th, 1992. (The 5-Day Seminar is a continuation of the 2-Day with more personalized attention focused on your company's marketing systems.) Both seminars are held in beautiful Clearwater, Florida. Seating for both seminars is limited, so if you're even remotely interested in learning how to make your marketing more powerful — **Call Now (813) 596-4966!**

Yes, Ted! Send me your "Free Direct Marketing Seminar Packet." This will, in greater detail, tell me everything I'll need to know about your Direct Marketing Seminar. I understand this is a no-strings-attached request, and I'm not obligated in any way, shape, or form. Please send my packet to :

Name:_____ Co. Name:_____
Address:_____ City, State, Zip:_____
Telephone Number: (   )   Fax Number: (   )

Mail this to: Nicholas Direct, Inc., 19918 Gulf Boulevard., #7, Dept. 55S2, Indian Shores, Florida, 34635. Or, you can fax this coupon to **(813) 596-6900.**

---

* *Direct marketing is a method of distribution that gets your product or service to your customer without the middle man. Direct marketing provides the most cost effective means of generating new business.*

Chapter Fourteen

Twelve Ways To Get Your Prospect's Attention

Direct marketers have several levels of competition to deal with. Of course, the main competition is from other products on the market.

Before you can state a case for your product, you first must get the attention of your prospects. Your first level of competition comes from other ads and mailings. If you can't get your market to read your material, you don't have a chance to sell your product.

How do you get people to stop and take notice of you? How do you keep them from looking at their other mail or reading another ad instead of yours?

You simply get their attention. Direct marketers rely on ad headlines to grab their readers. On direct mail packages they use teaser lines to hook their readers.

Consider your prospects, skimming through a magazine while relaxing, or going through the day's mail. You have to give them a message that makes them pause and want to read more. A good headline leads into the body copy or letter, and that's where the selling is done.

Unless you get their attention in the first place, you're wasting time writing body copy. A headline or teaser line is the most important part of your ad or mail package. In this chapter I'll show you a dozen different headline approaches that can help you get the attention of your readers.

A good headline does more than get attention. You also want to identify readers who are prospects for your product, and clearly show them the benefit of your product or service. Because you are doing so many different tasks with your headlines, you need to take great care when writing them. Often I'll fill pages while experimenting with possible headlines, and then I'll keep going back over the ideas looking for the best approach, the strongest, clearest appeal.

Starting with a blank piece of paper is hard. I think it helps to have guidelines for choosing headlines.

See how the features of your product fit into the following headline and teaser techniques. A new product that is the result of a technological breakthrough will probably use a headline approach that stresses the news value, the featured benefit or boastful claims. But, you wouldn't use a trick technique or an emotional approach to sell that product.

I've provided sample headlines in the checklist below. My product for these examples is a new light bulb that lasts 30 percent longer than normal light bulbs. Which techniques work best for this product?

Headline and Teaser Technique Checklist

1. *News.* "NEW LIGHT BULBS LAST 30% LONGER"
2. *Featured benefit.* "SAVE UP TO 30% ON LIGHTING COSTS"
3. *Boastful.* "TESTS SHOW ABC BULBS LAST LONGEST"
4. *Command.* "TRY THE LIGHT BULB PREFERRED BY FORTUNE 500 FIRMS"
5. *Emotional.* "WILL YOUR LIGHTS WORK WHEN YOUR FAMILY NEEDS THEM MOST?"
6. *Trick.* "THOMAS EDISON WOULDN'T BELIEVE IT"
7. *Curiosity.* "HOW OFTEN DO YOU CHANGE?"
8. *Slogan.* "ABC BULBS PUT YOU IN A GOOD LIGHT"

9. *Offer.* "TRY ABC LIGHT BULBS FREE FOR 30 DAYS"
10. *Information.* "MOST PEOPLE SPEND MORE MONEY THAN THEY NEED TO TO LIGHT THEIR HOMES"
11. *Testimonial.* "HOW I CUT MY LIGHTING COSTS BY 30%"
12. *Prediction.* "FIVE YEARS FROM NOW, ALL LIGHT BULBS WILL BE MADE LIKE ABC BULBS"

In the examples above you can see that some of the headlines or teasers combine approaches. For instance, the prediction headline could be seen as either a prediction or boasting. Don't be overly concerned about fitting your headlines into slots. The checklist is intended to be used as a guideline for your own creative process.

As you write headlines, choose words that will have the effect you want on your readers. Research shows that some specific words create interest and excitement in most readers. Here are some of the words you should try to put into your headlines:

NEW	FREE
HOW-TO	ANNOUNCING
EASY	WANTED
AT LAST	MONEY
WORRIES	NOW
FAMILY	CHILDREN
YOU	SAVE
BEST	

For direct marketers, the best word to use is *You.* Weigh the effects of different words. Let's say you're selling ABC Light Bulbs. You've decided to feature the benefit of saving 30 percent on light bulbs. You can make a list of different ways to say that:

"SAVE 30% ON LIGHT BULBS"

"HOW TO SAVE 30% ON LIGHT BULBS"

"NOW YOU CAN SAVE 30% ON LIGHT BULBS"

"ANNOUNCING—A NEW LIGHT BULB THAT CAN SAVE YOU UP TO 30%"

"AT LAST, A LIGHT BULB THAT CAN SAVE YOU MONEY"

There are many ways to say the same thing, and this approach may not even be the best one for the light bulbs! Trying different wordings gives you a chance to let your creativity and selling sense come out.

What you're trying to do is come up with a headline that makes it almost impossible for your prospects to pass by your ad or letter without reading it. Copywriters call these ideas *grabbers, hooks, stoppers* or *zingers.* Writers who are able to produce such copy can almost name their price. "Big ideas" are in demand. Many writers can come up with clear copy, but if you can develop truly unique selling concepts, you have a great future in direct marketing. To get you started on that road, let's look more closely at headline and teaser techniques.

News

When writing a news headline, you are telling your readers that you have a noteworthy product. Many people are interested in new developments, especially if there is a benefit in it for them.

You will be using newswriter techniques as you think out and prepare your ad. Ask yourself the questions a reporter asks before writing a story. By doing so you will see if there really is a news handle, and who is affected by the news. Nothing's worse than a news story that fizzles, causing readers to say, "So what?" after reading it.

To find out where the news is, ask yourself the following:

WHO introduced this development? Who discovered its newsworthy properties? Who will benefit most from it?

WHAT has newsworthy value? Should the writer focus on the product, the firm behind it, the persons benefiting from it or some other aspect of the story?

WHEN was this new product or service developed? When will it be available?

WHERE did this new product or service come from? Is there anything unique about its origin or place of use?

WHY is the new development newsworthy?

HOW is this product or service used?

By going through these stock news-gathering questions you can start putting together headlines. Without such an exercise to sharpen your news instinct, you can end up with a very dry headline or teaser. That often happens when you haven't worked hard enough to find the news *hook* that makes your story exciting.

Let's say you're writing an ad for a new painkiller. You could write a headline like this:

ABC CORP. INTRODUCES NEW PAINKILLER

That's factual, but it isn't interesting. You won't grab people and keep them reading your ad. Few will see the benefits important to them.

Go deeper into the story. Get specific. You'll come up with a headline more like this one:

TWO OUT OF THREE DOCTORS RECOMMEND NEW PAINKILLER

That's a stopper. Readers can imagine such a product helping them. Many of them will want to find out about what you're selling. That still might not be the best headline for the product. Use the questions outlined above to help you develop more specific approaches, such as the following:

DOCTORS REPORT NEW PAINKILLER WORKS FASTER THAN ASPIRIN

NEW STUDY REVEALS SECRET OF PAIN RELIEF

NOW AVAILABLE IN U.S.—THE PAIN RELIEVER USED TO HELP ARTHRITIS SUFFERERS THROUGHOUT EUROPE

Depending on the needs of your audience, you'll choose the news hook that has the most powerful effect on them. Then work with the words so that your news hook actually starts the job of selling. For instance, when stating that "two out of three doctors recommend" your new painkiller, you are simultaneously providing facts and a product endorsement.

Many of the interest-promoting words I listed earlier can be worked into news headlines. NEW, ANNOUNCING, INTRODUCING, AT LAST and NOW are examples. Having something new is interesting and exciting. Using a news headline will let you capitalize on that. One note of caution is in order. Be a good newswriter. Make sure that you can back up what your headline states. If you can't, your ad will lack authority, and your sales will suffer.

Some copywriters try to capture attention by making claims that the body copy can't support. That's unfortunate, and it's one reason why many consumers say they don't believe advertising. Consequently, they try to ignore it. If your voice becomes too loud or shrill, many people simply won't listen to you.

Featured Benefit

Use a featured benefit headline when you have a Unique Selling Proposition. When your product is better than the competition's, it's usually enough just to say so. If your light bulbs last longer than anyone else's, let the world know.

As we've seen earlier, your product might have several important benefits. If you can isolate which benefit appeals to different customers, you can write several ads or mailing pieces. In that way you'll target each benefit to the right group of prospects.

You can feature a benefit by citing a solution your product provides to a specific problem. Here are some examples:

ABC CUTS EXPENSES BY 30%—HERE'S HOW THE SMITH CO. DID IT

NOW YOUR GIFT-GIVING CAN BE TAKEN CARE OF BY EXPERTS: NEW METHOD SOLVES CHRISTMAS SHOPPING IN MINUTES

Another way to feature a benefit is to start your headline with the word *Why*.

WHY ABC PRODUCT OWNERS SAVE ON ENERGY COSTS

WHY ABC PRODUCTS REQUIRE NO MAINTENANCE

Straightforward statements are needed when writing featured benefit headlines. You don't need to be clever to attract attention when you're selling a strong benefit.

If you don't have a Unique Selling Proposition, you can still use the featured benefit headline. In this instance, however, you'll be putting a twist on the sales technique. Instead of featuring a benefit, focus on a unique aspect within your offer:

WIN A FREE TRIP TO JAMAICA!

Your readers don't even know what your product is, but there's a good chance they will keep reading your ad or mailer. Having a unique offer can create more excitement than your product does. Sometimes this strategy makes sense.

Reader's Digest, for instance, routinely offers sweepstakes to promote subscriptions. Perhaps they recognize that the product is well-known. Just selling the magazine to prospects won't create a lot of excitement. It's not new. You can't write a news headline, and you won't dazzle too many persons by touting its unique benefits.

What the *Digest* marketers realize is that a sweepstakes increases response to a direct mail offer. With the number of mailings they do, response will be great enough to support the cost of paying for nice sweepstakes prizes.

I generally prefer a direct selling approach. At times, however, it's appropriate to sell your product indirectly, like *Reader's Digest* does when pushing its sweepstakes.

Boastful

News and featured benefit headlines are used when you can pick out specific selling points. Be direct when using them. Make your point plainly.

Sometimes you can't isolate a specific selling point. You can't write a news headline saying your product features a unique development, and you can't write a benefit headline describing how your product outshines the competition.

Let's say you have a good product that competes well but has no outstanding features. In these cases your writing will have to be more clever. You won't be able simply to announce your product's qualifications. Other methods will be used to attract readers.

One method is the boastful approach. I don't mean boastful in the sense of making inaccurate claims. A boastful headline is one in which you make a positive, yet general statement about your product. It's different from news and featured benefit headlines simply because it's not specific. It's, well, *boastful*.

A boastful headline creates a positive selling climate. This type of headline lets your readers know what your product is. In that way you qualify prospects. By letting prospects know your product compares favorably with the competition, you're inviting them to read on.

Without offering a specific reason to buy your product, you want to make readers feel good about you. To write such a headline, try out different adjectives with your product. Look at ways of putting it in a nice light. Below are some examples. Because the boastful headline is general, I've left out specific product references in the examples. You could literally put almost any product into these headlines and use them as is.

AMERICA'S FAVORITE ____
EVERYTHING YOU WANT IN A ___
____ JUST LIKE MOM USED TO MAKE

You get the idea. Boastful headlines generally should be avoided in direct selling. Advertisers use them effectively for two types of clients. First, such headlines are used with general consumer products such as soap or beer, where there often is little difference among competitors. In these cases, all you can do is try to put your product name out in a favorable light and hope to gain market share on the retail level.

High-priced, luxury items also use the boastful headline to accentuate their snob appeal. Expensive cars and Scotch can attract buyers simply by saying they're the most expensive product on the market.

Such products aren't sold directly by the ad or mailing. If you want people to send you an order after reading your ad, you need a product with a specific advantage. If you don't have a unique feature, come up with a special offer to feature in the headline.

Because of their general nature, boastful headlines don't cause people to take action. That's what direct marketing is all about.

Command

Command headlines are more suited to direct marketing than boastful beginnings. As the name implies, a command headline encourages action:

BUY TWO, GET ONE FREE
ACT NOW TO FIND OUT HOW TO DOUBLE YOUR MONEY IN THE STOCK MARKET

If you want someone to do something, tell them. Be direct. However, the command doesn't have to be of the "Place your order now" variety:

USE ____ AND LOOK TEN YEARS YOUNGER
TELL YOUR BOSS HOW TO MAKE MORE MONEY
DON'T MISS THIS CHANCE TO TAKE AN ALL-EXPENSE PAID VACATION

Whether or not your headline asks for the order, you'll need to imply benefits for your customers while commanding them. Make sure your benefits are specific and concrete. You can't expect someone to do what you ask until they see how it will help them.

Don't make your commands too outrageous. You can turn people off by asking too much. Make sure your request is reasonable. Your command will be ignored unless you can expand on and explain the product benefits in the rest of the ad or mailing.

Finally, make sure your command is positive by giving readers a strong option. Don't scold them by making commands such as the ones below:

QUIT WASTING TIME
DON'T RELY ON CUT-RATE MATERIALS
TAKE VITAMINS TO IMPROVE YOUR HEALTH

Such headlines imply that your prospects are making poor choices. They're insulting. Instead, let your command strongly suggest an exciting offer that can help them.

Emotional

Selling is an emotional appeal. You'll get few people to buy unless they believe your product will somehow make them feel better. You want prospects to know that your product will make them more secure, more popular or more confident.

Usually this appeal is in the background, but with some products, the emotional benefits can be major selling points. When that's the case, go ahead and make your headline a straight emotional appeal.

Personal items, such as perfume and toothpaste, lend themselves to this treatment. Insurance is another product often sold by an emotional appeal. It's more effective to say:

YOU CAN MAKE YOUR FAMILY'S FUTURE MORE SECURE

than it is to state:

YOU CAN SAVE TEN PERCENT ON LIFE INSURANCE

Have you ever heard anyone selling deodorant because it costs less? Of course not, money isn't the main concern when someone makes that purchase.

Emotional headlines are put together in several ways. You can be direct by stating that a product will cause something good to happen in a customer's life:

HE NOTICED THE SOFTNESS WHEN I STARTED USING ABC LOTION

Or, you can take the same product and be less direct. In the example below we're still selling lotion, but the prospect gets hooked with the purely emotional headline. In order to find out what you're selling, he or she has to keep reading. That's okay, because a good emotional headline will capture a reader's attention.

"HONEY, YOUR SKIN FEELS SOFTER TONIGHT"

If you use a testimonial, such as the one in the example above, make sure that it sounds like something a real person would say. For that reason you should generally make the testimonial a purely emotional statement. Don't try to mention the product, as we do below:

"HONEY, YOUR SKIN FEELS SOFTER SINCE YOU STARTED USING ABC LOTION"

Most people would recognize that as an unrealistic statement. It sounds like something a copywriter thought up and not what a real person would say. It loses its emotional appeal, and the ad loses some credibility.

A well-written testimonial creates credibility. By making the ad or letter very personal, you can get rapport quickly with readers, and guide them to make a buying decision. Your emotional headline can be exaggerated for effect if you're not using a testimonial style. When you're making an emotional point, readers won't say it's unrealistic if you aren't scientifically accurate. You can try something like:

ENCHANT YOUR HUSBAND WITH SOFTNESS

Everyone knows your spouse won't be literally *enchanted*. Instead they'll see your point by understanding that you're describing an emotional state. And, soft hands, admittedly, can lead to that state.

Be aware of what you're doing when using emotional headlines. Try them out on uninterested parties to see if the headlines are understandable and believable. Be committed to what you're doing. For instance, don't try to combine news or benefit approaches with the emotional, or you'll come out with something like this:

ENCHANT YOUR HUSBAND WITH 10% SOFTER HANDS

Such a statement just doesn't work. When you use the technique correctly on the right product, an emotional headline can work well.

Trick

A trick headline catches the reader's attention while telling nothing about the product. An example would be an envelope imprinted with an illustration of an optical illusion. Your trick teaser line would be, "What do you see here?" Inside, the copy would explain why most people are fooled by the illusion.

Only at that point would the product be introduced. You might say something like, "Many buyers of (generic product) also don't look carefully enough." You could then talk about your specific product.

In addition to insulting the reader's intelligence, you can see that it takes a long time to get around to selling your product. What the copywriter hopes is that readers will be intrigued by the trick. To learn more about it, they'll read about the product.

Direct mail copywriters often use trick teaser lines, but I prefer more direct ways of selling. Use this technique only if you can't push a benefit, testimonial, news item, offer or emotional appeal. An indirect approach isn't the best way to get sales.

Curiosity

Curiosity headlines differ from trick ones in that the headline has something to do with the product. You are trying to get the readers involved with your product by making them curious about it.

You can create a curiosity headline by putting your product in a different light than that in which it's usually found. Here are some examples:

WHEN WAS THE LAST TIME YOU THANKED YOUR BLANKET?

TEN REASONS NOT TO BUY AN IRA AT ABC BANK

You can see from these examples that no strong selling point is coming across. When you're trying to get prospects to order, you should always try to emphasize benefits and the offer. Here you're just counting on curiosity keeping enough prospects reading, with the hope that if they read the rest of your ad, they'll send in an order. Try this method only if you don't have something concrete to base your headline or teaser on.

I'm not saying you can't be inventive or humorous when writing benefit or information headlines. Just make sure, though, that your emphasis is on how your product will specifically help your prospects. If you're off, then sales will most likely suffer.

Slogan

Headlines using company slogans try to encourage sales by keeping a firm's name in prospects' minds. Slogans are often used to promote items that don't have any advantage over their competitors.

Slogan headlines should be considered by direct marketing copywriters in some situations. First, you need to have an interesting company name that helps sell the product. Examples are Geico Insurance and Ugly Duckling Rent-A-Car. As mentioned in the previous chapter, Geico's name stands for Government Employees Insurance Company. By causing prospects to identify immediately with the firm, the Geico name helps sell insurance.

Ugly Duckling is also a company name that sells. It describes in an interesting way the company's service—renting used cars at discount rates. Here's a specific example of a slogan headline:

BIG ISLAND TOURS BRINGS THE SUN A LITTLE CLOSER TO YOU

Since most travel agents and tour companies appear fairly similar, the presence of a slogan makes this company memorable. Mailing a letter to affluent neighborhoods with that as a teaser could be effective. If someone is thinking of taking a winter trip, receiving that letter in the fall will grab their interest. Also, such a teaser captures the special feeling people have about a long-awaited vacation to a tropical island.

Consider using a slogan headline if you have a name and a slogan that sells your product or service. As you repeat your slogan, you hope your firm's name becomes established in your customers' minds. Whenever people think about taking a trip to the Caribbean, Big Island Tours wants its name to be remembered.

Slogan headlines are generally used to reinforce retail products. When a customer goes into a store to buy an item, the manufacturer of the item wants its name to be remembered. Repeating the slogan throughout ad campaigns may help the manufacturer gain market share. However, this is not a technique used frequently in direct response selling.

Offer

From this study of headlines you can most likely see that effective direct selling gets right to the point. You don't have to be cute. Often the best ad simply states the benefit or news item.

Powerful ads also can just state the offer in a headline. Here are some examples:

TRY THIS NEW LABOR-SAVING DEVICE FOR 60 DAYS WITHOUT RISKING ONE CENT

OPEN UP YOUR OWN IRA FOR ONLY $200

Notice how the copywriter strengthened the headline by using the words *new* and *your* to attract reader interest. You can present your offer in other ways, and see how readers react. For instance, put your offer in the first person:

I'LL LET YOU TRY THIS LABOR-SAVING DEVICE FOR 60 DAYS WITHOUT RISKING A CENT

In this case, you're speaking directly to the reader. Your sales pitch has the ring of a person talking to you; it's harder to ignore. Readers can trust what they read when there seems to be a person behind the words.

Note also that the writer has featured a benefit by mentioning a "labor-saving device." That's a good trick. Reader interest is stimulated by the headline, desired prospects are identified, a benefit is given and a clear offer is made.

To see if an offer headline will work for you, write your offer down on a piece of paper. If it sounds exciting, play with the words to improve it. Tell about the product. Or identify who can benefit from it.

Information

Another way to select your audience is by offering specific information. If someone thinks you know something that can help them, they'll keep reading. Here are some examples:

HOW TO INCORPORATE YOUR COMPANY IN LESS THAN 15 MINUTES

WHAT 500 PROSPECTS WANT FROM YOU

Provide specific facts and figures whenever possible. Doing so makes your headline more concrete:

FIVE WAYS TO SELECT A TAX SHELTER THAT WORKS

141 IDEAS FROM SALES EXPERTS ON WRITING MORE EFFECTIVE HEADLINES

One way to see if an information headline fits your product is to write a headline that begins with the words *How*, *How I*, or *How You*. Also, use the word *To* for identifying an audience that wants to know something you can tell them about:

TO YOUNG PEOPLE WANTING MORE THAN JUST A JOB AFTER COLLEGE

ADVICE TO BUSINESS OWNERS WHO NEED MORE HOURS IN A DAY

Guide your readers. Assume they want the information you're offering. Notice in the example below that we ask *Which*, not *Whether*.

WHICH OF THESE HELPFUL BROCHURES ON INCREASING SALES AND CASH FLOW WOULD YOU LIKE ME TO SEND YOU ABSOLUTELY FREE?

You can also experiment as you test headlines and teasers. For instance, which of the following examples do you think would pull best? Our first one tells what information is available in a very brief form. It's more of a caption than a headline. The next headline inserts more personal contact:

HOTTEST NEW BUSINESS IDEAS OF THE YEAR

LET ME SEND YOU 12 OF THE HOTTEST NEW BUSINESS IDEAS OF THE YEAR

Some direct sellers offer information as part of a two-step selling process. Don't feel you have to use an information headline just because that's what your offer revolves around. For instance, sellers of expensive items looking for leads will often offer a brochure. Still, they might choose to feature a benefit in their headline and describe the brochure offer at the close of the ad.

Other direct marketers wishing to build their lists will offer a brochure, and make that offer in the headline. Obviously that's because they're looking for people who like to receive—and presumably order from—mail order catalogs.

Since these direct marketers are going for a general audience, they don't need to qualify their prospects except to say what kind of merchandise is in the brochure. On the other hand, the maker of expensive business equipment would want to explain his product benefits first, and send brochures only to qualified prospects.

Testimonial

As we've mentioned before, it's good to establish personal contact with your readers. A testimonial ad does this. Just because you are telling a story, you'll tend to keep many prospects reading.

Perhaps the most famous testimonial ad is "They Laughed When I Sat Down at the Piano...." John Caples wrote the ad to promote music lessons by mail. In it he describes a party scene in which the ad's narrator, who is known as a jokester, sits down at the piano after an accomplished musician finishes playing for their friends.

Caples goes on to describe how everyone at the party assumes he's putting them on, and they all get ready for a laugh. They are then amazed when he starts playing classical music beautifully.

The narrator's friends want to know how he learned to play so well in such a short time. He of course tells them about the lessons he took by mail. As the ad ends, readers are invited to send in the coupon, ostensibly to learn how they can have a similar experience.

What if Caples had written the ad without using a testimonial? It would have been weaker to say, "Your friends will be amazed when you show them in a few short weeks what complicated pieces you can play."

Using the testimonial made the ad entertaining. Readers could put themselves into the ad. Without the story line, the ad would have lacked power.

Testimonial ads can provide credibility when your ad needs to make a big claim. Which of these do you think works best?

"HOW I MADE $1 MILLION IN THE STOCK MARKET—WITHOUT A COLLEGE DEGREE"

NOW ALMOST ANYONE CAN MAKE $1 MILLION IN THE STOCK MARKET BY FOLLOWING NEW STRATEGY

Using the testimonial approach listed first makes more sense. If someone states they can teach anyone how to get wealthy in the stock market, we automatically think that's a farfetched claim. But, if someone says they did it, we aren't going to assume they're lying. We have to admit it's possible, and we wonder how they did it. We keep reading the ad.

Testimonials can add credibility and emotion to your ads, and those are keys to getting direct response orders.

You can write testimonials in various ways. Look at the differences in the following examples:

HOW THE SMITH COMPANY CUT LEGAL COSTS BY 50%

MY SECRET FOR CUTTING LEGAL COSTS BY 50%

In the first example, the copywriter tells a story about the Smith Company. In the second headline, the voice of the advertiser is used. Usually direct marketing ads use testimonials as a means of letting advertisers tell their stories. Sometimes that isn't appropriate. For instance, Caples's ad wouldn't have worked if the testimonial consisted of the head of the music company describing how he taught himself to play the piano. It was much more effective using an everyday person to whom all readers could feel close.

That's also the case with the ad about the Smith Company. The advertiser wants to describe how a business benefited from his services. However, if his claims about his services were almost unbelievable, it would be best for him to vouch for himself and his firm by being the voice of the testimonial.

Finally, you can use the testimony of a third party in your ads. Well-known persons such as athletes or entertainers often are used for such testimonials. Since direct response is a selling tool, generating interest by using celebrities usually isn't effective. Direct response ads and mailing pieces need more selling power than that.

Predictions

The use of prediction headlines can be effective, although the range of products they should be used with is narrow. Anyone willing to go out on a limb and make a prediction is interesting. People will want to read what they say. Here are some sample prediction headlines:

FIVE TRENDS THAT CAN AFFECT YOUR BUSINESS PROFITS THIS YEAR

EMERGING OPPORTUNITIES IN OIL STOCKS—WILL YOU MISS THEM?

If your predictions make sense, readers will feel a bond to you and your ideas. You'll gain expert status in their eyes, and they'll be pleased to look to you for advice or products to help them take advantage of what the future holds.

Just make sure your product or service supports the idea of you as a futurist. High-tech equipment undoubtedly can be sold with a prediction headline. It makes the point that your products are ahead of their time. Information services, such as newsletters, can also use prediction headlines effectively. The advice they contain must help subscribers plan for the future.

In this chapter I've given you some tools to help capture the attention of your readers. You have to do more to get an order. In the next chapter, we'll look at how to keep selling in the body copy of your ad.

Headline / Product Matching

HEADLINE TYPE	EXAMPLE	REASONING
News	SCIENTISTS SAY THE XYZ COMPUTER IS FASTER THAN THE IBM-PC	Technical products can be sold as scientific advances.
Benefit	NOW YOU CAN DO THREE JOBS WITH ONE TOOL	A product with a well-known purpose can be sold as an improved model.
Command	TRY MACHO COLOGNE. IF YOU DARE.	Products that aren't necessities can gain more urgency with a command headline.
Emotional	WHEN YOU'RE HOT, SOFT-E-WIPES ARE AS SOOTHING AS A SUMMER BREEZE.	Personal products can be sold by appealing to the emotions and senses.
Offer	TRY THIS DESK CALCULATOR FREE FOR 30 DAYS	If you don't have a benefit to sell, you can mention the offer you're making on your familiar product.
Testimonial	"I LOST 50 POUNDS IN THREE MONTHS."	Extreme claims are made believable when they're part of a real person's experience.

Certain products easily lend themselves to specific headline types. Here are some examples and reasons why.

Chapter Fifteen

Writing Print Ads That Sell

Once you've decided on your headline, it's time to choose the best approach to writing the body copy. How do you organize and present material in your ad?

Often you'll take the lead from your headline. Your first paragraphs will flow from your head. In the last chapter we studied a dozen headline-writing techniques. There are many more ways to present information about your product in the copy. Let's look at some proven ways to make ads that sell.

Rule Number One

Remember that there aren't any ironclad rules, although some principles have worked time and again. Your basic concerns are: to say what you need in order to sell your product or service, to say it in an interesting way so that you won't lose readers midway through the ad and to ask for the order. In direct selling, you must get readers to act now.

Direct response ads must be different from traditional ads. Research shows that the body copy of most ads isn't even read. Advertisers are content with prospects seeing the headline, illustration and the company name. That exposure alone will cause many of the *glancers* to choose the advertised product over others when shopping.

You probably do the same. When going through a magazine, how often do you take the time to read all the copy in an ad? Almost never, I expect.

Yet that response won't be enough if you're selling through your ads. You have to grab your readers, first with the headline and then with the copy. The selling must continue all the way to the point where you ask your readers to order now. If you don't have the ability to hold people's attention with your writing, find someone who can.

One way to help your current writing is to look at the results of previous ads for the product. See what worked, as well as what didn't. Look at the differences between profitable and losing ads.

What if there aren't any previous ads for the product or service you're writing about? If that's the case, examine direct response ads for other products you like. See if any of them contain an idea you can adapt to what you're selling.

I'm not suggesting you copy anyone else's work—that's illegal. But, you can find inspiration from others. See how they approached writing problems. Dissect the ads. How do the ads you like keep people reading?

As we saw in the last chapter, many techniques can be used. If your product has outstanding features, keep talking about them. If it's based on a new development, describe its impact for your readers. Or if it helps solve a particular situation, weave a story based on such an experience. Talk with people who use the product. Find out how it helps them—and then create an ad that conveys that information to others in a compelling way.

Putting It Together

You can use different tools to make your ad effective. Once you understand the purpose of each element, it's easier to put the most appropriate material into those sections. As we've noted before, your headline is your stopper. Don't run a headline until you're sure it will make people want to read your ad.

What if your product has many selling points? Put the strongest one in the headline, and then run subheads throughout your ad. Each subhead will point out another product benefit. Body copy underneath the subheads will describe each feature.

Already you can see the ad almost outlining itself, but there are other elements to consider. Perhaps your ad would benefit from an illustration. Once again, your choice will depend on what message you are giving your readers. Use an illustration that reinforces what the copy is saying. If a picture is worth a thousand words, then choose your picture carefully.

It's not hard. If you're selling through a testimonial, use a picture of the person represented in the ad. Since I'm president of my publishing firm, I often write testimonial copy and include my picture. In that way my readers can see that I stand behind my products. Furthermore, I'm a successful businessperson who is telling other entrepreneurs about products that can help them.

If your product has unique technical features, show them in a photo. You can convince more people that you have a better mousetrap, office equipment or power tools by showing pictures of your product. Preferably show your product in action. Put a person in the picture to create more interest. Help your readers to imagine themselves using your product by showing another person happily or profitably using it.

If your ad creates a situation and shows your product or services resolving the conflict or problem in the situation, you have a different illustration opportunity. Consider using an illustration that shows the happy resolution of the problem.

Use a photo if your story is realistic. If your story is more abstract, a drawing might be better. You want readers to be able to place themselves in the situation. For instance, ads for cold remedies or dancing classes can use photos. An ad such as "They Laughed When I Sat Down at the Piano" should rely on art. Here you're creating a fictional setting. Printing a photo showing a man at the piano would be inappropriate. Using a drawing is better in that case.

Will Anyone Remember You?

You can see how the elements of your ad are starting to fit together. Use them to highlight whatever is most important in your message to prospects. You might feel you don't need an illustration; instead you'd like to emphasize your company's name. In that case you would put your firm's name and logo in large type. Generally this goes at the bottom of the ad, although it could also be in the headline.

Don't be shy about promoting your company. Remember that you are going to keep coming back to your customers again and again, seeking more orders from them. You want them to know your company's name. You want them to see your products mentally and feel good about them whenever they see your name on follow-up mailings.

You might say, "Why should I promote my company? It's small and young. Few people know about it. I'm not famous." Well, what better reason do you need for promoting yourself? If you do enough advertising, you will become famous.

Don't feel like you have to be a celebrity. You don't have to be Frank Perdue, Orville Redenbacher or Lee Iacocca. You just want customers who know enough about your firm to want to keep buying.

Some companies combine a slogan with the company name. It enhances the process of positioning your firm in the minds of your customers. Having a slogan provides a handle, a way for customers to remember what your company stands for.

You might also want to have a distinctive logo type or company symbol. Everyone recognizes the Coca-Cola logo, largely because it's used in their advertising. You want your customers to recognize your firm as quickly as they do Coca-Cola.

Having a descriptive and memorable product name also is advantageous. A good name helps sell your product. Don't lose sight of that goal. Don't blow up your company's name and then lessen the amount of selling you can do for the product. Use all the elements in your ad to reinforce your selling points.

Look at your strengths. Emphasize them. The name of my publishing company, Enterprise Publishing, was intended to state our purpose. It's always been easy for customers to remember, and it's unique. By itself, however the name couldn't do a lot of selling.

My ads haven't pushed the company name and logo. Instead I've emphasized my money-back guarantee, because that's a selling point. At times I've put the guarantee in larger type, or placed a fancy border around it to attract the reader's attention.

Do the same with your ads. Use headlines, subheads and graphics to point out whatever makes your product worth buying. Give your readers all they need to make a buying decision, and do it in an interesting way. Although you need to remain very serious about selling, keep in mind that entertainment can bring in readers.

You don't have to be a creative genius to be interesting or entertaining. Tie your copy into the needs of your readers. If they like to fish, drop references to fishing throughout your ads. Create interest by tying your product into a recent current event, the season or a holiday. You can add immediacy to ads just by mentioning your *special spring offer*.

Make sure that interest-creating devices are right for your prospects. For instance, calling attention to special spring savings would work for a firm selling clothes. Using the seasonal term identifies the type of clothing in the offer—spring clothes. In that way it selects readers who are in the market to buy light-weight goods.

Additionally the seasonal reference adds immediacy to the offer. It does so by pointing out that fashions change—both because of the weather and the new lines introduced by designers each year. By mentioning spring, you are hoping to arouse interest in fashion-conscious people. You are telling them to look at your goods if they want to see what's in fashion this coming season.

Mentioning spring savings to businesspeople, however, probably won't increase your sales. Your reference will mean nothing to them, and most likely will just go in one ear and out the other. Spring is neutral to businesspeople; it won't urge them to act.

Take the same idea and adapt it to the business market. Tell your prospects about a special year-end offer, and you should get more attention. The end of the year means that businesses are thinking about taxes for the last 12 months. Many companies will take advantage of a sale to buy goods they won't use immediately, because doing so gives them a tax break.

You can be entertaining by mentioning current events related to your product or service. Just make sure it sells. When I write copy I often mention how recently passed laws relate to my products. My ads gain authority and immediacy when the reader sees that my company's books are up-to-date.

Consumer products can make similar tie-ins, and they can be more whimsical about it than I can with my business products. Try anything as long as your references help you select your audience and sell to them.

Having a clever tie-in is a device that encourages readers to keep reading just to find out what you do with it. You must keep the momentum going in your body copy. You've gotten your readers' attention from the headline. How do you smoothly move into sales copy without losing them?

Smooth Selling

Perhaps the easiest method is to expand on your headline as you start the body copy. Generally this technique works best if you are using a featured benefit or news headline. Here's an example of a featured benefit headline and an opening sentence that keeps the idea going:

ABC DISCOUNT BROKERAGE HELPS INVESTORS AVOID HIGH COMMISSIONS

You can save money every time you buy or sell stocks with the help of the professionals at ABC Discount Brokerage.

You also can twist the featured benefit headline to pose a problem, and tell readers that your product provides a solution. Here's an example of headline and introductory copy:

ARE STOCK COMMISSIONS ROBBING YOU? HERE'S HOW INVESTORS ARE KEEPING THEIR SHARE

Too often a good gain in the stock market is lost after the brokerage firm takes commissions from both ends of the transaction. But that doesn't have to be the case. ABC Discount Brokerage is helping thousands of investors hang onto almost all of their investment gains.

From there the copy could go on to other selling points—telling how easy it is to use a discount broker and how many years ABC has been serving clients. Or, the copy for the entire ad could reinforce the main point of telling readers how much they can save in commissions.

Such choices depend on what you think your prospects need to hear in order to make a buying decision, and on how much ad space you have.

You can see how the ad progresses from the headline. If your headline describes a unique product—whether it's a computer printer or homemade jelly—use the body copy to give specifics. Back up the claim of uniqueness. Or, if you pose a situation in the headline, develop that story in the copy.

Another proven method is to start your ad by referring to or quoting an authority. Here's how I started one of my winning ads:

THE ULTIMATE TAX SHELTER

Everyone looks for tax shelters. But which one is the best?

Tax experts refer to the small, privately owned corporation as "The Ultimate Tax Shelter."

By quoting *tax experts*, I give my ad a ring of authority. There are other writing methods you can use to work on your readers' psyches; one is to challenge them. Here's an example:

NOT EVERYONE CAN PICK THEIR OWN STOCK BUYS

But the experienced investor used to making decisions can save money when trading stocks through ABC Discount Brokerage.

Together the lead and headline hook the reader in the above examples. What you're doing is making a convincing case about general points—the advantages of incorporating and why someone should buy stocks through a discount broker.

Once the reader sees your general point, it's easy for you to switch the focus of the ad to the specific product or service you're selling. In direct response ads, the firm's president often speaks for the product. It's another way of having an authoritative person vouch for the product.

In my own ads I make the case for incorporating, then introduce myself like this:

> My name is Ted Nicholas. Seventeen years ago, after successfully launching 18 corporations, I wrote a book called *How To Form Your Own Corporation Without a Lawyer for Under $75*. It's become one of the best-selling business books of all time, helping more than 900,000 people to incorporate easily, at minimum expense.

Because my product is for business owners, I first explain why the tax laws favor corporations over individuals. After telling readers why they should incorporate, I show them how to do it. Reader concerns lessened as I explained that I've helped over half a million persons form corporations of their own.

Other marketers selling consumer goods don't need to start by quoting the tax laws or any other authority. It's fine for them to start right off by using their own *voice* in the ad to make the offer.

One way of doing this is with a *Me-You* statement. Me-You statements give you a direct way to make an offer. Here's an example:

GIVE ME 5 MINUTES TO SHOW YOU HOW MUCH YOU CAN SAVE ON STOCK TRADES

Call up any ABC Discount Brokerage office and tell us what your last stock transaction was. We'll tell you how much the ABC discounted commission would be on that trade. I'm certain you'll find that we can save you money.

Many times a direct response marketer will come across almost as an eccentric in an ad. Although I would never do that when advertising Enterprise Publishing products, the technique does have its place. Generally it's used by sellers of consumer goods. When done effectively, the ads present the firm's president as a person who does things differently in order to obtain unique values for his customers. Here's an extreme example of that kind of ad:

"I WANT TO GIVE THEM AWAY, BUT MY WIFE WON'T LET ME!"

There is a middle ground, one that interests and sells your readers without being too dry and technical or too flamboyant. Generally it's called third-party influence selling. What that involves is using testimonials from your previous customers to convince your prospects. Here's an example:

HOW ABC DISCOUNT BROKERAGE CAN SAVE YOU MONEY

> "Dear Sirs: Recently I added up all the money I saved since I started using your services two years ago. Was I ever surprised! ABC Discount Brokerage has made a big difference in the size of my investment portfolio."
>
> J.P., Augusta, GA

After using this approach in the lead, you have to change styles. You must go back to straight copy. Keeping a testimonial going for very long is tough—it's hard to make it seem believable. Your sales copy will have to mention points that someone writing a letter wouldn't bring up.

What you can do is relate your selling copy to the testimonial. Try something like this:

Every month we get letters like this. ABC Discount Brokerage has helped thousands of investors keep their hard-earned investment dollars for the past 30 years.

Starting To Sell

What you have done is built a bridge from the testimonial to sales copy about the brokerage firm. A reader will follow you without really noticing that you've gone from an interesting headline to a testimonial backing it up, and then on to sales copy about the company and its services.

You'll use the same principle no matter what type of headline and lead you choose. When writing, recognize that your headline is a stopper, your lead expands on it in an interesting way, and sooner or later you have to switch to sales copy.

In direct response the headline and lead often introduce a unique benefit or a problem. A way to get into selling copy is to tell the story behind the product or service offering the benefit or solving the problem. Remember the ad about "the miracle from Germany"? In it the writer keeps the reader interested by telling the story of how the unique shoes were found by the company's owner. What he's really doing, however, is getting across all the benefits of the shoes.

A story helps to keep readers interested while you explain how such an extraordinary value became available. You can do your selling without the reader minding—or even noticing.

You're aware of what you're doing. You can pack selling into your writing without being obtrusive. It's not easy, but below are some ideas that have worked for me and other successful pros.

1. *Have a sense of urgency.* You don't have to be breathless, but remember that you are trying to get your prospects to act immediately. Having a sense of urgency means you won't be shy about giving your prospects advice or telling them what course of action to take.

Urgency will be heightened as you pile on reasons why the prospect should buy. Tell them the happy results that will be theirs after purchasing your product or service.

2. *Use short sentences.* Your writing will have more power if you use short sentences. Your appeals will be clear and direct. Your reasoning will be straightforward.

If you lose a prospect while he or she reads the ad, you've probably lost a sale. You don't want someone to look up from your writing and say, "I don't get it." Good selling is uncomplicated.

3. *Be believable.* Many people don't believe advertising, because many ads are unbelievable. Don't get carried away. Common copy mistakes are testimonials that don't ring true and claims that promise too much.

If you're selling improved soap, tell people you can get their clothes cleaner. Don't aggrandize. Meeting a need is sufficient. Some copywriters would make such an ad sound like a technological breakthrough that rivals the polio vaccine.

One way to check your ad's believability is to try reading it out loud. Portions that don't flow naturally or logically will come out sounding stilted. Direct response needs to be easy to read. You have to sound like you're talking to someone you care about when writing this type of copy.

4. *Get specific.* Nothing gives your writing as much power as good examples. Don't just say you sell big grapefruit; provide dimensions. Show a photo comparing your grapefruit to store-bought grapefruit. Doing so makes your writing more concrete. Your product then seems more real.

Now go one step further. Attach a benefit to every specific feature you mention. Let your prospects know that every detail of your product or service has been designed to please them or to help them reach their goals. Let's say you're selling wallets. Don't just tell prospects they're made of leather. Say "Crafted totally from leather, for years of beautiful use." In one sentence you're letting prospects know what the wallets are made of and reminding them that they are both sturdy and good-looking.

The above example is called *reason-why* copy. If your prospects get to the end of the ad and still aren't sure about buying, you're hoping they will remember that the wallet is made of leather. The prospects are reminded that the wallet will last a long time, and because of that it's a good value. You're giving them reasons to buy.

Buying decisions aren't logical. Many purchases are made for emotional reasons. In addition to your reason-why copy, tell prospects how your product or service will benefit them emotionally. In an ad for wallets you could say: "ABC Wallets are a great Christmas gift idea. You'll be remembered for years when you give an all-leather ABC Wallet."

You can use other means to convince your prospects to buy. One method involves showing the results of a test. Timex watches, Diehard batteries and most recently, Pepsi and Coca-Cola have featured self-administered tests in their ads. By showing the results of such tests to prospects you can offer *proof* that your product is the wisest choice.

A guarantee provides further reinforcement of your product. Every direct response item should have some sort of guarantee. You can't expect people to buy from you sight unseen unless you assure them that you will return their money, no questions asked, if they are dissatisfied for any reason.

Providing information about your company and product also reassures prospects. You don't want to bore anyone by talking about yourself. Instead, tell how your company has evolved to meet customer needs. Describe how you've worked for years to develop a secret recipe or to find an exporter in a far-off land who supplies great products at a low price.

Here you can use testimonials to back up your firm's story. Letters from satisfied customers can help you write the lead, as we showed earlier. Or, place the letters into the body copy to help back up product claims. You can identify persons giving testimonials by name or by initials. You should also add information about where they live or what they do.

Showing where your customers live helps establish you as a national firm, while also targeting your audience. If your market is mostly urban dwellers, pick testimonials from New York and San Francisco to put in your ads. If you're selling to people in smaller towns, choose Boise and Biloxi.

Sometimes it makes more sense to omit where your satisfied customers live and instead tell what they do. Here are some examples:

> "Your photocopying paper saves us 25 percent compared to the manufacturer's price."
>
> *B.K., law firm partner*

> "My nails last longer and have more shine with ABC polish."
>
> *J.L., commercial artist*

Testimonials provide proof of your popularity, and they also say something about the value in your products. You can back this up even more by weaving specific facts about your company into the ad. Tell how long you've been in business, how many customers you've served or how much of your work is repeat business to satisfied customers. All of these are powerful persuading points to someone just learning about your firm. Use them to your advantage.

Another form of testimonial is using an expert to make a favorable comment about your product. "ABC Soap is recommended by most washing machine manufacturers" is an example. Find an expert who will impress your prospects, or tell about any awards your product has won.

As you can see, there are many elements to draw on when writing an ad. Get the prospect's attention. Appeal to both logic and emotion. Use various techniques to persuade. One additional proven advertising method is the power of repetition. If you have a strong point, keep driving it home. You have to do so. Many readers skim and won't pick up everything you've written if you only say it once. Others might read your point, but not accept or grasp it immediately.

Use repetition creatively. Don't bore your readers. Keep going over important messages, but phrase them differently each time you bring up the point.

If you're offering free information, tell your readers. Later tell them you'll send them the booklet without charge. Finally, tell them they don't have to spend a dime to get the information you have for them.

By doing that, your chances for success are increased.

If you're offering something for sale, you have to do more to get your prospects to buy. Your prospects might admit your product is well-made, has certain benefits and is well-accepted. Yet they'll still put off making a purchase. They won't feel that now is the time for them to buy. On the other hand, you want them to buy now. How can you help make that happen?

One tactic is to show prospects what a bargain they're getting. Mention throughout the ad that you're offering a special low price. Tell what the price was previously. Add how many people bought at the original, higher price. In that way you're saying that you're offering a greater bargain now. Any markdown sale lends itself to this treatment. In this way you're finding a dramatic means of letting people know what a good price you're offering them.

Add believability to your price claims by giving reasons for the low prices. Many car dealers justify sales by saying they're "overstocked, and just received another shipment. Everything has to go." Retailers might say they have to clear out the winter clothes in order to show their spring collection. Specialty shops will explain that their buyer just got back from the Far East, after finding some fabulous new sources offering lower prices, or that currency devaluation is making imports cheaper.

You can go too far in this tact. Some mail order firms will tell prospects they're making a special offer as part of a marketing research effort. In reality the price isn't that special. Telling people they're getting a good deal because of a unique promotion is enough to get many prospects to buy.

More responsible direct response sellers may advertise special prices because a manufacturer is discontinuing a line. Perhaps the technology has changed, and the maker wants to bring out a new model. In this instance a direct response seller can offer great prices to persons who don't mind buying older technology. Always give the reason for your price reduction; doing so makes a fabulous price believable.

If you aren't selling at a reduced price, tell your prospects how your product can save money. Let your prospects know what they'd pay for a product or service comparable to yours. Ads for my book on incorporating describe how lawyers charge $300-$1,000 for what I'm offering at less than $100.

That doesn't even count the money people save in taxes after they've used my book to help incorporate their businesses. You can see that I'm showing prospects what a bargain I'm offering them.

If you're selling a product that will be used often over a span of time, tell your readers how much it costs per day or per week. If you're selling cable TV services, a charge of $15 a month might seem high to some people. If you describe the offer in terms of "only 50 cents a day to watch great movies and sports," you're putting the offer in a different light.

A similar method compares your price to something else of known value. Our cable TV service would probably go on to add that its monthly fee amounts to "what it costs to take your family out to see a single movie in a theater." Now that's getting persuasive.

If your product has less tangible worth, tell how much money it has made or saved others. A self-help course would fit into this mold.

Giving your prospects something of exceptional value isn't enough. You should also show them how easy it is to use.

Almost everyone dislikes change even if they know it's a change for the better. Look at people's habits. You can tell them how to be more efficient or save money, and many persons won't act because it's simply too much effort for them to change.

That's human nature, and it's what you're going up against when you try to sell people something they've never bought before. Too many marketers don't realize this trait and get frustrated as a result. They know they have a wonderful product. They know it's a great value and that it can help their customers, but not very many buy. "If only I could get people to try it," moan the sellers. Yet they don't realize they could get people to buy. To do so they just have to make it seem easy for customers to use.

Let's say you're selling tulips and other bulbs that you import from Holland. In your ad you describe how beautiful the bulbs look. You tell how your company has been importing only the finest bulbs for decades. Included are testimonials from customers and a guarantee that assures prospects that 95 percent of the bulbs will bloom, or their money will be refunded. Finally, you let people know what great prices you have by telling them how much they'll save because you import in large quantities.

What more do you need to make a sale? You need to remember to make it easy for the customer to buy. Do so by telling them that with every order they get a free booklet that simplifies bulb planting. In it they'll see when to plant, where in their yards to plant, how deep to place the bulbs, how close together to put them and how to care for them after planting.

The booklet is the clincher. It shows someone who has never planted anything how to have beautiful Holland bulbs blooming in the yard without having to go to the library or nursery for help.

Make it easy for people to buy. If you're selling clothes and don't know a size, explain how prospects should measure themselves. L.L. Bean tells people to trace around their foot and send the piece of paper with their order to ensure that their boots will fit. That's a sure selling technique. Almost everyone wears different shoe sizes on different brands of shoes, but tracing your foot means that Bean's will fit perfectly. That's reassuring, and it makes it easier for someone to order.

Make your coupon simple to read and fill out. If you have an 800 number, promote it. Give your prospects a sense of urgency. Make your offer contingent upon their ordering within a certain time length. You'll gain more than you'll lose with this tactic. If your prospects don't order soon in direct response, they never will. Few people will keep your ad on their desk for weeks and then decide to order. If you can't get them to order soon, as time passes they'll realize they actually can get along fine without your product.

Finally, if you think you need more to get prospects to order, consider adding to your offer. Special financing is one option and so is a rebate. Sometimes it helps to add that supplies are limited. Tell your readers that if they want to take advantage of this special offer, they need to act soon.

If you've done your job well, they will. In the next chapter we'll apply some of these principles to writing direct mail letters.

Chapter Sixteen

Writing Direct Mail Letters That Sell

Direct mail is the most expensive way to advertise. You can spend less money and reach more people with TV, or by placing space ads in newspapers or magazines.

Because of the high costs, you must know what you're doing if you're going to use direct mail to sell products or services. If you don't, you can lose a lot of money quickly.

The Cost of Freedom

Selling by direct mail gives you freedom. You have no size limits. It's not like a space ad with set borders. A direct mail piece can be anything from an insert in a billing statement to a four-color, glossy-stock catalog. What does that mean to you? To begin with, you can pick formats that will help you sell to your target audience.

Let's say you have a fur store. If you're selling furs for evening wear, you would want a traditional-looking brochure or catalog. You'd use color photos and glossy paper to project a classy image. In this way you'd be putting your products in the best light to sell to persons looking for high-class, expensive furs.

What if you are selling fur coats designed more for warmth than beauty? You could save money by abandoning the color shots and slick paper. You'd still probably use a catalog, although it wouldn't be lavish. You could use your savings to rent more names.

If you were selling *fun furs,* you might invent your own format. Someone in the market for an outlandish product would be attracted to a direct mail piece that folds out into a small poster, for instance.

Finally, you might be offering novelty fur items, such as a fur-lined pencil holder. In this case you could sell to a broad base of consumers by putting a stuffer in charge card bills sent out by banks.

What I'm getting at is that no one approach is right. Before committing to a direct mail format, check what it will cost to produce the mail piece. Unless you're a gambler, you need to be fairly certain you can make enough money from orders to pay for your marketing and then have a profit.

Do It Right

Don't cut corners. Many firms trying to get into direct mail will try to save money. As a result, they don't get enough back from their efforts to meet expenses. After seeing these losses for awhile, they decide that direct mail isn't suited for their business.

These firms often have made one of two common cost-cutting mistakes. First, they get someone who has never written direct mail copy to put together their package. Second, they mail out a package that lacks some of the selling elements direct marketers traditionally have found necessary to be effective.

Don't try a direct mail campaign unless you have a copywriter who's experienced and successful in that medium. If you can, choose one who's been effective in selling products or services similar to yours.

Many direct marketers prefer, as I did, to get started in space ads before trying direct mail. A small firm can begin by placing small ads. Even classified ads can be effective. You can learn about direct response in this manner without spending large sums, and you'll be building your mailing lists.

If you aren't used to direct response selling, your marketing staff will probably start off by suggesting vague ads. A seller of stereo equipment and calculators might advertise the following:

FOR ALL YOUR ELECTRONICS NEEDS

Hopefully this advertiser will realize before

losing too much money that a specific offer must be made to a set target audience. Even if you think you can be all things to all people, you should present yourself as a specialist in your advertising. Customers want to think that you have plenty of experience serving people just like themselves.

As a beginning direct marketer, you can test ads to learn how to come up with effective offers. One firm I know sent out mailings and produced ads that told about their products and how to use them. Results were fine, but not spectacular. When they wrote an ad with the headline *BUY TWO, GET ONE FREE*, their results were better. Offering bulk discounts had been part of this business for years, but it took awhile for them to realize that it was a strong selling point for their direct marketing work.

Ads can teach you these lessons—as they did me. Direct mail can be profitable—but, as I said earlier, it is expensive. Make sure you have enough money to commit to the project before starting.

Persons who have other avenues of selling can enter direct mail on a smaller scale. For them, direct marketing can reinforce other selling methods. To see how to use direct mail packages, let's look at four ways of selling through the mail.

1. *Stuffers and other inserts.* Retail store owners often begin direct mail efforts by putting stuffers into bills. Since these customers know your store and are charge card users, they're good prospects for buying through the mail as well as in the store. A stuffer encourages customers to place an order on a special item.

Give the buyers a coupon and a phone number. In that way they can choose whether to phone in their new order or mail back the coupon. Either way, customers will probably use their charge card when placing another order.

If such efforts are successful for the retailer, he or she can rent the names of persons similar to those in-house accounts. Since those prospects won't be familiar with the store, however, the retailer will need to send more than just a stuffer to sell them.

Most likely the retailer will choose to send a catalog or a full direct mail package. Both of these tools have enough selling power to convince people who have never shopped in a store to buy from it through the mail.

Other types of inserts are used just to create store traffic. Putting an ad insert in a local paper describing a weekend sale on seasonal products, for example, should boost sales.

To encourage action on the part of prospects, you can include a coupon that can be redeemed for discounts or a free prize. By forcing readers to cut out and save the coupon, you are making them reinforce their desire to stop by your store.

2. *Self-mailers.* A company that makes most of its sales through other means can bring in extra sales with self-mailers.

A self-mailer is a sales piece that can be folded, sealed, addressed and stamped. You save money on production, handling and postage when using self-mailers instead of traditional direct mail packages in envelopes. It's much more expensive to put out the mail package with letter, coupon, small brochure, outside envelope and a business reply envelope.

A self-mailer is generally a sales brochure containing an order form that can be torn out and mailed in.

Who should use a self-mailer? Consider a candle manufacturing company. They have a sales force calling on gift shops and drug and department stores. Additionally, the company sells directly to restaurants and other accounts, mostly in bulk.

Because of the different markets they sell to, this candle company is fairly well-known. A self-mailer from this company will be noticed by many persons, and the company can find appropriate mailing lists easily. A simpler way to start would be to mail brochures describing new products to current accounts.

Although sending just a stuffer in bills can work with personal customers, business accounts usually won't buy from a stuffer alone. In the first place, the person cutting the check to pay the bill won't be the person making the buying decision. Decisions made in a business often must be justified to others. For that reason a prospect would need more information than a stuffer can give in order to make an order.

A self-mailer can also show many products. In that way prospects can see how complete your line is. At the same time you can make offers encouraging bulk or multiple sales. Consider using self-mailers if your company has a well-known name, a good product line and if you can find mailing lists or have good in-house lists.

Self-mailers also can be used to back up a sales force. In essence, a self-mailer provides information leading to sales when you have other things going for you. If you want to sell to prospects who haven't heard of you, use one of the following two tools.

3. *A direct mail package.* Many elements can be in a direct mail package. It is a self-contained

sales kit. No store, salesperson or advertising is needed to get a sale.

First is the envelope with the teaser message. Use it to create interest in what you're offering inside. Some direct mailers do just the opposite to get prospects to open the envelope. A plain white envelope, a personal return address and a first-class stamp will cause many people who might otherwise throw out your letter to look at it.

Next comes the sales letter. Use that to amplify on your envelope teaser, explain your offer and ask for the order. Often another letter, small brochure or other item is included to support what's stated in the letter.

Your package will contain an order form. Research shows having the form as a separate item creates better results. Finally, you'll include a business reply envelope for your customers to send back their orders.

4. *Catalogs.* Because of their high costs for production and mailing, catalogs should be sent only to two groups: your best customers, (those who buy often) and known catalog buyers. If you send your best customers a catalog, they should use it to make more orders. If you don't have an in-house list, consider sending a catalog to persons who are known buyers from catalogs. Since catalogs are expensive to produce and mail, they carry some risk. Generally catalogs are used by firms who have experience in the direct response business.

Building Your Package

After deciding which tools will best help your direct marketing efforts, you have to produce them. Let's begin by looking at the premier direct marketing tool—the sales letter.

Start your letter by expanding on your envelope teaser line or inside headline. If you've gotten your prospect's attention, you won't lose many readers by giving more details in the first paragraph. Your teaser at the letter's top usually will be one of two general types. It will either give a benefit or make an offer.

Try different methods for presenting your headline and first paragraph. See which has the most grabbing power. Here are some ways to start your letter:

1. *NEWS:* Announcing a new way to keep your payroll. Companies are saving up to 30 percent when compared to hiring an outside service.

2. *TESTIMONIAL:* Smith Co. saved more than $35,000 last year with our new payroll system.

3. *PREDICTION:* Businesses must find new ways to meet federal payroll regulations. Changes in the law on January 1 now make keeping up expensive and nearly impossible.

4. *OFFER:* Let me send you a free booklet describing how you can save up to 30 percent on payroll expenses.

You can see these are examples of techniques similar to those in writing space ads. What I'd like to point out is that each technique is used to push either a benefit to the reader or to sell the offer.

Which one best suits you? That's where your creativity and knowledge of your prospects come in. Try different ways of presenting your story. If you think you've found a winner, test it. Mail two different packages to names on the same list and compare results. If you have a customer list with a fairly regular response rate, try the new package on some of them. See if it pulls better than other mailings you've done to that list.

Your letter should expand on both the offer and benefits available to your prospect. Although you will emphasize offer or benefits in your headline and lead, you should explain both thoroughly in the letter.

Be compelling, yet believable. Make your benefits as strong as possible, and then make them believable by including testimonials from previous customers. Add your personal promise that the product or service will be very helpful to your prospects.

Expand on your offer by sweetening it throughout the letter, or put other inserts in your mail package that make the offer stronger. Let's consider the firm offering the payroll system. They could mention in their letter that persons ordering now will receive a special report updating recent law changes affecting the taxation of corporate fringe benefits.

Include a money-back, no questions asked guarantee. Tell readers that you are offering that guarantee because you're so sure they'll be thrilled with your product and won't consider parting with it.

Add that the special report is theirs even if the prospects return the payroll system for a refund. Keep convincing your prospects that the offer is a good one by telling them how much others have paid for the product.

Finally, encourage action in two ways. First, tell prospects what they'll lose by not ordering. In that way you'll get a chance to describe the benefits again. Second, put a time limit on the offer. Tell prospects that supplies are limited, or that these prices are good for only a set time, such as seven or ten days from the time they receive your letter.

All of this selling must be done in a way that keeps your reader interested. The simplest way to do this is to continue to write in terms of what a great offer this is and how your product or service will meet the reader's needs. In order to be believable you must also weave in statements that back up your claims.

Don't worry about repeating points in the letter. Remember that many readers are just skimming. If you only mention a point once, some will miss it. You have to keep pushing your product's benefits in order to convince your prospects. Unless you remind them several times about what your product can do for them, they might not order.

Here's an outline for a direct mail letter that shows one way of putting all this together:

1. Describe the problem facing your prospects.
2. Tell why that problem won't go away. Add that it may become more bothersome.
3. Tell the benefit your product or service provides that solves or eases this problem.
4. Describe how easy and affordable your solution is.
5. Back up that statement with testimonials from current customers.
6. Now that your prospects see and believe your benefit, start pushing the deal. Tell them how much previous customers have gladly paid for this product or service, and then tell how much lower the price is in your current offer—if the prospect acts now.
7. Sweeten the deal. Offer an additional free bonus product if the prospect orders soon.
8. Give prospects your personal promise that the product or service will provide the benefits you're describing in the letter.
9. Add your money-back, no questions asked guarantee for additional reassurance.
10. Stress that action must be taken now. Tell prospects that there is a time limit on this exceptional offer.
11. Tell what prospects will lose if they pass up purchasing your product or service.
12. As a postscript to your letter, you can repeat the benefit or the offer or sweeten the deal even more. Often I find it's best at that point just to encourage action. Tell prospects to send no money now but to make sure their name and address are correct on the mailing label. Ask the prospect to peel the label off, place it on the order coupon and mail it in the enclosed business reply envelope.

Add that you'll ship within 24 hours of receipt. Give prospects a certain amount of time to examine the product. If they aren't happy, they can send the product back. If they are, you'll bill them when the examination period is up. Either way, the free bonus for *ordering now* is theirs.

You're making it easy to order. You aren't telling people to write a check. If you did, it could make them think twice about ordering. Instead, you're telling your prospects simply to make sure their name and address are correct on the mailing label, and to put that label on the order form.

Give your readers a token to put in a slot or a sticker to affix on the order form. One of the proven principles of direct mail is that response rates improve if you can get the prospect to physically do something with your package.

Perhaps prospects have fun when they're given an action to take. Maybe it's easier for them to make a mental commitment to buy your product if they've taken an action. At any rate, it works.

Now the simplest way to follow this idea is by having a prospect peel off an address label and stick it on the order form. Die cutting tokens and slots in order cards is very expensive, and yet that extra money spent in production comes back to many direct marketers who use those techniques. For most direct response mailers, I'd suggest sticking to having your prospects peel and affix their address labels.

For more selling power, add your brochure to the letter. Never send a brochure without a letter, however. Enclosing a letter gives your brochure the personal touch needed to get orders.

As we said earlier, you can add other inserts to the package to restate your offer and benefits in different ways. One example is to enclose a small piece of folded paper inscribed with, "*Read This Only If You've Decided Not To Order.*" Inside the company president can express disbelief that anyone would ignore a product with so many benefits. The offer and the money-back guarantee would be stressed again. Push the benefits and the no-risk offer to the prospect.

You also can use an insert to keep sweetening the deal. Add another free bonus for customers enclosing payment with the order, for instance.

Weighty Information

Can all this information overwhelm readers? It can *only for those who aren't interested*. If you can clearly state your benefit and offer in a way that attracts attention, your prospects will be pleased to read your package. They will believe that you can help them with a problem they have.

I want to stress that although the outline discussed previously is a moneymaker, it's only the beginning for a creative pro. Many successful direct mail pieces—I'm talking about letters that have been used for more than 20 years with only minor changes—take the original outline and attach twists to it.

You could call these twists gimmicks; they're methods to zero in on your readers and make them feel as though you are writing personally to them. For example, a marketer tells his upscale readers as he closes the offer that he is writing to them because they are successful and intelligent. He wants input from this select group before marketing to the population as a whole. He asks them to order soon, and if they're dissatisfied, to please take the time to write him a personal note explaining why the product didn't merit their approval.

This company has singled out its prospects by telling them that they're special. The letter encourages action by saying that the company needs the prospects to order and to let him know if they're dissatisfied before the company does any mass mailings.

Another such technique is to weave throughout the letter predictions on matters of importance to your prospect that relate to your product. One financial newsletter touts its direct mail package with a list of economic predictions. Many investors will read the letter because they're interested in the predictions.

In between predictions the publisher tells how much money the newsletter makes for its subscribers by offering them such information regularly. All the usual benefit and offer material is included. The prediction format helps get qualified prospects to read the piece.

Attention Getters

Look for similar twists on an ordinary sales letter that can make it pull extra hard for you. You're looking for a way to present the sales information uniquely. You're looking for ways to hold your readers's attention while telling them why they should buy your product. One way to do this is by writing your sales letter in the form of a story. We looked closely at that writing technique in the chapter on space ads.

"They Laughed When I Sat Down at the Piano" is an example. As discussed earlier, the writer of this letter describes how the product—music lessons—changed how his friends viewed him socially.

Using the story approach enabled the ad to appeal directly to the emotions of the readers. By choosing the technique, the writer acknowledged that one reason people buy music lessons is to enjoy the popularity that comes from being an entertainer.

By writing a story, you are showing the benefits of the lessons. A headline such as "Now You Can Impress Your Friends at Parties" doesn't grab a reader's emotions. In fact, it sounds a little silly. By representing what could happen with a story, your readers will be swept along.

Even if you choose not to use the story approach, it's good to know what the emotional appeals are behind your product or service. No matter how good the deal you're offering, your prospects will buy at least partially for emotional reasons.

Let's say you can somehow sell IBM PCs at 30 percent below retail. In your letter you'll push price and the product's quality reputation. You'll tell your prospects all the jobs that will become easier or quicker with the use of a computer.

The computer still costs a lot of money. In spite of the good price, the many benefits, solid reputation of the product and a great offer, you need to include emotional appeals to get someone to buy. What are emotional appeals? They are the benefits to a person's life-style that your product offers.

In the case of the computer, your prospects won't buy the computer just because it adds numbers quickly. They'll decide to buy when you tell them that a computer can balance a checkbook with ease, freeing them from that chore and enabling them to spend more time with their family or a hobby.

You can't go wrong by pointing out such appeals. Turn every product feature into a specific benefit. Don't just tell a prospect that the dress you're offering is made of silk. Tell her how soft the silk will feel as she wears it. And then go further. Describe how wearing such a dress will make your prospect look and feel her best—whether she wears it at a party or to the office.

Specific information gives your description more selling power. By telling exactly what kind of silk is in the dress, you make it seem more special. Which of the following has more sales power?

SILK
IMPORTED SILK
100% IMPORTED SILK
100% IMPORTED CATHAY SILK

I'd say you get the most mileage out of the last example. Using it lets you make the dress appear unique while providing more product information. In fact, you might go from a specific description to another product benefit.

Tell your prospects that, despite any apprehensions they might have about silk dresses, the fabric your silk dress is made from is easy to take care of. Keep piling on the benefits.

How To Keep Prospects Reading

Benefits are important to sell your product, and emotional pulls will help you get your prospects to order. Much of the excitement of your letter will come from the offer.

If you think your letter is getting a bit dry before you've finished telling about the product, add to your offer. Let's say you're selling by mail the silk dresses we mentioned earlier. If you use a two-page letter to get in all the selling information needed by prospects, you might just give a portion of your offer early on the first page. Mention the great price you have, for instance.

Then at the top of the second page, put in the following:

FREE BONUS OFFER—
CALICO MAKEUP KIT

If you order within five days we'll send you as a free bonus a calico-pattern makeup bag, made especially for our customers. You can't find a makeup bag like it anywhere for under $15! You'll love its soft cotton exterior. Our calico makeup bag is a natural for travelers. And it's a great hit with our customers, who wear our Cathay Silk dresses in style and comfort all over the globe.

That will attract attention. It will cause readers who are thinking about putting down the letter to keep going. It will cause others who are just skimming the letter to look more carefully at what you say on the second page. Your goals will then be met. Add to your offer halfway through a letter to keep the interest of your readers high. Without that interest they won't read your letter, and if no one reads your letter, you won't get many sales.

In your letter you must have a mix of benefits from your product and facts about your offer. You need both. Customers will buy after they're convinced that your offer has more benefits than cost.

Half of your job is to say how many benefits the product has, and the other half is to tell how low the price is. Do these two things, and add some emotional appeal. You'll be on your way to putting together a successful letter.

We've looked at ads, self-mailers and the traditional direct mail package: envelope, letter, brochure, order form and return envelope. One last direct mail selling tool fits in here. That's the catalog.

Approach catalogs cautiously. You shouldn't attempt one unless you have a large mailing list; many of the costs of putting together a catalog will be present whether you print one or one million copies. If you only mail a few thousand catalogs, you'll have to get back a significant number of orders in order to pay for the design and illustration work that goes into catalogs. Your customer mailing list needs to be at least in the tens of thousands before you should attempt a catalog.

Carefully choose the merchandise that goes into a catalog. Your best bet is to use products that sold well in previous offerings through ads, self-mailers and direct mail packages. You also can save some money by using photos or art previously shown in ads and mail packages.

Make sure that the anticipated return will cover your production and mailing costs. Do this by mailing selectively. Start by going only to your customer lists or to persons who have bought similar products from other catalogs.

Look even more carefully at these lists. Part of your in-house list might be names of persons responding to a promotional offer. Such persons might not be good prospects to buy from your catalog, unless you've told them in the promotion that you'll send a catalog with their order. They might be interested solely in the low-cost promotional item. If your catalog is filled with much costlier items, you should test these promo item names before mailing to all of them.

For that reason it's good to have a fairly narrow catalog. Stick to one general area of merchandise—cotton clothes, home hardware equipment and office supplies are examples. Don't stray from the formula that has brought in your current customers. Try to give them more of the same.

Some of your toughest catalog decisions will involve adding new products. Don't assume something you like will be a big success and automatically give it a full page. When you're writing the checks, you can't be too cautious. Rely on products you know you can sell to your customers.

Look at your product mix. You need some variety in merchandise and price. If you include too many low-priced items, your average order might prove too small to cover your costs.

Carefully track catalog returns. Know how much money each item has brought in. You can weed out the nonperformers, and give strong products more space in the next catalog.

When writing catalog copy, you don't have the space for each item that's available in a direct mail letter. You can't come up with a special offer on each item. Since you're mailing primarily to previous customers, however, you don't have to sell as hard. Your products and company name are known by most of these persons. You're just giving them the opportunity to enjoy again the benefits of your products.

Your copy will be fairly straightforward. Since your prospects can't examine the products, tell them about the features. It's important to mention several selling points for each product. Different customers will consider different features important to them. For instance, if you made a catalog of silk dresses you'd let customers know about fabric, care, construction, styling and colors available. Use action words. Put your prospect *in* the dress, as in the following example:

> You'll understand why silk has always been the choice of royalty with our Spring Silk dress. Designed exclusively for us from 100% imported Cathay Silk. Pastel floral design is right for both office and evening wear. Specify pink, yellow or taupe. Reinforced yoke neck and zip back. Machine washable. Easy care instructions included.

When combined with a good photo, that's all the information a prospect needs to order. In fact it's a pretty good selling piece, if the price is right and that it's mailed to qualified prospects.

Putting It Together

Together we've examined quite a few means of direct selling. How do you choose and manage these different tools to build a business? You might pick one for a specific task, as we mentioned earlier.

You could use an inexpensive self-mailer to support the efforts of a field sales staff. Such mailers can keep your name in front of customers when the rep is in the next town. They can make special offers and generate leads for your reps.

If you're just starting a business, how do you get into direct mail? If you have at least one product, a good offer and a well-defined target market, you will learn from experience how to grow your business.

Generally you'll start with space ads, just as I did. Space ads work because most magazines today have fairly narrow audiences. You can find magazines whose readers will be interested in what you're offering. Space ads also help new companies because you can buy an ad that fits your budget. If you don't have the money for a full-page ad, start smaller. Consider buying space in the regional edition. If it's successful, use your profits to go for a bigger ad next time.

At this point most of your earnings will go back into the business. You're in the growth phase. Specifically, you're trying to develop a large mailing list of satisfied customers. Once you've done that the space ads become secondary. You can then go to more expensive direct mail letters and catalogs to get more orders from the customers you brought in with ads.

At the start of this chapter we mentioned the heavy expenses connected with direct mail. Because of those costs, it's hard to make a profit mailing to prospects who don't know you. Wait until you have a customer list of 100,000 or more. You'll then be able to afford the cost of producing a direct mail package.

Printing costs per unit drop drastically as you print higher quantities. Most of the cost of printing is in preparation, so you don't have to spend much to keep the press running. The art and copy expenses will be the same no matter how many you print. As you print more, the unit cost drops, making it easier for you to make a profit.

Start with small space ads. Go to costlier direct mail only when you have enough customers to justify that step.

Here's a trade trick you can use no matter how young or old your direct marketing business is. In all stages of direct mail you can use a self-mailer as a *bounceback*. Whenever shipping any item, include a brochure with a coupon. Your customer will open the package, be delighted with the product and be open-minded about ordering from you again. Use a bounceback to approach customers with another special offer while they're thinking good thoughts about your company and products.

Not every ad or direct mail piece will be a winner. But in direct response you can cut your losses. If an ad, magazine, mail piece or list doesn't work, drop it. When you develop a winner, *roll it out.*

Go to outside mailing lists to increase your sales, but remember that your expenses will increase. For every thousand names rented, you'll pay at least $30, and with rented lists your sales will drop at least 15 percent from what you realized from your customer lists. If you mail to your own lists first, however, many of the production costs will already have been paid.

You can grow quickly if you have a profitable mail piece and can find lists of persons like your customers. As you find more products, you can develop a catalog. Your business will be taking another step. By then you'll have a lot of experience behind you. You'll know what products, offers and media work. You'll have successful marketing pieces and a large customer list.

Usually you'll start with a small catalog, a *minicatalog*. Begin by mailing to your customers. Once you've developed a profitable catalog, once again mail to outside lists.

Before you spend money on mailings, you need to understand how to make your ads, direct mail pieces and catalogs visually appealing. We'll look at how to do that in the next chapter.

The next pages show samples of direct response components from successful packages I have written.

136 The Golden Mailbox

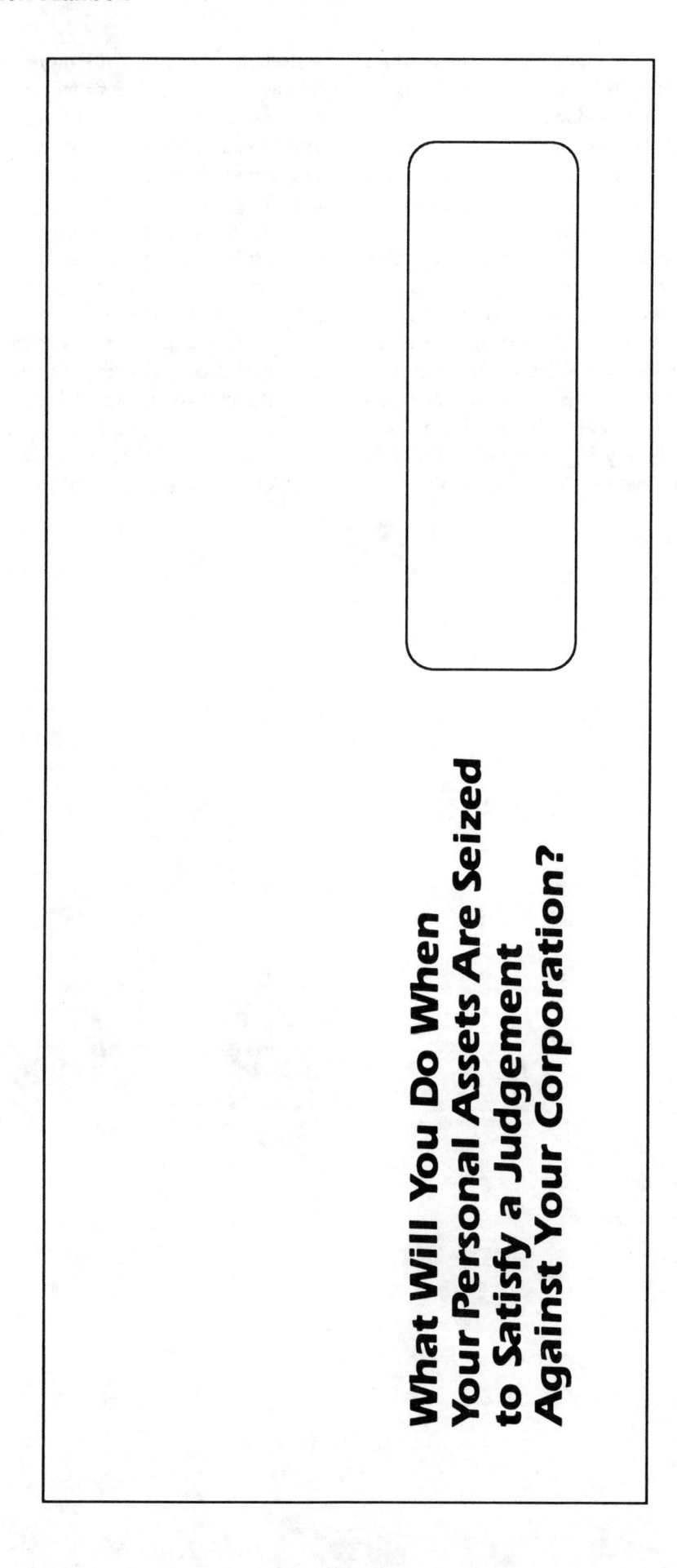

What Will You Do When Your Personal Assets Are Seized to Satisfy a Judgement Against Your Corporation?

16 / *Writing Direct Mail Letters That Sell*   **137**

SAMPLE FORM

Here is a sample form—one of the 92 you will find in *The Complete Book of Corporate Forms*. Notice the high-quality paper, and how easy it is to fill in the blanks. With your copy of the book comes permission to reproduce and use any form. Incidentally, the typestyle matches the IBM typewriter, so each document will look even more authentic when you fill in the blanks.

RESOLUTION OF BOARD OF DIRECTORS OF

_____

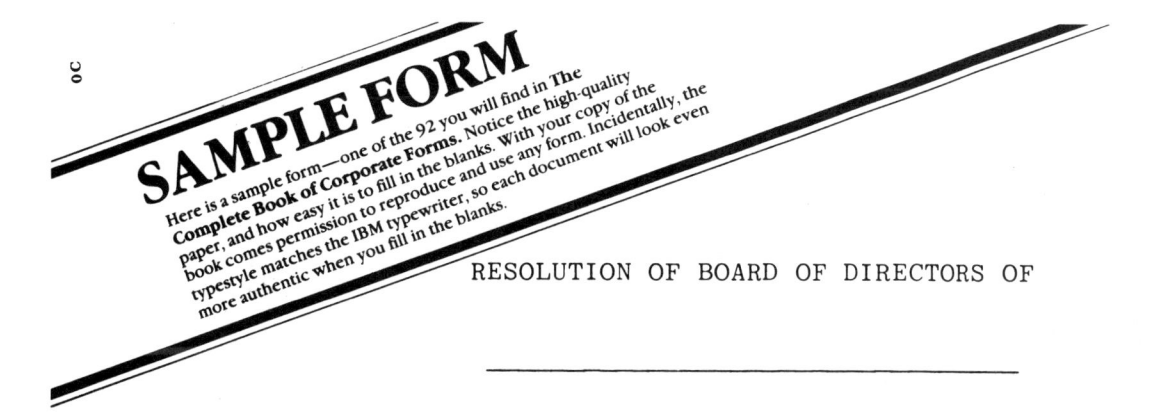

WHEREAS, the Board of Directors has carefully considered the advisability of purchasing a membership in
Country Club, for   , and

WHEREAS, it was determined that such membership would be desirable and beneficial to this Company in that it would provide a place for entertaining visitors, customers, members of the press, and the like, thereby increasing the Company's goodwill, improving its public relations, and increasing its business, and

WHEREAS,   , as officer in charge of public relations, will have the primary responsibility and duty of seeing to the accommodations and entertainment of such visitors, customers and the like, and

WHEREAS, the expenses involved in such entertainment, etc., are properly those of the Company and not of a private individual, be it

RESOLVED, That as a step to maintain and increase the Company's business,   is hereby authorized to apply for membership in   Country Club for the year   and to obtain reimbursement from the Company for any dues or initiation fees thereby incurred, and

RESOLVED FURTHER, That   is hereby authorized to obtain reimbursement from the Company for all expenses incurred at   Country Club during

Authorizing Purchase of Country Club Membership for Company Vice President   Form 5010

the year in connection with the entertainment, accommodations, meals, etc., of the Company's guests, including, but not limited to, expenses for lodging and meals, bar bills, greens fees, caddy fees, rental or purchase of sporting equipment, locker fees, and tips, and including   own such expenses.

    I,   , do hereby certify that I am the duly elected and qualified Secretary and the keeper of the records and corporate seal of   , a corporation organized and existing under the laws of the State of   , and that the above is a true and correct copy of a resolution duly adopted at a meeting of the Board of Directors thereof, convened and held in accordance with law and the Bylaws of said Corporation on   , 19   , and that such resolution is now in full force and effect.

    IN WITNESS WHEREOF, I have affixed my name as Secretary and have caused the corporate seal of said Corporation to be hereunto affixed, this   day of   , 19

_____
Secretary

Send Today For The Complete Book of Corporate Forms
30-DAY TRIAL NO RISK OFFER!

What Will You Do When Your Personal Assets Are Seized to Satisfy a Judgement Against Your Corporation?

Your corporate shield is one of your biggest assets. It's especially valuable during any business catastrophe. But this legal "veil" could be pierced.

If this happened, your personal liability protection and all the tax benefits through owning a corporation could be wiped out overnight. This means you could be forced to sell your personal home, automobile, cash, etc. to satisfy the judgement.

Does this seem far-fetched? It's not. All the I.R.S. has to do is pay you a routine visit. When they examine your corporate records they may discover deficiencies.

If you haven't kept complete and accurate minutes and other documents, your troubles could start almost immediately. Of course, if you are like most small corporate owners your main concern is the operation of your business. That's understandable. Keeping records at first just doesn't seem like a good use of your time.

However, under the alter-ego doctrine developed by the courts, the personal assets of a shareholder may be seized for satisfaction of a judgement against the corporation. That occurs only if the affairs of the corporation have not been managed in such a way to keep its identity separate from you.

Formalities must be observed even in the small individually owned and run corporation.

If your corporation's corporate veil were pierced, you also risk losing the important tax benefits to which the law entitles you.

When you figure in this loss along with losing your personal liability protection, it's just not worth the risk.

No business action has become as important as documenting your corporate actions. You've heard it a million times. The importance of getting it in writing! Up until recently it's been a big hassle to do so.

Banks, insurance companies and various state and federal agencies, besides the I.R.S., all require notarized authorization to grant loans, buy property and equipment, enter into leases and even to sell assets. And other problems can be equally devastating. The reason? The owner didn't document important transactions. The small business owner simply has to

(Over, please)

"Get It In Writing."

Here are some recent "horror stories" direct from actual court cases.

- Joseph P. obtained a loan from his corporation without the proper loan documents and corporate minutes. As a result, the court required him to pay additional taxes of $27,111.60. He narrowly escaped a penalty of $13,555.80.

- B.W.C., Inc. was forced to pay $106,358.61 of accumulated earnings tax because its corporate minutes were incomplete. They expressed "no specific, definite, or feasible plans" to justify accumulating earnings, according to the court.

Keeping records has always been a bother, and an expensive one, especially for small companies. Most entrepreneurs do not like to spend time keeping records -- probably because no one ever became rich by keeping records.

In a small one-person business, it seems downright silly to keep records of stockholder meetings and board of directors meetings...keeping minutes...taking notes...adopting resolutions...isn't it all just a waste of time?

Not if you ask any of the thousands of entrepreneurs who have lost fortunes because they failed to keep records.

You should look at corporate recordkeeping chores this way: It's part of the price you pay to get the tax benefits and personal protection from having a corporation.

A corporation does not exist except on paper, through its charter, by-laws, stock certificates, resolutions, etc.

Anything you do as an officer or director has to be duly authorized and evidenced by a resolution of the stockholders or the board, or by both in some cases.

It makes no difference if there is only one stockholder or one million stockholders. The rules are basically the same.

You can hire a lawyer, like big companies do, and pay $100 or more just to prepare one form.

But you may need, at minimum, a dozen or more documents to keep your corporation alive and functioning for just one year.

This type of work is the bread and butter for many corporation lawyers. Most of the work can be done by their secretaries, yet they will charge you enormous sums because they know how important the forms are to you and your business.

Lawyers know that the I.R.S. will insist that you have the corporate records to prove that you are entitled to all the tax breaks from having a corporation.

There is now a way for you to solve your corporate recordkeeping problems -- without a lawyer, without paying big fees, and without spending a lot of time.

THE COMPLETE BOOK OF CORPORATE FORMS was prepared by Ted Nicholas.

Nicholas is the author of the best-seller, HOW TO FORM YOUR OWN CORPORATION WITHOUT A LAWYER FOR UNDER $75. This book has become the largest single source of new corporations in America. It has revolutionized the business of forming new corporations by making the process simple, easy and inexpensive.

But forming a corporation is only the first step toward building the "ultimate tax shelter."

Through carelessness or neglect, <u>many people are denied their rightful benefits</u> from their own corporation.

Ted Nicholas saw that many, many business owners need more help after they incorporate. They didn't know how to turn their corporation into the ultimate tax shelter.

And so, he prepared THE COMPLETE BOOK OF CORPORATE FORMS. Virtually all the forms you will ever need are all ready for you. Everything is simplified. Either you or your secretary can complete any form in minutes. All you do is fill in a few blanks and insert the completed forms in your record book.

When you own this new book, <u>you are granted permission to reproduce every form</u>.

<u>If you are behind on keeping good corporate records</u>, now you can catch up in no time. Just complete a few blanks for the things you've already done in the company. It's legal and it works.

Best of all, the price is less <u>than you would pay a lawyer for one hour of counseling</u>.

Here is just a sampling of what you'll receive:

* Minutes of Stockholder Meetings
* Minutes of Directors Meetings
* Minutes of Special Meetings
  (Any of the minutes can be used
  whether you are the only stockholder
  or director or there are other
  shareholders.)
* Amendments to Articles of Incorporation
* Amendments to By-Laws
* Change in Membership of the Board

<u>You will also receive all the stockholder and directors resolutions you will need to take any major business action</u>, including:

- Negotiation of contractors
- Authorizing of loans to corporation
- Approval of corporate loans <u>to you</u>
- Designation of purchasing agent
  (Some suppliers may want to know who
  is authorized to buy from them.)

(Over, please)

- Setting your salary
- Director's fees
- Authorizing your expense account
- Mergers
- Sale of corporate assets
- Dissolution
- Bankruptcy
- Declaring dividends
- Appointment of attorney or accountant

Plus, you'll receive the forms needed to authorize any of these tax-saving fringe benefits:

- Pension or profit-sharing plans
- Medical and dental reimbursement plans
- Sick pay plans
- **Split-dollar life insurance**
- Educational loan program
- Scholarship aid program
- Stock options
- Group life insurance
- Financial counseling plan
- Group legal services
- Christmas bonus, special bonuses

Just one of the above forms can save you hundreds of dollars in legal fees .....

This entire 8½ x 11, loose leaf collection of simplified forms (over 150 pages of forms), clear instructions for their use, as well as samples of completed forms, sells for only $69.95, plus $4.50 for UPS shipping and handling. It comes in a luxurious gold embossed binder as well.

As with all Enterprise · Dearborn products, it sells under an iron-clad 30-day money-back guarantee. After you examine the collection, if for any reason you are not pleased, return it for a prompt and courteous refund. Take a moment to place your order now, and immediately begin saving time and money.

Complete the enclosed free trial request and mail for rapid delivery.

Sincerely,

M. R. Buchanan
President

P.S. Your corporate shield is a valuable asset. Help protect yourself for a nominal tax deductible cost.

POSTAGE REQUIRED

ENTERPRISE • DEARBORN
520 North Dearborn Street
Chicago, Illinois 60610-4354

Part of the price you pay to get the tax benefits and personal liability protection from having a corporation is keeping good records.

But corporate records don't have to be a problem—not any longer.

The Complete Book Of Corporate Forms make the task simple—fast and inexpensive.

Virtually all the forms you will ever need are included with samples and instructions for their use. All you need to do is fill in the blanks.

Order this remarkable collection at our risk, on approval, and see for yourself how easy the job can be.

The Complete Book of Corporate Forms by Ted Nicholas

16 / Writing Direct Mail Letters That Sell   145

FREE TRIAL REQUEST

Please rush me **The Complete Book Of Corporate Forms** by Ted Nicholas at $69.95 plus $4.50 for UPS shipping and handling. I understand that if for any reason I am not satisfied after examining its contents for 30 days, I may return it for a prompt and courteous refund.

Charge To: ☐ Visa   ☐ MasterCard
☐ Check Enclosed
☐ American Express   ☐ Diners Club/Carte Blanche   Exp. Date _____

Acct. No. _____ Initials _____

☐ I'd also like the best seller **How To Form Your Own Corporation Without a Lawyer For Under $75** at $19.95 plus $2.50 shipping and handling.

Enterprise • Dearborn
520 N. Dearborn St.
Chicago, IL 60610

©1992 Enterprise • Dearborn

C0(02)2142K

A few of the benefits of owning
The Complete Book Of Corporate Forms :

• Reduce or eliminate Corporate legal fees

• Cut time spent on corporate "window dressing"

• Simplify record keeping process

• A handy reminder of what needs to be done each year

• Be prepared for IRS review of your corporate status

• Have virtually all the forms you will ever need at a price less than paying a lawyer for one hour of time.

Chapter Seventeen

How To Get Noticed

Almost every direct marketer has a horror story involving artwork. For some it's the ad produced in reverse type, which no one could read. Others have sent out direct mail pieces and received as many complaints about space on their return cards for writing in an address as they did orders.

Your graphics have to be managed. Just as you choose words that help you sell, you also pick type, color and layouts that present your products in ways that will bring in orders.

Setting the Mood

If you're trying to put emotional appeals into your ad or letter, then you're doing well. Also recognize that the typestyle you choose will have a lot to do with how your prospects feel when reading your offer.

Just as your words are designed to suit your offer, product and prospects, your design must also be calculated in its effect. You'll choose a traditional typestyle, for example, if you're selling life insurance. You want to give your firm an image of stability and dependability. Your layout will also be clear and straightforward. Since financial matters are serious, you don't want anything in the ad or letter that might unconsciously confuse or upset readers.

As you design the ad itself, you'll pick a slightly larger type size than normal. Many of your prospects will be elderly. Providing large size type will make your offer easier to read.

That's what you want. Graphics are designed to attract attention. You want to draw readers in with your graphics, just as you do with your headlines. Unless you can get people to read, you won't get many orders.

Highbrow or Lowbrow?

You can have lots of healthy disagreements about art, just as you can about writing. I'll not give you many hard and fast rules about what works. Instead, I'll make the same sort of suggestions I did when we looked at how to write ads and letters. You'll need to understand the many different approaches that are available and try to choose the most appropriate technique, depending on the marketing situation you're in.

Let's say you're selling the IBM PCs mentioned in the last chapter, and you can choose whether you want to sell to corporations or individuals. In either case your marketing piece will describe the benefits of the computers. You'll use testimonials and make your offer in a convincing way.

The tone will be different when writing for a businessperson than when you're approaching an at-home user. Business users will want a more dignified approach and more technical details. How you use product information, your choice of words and the typography and layout of the mail package will be determined by the audience you're going after.

To help you decide how to make your marketing piece most effective, look at where the letter or ad will be read. A business desk is much different from the kitchen table. Consider what will be competing for your prospect's attention.

Dress Your Mailing Appropriately

A general rule for graphics is to try to stand out without being jarring. If you mailed your computer offer to business prospects and put it in an orange envelope, they probably would toss it out without opening it. Such a treatment is obtrusive. It's too much. Your mailing most likely would be noticed negatively by the prospect. You'd be much better off with something that looks more like a business letter. Put on a teaser to make the offer: "You can save up to 30 percent on IBM PCs". Most businesspersons considering a computer purchase will open the envelope.

Now think about your home users. You can work harder to get their attention. They want to relax after a day's work, or they want to prepare dinner for their families. Perhaps the TV is blaring from the next room. Because of the environment they're in, your presentation can be more ostentatious. Your at-home prospects aren't in the same mood as the businessperson who's dressed in a suit, sitting in an office and making measured decisions.

Your prospects at home are tired or harried. Put color on your envelope, or use a nonstandard size for the mailing piece. Write on the envelope:

LOWEST PRICES EVER ON IBM PCs!

Finding the Right Type

Inside you want to project the image of a firm that provides the best in high technology products. You'll choose a design and typeface totally different from what the life insurance company picked.

As in all aspects of direct marketing, it's great to look at what your competition's doing before making any final decisions concerning your product. By doing so you can pick up some helpful ideas. From a design standpoint, you can see what you're up against. It's a way of determining what else is on your prospects' desks and kitchen tables. You'll do well if you can come up with a look that's fresher. You want to be more compelling in offer, words and graphics.

I won't provide a design course here. But I will identify the important graphic elements of direct marketing media, and show you techniques for using art as a selling tool.

Let's start by looking at space ads. As with all direct marketing media, you want to attract attention and hold it while presenting your sales pitch. Then make it easy to order.

In space ads you must pay particular attention to the flow of your ad. Since your entire presentation is laying flat on the page of a publication, it has to look like a complete unit. If you don't lead readers graphically, you'll lose them. At best they'll skip over parts of your ad.

Remember again the competition you're up against. In a publication you're competing against the other ads and editorial material. If your piece doesn't measure up, it's very easy for your prospect to turn the page and read something else.

One reason many direct marketers start successfully with classified ads is that graphic decisions are limited. For that reason there's less chance to make a mistake. As you know, in direct response advertising you have to pay for your mistakes. By starting with classifieds you can learn how to get prospects to respond without spending too much. Most classifieds are fairly similar—interested prospects skim them, looking for ads on products they're after.

As you progress to display ads, use the following formula to help make your ad flow. Start with an illustration, if you want to use one. Show the product in use. In that way you'll graphically display a selling point. If you are selling a service, include a picture of yourself. Pictures increase appeal—everyone's curious about other people.

Use a picture of yourself to draw readers in if the ad copy is written from your vantage point. In that way you're making contact with your prospects. As they read they'll picture you saying to them what you've written. By the time they get to your guarantee, they'll feel as though they know you. What's more, they'll tend to trust your guarantee.

Next, go to the headline. Use it to create interest, sell product benefits or make your offer. Then expand on that idea in your copy. Let subheads break the copy up into smaller pieces. Subheads can illustrate secondary points about the product or offer. Use them as headlines for selling points that aren't important enough to make up your primary headline.

Suppose you're selling those computers in space ads. Your headline might be:

LOWEST PRICES EVER ON IBM PCs

Use that in the headline because it's your strongest selling point. Subheads would go into other sales points. Here are some examples:

IBM PC—FAVORED BY
FORTUNE 500 COMPANIES
A COMPUTER THAT WILL
GROW WITH YOU
EXTENDED WARRANTY TO
OUR CUSTOMERS
ORDER NOW AND RECEIVE
FREE SOFTWARE

Since it's your ad, you'll agonize over the wording. Many of the publication's readers, however, will just skim. Recognize this, and make sure that your offer can be understood just by reading the headline and subheads. If it can't, then many prospects won't bother reading the body copy.

Use a typestyle compatible with the publication. Some mail order firms try to make their ads look like editorial material. Generally the publication will make these advertisers put the words *advertisement* in small type at the top and bottom of the ad. Despite this, it's a technique that works. What the advertiser wants to do is gain more credibility in the reader's mind by appearing more like a feature article than an ad.

If you are planning your own ad rather than copying the magazine's design, keep the following in mind:

1. *Use upper and lower case letters in headlines.* Look at an example in upper case only. You'll find it's too hard to read. That would defeat your first goal.

2. *Avoid using reverse type anywhere in your ad.* White type on a black background is difficult to read.

3. *Sans serif type should be used only in headlines and subheads.* Serifs make type easier to read. Examples of serif and sans serif type are found at the end of this chapter.

4. *Stick with one typeface for headlines and one for body copy.* Too many typefaces make for difficult reading. Instead of making your ad more exciting, it tends to make it look sloppy and unprofessional.

5. *Make sure your typeface is large enough.* Use at least 9 point type, with a point of *leading* between lines. You need this for readability. In fact, before picking any type for either body copy or headlines, insist on seeing samples in the size your type will appear.

6. *Don't put dots around your coupon.* When people see dots their mind says, "Connect them." Dashes mean "Cut here." Always put dashes around your coupon to encourage readers to cut it out and send it in.

Another tip is to place a final layout of your ad on a page in the publication where the ad will appear. Imagine how it will look when surrounded by other ads and articles. Will your ad be noticed? Does it compare favorably with others in that publication? If not, you should rework the ad before running it.

Pay particular attention to your coupon. Make sure it repeats your offer briefly—and personally. If someone just reads your headline and then goes to the coupon, you want the deal to be understandable.

If someone reads the ad, cuts out the coupon and stuffs it into a pocket, you want to make sure that he or she remembers why the coupon was clipped when it is discovered in that pocket a week later. Put your address on the coupon for the same reason. Tell your customers to print clearly. If you can't read their addresses, no one will be satisfied.

Adding a personal touch shifts your customers' attention from the fact that they're making a purchase. To captivate your prospects, make your coupon sound more like they are making a fun discovery than buying a product. Here's an example:

YES! SEND ME 12 ISSUES OF MARKETER'S MONTHLY FOR ONLY $19.95—30% OFF THE NEWSSTAND PRICE.

Have enough room to get the customer address information you need. If there are any purchase options such as credit cards or bill-me-later, they should be easy for the customer to select. Provide a box where the chosen option can be checked.

If you don't have enough room in your ad to put in a coupon, don't despair. In fact, it's best to face up to your lack of space rather than trying to put a coupon in an area that is too small to write in. Many prospects will turn away from such a task—no one likes being asked to do something difficult.

One workable alternative is to print a message at the bottom of your ad that is similar to this: "To order, tear out this ad and print your name and address in the margin. Send it with check or money order for ($ amount) to (your address)."

An order request like that actually could pull very well for you. It encourages immediate action by the prospect, and it gets the prospect involved, which always increases results. Asking prospects to tear out an ad, write their names in the margin and mail it in with a check is an effective involvement device.

Art To Sell By

One area of direct marketing where art plays a big role is in the use of brochures, flyers and circulars. Producing a brochure to accompany your sales letter is time-consuming and expensive. It will give you an idea of the effort required by firms selling through catalogs.

Remember that your brochure will be secondary to your letter. Your letter spells out the offer and provides more of a personal approach than a flyer does. Why use a flyer then? Primarily because a brochure or flyer can make your offer seem more authoritative.

Picture your prospects just as they've finished reading your direct mail letter. They don't know you. They're thinking, "Can I really believe this person?" To them, your offer almost seems too good to be true.

Then they pick up your brochure. It's printed on nice paper—perhaps a glossy stock. Maybe it's in color. All this is designed to make your brochure seem to represent a product and company that are very stable and real.

Your copy in the brochure will mention the offer, yet it won't sell as hard as your letter does. You want the brochure to seem more like a factual description than a sales piece. Actually your brochure's doing quite a bit of selling by answering some objections still lingering in your prospects' minds.

Do this by using illustrations that show your product or service. Show the product in use. If applicable, consider printing *before and after* photos. Always put captions under your photos or artwork. You want prospects to understand what you're showing them. Once again, make it easy on your prospects. Many of them will be skimming. Let your brochure be complete for those who see only the headlines, illustrations and captions.

Color always creates interest. Your artist will suggest color for excitement. Here's where you need to avoid becoming too excited yourself. Color, glossy paper and odd sizes do attract more attention than a black-and-white, letter-sized piece. But get complete costs for the quantities you'll be printing before making any decisions.

Figure how much more money you'll have to bring in per thousand pieces mailed in order to pay for fancy printing or paper. If you think the money will come back to you, then spend it.

When designing your brochure, remember:

1. *Use the front cover of the brochure to create interest.* A brochure's cover can be compared to the outside envelope of a direct mail package. If no one opens it, you lose.

Try to use some device to make readers curious about what's inside. Often you can borrow a technique used on the outside envelope: write a teaser line on the cover of your brochure. Make prospects want to know what's inside. Make them eager to read your brochure and take in the information on your product.

Teaser lines can be founded purely on a curiosity appeal, but not everyone responds to that. Since a curiosity teaser doesn't mention the product, you'll disappoint some readers who will open your brochure thinking that you're writing about something entirely different from what your product actually is. Use the teaser to tantalize your prospects while qualifying them. Often the cover illustration can help in this task.

Let's say you're selling investment real estate to middle-aged investors. Your cover illustration could show a close-up of a couple in your target market's age bracket. It could show that couple in front of some investment real estate or it could be more general and just have artwork showing piles of money.

Similarly your teaser could be a general line, such as "Here's a way others have made up to 33 percent annually on their money." You could identify the investment vehicle in the teaser—"Apartment buildings in America's fastest-growing cities now offer unique opportunities for investors."

I prefer identifying your product in most cases. You can be compelling without *tricking* your prospects with a teaser line.

2. *Use the full size of the paper graphically.* When your prospects unfold the brochure, they should be impressed. Don't fall into the trap of designing your flyer panel by panel. Your brochure will be more striking if you can get readers to open it up entirely. Even if your flyer is just one page folded over, treat both inside panels as a single unit. Let your headline, and possibly your illustration, flow across the whole page. Don't let the page fold block your design.

Using the whole page lets your type and illustrations be larger than if you stayed within the panel boundaries. Getting readers to open up the brochure gets them more involved in reading it.

3. *One of the easiest methods for designing ads and brochures is the grid method.* When using the grid, you keep all elements within imaginary blocks. Your design will appear clean and evenly balanced. Your information will be easy to read. Your copy and illustrations will guide the reader's eye from point to point. You'll avoid jarring the reader.

4. *Use the brochure to describe and show product features.* In the sales letter you talk about product features in terms of how they can help the prospects realize their dreams.

A brochure needs to be more technical and less emotional. Use the space to show and describe exactly what your product or service is made of. Explain the beneficial effects found by users in fairly straightforward terms.

A brochure is a good place to quote from testimonial letters. If you need testimonials, write a letter to 100 of your customers. Ask them what they like and dislike about the product. You'll gain useful information for your business, and you should get some good testimonials. If you don't, your product probably needs more than a brochure can do.

> 5. *Always include your address and phone number.* Put them on every piece in your direct mail package. Do this in case part of the package gets lost or misplaced. Often your prospects will throw out the letter after reading it. But they might keep the more informative brochure. Make sure they can order at a future date—or at least contact you—just from the information on your circular.

You might think at first that direct mail letters don't require much art support. Nothing could be further from the truth. As you've seen up to now, what appears to be a simple letter is actually a planned, coordinated selling tool. Just as the words are thought out, so is the design. If you just typed your direct response letter, had it printed and mailed it, I can guarantee that response to it would be disappointing. Although your words might be the best ones possible, you must also use art to help guide your readers.

Making Art Letter Perfect

Effective letters match the art with all the other sales elements in your package. You can treat a letter almost like a space ad that's in a letter format. If there's a strong selling point, put a headline at the top of your letter. Here are some examples:

HERE'S THE OFFER IBM DIDN'T WANT US TO MAKE

AT LAST! A PORTABLE, AFFORDABLE VCR

INVESTORS WHO FOLLOWED OUR ADVICE LAST YEAR ARE 35% RICHER TODAY

If you have a strong emotional appeal, start with a paragraph emphasizing that. Set if off from the rest of your letter both by positioning it above the salutation and by using a different type style. Here's an example:

> *Since we last wrote you, the toxic dumping problem in our community has doubled. New chemicals have appeared in our streams. And a report from the State University says long-term health problems for residents are possible.*

Dear Neighbor:
Now more than ever, the Toxic Waste Fund needs your help.

Once you get into the body copy of the letter, keep the personal appeal by making sure that it looks like a letter. Always indent paragraphs for easy reading, and print in a typewriter face. Don't typeset your direct mail letters. Using these techniques will help you keep prospects reading while you're selling your product and making your offer.

Make art choices purposefully. Don't just throw color in a letter, or put in other elements merely to heighten your reader's excitement level. Use art to clarify key points. Here's how:

> 1. *Use short paragraphs.* Try not to go over eight lines; shorter is even better. Long blocks of copy are hard to read. Often prospects will skip longer paragraphs—or unconsciously use them as excuses for putting your letter down.

Don't let that happen to you. Short paragraphs are more inviting. Visually they don't ask too much of readers.

> 2. *Break out key points with subheads.* Just as you do in space ads, draw attention to selling points throughout your letter with subheads. After you've drawn your reader's attention, develop the point more fully in the copy beneath the subheads.
>
> 3. *Follow up on the envelope teaser copy in your letter's headline or lead paragraph.* Many of your readers will be looking at your letter because the outside envelope's teaser enticed them. Get these prospects into the flow of your letter. Do so by expanding on your teaser at the start of the letter, or by making that point the emphasis of your headline on the top of the letter's first page.
>
> 4. *Use a second color—sparingly.* A second color won't raise your printing costs by much. For most direct marketers, the money spent on a second color will come back in orders.

What do you do with that color? Use it as a highlight. Place it on key words and phrases. You'll make them pop off the page—and into your prospects' minds. It's an easy way to ensure that ideas become more memorable.

> 5. *Put in personal accents.* One effective method is to have an artist draw attention to your offer by underlining it in freehand.

Instead of having a perfectly printed letter, you then have one that looks as though someone marked on it. All of a sudden it's more personal.

Other accent devices include drawing an arrow in the margin to point out an important paragraph. Or write comments in the margin, such as "Best Value." Usually these personal accents will also be printed in your second color.

Like all art techniques, this can be overdone, but it's worthwhile to experiment with your letter. See how it changes as you use your white space to put personal comments in your letter.

> 6. *Try capital letters for emphasis.* Here's another way to put attention where you want it. Since your reader won't go over every word, you want to show them where the important ones are. Just as good salespeople use their voices to show prospects what points are the most important in their message, you can use capital letters to do the same for you.

If you choose not to use a second color, capital letters will be important selling tools.

Many other selling tools are available once you understand the business. For instance, use your order form to repeat your offer. Then encourage customers to spend even more. Your costs are fixed for an ad or mailing. If you can increase sales 10 percent, your profit could go up much higher—to say 25 percent.

You can get these better returns in several ways. Put in a *good-better-best* line of merchandise, as previously discussed. Others offer discounts for bigger orders. You've probably seen these in magazine subscription offers. If you sign up for two years, you pay less per issue than with the one-year offer.

Also try rewarding your customers by offering a free gift when their orders go above a certain amount. The gift won't be very expensive for you, but such an incentive often can increase your total sales by about ten percent. Since your customers like your products, giving them a reason to buy more is often successful.

Keeping Artists on Track

Hopefully you can see why managing your artists is crucial. Using professional artists is as important as finding good writing help. In fact, when selecting artists you should question them along the same lines I suggested for interviewing copywriters.

One of the most important factors is finding artists who have worked on projects nearly identical to yours. An artist or writer without a successful track record could receive a good practical education at your expense. If you're paying for the mailing, make sure beforehand that your creative help knows exactly what they're doing.

You also need to watch over the pros. Let them be creative, by all means, but make sure that what they produce will sell for you. You should be the best judge of how to sell your products or services to your prospects. Make a list of the items that you need on the order form. Don't allow artists to design something simply on the basis of what pleases them.

From such a list your creative help should be able to develop a package that's unique to you. Tell them as much as you can about your company's products and customers. Work with creative people to develop selling pieces that stand out from everything else in your prospects' mailboxes and favorite publications. You need to be sure that your package has visual appeal, or your words too often will be glossed over.

Make sure that the package's appeal fits your product and prospects. A catalog of low-priced consumer items should appear light and breezy. You want to make catalog shopping fun and easy. Since many of your prospects work, they'll be reminded throughout to use your 800 number for easier ordering.

On the other hand, a company selling expensive items will be less relaxed in its visuals. Prospects for costlier goods will want a more serious presentation of the merchandise. Copy and art will be fairly straightforward, recognizing that these prospects don't expect their shopping to be *fun.*

One art decision you'll make when putting out a catalog is whether to use art or photos, and how to present the items. If you are using photos, you'll have to choose what to place in the background of your shots. Usually you'll develop a scene that suggests the strongest selling point to your prospects.

Suppose your catalog sells watches and clocks. To suggest how accurate they are, picture one with a background showing the intricate inner workings of the timepieces. To show off their beauty, surround another with gold or leather work, suggesting expert craftsmanship. You could put them next to objects to help identify how large or small they are, if that's a selling point. Or, picture one on a wall or desk in a home or office to show how they help decorate a room.

That isn't the only method of presenting catalog merchandise. One clothing seller I know chooses not to use models. For years this firm successfully has shown photos of the clothing, leaving the rest to the buyer's imagination. Pick the art treatment that best sells your items to your prospects.

Where you position your merchandise in the catalog's layout affects sales. Front and back covers will move merchandise. Put your strongest items there—especially if they also can represent to your readers the sort of items to be found in the rest of your catalog. Your cover should qualify prospects. Something in your cover art should appeal to your target prospects. If that's the case, your prospects will find it hard to resist opening the catalog and looking over the rest of your offerings.

Items shown on the inside covers, the first few catalog pages and on or around the order forms should also do well.

You'll also have to decide how much space to give each piece of merchandise in a catalog. Be conservative. Don't assume a new item will be extremely successful and put it on your cover. Catalogs are expensive ventures. Most of your catalog offerings should have been tested before in space ads or mailings. From these test results you should be able to figure their relative pulling power and accordingly allot each item catalog space.

Cataloging Sales

Compile the results of each catalog page carefully to see how much money each item brought in. After doing a mailing you'll probably want to alter the space given to some entries in your next catalog. Poor performers will be discarded from future catalogs and replaced by new items. Each new catalog generally will have 20 percent new merchandise in it.

When designing catalog pages, follow the tip I offered for brochure design. Use the whole spread. Don't design just a page. Instead, design across the gutter (the middle fold) of your catalog. Encourage readers to open it up and get involved. Use the extra space to be more visually compelling.

Another decision you need to make concerns the size of your brochure, catalog or letter. You need to balance production costs against selling strength. A longer letter or brochure could bring in more sales, but it will also cost more to design, write, print—and possibly be more expensive to mail.

Color and paper choices also involve making decisions about the cost of your creative efforts. In the next chapter we'll consider how to make such production choices while also making creative ones. As always, we'll focus on finding what will bring in the most sales.

Chapter Eighteen

Managing Production Costs

As you move from writing to designing and then to printing your package, you'll deal with a lot of people. Not all of them will understand your vantage point. In fact, many of the people you'll manage won't really know what makes your direct mail piece a selling tool.

You have to recognize that the people you're dealing with have their own biases and interests, which means your needs won't necessarily come first. Your copywriter, for instance, might get lazy. He or she could write a short letter, ad or self-mailer—one that doesn't do a complete selling job or won't work as well as it could.

Your artist might want to put an embossed cover on a brochure, or add a fifth color to a four-color catalog. He or she might want to make the piece look great without thinking how much it will cost and how much selling power you'll get for the money.

Your printers might push certain types of paper because they've got boxes of it sitting in their warehouses.

Don't get me wrong. Printers, artists and writers are important parts of the direct response business, but they must be managed so that their collective talents develop the kind of marketing products you need. It's up to you to make sure your creative team is managed to meet your selling goals.

As with writing or art techniques, there are no set answers to effective production. Everyone works differently, and no one has a monopoly on success. In this chapter we'll look at some of the decisions you'll have to make before producing a direct mail package. You'll become familiar with the terms you'll need to know in order to make good choices.

Cost-Cutting Guidelines

Before getting into specifics, let's look at some general principles worth considering. Experience shows that the ideas below can help guide your thinking in profitable ways.

1. *Be conservative.* In general, don't spend more money than you have to. If you think two colors will place your product in a good light, don't use four.

You'll find it much easier to upgrade a package than it is to downgrade one. Let's go back to the four-color example. Suppose you're doing a catalog and decide to print four colors on the cover. You'd have to hire a color photographer. Your artist would also spend more time on design, since color would provide more options.

Your primary expenses would be the costs of color separations and printing. Color separations use a photographic process to prepare four plates for the printer. Each plate is designed to be printed with one of the primary colors—red, yellow and blue. Along with the black plate, they are used to reproduce the color cover.

Because the printing process requires four different plates for the cover, those pages must actually go through the press four times. That raises your costs.

Let's say you printed a four-color cover, and the catalog didn't produce the sales you'd hoped for. In your analysis you find that despite the extra color, the merchandise on the covers didn't generate more sales than you would have expected with a two-color cover. In fact, you figure that if you'd gone with a two-color cover, you would have saved enough money to make the catalog a success.

Unfortunately, though, it's too late to go back. You've already spent the money on the separations and the printing. If you switched to a two-color format on your next catalog, your customers might notice the difference. It could change their perception of your firm. Whereas they might have been perfectly happy had you originally sent a two-color catalog.

Even if you decide to go to two colors now, you'll have to remake your cover art and printing plates to fit that format. Just doing that will cost you hundreds of dollars, if not more.

My point is that it would have been more profitable to have run a two-color cover in the first place. It's now costly and a bit treacherous to try to switch down from four colors to two.

A general rule for marketers is to start small. If it works on a small scale, you can spend more the next time. Whether you're renting lists, buying space or choosing production techniques, start small. Don't fall into the trap of wanting *the best* and spending more than is necessary to accomplish your marketing task.

The other extreme is that you might pinch pennies so hard that your mailing isn't competitive. To avoid this problem, consider the next two guidelines.

> 2. *Look closely at your prospects when deciding on a production process.* Match your package to what your prospects are used to. Doing so will give your prospects a comfortable feeling. Many direct marketing prospects enjoy receiving catalogs in the mail. As they get them, they can tell by a glance what's being offered and whether or not they're interested in looking further.

If you offered your wares in a different format than a catalog, you'd encounter resistance. Prospects often would react with a "What's this?" comment. It would be like a grocer selling food in different sizes and quantities than usual. From force of habit, many persons wouldn't feel comfortable shopping there. The same is true of direct response buyers. Make your marketing piece seem *comfortable* to your prospects.

If you're mailing to conservative businesspeople, use words and art that differ from those in a mailing to teenagers. Stay conservative. Don't try too hard to be different.

At the same time you want a marketing piece to stand out. That's the challenge you must issue to your creative staff. It's easy for creative people to claim they need glossy paper or another color to be effective. What you have to do is tell them what the creative parameters are, and then expect your creative people to work within them to make something memorable.

Perhaps the best method of determining how well your creative staff is doing comes from applying the next rule.

> 3. *Take a careful look at your competition.* I'll give you two reasons for doing this. First, you should assume that your competitors know what they're doing. Perhaps you can learn something from them.

Secondly, avoid making a mistake. Let's say you have dreamed up a new marketing approach that you think is really unique, and you can't imagine why it wouldn't work.

You might be on to something big, but the fact that no one else is doing what you've thought of should cause you to pause a bit. Your competition probably isn't dumb. Perhaps what has occurred to you has already been tried and abandoned by others.

Often there's a good business reason why your idea isn't being used by others. If you can discover this without spending the money to try your idea, you're ahead of the game.

Don't drop your original ideas, but scrutinize them. If they hold up, then test them. Start marketing on a small scale, and measure the results. Don't be afraid that one of your competitors will steal your idea and market it in a big way before you can.

If your idea is good enough to make more money than your current marketing does, it will be able to withstand imitation. That's a normal part of any business. Don't allow the fear of imitation to force you into ill-advised marketing moves.

My second reason for you to watch what your competition is doing is the simple fact that they are your competition. You're going after the same customers. In direct marketing you'll be using some of the same publications for ads and renting from the same mailing lists as your competitors.

How will your mutual prospects respond if your ads appear in the same magazine? Who will receive the order if your direct mail package and a competitor's arrive on the same day in a prospect's home?

Much of your firm's income will come from taking business away from other direct response firms. You're not really competing against local retailers. You're competing against other direct marketing companies. I'm assuming here that your offer can beat what retailers are offering your prospects. If that's not the case, you shouldn't be in direct response.

Unless you develop lists to which no one else is mailing, perhaps through promotional offers or space ads, you're competing with other direct mail firms. Before producing and mailing anything, make sure that your product is better than the others.

Here's where you must walk a fine line—balancing costs, trying to maintain a format your prospects are comfortable with and at the same time standing out as unique. To help you make these production decisions, let's look at the choices available to you.

One thing you'll soon realize is that production choices can transform your company's image. You can be in business only a short time and have very slick-looking marketing materials. Of course, most new firms don't have the money to do that. And such aids don't necessarily produce sales. Direct marketing pros know that results come from good offers, good writing and good media selection. Here's what adman David Ogilvy has to say about the need for big budgets in his book *Ogilvy on Advertising*:

"One day a man walked into a London agency and asked to see the boss. He had bought a country house and was about to open it as a hotel. Could the agency help him to get customers? He had $500 to spend. Not surprisingly, the head of the agency turned him over to the office boy, who happened to be the author of this book. I invested his money in penny postcards and mailed them to well-heeled people living in the neighborhood. Six weeks later the hotel opened to a full house. I had tasted blood."

David Ogilvy, who went on to form the worldwide firm of Ogilvy & Mather, calls direct mail "my first love and secret weapon." He adds the following in his book:

"From that day on, I have been a voice crying in the wilderness, trying to persuade the advertising establishment to take direct mail more seriously and to stop treating its practitioners as noncommissioned officers. It was my secret weapon in the avalanche of new business acquisitions which made Ogilvy & Mather an instant success."

Obviously you don't have to have a fortune to get results. Let's look at ways to maximize production expenses. My first principle is to shop carefully. Unfortunately, many new marketers tend to let go of the process once they get to the production phase. They just turn it over to someone and say, "print it."

Probably this is because they don't know much about production. Unsure of what questions to ask and what to look for, they instead trust production people rather blindly. They can run into the same sort of problems that come up when writers and artists are left to work without direct suggestions.

Perhaps many marketers enjoy working with the writers and artists more than they do discussing the job with printers. Remember, however, that the quality of your printer's work will directly affect how your prospects view you.

You need to know the capabilities and prices of production people. Let's begin that process by looking at the primary methods of printing.

1. *Letterpress prints much like a typewriter works.* Ink is placed on raised surfaces and then transferred to the paper. Although letterpress is available in many places, it is generally considered obsolete. Because of the high cost of printing presses, however, letterpress continues to hang on.

Newspapers used to be printed on giant letterpress machines. Some large metropolitan papers years ago spent lots of money to buy their own presses. Now they can't afford to give them up.

As other printing techniques emerged, the importance of letterpress declined. Printing in color isn't practical with letterpress for newspapers, and the ink is sometimes too thick, causing it to come off on the hands of readers. Some newspapers are stuck with letterpress printers that are essentially white elephants. In the same way, you can easily find printers whose operation isn't right for you.

2. *Lithography uses a flat plate for printing, in contrast with the raised surface employed in letterpress.* Areas on a lithographic plate receive or repel ink, depending upon how they've been treated chemically. Ink from the plate is transferred to a smooth rubber *blanket*. Finally, the image is offset from the blanket to the paper running through the press. Because of this process, lithography is generally referred to as offset printing.

Offset printing is more precise than letterpress. It requires less ink, and distributes it more evenly. Reproduction of black-and-white photos is better on offset printers.

Additionally, offset printing has lower prep costs than letterpress. Prep costs refer to the time it takes to get a press ready to run a job. Cleaning the machine, filling it with ink and other fluids and installing the printing plates and paper are some of the components of prep costs.

This is an important concept for printers. Prep time is down time for their presses—a time when they aren't doing any printing. In that way it's costly to printers. You need to understand it, too. If you can make your printers more effective, they will pass the savings on to you.

Prep costs, or *make ready*, are the reason small printing jobs are so expensive. Presses must be set up the same way no matter if 100 or 1,000,000 copies are being printed. If you can save up your printing so that several jobs can be done at once, you'll save money.

3. *Gravure can be seen as the opposite of letterpress.* Ink is put into a depression on a plate, and then transferred to the paper. Rotogravure is probably the best technique for printing color photographs, especially for long runs. Rotogravure is a good printing choice for four-color magazines with subscribers in the tens of thousands or above.

4. *Screen printing uses a stencil and a squeegee to apply paint.* With this technique you can apply bright colors, which don't fade, on a variety of materials. Posters, bumper stickers, billboards, point-of-purchase displays and even glass bottles and other packages can accept screen prints.

Direct marketers would use a screen printer if they wanted to personalize some of their merchandise by applying the company logo.

5. *Flexography combines letterpress and rotogravure techniques.* Generally flexography is used to imprint items that don't need the quality found with screen printing, such as corrugated boxes and candy wrappers. A direct marketer should use this technique in the same manner—for printing on lower-quality packaging.

Picking a Face No One Will Forget

Although we've discussed before how to pick type that suits your project, we haven't looked at the production aspects. When choosing and buying type, it is described in terms of its *face*—or design—and its *points*, which describe the size in which the type will be printed. Examples are: 10 point Times and 32 point Helvetica. Your artist can supply samples of different faces and points.

Here you have lots of freedom. You can choose the typeface that best sets off your marketing piece from hundreds of styles. You can pick type sizes from very small to banner headline size. If you want another way to think of type sizing, just remember that 72 points equals one inch in letter height.

In your body type you'll have *leading*, which is the amount of space between lines. Ask your compositor to show you several lines of the same size type with different amounts of leading. When working within the confines of a space ad, you might have trouble fitting everything in without sacrificing readability. If you're in this bind, experiment by changing the type size and leading. At times you can go to smaller type with more leading and save space without compromising readability. By the way, blocks of copy are measured by artists and printers in terms of *picas*. Six picas equal one inch.

Typesetting will be done by a compositor using a computer. Shop around when looking for typesetters. Each of them will differ in terms of the number of typefaces they can offer, their speed and accuracy or number of typesetting errors. Decide what's best for your needs. You might use different typesetters for different jobs. Some typesetters can compose a page from your layout on their computer and then print it out. Doing so saves your artist the time-consuming task of cutting and pasting type to fit the layout.

If your artist is going to cut and paste, make sure the typesetter supplies you with photocopies of the type. Artists use the photocopies to size, or *dummy* the type to make sure it fits the space correctly. Once the layout is dummied, the artists are ready to actually paste up the ad, using the actual set type. Having a photocopy allows them to work with the type without messing it up.

Black-and-white photos must be converted to *halftones* before printing. In this process the photo is changed into a series of black dots on white space. Because they're so small, the dots can't be seen without close inspection. It's the way gray tones are made when printing with black ink. Halftones are much less expensive than color separations. You can also get them faster.

Artwork doesn't need to be shot as a halftone. Generally the artist will reproduce the art to size using a *photostat* or *velox* machine. Your artist will then paste that reproduction onto the finished *art board*, also called a *mechanical*, or *camera-ready art*. Your printer will use that board containing type and halftones to make the plate for printing.

A paper overlay will be used to mark where additional colors will be printed, and a sample of the color will be attached to the art so the printer can accurately reproduce it. Usually a system developed by Pantone is used to label the colors, so that the artist and printer both know exactly what the color is.

Spotting Printing Problems

Most direct marketers will have the majority of their printing done on an offset press. No matter what printing process is used, there are some easy ways to see if your printer is doing a good job.

If you've never used a printer before, I'd suggest being there while your project is being printed—especially if it's a long run. You want to be able to spot problems, and correct them while the press is going. It's much harder on everyone if you decide a job is unacceptable after all the work has been done.

When you're looking at black-and-white printing, check both the printed image and the unprinted areas. What's printed should have a uniform, smooth layer of ink. The white space should be *free* of ink.

Check details such as the serifs on a letter *a* or the downstroke on a lower case *g*. Make sure the serifs are printed clearly. Here's a list of other problems common to offset printing:

- Blotches on the surface of areas that should be one tone
- Areas that have either too much or too little ink in what should be solid
- White spots or pinholes in solid tones; nonprinting spots in solid areas; *hickies*—dark spots within a white circle
- Ghost images that repeat other printed areas in either light or dark patterns
- A light color tint that bleeds into white space

Many of these problems are caused by dirty plates or poor ink. For that reason, they can be corrected during the printing process. When you're printing in color, watch for two additional problems.

1. First, make sure that the colors are in register. As one color is printed on top of another, the plates must align exactly. If they aren't, colors will overlap. Look at the edges of a color block to check for registration. You don't want to see one shade jutting out by itself. If that's the case, that plate is out of register.
2. Check for faithful reproduction of the color you want. Bring your original art, and compare that with what's being printed. Colors can get off if the printer is applying too much or too little of one shade. Color work is difficult; make sure you choose your printer with care when you need to print in more than one color.

Feeding Your Printer

When choosing printers, find out if their presses are *sheet-fed* or *web-fed*. Sheet-fed presses print single sheets of paper, one at a time. Web-fed presses print on a large roll of paper. You'll probably use sheet-feed printers. Web-fed presses are faster, but they are only economical when printing a very large run.

Both techniques are available for letterpress and offset printing. Presses can print on paper six feet or more in width. At that point the paper is folded, bound and trimmed to finish your product. Remember that your sheets might be six feet wide. Your brochure or letter probably won't be that size. Printers find that using paper that big can save them time. Several pages can be printed at once.

Your printer can probably fit your brochure on one sheet. One side is printed, the paper is turned, and the other side then goes through. The sheet is designed so that it can be folded, or *gathered*, in the right sequence for reading.

Each sheet is called a *signature*. Your artist will work with the printer to make sure the design fits in a standard signature size. If you want an 18-page catalog, but the signature only takes 16 pages, you'll save a lot of money by cutting out two pages. In that way you'll just be printing one signature. If you insist on the 18 pages, you'll have to print a second signature just to get the last two pages. Your costs will escalate, and your extra returns from those two pages probably wouldn't justify the expense.

That's why it's good to have an idea of how you'll produce your package even before designing it. If you'd hired an artist, worked up an 18-page catalog, shot photos and made color separations before finding out that you need to take out two pages, you'd have a lot of work to redo.

Grading Papers

Another decision you'll have to make is what type of paper to use. Listed below are some standard grades. Talk with your printer to learn prices.

- *Bond paper* is normally used in business correspondence.
- *Coated paper* gives you both better print quality and a classier overall look. Many types of coatings are available, and they do add substantially to your cost.

- *Text paper* is used for announcements, invitations and brochures. Its texture and colors give artists plenty of freedom, but it's also very costly.
- *Coated* and *text papers* in heavier weights are called cover papers. You can find them in many different textures, colors and finishes. They can add a classy touch when used as a brochure cover.
- *Book paper* is found in books and many other types of printing. Its reasonable cost and wide range of weights make it useful for a variety of jobs. It can be either coated or uncoated.
- *Index paper* is a heavy paper that is also inexpensive. Its ability to take printing is good; use it when you want a stiff paper but not a real classy look and feel.

You're often better off choosing your paper early in the project for two reasons. First, paper comes in standard sizes. You should design your package so that you use the whole sheet. If you don't, you'll just be cutting off extra paper. Make sure the size of your signature is standard for the kind of paper you want.

Second, you'll buy better when you order early. With the wide range of sizes, weights, textures, colors and coatings, no paper supplier has it all. It's no fun to have a brochure on a tight production schedule printed on your second choice of paper. Ordering before you take the brochure to the printer will allow you better selection of stock.

Other Production Costs

When choosing printers you must also know their capability for finishing the project after it's been printed. Folding, collating, binding and trimming require special equipment, take time and cost money.

When printers don't have the proper folding machine for your needs, they might have to farm out the job. Find out if that's the case. Also find out the cost and time required for that. Printing is only part of the total job. Don't allow yourself to be surprised by unexpected delays or expenses when the actual printing process is over. Negotiate the terms of the total job from the start.

For a direct mail package you might choose a bond paper for your letter, perhaps a 60-pound paper weight. If you had a four-page letter, you could put the whole thing on 11" x 17" paper. For printing purposes, though, you'd buy paper in a standard 23" x 35" size and have a signature you could fit two letters on at a time.

You'd choose a second color for emphasis—maybe red or purple if you were mailing to consumers and blue if you were approaching a business market.

Your brochure would be smaller in size. Let's say 4" x 9". Again, you'd buy paper in the standard 25" x 38" size, and fit a dozen on your signature. You'd use a book paper, or your printer might just refer to it as offset paper. If you were printing color photos in the brochure, you'd want a coated stock. For a short letter repeating the offer, use uncoated paper.

You'd talk with your printer about coordinating the second color in the letter with any color in the brochure or outside envelope. You'd want to match the envelope's color to the color in the letter in order to lead your readers' eyes into your letter.

Additionally, you would save money by using the same color. Your printer wouldn't have to clean the press and put in another color before printing each item. He or she could go straight from printing the letter to working on the outside envelope without any press down time.

For your coupon you'd also coordinate colors. Paper for the coupon could be a text or heavy book stock. You'd want it to look nice and substantial, but don't make it too fancy, like a formal invitation. You could unconsciously give the impression that the paper is too nice to write on, and your prospects might feel uncomfortable filling it out.

Make sure your coupon and order form sizes are geared both to the dimensions of your outer envelope and your reply envelope. Neither should be folded. Your outer envelope will be larger, and the return envelope and coupon will fit inside. Your order form can be torn off the coupon and inserted into the return envelope.

Once again, you'll probably want to pick a standard-sized envelope to save money. Such envelopes are manufactured in bulk. An odd-sized envelope would require a readjustment of the the folding machines. You would, of course, pay extra for that.

Some direct marketers, however, have been successful paying more for oversized envelopes. What they theorize is that the bigger envelope stands out in the mail. More prospects will pick it up, notice the teaser and open it up. I'd suggest testing this on your lists if you're interested. It would probably work better on consumer lists than with businesspeople.

You would also choose the type of paper for the envelope. Here are some of the choices:

1. *Commercial envelopes* are normally made for business correspondence and can come in many sizes and paper types.
2. *Bankers flap* or *wallet flap* envelopes are similar to commercial envelopes but are made thicker and stronger to carry more bulk. For that reason they're suited to the needs of direct mail sellers.
3. *Window envelopes* are often chosen for the outside envelope so that the address label can be affixed to the inner coupon. With that setup you can ask the prospect to affix the label to the order form and place it in the reply envelope. Make it easy for the prospect to order, and you can track the sale to the list by looking at the code on the label. You won't have problems with illegible addresses and won't have to reenter the name into your computer.

There is one problem with window envelopes—most peoples know that they contain a direct mail offer or a bill. Window envelopes make your mailing appear less personal than commercial-style envelopes do. For many direct response marketers they're a necessary part of doing business. Weigh the pros and cons for yourself after considering how your prospects will respond. It's another part of direct sales you should consider testing. Like commercial envelopes, you can get window envelopes in a variety of standard sizes, some of which are shown in the Appendix.

4. *Booklet envelopes* are larger than commercial envelopes. These envelopes are often ideal for direct mail packages. Because of their size, booklet envelopes are well-suited for direct sellers. Consider using them especially if you have a large brochure that you don't want folded too small.
5. *Self-sealing envelopes* make handling easier. A large expense for direct mail marketers is the cost of stuffing, sealing and affixing postage on their packages. You can cut down on this expense by specifying self-sealing envelopes. An adhesive makes the flaps stick when pressed together. Since no moisture is needed, sealing can be done quickly by machine. Generally self-sealers are slightly smaller than booklet envelopes.

After specifically determining your needs, get bids from at least three printers. Explain the job to each one. Determine which printing company has the equipment and experience best suited to your project. Also listen to your printers. They often will have ideas on how to make the production process quicker or less expensive.

Work up the job specifications for your printer. In that way both of you will understand exactly what the job requires. Once you decide which printer to use, the specifications will be put into a purchase order (P.O.). This is a very important piece of paper. The P.O. is the contract between the printer and yourself. If any problems come up with the job, the purchase order will determine who's in the right. If your printer doesn't follow the specifications on the order, you can refuse to pay for the job.

The purchase order is used by printers to tell their pressmen, finishers and shippers what to do. After you get to know a printer, you might just deal directly with the sales rep on easy jobs. The rep is going to hand your purchase order and art over to the people doing the actual work. Make sure they can understand from the P.O. what the job entails. Spell out exactly what you want in order to ensure a job well done. Here are the items that should be included in your P.O.:

1. *Client name.* Tell who you are.
2. *Job description.* Tell if the job is a letter, brochure, stuffer or whatever. Also give the job's name in order to further identify the work, in case the P.O. gets separated from the art. For instance, you might write, *Direct mail letter for Peterborough Silverware.*
3. *Quantity.* Specify how many you want printed.
4. *Size.* Tell what the finished size will be. If your project has different parts, identify them separately. For a brochure you could specify, "16 pages plus cover—4" x 9"."
5. *Stock.* List the type of paper each element will be printed on. As in the brochure above, put down separately what the cover and text stocks will be.
6. *Printing.* Specify the technique and ink color to be used. Refer the printer to the layout. Also mention any special observations, such as borders that *bleed*, or have printing all the way to the edge of the page.
7. *Finishing.* Tell what you want to happen after the piece is printed. Folding and binding or fastening instructions belong here.
8. *Proofs.* Tell who is to receive the bluelines or color proofs. Blues and proofs show how the

project will look before actually printing. It's your final time to check. Blues are used on black-and-white jobs, and are so named because they are a light blue color. Inspect them to make sure that the plate used for printing doesn't have any flaws on it. If it does, circle them. Look for specks on the negative, which show up when printed. Also make sure that no pieces of type have moved on your finished art during the platemaking process. This is also your last chance to check for typos.

9. *Due dates*. Specify when you expect to see the blues or proofs. Also state when the final project is to be delivered.

10. *Samples*. If you won't be mailing from your offices, you'll want samples sent to you while the rest of the job is sent to the mailing house. List the number of samples you want sent separately to your firm.

11. *Packing and shipping*. Tell how you want it packaged. Is it to be boxed, banded, shrink-wrapped or packed loose? Also specify where the final product is to be shipped.

When your purchase order has all the above elements, you should keep mistakes to a minimum. In the next chapter we'll look at what to do with your marketing material once it's been printed.

Chapter Nineteen

How To Fulfill Orders

Even after you've mailed your marketing pieces or had your ads published, more expenses must be managed. Orders must be shipped quickly after you've received them. You must have people, inventory and equipment ready to accomplish this. If your operation gets very big, the costs of fulfilling orders become considerable.

Here's yet another reason why newcomers to direct mail should start small. I was able to fulfill my orders out of my basement when I began. At the time I didn't know much about mailing regulations, warehousing or computer systems. As my firm grew I learned, but if I had started with a full catalog of different items to fulfill, the first year would have been a lot tougher.

Keeping Things Orderly

You'll have to carry inventory on most of your items. Some products can be drop-shipped from the manufacturer to the customer, but you need a good reason to ask the manufacturer to do this. Most merchandise won't require drop shipments unless it's expensive, heavy or requires custom work on each order by the maker.

Don't expect manufacturers to keep inventory for you. You'll have to have space for holding stock and methods for finding, packaging and mailing the merchandise. You'll also have to keep records of your receipts and note where the orders came from. We'll look at how to manage these challenges.

Any system must be fairly simple. Many mail order firms double their employees during the Christmas buying season—from August through December. You won't have much time to train part-time workers then. Make sure glitches in your fulfillment process are kept to a minimum, so that you can keep things flowing smoothly.

Staying on top of things is one of the best ways to avoid problems. Let's consider inventory. You need to have enough so that your customers don't get upset when you backorder their goods. You don't want to order so much that you strain cash flow, take up too much warehouse space or get stuck with a lot of items that don't move.

I can't give you a rule for how much inventory to keep. You'll have to decide after analyzing your own sales figures. But as you do so, here are some concepts to keep in mind:

1. *How much do you think you can sell?* See how the product—or similar ones if this is a new item—has sold in the past. Then look at your upcoming marketing schedule to see how much exposure you'll be giving this item.

If you've kept good records of past sales, you should be able to judge how much you can move in the next 30 to 60 days. Keep enough of any order on hand so that you don't have to backorder more than three percent of your orders.

2. *How difficult is the item to get?* An importer might want to order extra in order to have a buffer in case shipping is delayed. Others need to know how quickly suppliers can ship their orders before deciding on quantities.

Here again it pays to be prudent. Don't buy a lot of an item you think might catch on as a fad. Test such goods. Save your big purchases for your bread and butter—the products you sell every day. Don't risk too much money on a speculative item.

3. *What season is it?* In direct mail the seasons can affect both your own orders and the ability

of manufacturers to keep you in stock. Some goods, such as fruit, are available only at certain times of the year. Others, such as clothes, are sold at specific seasons. Take these differences into account when planning inventory.

Start a tickler file, or write on your calendar when to order seasonal goods. If you order too few or too late, you might not be able to get your inventory caught up again until next year.

4. *Does the product have a good profit margin?* Products with high margins cost you less to store. If a gadget costs you $5, and you can sell it for $12, then 100 units will bring you $700. If the gadget cost $7, yet could only be sold for $12, then 100 units is worth only $500 in profit.

Keeping the higher-cost item in stock isn't as valuable to you. Don't stock your warehouse with any more low-margin items than you must. Try to get rid of them, and fill that space with more profitable goods.

5. *How many can you afford to buy?* Stocking expensive items can put a crimp in your cash flow. If the items sit there, your investment in them isn't making any money.

Before marketing costlier goods, make sure your business can afford to do so.

6. *Do you have enough space?* This seems obvious, but you can get into trouble by ordering goods without checking to see if you can hold them all. If you can't, you either have to find more space quickly, or get rid of some of your inventory fast. The more items you stock, the more difficult it becomes to give each one the right amount of space.

Most direct mail businesses turn over their inventory at least six times a year. Let's say your business does $200,000 in sales annually. Your profit margin is 50 percent, so your total cost of goods over a year is $100,000. At no time should you stock more than one-sixth of that. Your inventory value in this case should not exceed $16,666.

Problems can arise when juggling cash flow, seasonal needs and space limitations. That's why I suggest careful management of your inventory.

If you start with a single product, that item will probably be your number one seller for years. That's what happened to me. If that happens with your business, your inventory will consist mainly of your first product.

You'll only get into problems if you overstock on merchandise that either isn't moving or isn't profitable. Be aware that the 80/20 rule applies to inventory. Eighty percent of your sales will come from twenty percent of the items available. As long as your inventory reflects that balance, your cash flow will be fine.

New Methods Aid Cash Flow

Another method has come into vogue with manufacturers that can be a real help to smart direct marketers. It's called *Just In Time* inventory. Using this method you figure when you'll need items and arrange for delivery "just in time." Doing so cuts down on costs dramatically. What you want to do then is sell the items almost immediately. In that way your need for inventory space is reduced. You might even be able to collect from your customers before having to pay your suppliers. You shouldn't have any cash flow problems then. You can grow without having to borrow money for inventory, because you'll pay suppliers directly out of sales.

To set up such a system you'd need to have predictable sales and suppliers. I'd suggest making sure you have a local supplier to help you if you got more orders than you expected and needed more inventory quickly.

Other inventory problems must be managed if you are to be successful. One is finding ways to get rid of merchandise that doesn't sell. Just as all ads or direct mail pieces don't work, all products you promote won't sell. That can make for tough times.

You can take products out of your promotional literature because they aren't moving, but they're still sitting in your warehouse. One way to get rid of such items is to reduce prices and find a new market for them. Local retailers and wholesalers might be interested in what's stuck in your storage space.

Try to make any such sales on a cash basis and goods accepted as is. If you're trying to thin out your inventory by offering low prices, you can't tolerate many bad debts or returns.

Discovering Fulfillment

Any time first-time customers send in an order, all they know about you will be based on an ad or mailing. Fulfillment is the process of handling that order. More importantly, it's the first time your new customers will come in contact with your company apart from your marketing material. If you don't treat your customers well, you'll lose many of the positive effects developed in your marketing.

Have you ever seen an ad for a store and decided to go into it—only to be disappointed? Perhaps the merchandise wasn't what you expected, or the salesperson wasn't helpful enough. At any rate, you might have decided on the spot not to come back to that store.

On the other hand, you might have other stores that are your favorites. The products have good value, and the salespeople know just the right way to help. I'll bet you go to stores like that as much as possible—and probably wish you knew a few more like them.

You can apply the same analysis to direct marketing firms. If their merchandise or service is disappointing, customers won't order again. We've said before that most profits will come from repeat orders. Any method that encourages customers to buy again is worth looking into. Here we'll consider how to manage that function from the fulfillment end. Let's look first at the objectives of a good fulfillment operation:

1. *Make the customer happy.* Mail order customers often buy on impulse. If the order isn't received promptly, they might purchase a similar item in a retail store or decide they don't need what you're selling after all. Make sure your orders are delivered promptly and neatly. Some students of the business say that shipping quickly can keep returns down by one-third, or more.

Fulfillment should also make sure that every aspect of the purchase is clear to the buyer. Your invoice should be easy to read. Give your customers the feeling that the company will settle any disputes quickly and fairly. Tell them what your policies on returns are and how to get in touch with you if they have a complaint. In that way fulfillment can alleviate consumer complaints to federal or state regulators.

2. *Be efficient.* As you grow, fulfillment will become more costly to your firm. Having waste in that department can erode your bottom line. Below are some general guidelines for rating a fulfillment department.

Depending on your system, each person in your fulfillment department should process as many as 500 orders a day. Customers should receive merchandise within two weeks after they sent their order. Complaints about lost or damaged goods are inevitable. Respond to such letters within five days. We stress customer service and try to respond to each letter on the day it is received. Finally, the ratio of returned goods will vary, depending on what you're selling.

Fulfilling Your Goals

Let your staff know you expect them to treat customers courteously. Let them know that your goal is repeat sales from happy customers. Then give your fulfillment people tools to handle most of their everyday functions. Order processing and shipping procedures and form letters will allow your staff to represent your firm efficiently in most situations that arise.

Be sure your fulfillment people understand your offer. Some of the customers might be confused about the product, terms or discounts. You want a staff that's able to help customers courteously. Doing so makes ordering easier and faster. It saves money for you and creates goodwill with your customers.

More direct marketers are taking orders by phone. Here you need to have bona fide salespeople at your end. Make sure they know what is and isn't in stock. If an item isn't available, your phone answerers should be able to suggest another item, and they should try to sell appropriate add-ons. For instance, if a woman calls and orders a blouse, they should suggest a scarf to go with it.

Having special phone offers also helps customers feel good about making an order, while at the same time increasing your total sale. Tell the woman who is buying a blouse that she also can get a tie for her husband at a price 20 percent lower than what's listed in your catalog.

Orders coming in through the mail should be dated and processed in batches of 50 to 100. Often a receptionist can open the envelopes as they come in and date the day's mail. Try using a color system to code the batches. Each day of the week will have a different color tag affixed to the batch. In that way your staff will know which orders to fulfill first when the batches arrive on their desks.

Workers going through the batches should check first to make certain that all the necessary information is included. Here's where having a simple, legible order form is a boon. If you don't design your order form so the information is organized, readable and complete, you'll pay for it in fulfillment. Your staff will have to try to find your customer's phone number and give them a call to get additional information. It's better to do it right the first time.

If it's a new customer, your fulfillment person will type a mailing label, or indicate to the data processor that an entry should be made for this customer. Then the fulfillment person will use a marker to circle the product code and quantity on the order form. Your packing person then can see quickly what to put in each box.

Before sending the order to the packing department, your fulfiller will choose a form letter to accompany the order. Having a letter with every order is important. You want your business to be as personal as possible. To that end, don't mail anything to your prospects or customers without enclosing a letter.

Not every situation can be met with a form letter. Train your staff to recognize that. Hopefully you'll have at least one person who can answer customer communications needing individual replies. Try not to shirk this responsibility. If both you and your competition are pretty even in most respects, you need to become better than they are in the *little matters*. Losing even a few customers through bad service can hurt profits—especially when you're just starting out.

Try to be fast, friendly and fair when dealing with customers. If you handle a few hundred orders a week, you can quickly build a customer list in the thousands. But if you lose customers every week, your business will suffer just as quickly.

It's interesting to note that some direct marketers report that customers who've written in with a complaint eventually reorder in a greater percentage than do regular customers. Treat complaints not as annoyances but as chances to make friends. After all, the letter writer cares enough about your company to write in the first place.

Letters Perfect

You can construct form letters to fit most of your needs. You'll save time by not making your fulfillers write individual letters. Customers will be happy to get answers quickly. Here are the main form letters you'll need:

1. *"Thank you for the order."* In this letter you say that the order is enclosed. You want your customers to know that you stand behind your merchandise—and you are concerned about customer satisfaction. Take this opportunity to thank your customer for their business, tell them how much you appreciate serving them and look forward to doing so again. Use this letter to add a personal touch to fulfillment.

2. *"Your order will be shipped as soon as possible."* Use this letter to send to persons whose merchandise is backordered. In the letter you should explain immediately that there will be a delay in the shipment of an order. At the top of the letter leave space to write in what the product is and when the expected shipping date will be.

Go on to say how you almost always ship within a few days—if that's the case. Add that you regret the delay with this order but welcome the opportunity to serve the customer again. Reassure your customer that you're sure service will be better next time.

If you're shipping later than when you promised in your promotional letter, or later than 30 days after receiving the order if no shipping date was promised, Federal Trade Commission regulations demand that you give customers the option of canceling their order. Sample letters covering this circumstance are in a later chapter.

3. *"Here's your late order."* When the backordered item comes in, attach this letter to the order. Once again you'll regret the delay, thank them for their patience, tell them how happy they'll be with the item and that you're eager to serve them again soon.

4. *"Our records indicate your order has been shipped."* Most of the inquiries you receive probably will be from persons saying they haven't received their order. Your fulfiller will go back to the sales record to see if that order was sent. If it was, the possibilities are as follows: a) a family member or business associate received the order and hasn't yet told your customer that it's arrived; b) it's somewhere in the mail or UPS system; c) the package was lost.

Generally the situation will fall under "a" or "b" above. If one of those is the case, everything will work out with time. Your customer will discover the package has already arrived and been taken by someone else who hasn't given it to them yet, or the package is en route and will get there shortly.

You should still write back to your customers. Tell them you've looked at your records and found that the merchandise described at the top of the letter was sent on the date also written in. Remind them that the mails can be slow. Ask them to wait another ten days to receive the package. If it hasn't arrived by then, tell them to mail back this letter with a note, and you'll reship.

5. *"We're reshipping your order."* If the order was lost, then the customer will send your note back after ten days. Rather than going to the trouble of tracing the order, assume the responsibility of satisfying your customers. Reship immediately.

Explain in this letter that the merchandise must have gotten lost. Tell your customer how much time it would take to trace the order. To get around all that, and ensure their satisfaction, you are reshipping the item. Apologize for the delay. Explain when you'll be sending out their new merchandise, so the customer will be able to estimate when it will arrive. Don't forget to remind them how you look forward to serving them again in the future.

6. *"Please confirm your order with us."* In this letter you'll tell the customer that your records don't indicate receiving an order from them. You'll ask them to write on the back of the letter the date and number on their cancelled check, or the date and transaction code on their charge card, along with its I.D. number.

Resist the temptation to be hard on the customer. In all likelihood they did send in their order. It probably got lost either in the mail or somewhere in your office. Few people are going to try to dupe you by claiming a false order. If they've gone to the trouble to write you, it's probably legitimate. Even if it's not, the time you could spend proving that isn't worth it.

Many direct marketers will reship an unrecorded order—if it's below a certain dollar amount—without asking for any verification from the customer.

7. *"We made a mistake."* From time to time your fulfillment department will make mistakes. When this happens you should own up to it, and make it right. Candor creates good will on the part of your customers. Everyone knows that accidents happen. Since they're aware of the mistake, accepting the blame is the least you can do.

Common mistakes include sending the wrong quantity or item or shipping later than usual. In these letters you'll apologize for any inconvenience you've caused your customer. Tell them also that you're sure you'll do better on their next order.

8. *"Here's your exchange."* If the lady doesn't like her new blouse, you'll want to do everything you can to make her happy. Perhaps it doesn't fit or the color wasn't what she imagined it would be. Perhaps it was too heavy or too light a fabric. An exchange is better than a refund because you don't lose the sale. Also, you've proven that you can keep the customer happy.

In order to help process exchanges quickly, have a form letter to go with them. Let your customers know how pleased you are that you can satisfy them and how much you look forward to serving them again.

9. *"Here's your refund."* Since direct mail offers always come with a money-back guarantee, you'll get some returns. Give these persons the same prompt response you give your other customers. Try to turn their refund into an order. You can do so by making an extraordinary offer on other merchandise.

What's often more effective is to give customers the option of choosing any product in your line. Make that option attractive by crediting them more than the amount of their original purchase if they use the money to order again rather than taking a refund.

Here's how it works. If the woman doesn't like the silk blouse and sends it back, write her a check for the amount of the blouse. In the letter tell her that she can cash the check, or use it to order from you again. To entice her to use it on another purchase, tell her you'll add 15 percent or 20 percent more to the amount if she spends the money on your merchandise. Write in the corner of her refund check what it's worth in goods from you.

This accomplishes several things. First, you're trying to make a customer happy. After all, she simply might have found a similar blouse and bought it before your package got to her home. You'll be better off financially giving her a break on another purchase. Assuming your markup is at least 50 percent, you'll still make money on the deal.

Keep records of the items coming back for exchanges or refunds. If one item seems to be causing a lot of dissatisfaction, look at it more closely. It might be poorly made. Perhaps your marketing misrepresents the product in some way, but sometimes it's a simpler problem. Maybe you're not packing it well enough, and it's getting damaged in shipping.

Test Yourself

A way to spot problems before getting customer complaints is by testing yourself. Have someone not affiliated with your company make some test orders. Pay a friend or relative to order items from you. Have them keep records concerning how quickly the order came, how fast exchanges or refunds were made and how soon inquiries were answered.

You should also have these people do the same test on your direct marketing competitors. Doing so will give you a benchmark. Let your staff know the results of these tests. Reward them for beating the competition. If you don't win, ask your staff and test customers how you can improve, and put their ideas into action.

Computerizing Your Business

Using a computer effectively is essential to direct marketing. You'll need one to keep sales records and maintain lists. Before shipping orders, your fulfillment staff will route them to data processing. If you're just starting out, your data processing department could consist of you or a family member on a fairly inexpensive personal computer.

A standard word processing program and perhaps a spreadsheet program will be fine at first. Eventually you might want software written to your exact specifications. Since that's a costly job, make sure your business is well-defined before committing your business procedures to disks.

Whether you run the computer yourself or hire someone to do so, you have to know what you want it to do. One of the timesaving properties of computers is their ability to generate reports giving you specific information. You should be able to quickly find out about sales over certain time periods, inventory levels for all items and the purchasing history of each customer. Finally, your system should be simple enough for almost anyone to learn how to use it.

When an order comes in, your computer operator will enter the person's name and address, the order, the method of payment and sales tax when applicable.

You'll want everything standardized to fit your computer format. All consumer addresses should fit on three lines. Commercial addresses will need another line for the company name. That might sound elementary, but if you don't follow that simple form, you'll mess up some orders. If an address extends over too many lines, it won't fit on your mailing label.

Along with the name and address you'll want to include information on the customer. What information you need is up to you. Decide what's important for you to know about each customer. The date of last purchase or the date when the customer's subscription expires are commonly coded.

Your business needs will dictate what other information you wish to keep on each customer. Telephone number, which ad or mailing the customer responded to, demographics of their neighborhood and size of company, in the case of business buyers, are examples. For all customers you'll want to keep records on their purchasing history in terms of recency, frequency and dollar amount. Not all of this will fit on the mailing label. Your computer operator can devise a form that will be entered next to each customer's mailing label to hold the information you need.

If you're building a large list, you'll want to match code each person. Match coding lets you create a code unique to each name. Perhaps you'll take the first letter from each word in the name and address. Look at this example

George Grayson
144 Shasta Heights Dr.
Mt. Vernon, NY 11111

Your match code would run along the top or bottom of the label as follows:

GG1SHDMVNY1

How can that possibly help your business? You'll use that code when merging and purging lists. Merging and purging eliminates duplicate names on your lists. Doing so allows you to cut mailing costs without losing any customers.

If someone orders from you several times, you'll want to record them only once in your customer files. Looking at names for duplicates won't work—there could be several George Graysons. By developing a code based on each customer's complete address everyone becomes unique. You can tell your computer to look through these codes and erase doubles.

Clean Lists Mean More Sales

Update your lists two to four times a year. If you wait and do it only once a year, 15 to 25 percent of your names and addresses will be incorrect. Because we're such a mobile society, it's hard to keep mailing lists up-to-date. Even the best lists will have approximately five percent wrong addresses just after you rent them.

More error than that spells trouble. Only a small percentage of your prospects will respond in the first place. You can't afford to lower that amount by up to 25 percent through mailing to wrong addresses. Remember, you're paying for printing and postage, too.

One way to keep your list clean is to write *Address Correction Requested* on mailing pieces. If the address is incorrect, the Postal Service will return the envelope to you with the right address. They charge for this service, so don't do it on every mailing. Ask for corrections on mailings to your main customer list every three to six months. Generally, it's not worth the cost of purging a rented list.

On most mailings you'll print *Postman—if addressee has moved, please deliver to current occupant.* Obviously it won't be as personal a communication without the correct name on the letter. Doing this won't cost anything, and you can guess that whoever lives in that house now has about the same demographic characteristics as your original prospect.

Finally, it's useful to have someone periodically go over your list to look for obvious entry mistakes—name misspellings and wrong zip codes do happen.

After you've entered the necessary information, you'll print labels. To save time you should print in batches. Send the labels to your packing people. You can avoid the problem of the wrong order form being matched to the wrong label by printing order information on the label. A code for the item and quantity can be included on each label. In this way you'll help the packing people and also retain the most recent order information on your computer.

Sales Records

Once you have over 25,000 names, you should consider hiring an outside computer service to maintain your list. You'll send them the order forms, and they'll send back labels. They will be the ones to provide the reports you'll want to help you see how your business is going. Here are the reports I suggest you have generated:

1. *A sales list.* With this list, you'll have a complete tally of the business you've done. All the orders sent out will be here. You might want this report every week. If you're just getting started, every other week should be sufficient. You can refer to this sales list to confirm shipment if a customer inquires about his or her order.
2. *Sales by item.* Here you can see which items moved over a time period. Such a report is essential for inventory control and to see what your best products are. Stay in tune with your customers by seeing which merchandise groups they prefer.

You might see a trend developing. Customers might start buying less for themselves and more for their children. You can also see when various seasonal merchandise is bought, in order to better time your marketing of those products. Finally, you can juggle the numbers. Estimate how raising or lowering prices on a certain item would have affected profits.

3. *Sales by media.* Here you can see which marketing efforts are working. You'll be getting the results to your tests on different packages and media.
4. *Sales by customer.* You can find out who your best customers are over time. A report singling out your biggest buyers—either by large single purchases or an accumulation over time—can be useful. Calling or writing these customers is a good idea. You want them to feel special, and they are. Having a few habitual customers can produce good steady business.

All these reports are doing is presenting your order information in different ways. Sorting through and organizing information is one thing computers are great at.

Keep Those Cards and Letters Coming

For large mailings, you might want to look at a complete fulfillment house for help. All you have to do is give them your mail package. Labeling, inserting, sealing and applying postage can all be done by fulfillment houses. Because they have the necessary equipment to send out mailings fast, fulfillment houses can be quite reasonably priced.

A fulfillment house can also help you arrange to rent your list to other direct marketing firms. For some companies, the income from list rental is what makes their businesses profitable.

You'll want to fulfill orders yourself. Since orders will be different, the automation offered by a fulfillment house won't help much in this situation. You'll need to equip your mailroom with a mail scale, tape, boxes and metering machines. Electronic mail scales are the fastest and most accurate. Some can be linked with metering machines. Weighing and dispensing postage can then take just one step. You can set the mail scale to figure the postage needed for first-class, third-class, international, parcel post or United Parcel Service delivery. Metering machines come in models to meet different needs. Some postmark, precancel, seal and stack envelopes. Others are designed to make labels for packages.

If you do third-class mailings, you'll need to presort your mail to Postal Service specifications. Presorting is done by zip codes. Even if you don't mail by third-class, the Postal Service offers some savings if you sort your mail. There's another benefit—saving time so your mail goes faster to waiting customers.

Direct marketers spend time blasting the Postal Service regulations. I think it's a better course to try to work with your local Postmaster, rather than being frustrated by what his or her staff does. Talk to them. Find out what you can do to make their job easier and faster. It might be little extra work for you to box or bag letters or packages going to the same Post Office, but doing so can save time.

Also learn when the best time is to drop mail. You might be able to save a day in shipping by delivering to the Post Office a few hours earlier, before their trucks leave.

Finally, you should subscribe to the monthly *Memo to Mailers,* put out by the Postal Service. Doing so will ensure that you'll know about any changes in regulations before you've metered and sealed your packages. You can get the newsletter free by writing: *Memo to Mailers*, P.O. Box 1, Linwood, NJ 07221.

Now that we've covered the basics of direct selling, we'll look in the next chapter at some tools that can help your business grow.

Chapter Twenty

Other Ways of Selling Directly

Up until now we've looked at traditional methods of direct selling. Space ads, direct mail packages and catalogs are the normal means of selling directly. You can build a business using one or more of those approaches. You find your prospects, and make your offer.

Many people have done that. At times when competition is especially keen, it seems like too many! Direct marketing methods make many businesses easier to enter. There are several factors behind the growth of direct selling.

With the growth of computer use, the cost of keeping mailing lists has dropped. The acceptance of zip codes allows you to use demographic data to pick your mail prospects. Offset printing allows smaller businesses to have high-quality work done at a reasonable cost. Specialized magazines deliver target audiences. The universal use of credit cards makes direct selling easier for the prospect. The discounting of long-distance telephone rates makes toll-free ordering a positive means of doing business for many direct marketing firms.

Not Lonely at the Top

Factors that made direct marketing attractive over the past 20 years have caused a rush into the use of this sales method. For the newcomer, it's hard to get noticed. You have to develop your business slowly. Do so by building a unique list, rather than renting the same lists everyone else uses. Let your customer base grow on your own efforts.

Direct marketers who go to outside lists too soon often get stung. Make sure you have a solid customer base before testing outside lists. As we've said before, the time-honored way of building that base is through space ads. That's how I started Enterprise Publishing.

I'd be remiss if I didn't let you know about other opportunities for building a direct selling business. In this chapter we'll look at techniques for finding new markets, selling through seminars, selling through public relations and telemarketing.

These are all legitimate business activities. You can build a firm based on any of them. I'd like to emphasize that. Unwisely, many companies treat such new selling tools as afterthoughts. If their main business revolves around putting out catalogs, public relations soon becomes a luxury. That's fine if the catalog business is profitable, but trouble can occur when a company tries to use some of these techniques without committing enough people, money or time to them. Don't make the mistake of thinking these activities won't require much work, or that they can be accomplished by people who already are busy.

If you want to branch out into one or more of these areas, come up with a business plan first. Define your expectations, and list what resources you have to offer to make the plan work. If you get started without a clear understanding of the necessary work and expected results, you can soon get discouraged. You might end up saying, "It just doesn't work for us," when you really haven't given these techniques a fair chance.

Recognize that you are involved in new business activities. Learn what's entailed—and then go to it. You could find that using the phone, the media or seminars will help make your firm more successful. It could be the way to find new customers, new ways of selling and new methods of showing how you're different from your competitors.

How To Find New Markets

Here's another reason why it pays to keep in close touch with your market. Don't just turn your orders over to your fulfillment staff. You need to go through the mail yourself.

Let's say you sell a consumer item, but you notice that some businesses buy from you, and they buy regularly, in bulk. Your eyes should light up when you see that. Now get some of those customers on the phone. Find out why they are buying what you tout as a consumer item. Are they reselling it to their customers? Maybe they're buying for personal use and just ordering from their business address.

You need to find out. If a new market is approaching you without your advertising having been directed at them, it could be a golden opportunity for you. Find out what the needs of the market are.

You might ask how you can attract and serve different types of customers if you have a narrow focus on your business. We've stressed all along the importance of finding and marketing toward a specific group, in order to set your firm apart.

Even though you've targeted your marketing, your product can still appeal to others, and they'll order from you. If you discover that there are plenty of others like these new customers, you might have found a secondary market for your goods.

Test any new market. See if you can find lists and publications targeted toward them. Rework your offer to suit this new group.

You might also need to change your packaging. For instance, the retailer who buys your unique consumer goods might love to have a point-of-purchase display. Offer it to retailers on a monthly consignment basis to see if you can get a new line of business going.

Approach such an endeavor slowly. Remember that you're building a new line of business. Your chances of success are good because the new line is closely related to your main work, but any new venture will be somewhat different. If you've been selling to consumers, repackaging, repricing and marketing to retailers has its own set of risks and rewards.

Don't get too excited about this new market. Remember to keep serving the customers who have been your bread and butter up until now. Of course, it's perfectly natural to be excited when you're imagining a whole new universe of potential customers!

Too many businesses don't temper that notion. They try to tackle the whole universe at once. Since they're not ready, they have to either give up or regroup. Always take things one step at a time. Don't try to do anything your company isn't ready for.

Premium Sales

One good source of secondary markets is the premium business. Premiums are giveaways or low-cost items used by companies to promote themselves. A firm might give a premium to its customers, employees or prospects—calendars, pencils, key chains, etc. with the company's logo printed on them.

Your entry into this market comes when you provide your unique line of goods as premiums. Find which ones are best suited to be premiums. Line up companies that can print on them, to individualize them for each premium buyer. Set bulk prices.

Your sales to this market will be to established firms. You won't have problems with collection. You won't have problems with returns. It does, however, take some work on your part in order to develop your line of premiums and to market them. You'll probably want to go to premium trade shows. If your merchandise applies specifically to one industry, go to its trade shows and consider advertising in the appropriate trade journals.

Other ways of developing new markets are limited only by your creativity. Besides seeing what new customers are buying from you, ask yourself who you'd appeal to if you changed your product. What if you sold it in different quantities, or on different terms? Play with the elements of your current marketing. Perhaps a slight change somewhere could open new doors for your company. If you can manage two markets, the second one can improve your company's profitability and increase its growth rate.

Seminar Selling

Seminars are an effective way to make selling presentations. Today many persons go to seminars in order to learn from experts. How does one sell products when the listeners want information?

Begin by remembering that people come to seminars because they have needs. They want to learn how to use a computer, write poetry or have more money. At the seminar you let them know that their needs can be met. Tie your product in with meeting those needs. A person who wants to use a computer effectively needs a computer or at least some software to make it more user-friendly. An aspiring poet would buy a book or newsletter describing techniques, describing markets and offering inspiration. Those wanting more money are ripe for the purchase of an investment.

To be nonthreatening to attendees, you mustn't come on like a salesperson. Appear only to be giving useful information. When your attendees see how your product can help them, they'll buy it. When presenting information, provide useful facts, but don't tell everything you know. If attendees learn all they need from your presentation, they may not buy your product. However, I always strive to provide more value than people expect.

Seminars aren't good ways to sell low-cost items. Most seminars will have fewer than 100 attendees. Of course, not all of those people will buy. If you're selling inexpensive goods, you probably won't gross enough to make it worthwhile.

Just as in any type of direct marketing, you need to pinpoint your prospects. Make sure to plan the seminar around their schedules. For instance, a noontime luncheon session might be best for businesspeople. If you also want their spouses to attend, plan your seminar for an evening.

Check a comprehensive calendar to see if your seminar is planned on any religious holidays. In addition, check the schedules of any groups that might be competing for your prospects' time. If your prospects are upper-middle class, make sure the local symphony isn't performing the night you have a seminar planned.

Don't give a seminar on weekend evenings. If you want to hold one after 6 p.m., choose a night when people normally don't go out. You'll want to keep your competition to a minimum. Tuesday and Thursdays are the best nights, followed by Wednesday and Monday.

One rule of seminar selling is that the longer you can hold the audience, the greater your chances of closing sales. You can do this in several ways. Hold a series of seminars over two or three evenings—or have one that lasts all day on Saturday.

Seminar techniques are often similar to selling strategies used in direct mail. Many seminars are open to the public and advertised in newspapers and on the radio. Your advertising is then like the tease line on the outer envelope of a direct mail package.

Once you've gathered attendees, you need to qualify them as good prospects before the selling really starts. To do this, the first night of a seminar often will be free. At that time the leader tells attendees what information will be given in the seminar, and invites them to come back on subsequent evenings to get that information. Many of the seminars telling how to buy real estate with no money down use this tool, but it can be effective for others as well.

By asking the attendees to come back for another night or two, seminar leaders are separating those truly interested from the curious. Another way to qualify attendees is by charging admission. In this instance the first night would be a free introduction. Meetings on the next two evenings would be subject to an admittance fee. Your fee isn't imposed as a revenue-generating device. Instead it's used to find serious prospects, and to ask them to make a commitment to your seminar. If they've paid for it, they'll tend to see your meetings as being important.

There are also ways to generate revenue from prospects who aren't completely serious. If you follow the method of having a preliminary session, you can offer an item for sale at the end of that meeting. Use it to get some money from the people who are somewhat interested but who aren't excited enough to come back for your other meetings.

If your seminar is a one-day affair, you probably would want to charge admission for the whole event. You probably shouldn't charge an admission fee when you're first beginning to do seminars. Frankly, it will take a while for you to work your presentation up to the point where you're worth paying for.

Many seminar givers see admission fees as a revenue producer. "If I can get 100 people paying $25 each," they say, "that's $2,500." They're missing the point. In seminars you charge money only as a means of qualifying attendees. In other words, you make people pay in order to ensure their involvement with what you're saying. Don't see fees as a way to cover the cost of your meeting room or advertising. If you can't make a lot more than that by selling your product to a small percentage of attendees, you shouldn't be holding seminars.

Picking the Best Spot

The meeting's location should be chosen carefully. Don't make your pick based on price. Consider your attendees. You want to find a place where they'll be comfortable. Depending on where you live and what you're offering in the seminar, this could be anyplace from the local high school auditorium to a hotel meeting room.

Most seminars are given in hotels. Doing so provides attendees plenty of safe parking. Most hotels are in well-known locations. Don't pick one that isn't. Remember that you'll have to tell people in your ads where the meeting will be. It's much easier to say, "the downtown Hilton," than it is to give complicated directions. If you meet at a hard to find place, you'll lose some of your prospects—especially if the meeting's at night. No one likes driving around in the dark, looking for a place they've never seen before.

Locations other than hotels can also work well. Look for a place that will make your meeting seem special. If you're selling to businesspeople, find a room in a new office building. Museums, community centers and resorts also rent meeting rooms. Make sure the room you pick is large enough to hold the expected crowd. Don't get too large a room; it won't look good if your space is less than half filled.

Specify to the person controlling the room what you need. Spell it out in writing. Here's a sample list:

Chairs should be placed in rows with an aisle up the middle. You should ask that the rows be slightly curved, so that the chairs on the end are in front of those in the middle of the row. Explain to the person you're working with that you'll be making a presentation that night. Ask that adjoining rooms not have dances or other loud activities scheduled.

You'll probably want a *podium* for notes, even if you walk around while talking to establish contact with your listeners. Ask for a lavaliere microphone. Use one even if you have a good voice. If you use an overhead projector in your presentation, place the screen at a 45-degree angle to the attendees so that the overhead will not block the audience's view.

Arrive early to test your *sound equipment*. Make sure everything's in place. Put a sign outside the door to let people know they're at the right spot. You'll need a table at the back of the room to display sales material and samples of your product.

If you've taken reservations, place another table at the entrance to your meeting room to sign in attendees. In that way you'll also have the names and addresses of your guests for follow-up. Encouraging reservations is a good way to ensure your crowd. Telling prospects they must reserve their spot makes the seminar seem more important. It will be marked more carefully on prospect calendars, and they'll look forward to hearing you. You'll also have fewer no-shows when you take reservations. On the day before your seminar, have someone on your staff call everyone who has reserved in order to remind them.

Filling the Room

Promote the meeting much as you'd sell any other product. Go to your customer list first. Let them know what an opportunity a seminar gives them—in it they'll learn how to solve some of their problems. Start out by giving seminars to your local customers in order to build your presentation skills and confidence. Marketing to them won't be that expensive. Once you see that seminar selling works for you, market to other persons with similar needs and desires. You'll find them just as you locate prospects for your normal direct selling activities.

Another way to build your speaking skills is by volunteering to speak to various groups. In fact, this is the way I recommend getting started in seminars. You can see if such sessions are effective for you without risking too much time or money.

Speaking before a group offers a pre-formed audience. You don't have to go to the time and expense of marketing your seminar in order to build a crowd. Getting the group together is probably the hardest part of putting on seminars. If you can find someone else to do that for you, you're way ahead.

Choose groups whose members can benefit from your products or services. If you sell to businesspeople, contact local trade and professional organizations. If you sell to consumers, market yourself to a shopping mall. Most malls sponsor events regularly to bring in customers. Talk with the special events coordinator at the mall, and convince him or her that you'll attract new customers to the mall and won't take any business away from stores.

One drawback to speaking before preformed groups is that they'll expect you to be less commercial. You'll have to delete references to your product. Be generic. But let listeners know that you have answers to their problems and that you can be reached during normal business hours. You'll get responses.

You can easily make a list of potential seminar-organizers. Charities, nonprofit groups, businesses looking for speakers for their workers, universities with speaker's bureaus, continuing education programs or resorts and retirement homes offering activities for residents and guests are some examples.

Seminars can also be promoted with the help of the media. Later in this chapter we'll look at ways to get on radio and TV talk shows, as well as how to get the press to write articles about your work.

Get Their Attention

Start off the seminar by introducing yourself and telling about your background. Relate the problems you'll be looking at which concern your audience. Let them know that you have solutions and why your experience qualifies you to offer help. What you are doing is talking about people's problems and the solutions you have for them.

Don't go too far. Since you're trying to sell a product or service, keep pointing to that. Don't give a complete solution to your listeners. Let them know that they will be helped by using your product or service to alleviate their problem. If you offer consulting services, don't give a lot of answers at the seminar. Let your audience know what they really need to do is call your office and make an appointment to see you.

Use other speakers to provide testimonials about your product or service. Additional guest speakers can talk about specialized points concerning your business. Use them to bolster your reputation for expertise. Your attendees will be impressed that you have associates with so much knowledge.

End the program by asking for the audience to comment on the meeting. Pass out cards, and stop talking. Give everyone a chance to fill out the cards. On them your attendees will record their impressions of your presentation and let you know more about their specific needs.

Of course you'll also ask for names and addresses on the cards. Tell the attendees what you'll be doing with the information. Most people at a seminar don't mind giving you information if they know what you are going to do with it. If you're going to send them material, say so, or tell them if someone from your office will be calling them within a week.

Leave time for questions at the end; this will get the audience involved. Here you can listen to individual concerns and let the audience know if your product or service could help. Direct attendees to your associates sitting at the table at the back of the room. On the table you'll have sales literature and samples of your product. Use the opportunity to talk about your prospects' needs and to close sales.

Read the comment cards after your seminar; they'll contain valuable information. You'll see what type of person is attending and what their needs are. With that feedback you probably can think of ways to be more effective in seminars. If you find you're attracting the wrong type of person, you might look at changing your marketing strategy.

Follow up immediately on your prospects, while they're still warm. You should contact them within two or three days. In fact, have your follow-up process planned and ready to go before you even start organizing the seminar.

Using Public Relations

When most small businesspeople think of public relations, they recall horror stories from colleagues. It's not uncommon for a public relations firm to talk a growing business into signing a contract that gives the P.R. firm a monthly retainer. Months pass, and the firm is always *working on* getting a story placed in the media. What actually happens doesn't justify the cost of the agency.

Don't misunderstand me. Public relations can be a profitable way to invest some time and money, but you have to approach it correctly. Here are some guidelines:

1. *Remember what makes up your bottom line.* In other words, don't take your eyes off your business in the pursuit of publicity.

That should be obvious. Too many business owners, however, unconsciously fall prey to the idea that "If I become famous, riches will follow." They spend their time trying to get on TV talk shows—as a result their business suffers.

2. *Have a plan.* Make sure it's a reasonable plan. What exactly do you expect public relations to do for your firm? How can you help make that happen?

Public relations means using the media to help get your message out to the public. You benefit in several ways. People tend to trust an article or show more than they do ads or mail pieces. If you're the guest on a talk show, you can generate interest in your business without sending out a single letter. Moreover, the interest is liable to be strong, since your prospects "heard it on TV." It's surprising the authority that words take on when they're in a published or broadcasted format.

Using the media can bring you good prospects without costing anything. Since the publication or broadcaster chose to report on you, the trust readers and viewers have in the media is transferred to you—and your product. Additionally, you are multiplying your sales power by being able to communicate with many people at once.

You have to remember that a TV show or magazine article is not a closing medium. Since you're in the direct marketing business, though, you have plenty of brochures and letters to send prospects. You'll be more effective if you design a piece to go specifically to persons who inquire as a result of hearing or reading about you. In it you'll mention the media you've appeared in, since that seems to be a selling point to these prospects.

3. *Use your offer as a selling tool to the media.* Reporters and producers are looking for

unique, interesting and newsworthy items with which to fill their space or air time. If you have built a noteworthy business, you're a natural for getting publicity.

Nevertheless, you have to know how to sell yourself. Do it the same way you sell prospects. Don't talk about yourself. Tell how you can help meet the media's needs. Of course, you won't be that blunt about it, but reporters are busy people. If you can help them, they'll use you as a source time and again.

Even being in the media just once can be worthwhile. Many publications regularly report on unique products, for instance. Being in a national consumer or trade publication can help your business. All of a sudden your small company can get national recognition. Not only will you receive inquiries and orders, you also can mention the publicity in future marketing materials. Let prospects know that you have been covered by the national or local media. It's a strategy similar to movie producers reprinting portions of positive reviews in their ads.

   4. *If your company is unique, you have something to offer the media.* How do you do it? First you must decide which media to approach. Then go after them in the right way. Just as direct marketing letters must be well-written to be effective, you need to know what you're doing in public relations. Remember that you're dealing with professionals.

Begin by writing down what group of people you want to communicate with through the media. Generally this will be your primary sales market. Here you must be specific, for the same reasons we discussed earlier about marketing. You might be tempted to say, "everyone will want my product."

That could be true, but the best marketing minds today believe that even large markets are composed of many smaller groups. Why do you think Coca-Cola sells new and classic versions of its most-famous soft drink, not to mention the many other types of drinks? Each one is aimed at a slightly different group. Mass marketers such as soft drink companies don't define themselves as selling to everyone at once. Everyone wants products that seem as though they're made especially for them.

That's where the direct marketer comes in. By now you have a unique product or service, or you have a special offer to make. You have something with which to capture the attention of your prospects.

Media people want to know about your product for just the same reason—it's interesting. Hopefully, it's fascinating, and it's unique. Of course, they're not going to use sales copy when they present your item. Instead, it will be shown as news.

When approaching the media you should use their language as much as possible. Never send your direct mail package. Instead, write a press release. With a release you phrase your message in news terms. Write it as you would a news story. If you've never had newswriting experience, get someone who has to write your press releases. Don't necessarily go to your direct mail writer; he or she might be a poor choice. Unless they've also written for news media, they might have a hard time getting away from sales copy.

Then again, you don't have to hire a high-priced public relations firm to get the job done. The P.R. needs of most firms can be met by choosing media, sending out press releases and then having someone knowledgeable about your firm call to follow up on the release.

How does one choose media? Start by looking at the publications you advertise in or rent names from. If they're good prospects for your sales material, the editors could also be interested in finding out more about you.

Get in touch with other media that are influential to your prospects. Start by finding out to whom you should write. What reporter would write a story that could use you as a source? Who produces the radio or TV talk show you're interested in appearing on? Who edits the magazine or newspaper column that might mention some of your firm's products? Call up the magazines, newspapers and radio and television stations you've chosen. Always check to be sure you have their names spelled correctly. Since media people must get the names of their sources right, they appreciate it when that courtesy is returned.

Your approach will depend somewhat on your goals. Here are some typical approaches:

   1. *If you simply want to talk about your product, send a press release.* In that release you'll be pitching a story angle. Tell about your product if it's newsworthy. Be factual and objective. Avoid using adjectives. If you're selling something based on a technological advance, you would write a story based mainly on the technology. You'd introduce your product when mentioning the uses of the advance.

   2. *If your whole company is unique, that could be the angle.* Stores have gotten national coverage by having an interesting outlook. If you sell nothing but items for left-handers, for

instance, you could get media coverage. If your company won an award, you might also get mentioned in a local publication. That probably won't get too many readers wanting to know more about you. Someone who wins a professional award isn't too compelling for most readers, since that doesn't address their needs directly.

3. *If you think you have some knowledge a reporter would find useful, include information about yourself with your press release.* Let's say your company is the largest direct marketer in the area. You'd probably want to let local business reporters know about that. Initially, they might like to do a story on your firm, but it is more likely that the reporters would see you as a source of information for any marketing article they're working on.

In that case you'd include a cover letter describing your background along with the press release. Include any previous press clippings. What you're trying to do is show the reporters that you are familiar with their needs. Reporters work on tight deadlines. Often they'll need some information or a quote to complete a story. At that time they'll think of people they know who will give them the information they need quickly, and in an interesting way. If you can be that person, you'll be held in high esteem by the media.

Meet the Press

Gear your press release to the readership of the publication. Let's say you sell gourmet chocolate products. A publication with general readership could be interested in a press release discussing all the different types of chocolate in the world. Your hope is that the magazines or newspaper would want to do an article based on that idea, and use you as a source. You would then be seen as a chocolate *expert*.

For a gourmet publication your release should be more specific. Perhaps you'd discuss one type of chocolate in detail. You'd tell its history, how it's prepared and put in some amusing anecdotes concerning this type of chocolate.

A press release on chocolate to a trade journal should address an aspect of the chocolate business. Whether you deal with manufacturing, importing or marketing, you'd be setting yourself up as an industry leader if the publication used your press release. A good release is exactly like a regular news story, except that you are the only person quoted. At times press releases are used as is by media when they don't have the time to go out and put other viewpoints in it. When that happens, you've done a good job of picking media and writing a release.

It's more likely that you'll have to call up the reporter or producer before any action will be taken. Remind them of the story idea you sent. Ask if there's anything else you can help them with.

If you want to write a magazine article, send a letter to the editor describing the article. Include information on the length, tone and slant of the piece. Study the magazine first so you'll be sure what the magazine prefers in the articles it prints. Tell about the availability of photos or illustrations. End by saying why you're qualified to write the piece and when you can have it finished. Enclose copies of any published writing you've done.

If you're asked to be a talk show guest, anticipate questions. Ask the interviewer what topics will be covered. Keep your answers short and relatively simple. Although you'll be a little more educational in interviews than in seminars, remember that you'd still like listeners to call you at your office for information on how you can help relieve their problems.

When you receive inquiries after an interview, put the names on your mailing list. You might want to track them to see if such leads pull better than rented names. If you hold seminars, you should invite the media. Doing so will give them a chance to see you as an expert, as a potential source.

Don't be discouraged if a lot doesn't happen at once. Promotional activity is like any marketing campaign. It takes time to get results. After all, you can't build a customer list overnight. You have to devote plenty of time and energy to the media before the effort will start to pay off. After a while you'll find that once the smaller publications have accepted you, the larger ones will want to talk with you. Around this time, you'll start feeling more at ease when talking with the press. You'll know more about what the press needs from you. As long as you're providing them with the information they want, they'll keep coming back. Such publicity can provide you with a good source of customers.

Dialing for Dollars

Telemarketing—or selling over the phone—can be an additional means of finding customers. Remember to apply the traditional direct selling rules when setting up a telemarketing operation. Segment your lists so that calls are made only to the best prospects.

Decide who your prospects are by finding out who buys over the phone. Telemarketers should keep careful records. Note everything that happens while selling over the phone. Hang ups and wrong numbers are a part of the business—just as wrong addresses are for direct mailers. Just as mailers know what percentage of marketing letters get returned, telemarketers need to analyze how their phone lists are working.

Study results to see if you're making less money than you could by marketing differently. Often telemarketing is used to support other sales efforts. Don't let that excuse poor performance. If a telemarketing operation isn't profitable, it should be changed or discontinued.

Keep your telemarketers motivated with commission compensation. On a chalkboard in the front of your phoning room, record who makes each sale. In that way you'll promote friendly competition among your telemarketers.

Some firms give telemarketers canned scripts to use. Others show them how to introduce the product and its benefits, and then let the telephone sales people work to uncover and meet the needs of their prospects. Obviously the latter approach demands trained telemarketing salespeople, and it can be a most effective means of selling expensive items. Your telemarketer might need to make several calls before closing a sale. As such, it's a way of selling costly items that require a personal sales approach. You can support your calls with direct mail. Experiment with sending the mail before and after the phone campaign.

Another way to get into telemarketing is by using a taped message hooked to a dialing machine. You can call prospects, give your taped presentation and invite them to leave their name and number at the end if they'd like more information. As a rule this method is used to generate leads for salespeople.

Anticipate the costs before getting into telemarketing. Fortunately, that's not too hard. Contact the phone companies for information on the different systems available and their costs. Again I'd suggest that you start small. Test telemarketing before making the commitment to buy a large system.

We've covered many of the work issues affecting direct sellers, but there are other aspects to being in business. Next, we'll consider some of the legal and ethical issues impacting direct marketers.

Chapter Twenty-one

Legal and Ethical Concerns

Trust is the basis of direct selling. Your customers can't walk into your showroom and inspect merchandise; they send you an order on faith. They hope the product will be what they expect and will arrive in a timely fashion.

Most of today's direct marketing firms know that. They also recognize that maintaining happy customers who will order repeatedly is their best method for reaching success.

In the past, however, some companies have taken advantage of customers through misleading ads. Today the odds of that happening are smaller. Consumers are better educated and have higher expectations. Legal and regulatory bodies also watch for abuses.

It makes sense from an ethical and business standpoint to conduct your work honestly. In this chapter we'll look at some areas that are more commonly prone to ethical mistakes. You should be aware of them, and form strict policies to let your workers know where you stand. Let's look first at possible abuse situations in ads and mail packages. Most of these involve making sure your claims are accurate.

Is your offer clear? A reasonable person should be able to easily understand your offer, even without reading every word of your ad or mail piece. Check the following areas for possible misunderstanding or misinterpretation: exactly what product or service is being offered, the specifications of that product or service, delivery date, price, terms of payment, obligations to make future purchases, return policy and guarantee.

Be certain that your offer can't be misconstrued. If it is misunderstood, you'll have plenty of angry customers to deal with, and you don't need that.

Earlier we discussed *gimmick* ads. A gimmick you must not use is making a misleading offer in order to bring in more sales. If you can't sell your goods or services in a straightforward, honest and open fashion, you shouldn't be in direct marketing.

Check the Facts in Your Offer

Unfortunately, the history of direct selling has some stories of misleading come-ons. Although the vast majority of direct marketers would never consider such activities, a stigma remains. For that reason alone you should make your offer as clear as possible. Don't give your prospects any reason to suspect your ability to deliver on what you've promised.

Do so by checking on your copywriters. Don't let them get carried away and claim too much. Put your product in the best possible light without being deceptive. Can you back up any claims made? Are the results you cite typical? Can your average customer expect to have the same experience with your product? You want to sell possibilities without misrepresenting your product's capabilities.

Let's say you offer a product that can help people lose weight. Perhaps you've found that 10 percent of the people who order from you lose more than 20 pounds. About half lose five to ten pounds. Ten percent lose two pounds or less. And one lady, Mrs. E. Biggs, actually dropped 45 pounds while using your product.

Obviously a typical, reasonable expectation for the product is a five-pound to ten-pound weight loss. Half of your customers fit into that category. What should you claim in your marketing material? Here are some possibilities:

177

MRS. E. BIGGS LOST 45 POUNDS!
YOU CAN LOSE OVER 25 POUNDS
LOSE 20 POUNDS OR MORE
LOSE 5 TO 10 POUNDS
LOSE 5 TO 10 POUNDS EASILY
MOST OF OUR CUSTOMERS LOSE AT LEAST 5 POUNDS

Although it can be argued that each of the above headline ideas is true, which ones are fair? Which are accurate? Which are realistic? A lot depends on how you present the product throughout your ad. If you let people know that Mrs. Biggs is an exceptional case, it's okay to tout her as a possibility. But, it's misleading if you tell Mrs. Biggs's story in the ad as though she's a typical customer of yours.

Be Picture Perfect

Additionally, be sure that your photos don't intentionally or unintentionally mislead. Don't create disheartened customers who are disappointed when your product arrives because the photo made your item seem much larger or because your copywriter's description implied that it was sturdier than it is.

Even if your words are truthful, look carefully at the implication you're giving readers. Be certain that your customer testimonials are authentic and that statements you pull from them aren't taken out of context. Don't go overboard, lest you be flooded with returns and complaints.

A similar situation arises with the use of test results. Use independent labs to verify the results of any tests. Make sure that you aren't misrepresenting the findings or their significance to your prospects.

Your ads and mailing pieces always should be in good taste. If you have vulgar or biased marketing material, you'll turn some of your prospects off—especially many general consumers. Some marketers cultivate a cluttered look, thinking that it will attract more attention. This can be a profitable strategy. Make sure, however, that you don't do anything shocking in order to attract attention. Practice courtesy at all times.

Remember that direct marketing is going into the homes and offices of others. You want to stand out, but you must also respect the privacy of the recipients. Telemarketers, for instance, shouldn't call at inconvenient times. When in doubt over a decision, always be cautious. Err on the side of courtesy and good taste.

One rule of thumb is to ask yourself if this is an ad or mailing piece that you'd like to send to your family or friends. Chances are you'll not want to do that if your offer is misleading or your presentation is lax in some other aspect. Take prices, for example. Some direct marketers make their offer seem better by saying it's half off the original price when they've never made any sales at the higher price. This is yet another gimmick to avoid.

Be careful when describing your reduced prices. You must have some basis for saying you're offering a product below its regular, previous, list or suggested price. Federal Trade Commission (FTC) regulations apply to this and many other situations noted in this chapter. If you don't apply proper ethical standards, you run the risk of having to face federal regulators as well as the ire of your own customers.

FTC rules state that your bargain price must be a reduction from an original price "...at which the article was offered to the public on a regular basis for a reasonably substantial period of time...." When that isn't the case, "the 'bargain' being advertised is a false one," says the FTC.

In addition, the FTC warns against telling prospects an article is being offered at a reduced price when that reduction is so small that it's insignificant. For instance, if your original price was $9.99 and you're now selling at $9.95, don't prepare an ad or mailing announcing "SALE!".

If you compare your price to your competition's, make certain you're accurate. Use your competitor's average price as a comparison—don't quote the highest price you can find. Make sure the item you're comparing your product to has comparable qualities. Similarly, if most of your competition sells below the manufacturer's suggested price, or list price, don't try to make your comparable price reduction sound like a great opportunity for buyers.

You should provide enough information for your prospects to make intelligent choices. To do otherwise is simply unethical. If an item you sell is imported, you should tell prospects where it's made. Not doing so would be omitting facts that could affect your prospects' buying decisions.

There's a large gray area within this topic. The purpose of advertising is to persuade. Copywriters aren't under obligation to objectively compare the product they're writing about to the competition, unless they're pointing out how their product beats those competitors.

Coca-Cola will claim "Coke Is It!" and no one expects them to add that half of the country's cola drinkers prefer Pepsi. Consumers know the Coke slogan is advertising. They recognize that it's an exaggerated statement.

You can get in trouble when misrepresenting information presented as fact. Before a soft drink maker can claim its beverage is better for you than the competition's, it would have to do something like add vitamins to the drink. You can't run down the competition without basis for the poor comparison.

Another potential problem comes from leaving out important facts. You don't have to point out your product's weak points, but don't hide them.

Questionable Selling Tactics

When decisions have to be made, many ethical issues come down to personal judgment. It's important to keep some things in mind. One involves the use of surveys to start a selling proposal. With this technique, a direct mail piece or telemarketer tells a prospect that a survey is being conducted on a certain subject. Such an approach causes prospects to relax and provide information about their needs and wants.

When the survey is completed, the marketer tells the prospect there is a product or service that might be helpful, judging from the prospect's survey answers.

Some direct marketers hold that you should tell the prospect that you represent a product before starting the survey. Others go right into the survey and then on to their sales pitch.

I believe that conducting a survey is a legitimate business activity for a direct marketer. Finding out about prospects' attitudes towards your product area is always useful. Direct marketers who conduct surveys certainly won't throw the information away. It's more than a sales tool to them. If a survey helps *break the ice* with a prospect before the selling begins, there's nothing wrong with that.

The ethical point in question is that you shouldn't use a survey to mask your selling intentions. Whether or not that means announcing upfront that you are a vendor as well as a poll-taker is up to you.

Free items pose similar dilemmas. Sellers will use conditional *free* items to encourage sales—if an order is made, the customer receives something free. This can be a real selling tool to give your prospects an incentive to buy. Free gifts should be appreciated by those who order, but once again, make sure that you aren't overstating the importance of the gift. Don't give away something of little value or use and then suggest that you're making an extraordinary offer.

If you offer free gifts with orders, don't increase the normal price or decrease the quality of the items being ordered. In fact, any other special offers should be scrutinized similarly. If you have a *buy one, get one free* offer, don't raise the price or lower the quality of the first item to make up for giving away a second one.

If you use sweepstakes to create interest in your products, they must be carried out ethically. All prizes you advertised must be awarded. Many states have laws dealing with sweepstakes; look at them before proceeding. Some states even outlaw sweepstakes, which is why sweepstakes marketed to a national audience will say that their offer is "void where prohibited by law." However, most direct marketing firms don't use sweepstakes to sell their goods.

Telling Customers How To Say "No"

No matter what or how you're selling, make sure your offer is understood. Some book and record clubs require that customers notify the company when they want out of the club. As long as they don't say anything, they will keep receiving merchandise—and bills. In direct marketing terms this is known as a *negative option*. Nothing is wrong with making such an offer as long as it's very clear to the customers what they're getting into. On such deals the FTC requires that you let customers know they must notify you when they want out of the arrangement. You also must tell them if there are any minimum purchase requirements, if there is an extra charge for postage and handling and how many order obligations there will be each year.

Customers must be told with each order how to cancel the service. They also must have at least ten days to send back the form specifying what they want. Individual states have laws governing negative option offers, so check your state to see what the requirements are.

Making It Perfectly Clear

Always clearly tell prospects what they are getting. If they must make a purchase to get a *free* item, state this plainly. If your prices are low because you're selling seconds, make sure that's clear to customers. Most won't care, and doing so actually makes your low prices more believable. You've given prospects a reason they can understand for being able to sell at lower prices than the competition's.

Don't give prospects false reasons for buying now. Don't say that prices will go up soon when in fact you have no plans to raise prices. Be careful about using the phrases, "Order now, quantities are limited." You could argue that quantities are always limited, but don't make it a selling point unless there's some basis to your claim. In other words, don't claim quantities are limited unless you think you won't be able to fill all the orders for that item.

Don't go to the other extreme, though, by making a great offer that you know you can't fulfill in the hope of getting leads for other sales. Doing this is *bait and switch* advertising, and it's illegal.

You can get close to bait and switch techniques if you aren't careful. Here's an example. Let's say you sell a range of car stereos priced from $74.99 to $199.99. You decide to run an ad describing your low prices. Your headline is:

CAR STEREOS FOR UNDER $79!

In the body copy, you describe the features of the more expensive models. Without telling readers that the one being mentioned in the copy costs more than $100, you invite inquiries. Naturally, people will get in touch with you, wanting a $79 car stereo with all the features you talk about. If you then tell them there's a misunderstanding and try to sell them the higher-priced model, you're guilty of bait and switch.

Be aware of potential problems. When renting your mailing lists, make sure they're going to reputable firms. You don't want your customers receiving deceptive or misleading offers. Even if they don't know that you were the one who provided their name to the unethical firm, they can be turned against ordering through the mail. Ultimately, that could hurt you as well.

Also, see your control of your list as your way of helping to regulate the direct selling industry. If direct marketers don't police the industry effectively, it's an invitation for more government intervention than is present now. In fact, proposed legislation has been put off at times when the Direct Marketing Association stepped in and assured lawmakers they could self-regulate the industry.

If you rent your lists to other direct marketers, give your customers an option to refuse having their names rented. Doing so allows them to retain their privacy. Look at it this way—you know their names, addresses, demographics and direct marketing buying habits, but you don't have the right to divulge that to anyone before first asking for the privilege.

Look at the Picture You're Presenting

Many prospects will read only part of your sales material. Don't force them to look for *fine print*.

Doing so will only create bad feelings—and a subsequent loss of sales.

Be careful when advertising a *free* item, when it's only available with a regular order. Don't mention the free aspect three times and the necessary order only once in your mail package. Be careful with your outside envelope's teaser line. If you're making a free gift with purchase offer, it's okay to mention the fact that you're offering a free gift. If you just mention the gift generically, prospects know they must read the inside material for full information.

Don't identify what the gift is on the outside envelope. That, in effect, completes the offer. Your prospect can assume there's nothing more to know.

Make sure you don't have a continuous free offer in your marketing. If that's the case, the FTC can rule that it's a combination offer. Money for the order then applies to both items, and you can't say that one is free. Don't make a free offer contingent upon a purchase for more than six months out of a year. If you make your offer all the time, it's not really special. To ensure that it's a special offer, don't get more than half of your revenue for a product you're selling from the free offer.

How New Is It?

Be careful when using the word *new*. Don't say your product is new when all you've done is redesigned the package. According to the FTC, "the word 'new' may be properly used only when the product so described is either entirely new or has been changed in a functionally significant and substantial respect."

Although the FTC admits that the length of time you can claim something is new depends upon the product and market, it generally holds that six months is the maximum time period during which a product can be marketed as new.

Other FTC regulations affect direct marketers on every order they take. Most important is the rule stating that orders must be shipped within 30 days of receiving the order. If you know you can't meet that deadline, you have to state in your marketing material when the order will be shipped. A statement such as, "Please allow six to eight weeks for delivery" is an example. However, don't say that you'll ship "as soon as possible." You must state a time when you'll ship. Your order form is your contract with customers.

If you can't meet either the 30-day deadline or the date you specified on your coupon, you must contact your customers. Tell them what has happened, and give a new date for expected shipment. Include a postage-paid reply card on which your customers can indicate that they will wait for the order to be shipped, or that they want a refund. Let them know that if you don't get the card back from them, and if your delay is less than 30 days, you'll assume they want the merchandise shipped at the later date. According to the FTC, if the delay is more than 30 days, no reply must be taken to mean that your customers want to cancel their orders and be refunded.

Guarantees are also watched by the FTC. Most direct marketers offer money back if the customer isn't totally satisfied. If you want time limits or any other constraints on your guarantee, make sure to put that in writing.

You also can get into problems with guarantees when you put the guarantee in your offer. Examples are "Guaranteed to save you 50%" or "We guarantee that our prices are the lowest you'll find." If you have any doubt about backing up these guarantees, don't use them, or at least tone them down. You could write "Guaranteed to save you money," in lieu of promising a 50 percent savings.

Taking out the word *guarantee* is probably the better solution. It's still a strong statement that your customers will save money. Let your testimonials back up that appeal. Leave your guarantee as an assurance that you'll take care of customers who are dissatisfied for any reason. Surely that's all anyone could expect of a guarantee. Don't paint yourself into a corner by *guaranteeing* too much.

If you offer warranties on some of your products, you must either enclose the full warranty with the offer, or state that you'll send a copy if so requested by a prospect.

Dry testing is a practice used by some direct marketers in which an offer is made before the product is available. Response to the offer then helps the marketer decide how to proceed. Be careful with such promotions to ensure that you aren't misleading prospects. From a practical standpoint, don't let your marketing staff talk you into doing test mailings to determine demand for a specific product. You should be able to decide from your own research if a certain product is in demand at the price you can offer it for.

Other points to thoroughly investigate before mailing involve Postal Service regulations. Because these regulations are so numerous and subject to change, I won't go into specifics here. Keep in mind that even experienced direct marketers have been surprised when the Postal Service informed them that their reply card was slightly too big, or that they had to use a lower mailing class because their offer gave more than a 50 percent saving.

It pays to take time to talk with your local Postmaster before mailing. Show him or her your package, and discuss your mailing needs. If you're going to drop a lot of mail, he or she will probably appreciate a chance to give ideas on how to make the mailing process easier on everyone.

Postal Service workers aren't the only government employees you'll deal with. More and more state governments are seeking to tax direct marketers. In such cases the states argue that mailings give a firm a *presence* in their state, even though the company has offices elsewhere. Sales and use taxes are then levied on the direct marketer. In the past direct sellers have successfully fought paying these taxes, but some cases have gone all the way to the United States Supreme Court.

You should retain legal counsel to determine which taxes you are legally liable for and in which states, if any, you should collect sales taxes or use taxes from customers. Generally you'll do so only from the residents of the state where your office is located.

Taxes are only one unpleasant drain on your cash flow. Just as you minimize tax losses, you should work to keep other business losses at a minimum. Have insurance that will cover the effects of disasters on your business. Fires, floods, tornadoes and theft should be covered.

Planning for the Impossible

To see what your potential losses are, take a moment and figure the replacement costs of your building, office equipment and inventory. Although no one anticipates catastrophes, you should be prepared for them. If you aren't, an unfortunate circumstance could put your business in a real bind.

Find out the types of coverage you should have. Do this by listing the potential business risks you face. Ask yourself and your associates what future events could harm the business. Some things, such as an increase in postal rates, can't be covered by insurance. Consider other problems that should be covered.

You might need to do some research, such as finding out how much it would cost to replace your computers if they were damaged or stolen. Talk with your insurance broker or agent. Find an independent agent who specializes in working with small businesses. He or she can help you find the best price as well as structure policies to your unique needs.

If you sell to consumers, your inventory probably will be much higher during the Christmas buying season than at any other time during the year. You then should insure your inventory on a *reporting basis*. Both coverage and premiums will be based on the dollar value of your inventory as reported at the end of each month.

Tell your agent what your concerns are. Look at the costs for covering them. Your agent should have creative ideas to help you get the most from your insurance money. You might be able to afford insurance only on the most expensive aspects of your business; other parts might have to go uninsured. After talking with your insurance advisor, you'll have a realistic picture of what you can cover and what the costs will be.

Your agent will also make suggestions on things you can do to lower your insurance costs and, in the process, lower your risk of loss as well. Using security devices to ward off theft is one example, yet there are other dangers. Look into fidelity bonding coverage to protect yourself against employee theft and fraud.

If your business is based on the activities of a few persons, you might want a key-person policy. This is a life insurance policy with your company as the beneficiary. Use such a policy to cover the principals in your firm, if losing one of them would hurt your business substantially.

This policy can be used to retain ownership of the firm. If you have a buy-sell agreement with a partner, a key-person policy can be used to buy the deceased's interest in the firm from his or her family.

Besides having adequate insurance, you'll need to have policies designed for limiting business losses from crime and fraud. You'll have to deal with both external crime, or break-ins, and the possibility of pilferage by your own employees. Areas of concern will include your inventory, mailing lists, business records, and computers and other equipment. Let's look at these concerns individually:

1. *Pilferage or theft by employees.* When hiring you should be on the lookout for a record indicating a background of theft or disrespect for an employer's property and interests. When in doubt, don't hire someone.

Let employees know that you will prosecute anyone caught stealing. Make it a company policy. Post signs to that effect. Create an attitude of individual responsibility by requiring employees to wear name tags. Have managers supervise areas prone to theft. If anyone is caught, prosecute.

Get a security expert to look at your building, and propose ways for protecting against break-ins and employee theft. Video cameras both inside and out might be recommended. Make sure your lighting, alarm system and barriers to entry are sufficient for when the building's not being used.

You can avoid theft by keeping people from temptation. Make sure people delivering goods are kept out of the warehouse. Small but valuable items should be kept locked at all times. Only trusted employees should have access to these products, including those who pack and ship them. Larger, expensive goods should be stored up high. In that way it would be difficult for an employee to take such goods without being seen.

Keep records of all shipments going out. At times employees will try to ship goods to someone who hasn't sent in an order. Control the supply of labels, to keep this from happening. If you exercise good sense and have the right procedures, you'll reduce much of the potential for problems.

2. *Computer protection.* Natural and human elements can damage computers. Your goal is to set up your system in a way that minimizes the possibility of either happening.

To avoid natural disasters, be careful where you put your computers. A ground floor location can make them susceptible to flooding, but don't put them above the third floor, which would make them less accessible to fire-fighting equipment. Fire detectors and an automatic sprinkler system should be in your computer room. Temperature and humidity controls should also be installed and maintained.

Place the computer room in the center of your floor. In that way, the hardware is farther away from intrusion by either the elements or human break-ins. Additionally, you can more easily supervise the area during working hours when the computers are enclosed in glass and in the middle of a floorplan.

Carefully screen new employees. Get fidelity bonds on workers who will be in the computer room. Let these employees know that any crime will be followed up by the bonding company. Also, let your workers know that it's illegal to steal trade secrets. Have them sign confidentiality contracts. Finally, make sure that several workers are aware of the intricacies of any given program. In that way the odds of it being tampered with are reduced.

Keep hard copies and backup disks or magnetic tapes in case of damage due to computer failure, natural disaster, employee mistakes or theft. Limit access to the computer room. Have everyone going in sign a log and record how long they were there and what tasks they were doing. Much of this advice involves common sense and good procedures, but following it can reduce the risk of a major problem.

> 3. *Mailing list security.* Your lists are probably your most important business possession. You need to guard against their theft or unauthorized use. Do so by protecting the computer tapes or disks on which they're stored. Use the guidelines mentioned above for computer security.

Be aware that others in your firm might be able to get access to your lists. A disgruntled employee could use your lists to start his or her own business, or sell the lists to one of your competitors.

Guard hard copies of your mailing list. Don't allow them to be circulated throughout the company. Put decoy names on the list to check for unauthorized use. Place the decoy names in all sections of your lists so that any partial use will be detected. Decoys are paid to make sure that they receive only mailings you've okayed.

> 4. *Safekeeping of business records.* Check with your accountant, attorney and banker to see which records need to be stored. You might be able to lower state sales taxes by keeping accurate sales records. Additionally, you'll want to keep some records for your own use in planning.

After choosing what you want to keep, decide where the documents should be stored and who should have access to them. You don't want your reports on markets, media and products getting into the wrong hands any more than you'd want your mailing lists stolen.

You'll need to have policies concerning what records to keep working copies of, and who gets to see those. You'll set timetables for when those documents are to be destroyed. Make sure that happens. Other documents will need to be kept in long-term storage. You'll need procedures for updating those documents—as well as having a timetable for disposing of older documents.

Don't just store your business records—use them to help your firm grow. One way of doing this is to graphically record expenses and profits. Recap monthly expenses in a chart. Under each month, write what you spent on lists, ads, artists, copywriters, utilities, postage and all other expenses. Check to see if any of the figures surprise you. If your costs are out of line anywhere, they'll affect your profits. You can also analyze your sales to see which areas of the business are most profitable. Find out what's dragging profits down.

Let your workers know what's going right in the business, and also tell them your concerns. You need their help in bringing costs into line.

Bad debt is a potential problem. Here again you need clear credit policies in order to minimize your risks. One way to avoid such problems is to require a check or credit card number with each order.

Many direct marketers have learned that they'll lose sales if they don't offer a *bill me later* option, yet those extra sales will include some persons who won't pay. If you're marketing to rented lists, find out what the bad debt percentage was in previous mailings. Check how many bad debts you received on your test mailing to that list before rolling out to more names.

When selling expensive items, you can afford to run a credit check before fulfilling any orders. Keep in mind that if you offer credit to your customers, you must follow strict federal guidelines.

Make certain that your order form is clear concerning what you expect from the customer; it is a contract between you and your customer. Have a signature line on your order form if there's space, to make the deal more binding. Also include a space for a phone number, in case you need to call.

Potential bad debts often can be spotted by looking at your filled-in coupons. Here are some signs of potential problems:

- Illegible handwriting
- Use of a Post Office box
- Omission of information: phone number, first name, signature or full address (even not including the word "Road")
- Incorrect addition of price
- Ordering a quantity or mix of items that is unusual
- Use of pencil or red ink
- Checks with low numbers, indicating a new account

To see if this type of rating system would work for you, have your fulfillment staff separate such orders from the rest. Fill some of them, and see what the results are. If you run into credit problems, you might want to make it a policy to reject orders with such characteristics.

When bad debts occur, have a set procedure. Each business will need a different timetable and plan. Basically you'll send form letters, make phone calls and perhaps turn the account over to a collection agency. You'll save time by having letters already written and phone calls scripted.

Your first letter should serve as a reminder of the account. The second letter will make an inquiry as to why the invoice hasn't been paid. In the next letter you'll demand payment, and finally notify the customer of further action you will take.

Use the business tools we've outlined in this chapter to run a good and profitable firm. Attention to some of the topics in this chapter could give your company the extra boost necessary to put profits where they should be.

Appendix

Ted Nicholas Space Ad

Enterprise • Dearborn Catalog Page

JS&A Space Ads

Enterprise • Dearborn Direct Mail Outside Envelope

Typestyle Samples

Point Size Chart

Sample Imposition/Signature

Envelope Size Chart

Printer Checklist

Order Form

Sample Press Release

Sample Option Notice

Sample Renewed Option Notice

The Ultimate Tax Shelter For ALL Incomes

by Ted Nicholas

Tax experts are calling a small, privately-owned corporation "the ultimate tax shelter."

Because government has recognized the important role of small business in our country, there are numerous laws favoring corporation owners. With the help of my book, anyone — from any income bracket — can take advantage of this readily available tax shelter.

Anyone Can Incorporate

Small, unincorporated businesses, enjoyable hobbies, part-time businesses, even existing jobs can be set up as full-fledged corporations. I've written HOW TO FORM YOUR OUR CORPORATION WITHOUT A LAWYER FOR UNDER $75, to show you the simplest, fastest and least expensive way to incorporate.

If you're intrigued with the thought of running your own corporation, even on a part-time basis, but don't have a specific idea in mind, I believe my book can stimulate you to action. It's important to remember that you don't need to have a big operation or business to benefit. Ninety-eight percent of businesses in the U.S. are small — often just one person working out of his home.

How You Benefit

Your initial investment can vary from zero to a few hundred or a few thousand dollars. I know it can be done because at age 22, with no capital, credit or experience, I incorporated my first company — a candy manufacturing concern and raised $96,000. From that starting point, grew a chain of 30 stores. You, too, can go as far as your determination and imagination will take you.

When you incorporate, you limit personal liability to your investment in the business. Your home, furniture, and car are not at risk. You can raise capital by borrowing or selling stock and still keep control of your business. You can put aside up to 25 percent of your income tax free into lucrative retirement, pension, and profit-sharing plans. Your own corporation enables you to maintain continuity and facilitate transfer of ownership. Many tax free fringe benefits can be arranged, such as the deductible health and life insurance programs. Medical and dental expenses for both you and every member of your family can become tax deductible to your corporation. If you wish, you may set up a non-profit corporation or foundation. You can even draw a salary while helping your favorite charity. If you prefer maximum privacy, you may operate anonymously under a pen name you can record for one dollar.

Startling Facts Revealed

Lawyers charge substantial fees for incorporation when often they prefer not to and I'll explain why. You'll discover why two-thirds of the New York and American Stock Exchange companies incorporate in Delaware — the state most friendly to corporations. You'll learn how you can have the same benefits as the largest corporations.

You'll be able to hold all corporate offices: President, Vice-President, and Secretary, if you wish.

What Readers Say

"I was quoted a legal fee of $1,000 each for three corporations I wanted to form. This book saved me almost $3,000!"
— *Joanne Strickland, Wilmington, DE*

"This book succeeds... because it fills a real need."
— *PUBLISHER'S WEEKLY*

"Please accept my many thanks for a great book and "Do It Yourself Kit" for the little guy to be able to incorporate without all the hassles and added expenses that normally transpire."
— *John Silvestri, Coral Springs, FL*

Free Bonus

As a bonus for ordering my book, HOW TO FORM YOUR OWN CORPORATION WITHOUT A LAWYER FOR UNDER $75, I'll send you absolutely free THE INCOME PLAN. This portfolio of valuable information which normally sells for $19.95 shows you how to convert almost any job into your own corporation. You could increase your take-home pay by up to 31 percent without an increase in salary. Employers will also save time and money on payroll records and withholding taxes.

My Personal Guarantee

If you are not completely satisfied with my book, return it undamaged within 30 days, and your money will be promptly refunded. And even if you do return it, THE INCOME PORTFOLIO is yours to keep.

Ted Nicholas

Save $300 to $1500

You'll save from $300 to $1500 simply by using the convenient tear-out forms included in my book. Everything you need is there: certificates of incorporation, minutes, by-laws, and complete instructions.

In a hurry? Orders may be faxed to Nicholas Direct, Inc. 302-529-7567 or mail coupon below.

Mail To:
Nicholas Direct, Inc. Dept.
1000 Oakfield Lane,
Wilmington, DE 19810

Please mail ___ copies of HOW TO FORM YOUR OWN CORPORATION WITHOUT A LAWYER FOR UNDER $75 by Ted Nicholas @ $19.95 plus a $2.95 postage and handling fee. It is my understanding if I am not completely satisfied with the book, I may return it within 30 days of receipt for a prompt refund and keep the Income Portfolio, normally $19.95, for my trouble.

___ I enclosed my check for $19.95 + $2.95 Shipping & Handling

___ Charge my ☐ Visa ☐ Mastercard ☐ AmEx

\# _____ exp. date _____
Signature _____
My name is _____
I live at _____
City _____ State ___ Zip Code ____

Fax credit card orders to:
1-302-529-7567

If coupon is missing, send orders to Nicholas Direct, Inc. 1000 Oakfield Lane, Wilmington, DE 19810

© Nicholas Direct, Inc. 1992

Over 200,000 copies of my first book were sold using this successful space ad.

I. The Emerging Entrepreneur

Starting a business for the first time? The emerging entrepreneur is actively planning and researching the feasibility of a new business venture.

Incorporate Yourself— and Discover America's Ultimate Tax Shelter

"...this book has helped more people to incorporate than all the lawyers on Wall Street put together."
— Ted Nicholas

OVER 900,000 SOLD!

How To Form Your Own Corporation Without A Lawyer For Under $75.00
Ted Nicholas
Fully Revised and Updated!

Catalog #5615-01   Price: $19.95

Imagine owning two tax deductible family cars. Imagine having tax deductible hobby expenses. And how about tax deductible life, health and income protection insurance? Tax deductible trips, and tax deductible meals.

These are just some of the remarkable fringe benefits that can be yours through the most powerful tax shelter in America today—owning your own corporation.

And better yet, thanks to the most recent changes in the tax rate, most successful business people will prefer the advantageous tax rates that a corporation can offer you over what the unincorporated business owner will have to pay.

Moreover, you'll limit your personal liability (so much is at risk anymore in today's lawsuit-happy society), raise capital more easily, and benefit from estate planning techniques that only a corporation can provide for you.

With this ready-to-use book on your side, *How To Form Your Own Corporation Without a Lawyer for Under $75*, you'll discover all the unique advantages of incorporating while at the same time learning how quick, easy and inexpensive the process can be. Avoid the hassle of lawyers and save from $300 to $3,000 in legal fees by following the simple instructions spelled out for you in this perennial bestselling book.

Join the thousands of other businesses which have followed the advice in this book. Written by Ted Nicholas, founder of Enterprise Publishing, Inc. and 22 other successful businesses, you'll discover how easy it really is to incorporate and protect your business assets, your family and your personal assets in the process.

Unlike popular opinion, incorporation is no longer the sole domain of "big business" or the Fortune 500 giants. In fact, it's the thousands of smaller companies, many just one-person operations, that are the leading edge in this increasingly popular business trend. Learn how easy it is for just about anybody to incorporate and how to take that important step *now*.

You'll also get a complete set of forms including a Certificate of Incorporation, Minutes, By-Laws ... everything you need, all for an incredibly low price.

How To Get Your Own Trademark and Protect Your Single Most Important Asset— Your Good Name

Discover step-by-step how easily you can do it yourself and save a fortune in legal fees. Includes ready-to-use tear-out forms for everything you need!

How To Get Your Own Trademark
From the Editors of Enterprise Publishing

Catalog #5615-02   Price: $24.95

The single most important asset of your business is the good name attached to your products and services.

If you have name recognition, customers will seek out that product or service by name. And that name may be of immeasurable value, even worth millions in the form of goodwill should you ever decide to sell your business.

The safest, most effective way to protect a name is to obtain a federal trademark. You are then in the best position to guard against strangers usurping your name.

Once your name is embraced by trademark protection, it can remain yours forever. All you need to do is use it and renew it every twenty years to protect it. You thus retain the exclusive right to that name in perpetuity.

How To Get Your Own Trademark, by the editors of Enterprise • Dearborn, shows you:
1 Why you and/or your business should obtain trademark protection
2 How easy and inexpensive it can be for you to obtain that protection yourself, without engaging costly legal or other professional assistance
3 The simple, straightforward steps you can take to ensure that once you obtain trademark protection, it's yours for as long as you want it
4 What to do if someone is infringing on your trademark
5 What to do if your trademark application is denied
6 How to get trademark protection in other countries
7 How to comply with trademark registration, with complete step-by-step instructions
8 How to use the trademark applications provided, complete with samples and tear-out forms

A word of warning: Many people believe that they have obtained name protection for their company when they incorporated. Not true! Get *all the facts* when you order your copy of this informative book today.

SAVE $1.00! FAX Your Credit Card Order 1-312-836-1021. Or Call Toll Free 800-554-4379.

5

Note how the products in the catalog complement each other. Products that appeal to the same target market help generate multiple sales.

Vision Breakthrough

When I put on the pair of glasses what I saw I could not believe. Nor will you.

They look like sunglasses.

By Joseph Sugarman

I am about to tell you a true story. If you believe me, you will be well rewarded. If you don't believe me, I will make it worth your while to change your mind. Let me explain.

Len is a friend of mine who knows good products. One day he called excited about a pair of sunglasses he owned. "It's so incredible," he said, "when you first look through a pair, you won't believe it."

"What will I see?" I asked. "What could be so incredible?"

Len continued, "When you put on these glasses, your vision improves. Objects appear sharper, more defined. Everything takes on an enhanced 3-D effect. And it's not my imagination. I just want you to see for yourself."

COULDN'T BELIEVE EYES

When I received the sunglasses and put them on I couldn't believe my eyes. I kept taking them off and putting them on to see if what I was seeing was indeed actually sharper or if my imagination was playing tricks on me. But my vision improved. It was obvious.

I kept putting on my $100 pair of sunglasses and comparing them. They didn't compare. I was very impressed. Everything appeared sharper, more defined and indeed had a greater 3-D look to it. But what did this product do that made my vision so much better? I found out.

The sunglasses (called BluBlockers) filter out the ultraviolet and blue spectrum light waves from the sun. Blue rays have one of the shortest wavelengths in the visible spectrum. As a result, the color blue will focus slightly in front of the retina which is the "focusing screen" in your eye. By blocking the blue from the sunlight through a special filtration process and only letting those rays through that indeed focus clearly on the retina, objects appear to be sharper and clearer.

The second reason is even more impressive. It is harmful to have ultra-violet rays fall on our eyes. Recognized as bad for skin, UV light is worse for eyes and is believed to play a role in many of today's eye diseases.

SUNGLASS DANGER

But what really surprised me was the danger in conventional sunglasses. Although they reduce the amount of light that enters our eyes, our pupils open wider and we allow more of the harmful blue and ultraviolet light into our eyes.

DON'T BE CONFUSED

There are many imitation sunglasses now being offered that claim to be as good or better than BluBlockers. Don't be confused. BluBlocker is the only sunglass with Malenium 99 lenses—the finest you can buy. Our quality frame can't compare to the others. Get the best with the original BluBlockers.

BluBlocker sunglasses use expensive Malenium-99™ lenses with a hard anti-scratch coating. You can't get any better lens.

The black, light-weight frame is one of the most comfortable I have worn and will comfortably contour to any size face. It compares with many of the $200 pairs you can buy from France or Italy.

There is a clip-on pair that weighs less than one ounce and fits over prescription lenses. All models include a padded carrying case and a one-year limited warranty.

I urge you to order a pair and experience your improved vision. Then take your old sunglasses and compare them to the BluBlocker sunglasses. See how much clearer and sharper objects appear with the BluBlocker pair—especially compared to the other cheaper pairs that do not remove all of the blue. If you don't see a dramatic difference in your vision—one so noticeable that you can tell immediately, then send them back anytime within 30 days and I will send you a prompt and courteous refund.

DRAMATIC DIFFERENCE

But from what I've personally witnessed, once you wear a pair, you'll love them.

Our eyes are very important to us. Protect them and at the same time improve your vision with the most incredible breakthrough in sunglasses since they were first introduced. Order a pair or two at no obligation, today.

Credit card holders call toll free and order by product number below or send a check plus $3 for postage and handling.
BluBlocker Sunglasses (2020FP) **$39.95**
Clip-On Model (2028FP) **39.95**
Note: Order any two pair and get the third pair FREE.

JS&A

One JS&A Plaza, Northbrook, Illinois 60062
CALL TOLL FREE 800 228-5000
IL residents add 7% sales tax. ©JS&A Group, Inc.,1987,88

Joe Sugarman sells mostly high-tech items through his innovative space advertising.

Stop Taking Vitamins

If you think the vitamins you are now taking are doing you any good, wait until you hear the latest news on why they may not.

Stop taking that innocent looking vitamin pill until you read this report.

By Joseph Sugarman

This may come as a shock. But according to the latest research, those vitamins that you take every day may be doing you absolutely no good. For example.

FACT: Vitamins should be taken after a meal—never before. The body must first have protein, fats, or carbohydrates in the digestive tract to properly break down the vitamins for proper absorption.

FACT: Your body has a need for a natural vitamin balance. Too much of one vitamin may cause another vitamin to be less effective. For example, vitamin A should be taken with vitamin E but excessive iron should not.

FACT: If you take too much calcium, you may deplete the magnesium in your system. And you need magnesium to convert food into energy.

FACT: Some vitamins are best taken in the morning and others at night. For example, the trace element chromium helps break down the sugar in your food which in turn creates energy—perfect to start the day. But at night you should take Calcium which has a relaxing effect—perfect for the evening.

FACT: Athletes or people who exercise a great deal need vitamins more than people who don't exercise. Vitamins are depleted at a much faster rate during exercise than during any other period of time.

But there was a series of other facts that surprised me too. For example, despite everything I've just mentioned on the care in taking vitamins, there are those people who need vitamins because of the mental or physical activity that they undergo. People on a diet, under stress, those who smoke, women who take contraceptives and even those who take medication—all rob their bodies of some of the essential vitamins and minerals that they need to help combat the various habits or conditions they are under.

And with vitamins in the proper balance and at the proper times, you may have more energy and vitality. Little changes may take place. Your nails may become stronger, your hair may become lustrous and your skin may remain more elastic which will keep you younger-looking longer.

DOCTORS HAD IDEA

About two years ago a group of doctors had an idea. They realized that many people were taking vitamins and not really noticing any difference in their health. They also realized that, based on the latest nutritional findings, the vitamins people were taking may not have been doing them any good.

So they formed a group of advisors consisting of nutritionists, dieticians, dermatologists, biochemists and physicians, and developed one of the most effective combinations of vitamins and minerals, formulated four tablets—one for the morning and one for the evening—and one for men and one for women and then started a test program that lasted over two years. The results speak for themselves.

It was ideal for weight loss programs and it was ideal for people under stress. It helped many increase their energy levels. Smokers benefited. Some under medication benefited. And before long MDR Fitness Corp., the company that had developed the program, became one of the fastest growing vitamin companies in the United States. And no wonder.

SEVERAL BENEFITS

With a fresh vitamin and mineral balance, taken in the right quantity in the right combination and at the right time, several obvious benefits occur. First, you may develop a better mental outlook because you've got the energy and the zest to accomplish more. As a result of the trace elements copper, zinc and manganese, your body is helped to make its natural anti-aging enzymes that keep you fit. Improvements in your vitality translate into everything from better job performance to a greater sense of well being.

JS&A has been selected by the vitamin company to introduce their medically formulated vitamin program. Every two months we send you a fresh two month's supply of 120 fitness tablets—one to be taken after breakfast and one after dinner.

During the first two months, you will have ample opportunity to notice the difference in your energy level, your appearance and your overall stamina. You should notice small changes. Your complexion may even take on a glow. Some of you may notice all of these changes and others may notice just a few. But you should notice some of them.

If for any reason, you do not notice a change, no problem. Just pick up your phone, and tell us not to send you any more vitamins. And if you're dissatisfied and ask for a refund, you won't even have to send the empty bottle back. It's yours free for just giving us the opportunity to introduce our vitamins. However, if you indeed do notice a difference (which we are confident you will), you'll automatically receive a two-month's supply every eight weeks.

ONE MORE INCENTIVE

I'm also going to give you one more incentive just to let me prove to you how powerful this program really is. I will send you a bonus gift of a fitness bag with your first order. This beautiful bag will hold all your fitness gear and it's great too for short vacation trips. It's a $20 value but it's yours free for just trying the vitamins. Even if you decide not to continue, you keep the fitness bag. I am so convinced that you will feel and see a difference when you take these vitamins that I am willing to gamble on it with this unusual offer.

Vitamins indeed are important. And with today's research and new nutrition technology, you have a greater chance to achieve the fitness and health levels that may have eluded you with the typical store vitamins or the poor advice we may get in health food stores or from friends. Here is a safe, risk-free way to get one of the best vitamin programs in the country, formulated by a physician, with the right combination of vitamins, minerals and trace elements, in a convenient program that assures you of delivery every two months. I personally take and highly recommend them. Order your trial quantity, today.

To order, credit card holders call toll free and ask for product number (shown in parentheses) or send a check and include $2.50 for delivery.

Men's Vitamins (1155FF2) $24
Women's Vitamins (1156FF2).......$24

JS&A

One JS&A Plaza, Northbrook, Illinois 60062
CALL TOLL FREE 800 228-5000
IL residents add 7% sales tax. ©JS&A Group, Inc.,1987

Sugarman's ads are long on copy... and longer on selling power.

Appendix 191

Protect Yourself and Save Legal Fees with a Book of Ready-to-Use Business Agreements

Open for valuable form enclosed absolutely *FREE*

Dennis Blitz
520 N. Dearborn St. #4
Chicago, IL 60610

E(2S)

This is an example of an outside envelope featuring "teaser" copy.

Typestyle Samples

Sans Serif Typestyle 1

Sans Serif Typestyle 2

Serif Typestyle 1

Serif Typestyle 2

Point Size Chart

Garamond 10
Garamond 12
Garamond 14
Garamond 18
Garamond 24
Garamond 48

Helvetica 10
Helvetica 12
Helvetica 14
Helvetica 18
Helvetica 24
Helvetica 48

Times Roman 10
Times Roman 12
Times Roman 14
Times Roman 18
Times Roman 24
Times Roman 48

194 Appendix

Sample Imposition/Signature

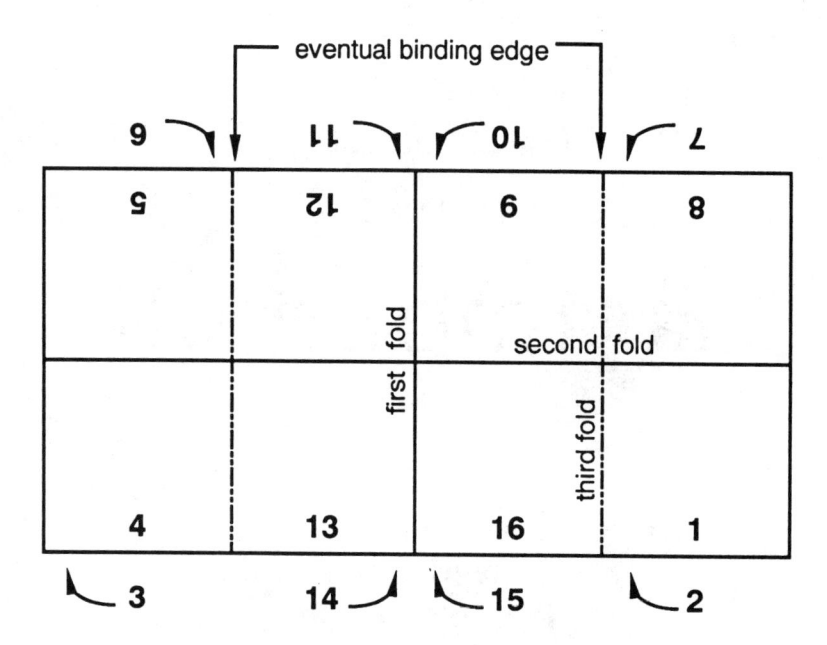

16-page imposition

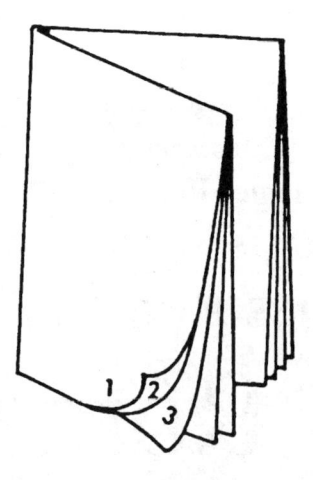

Signature after folding

Appendix 195

Envelope Size Chart

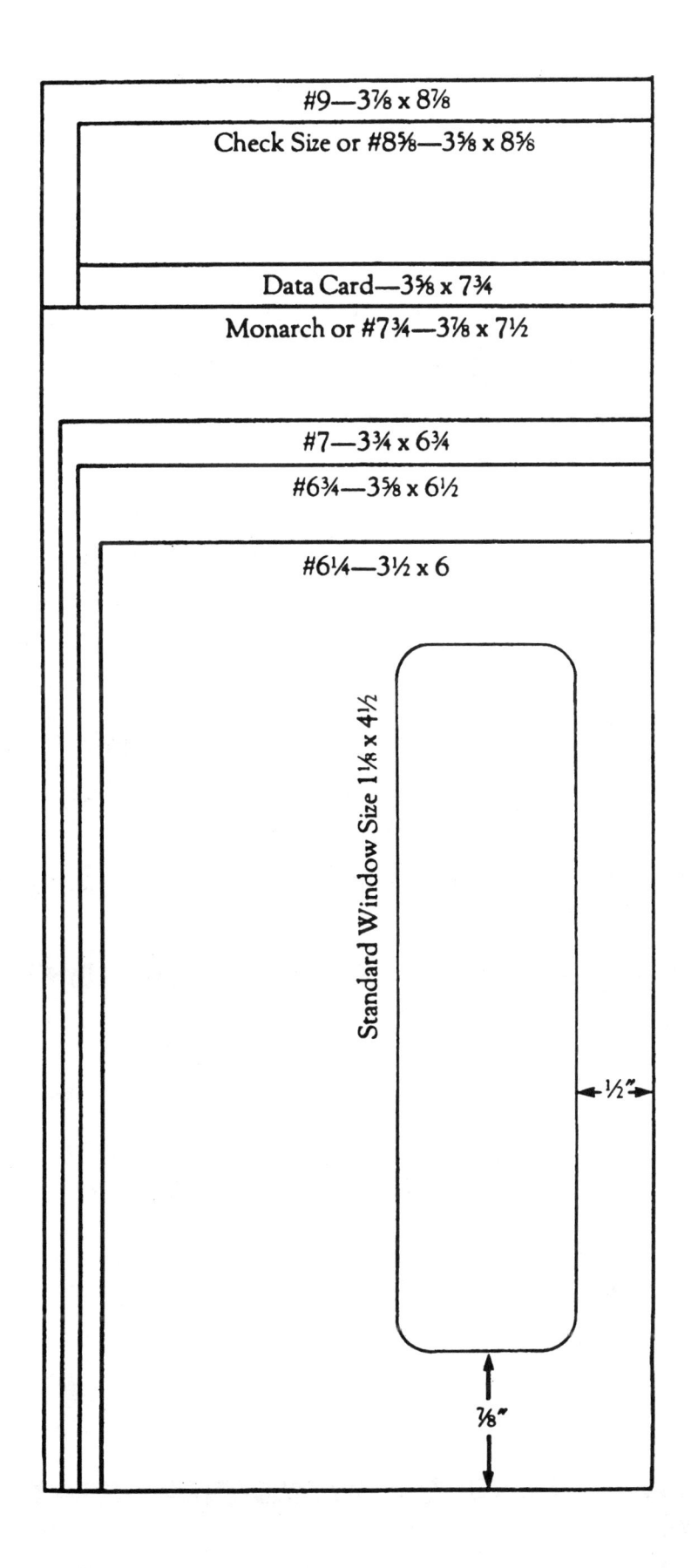

#9—3⅞ x 8⅞

Check Size or #8⅝—3⅝ x 8⅝

Data Card—3⅝ x 7¾

Monarch or #7¾—3⅞ x 7½

#7—3¾ x 6¾

#6¾—3⅝ x 6½

#6¼—3½ x 6

Standard Window Size 1⅛ x 4½

← ½" →

⅞"

Printer Checklist
How To Match the Printer to the Job

1. Find out if a printer has the equipment necessary to complete your job. Check on the kind of presses available and their sizes. Make sure your printer has the machinery needed to fold, bind and stuff your printing job.

2. Determine if the printer specializes in the type of printing you need. Doing so can save greatly on time and expense.

3. Ask for samples of finished print jobs similar to the one you want produced. Carefully check the works quality.

4. Investigate the printer's reputation for integrity and reliability.

5. Make sure the printer can guarantee the completed job by the date it's needed. Build in a two to three day safety margin for unexpected delays.

6. Listen to suggestions your printer may have on how to produce the best product for the least cost.

7. After getting at least three estimates, compare pricing carefully. Choose the printer offering the best overall service.

Appendix

Order Form

YOUR ENTERPRISE • DEARBORN PROSPERITY ORDER FORM

3 Convenient Ways to Order!

Save time—get your books faster—order by phone!
1-800-554-4379 In Illinois, 1-312-836-4400, ext 650
When ordering, please mention the code number on the label

Save time—and an additional $1.00—FAX your order!
FAX 312-836-1021
Please complete and use this Order Form when FAXing.

OR, COMPLETE THIS ORDER FORM AND TEAR OUT. MAIL IN THE ATTACHED ENVELOPE.

FREE BOOK OFFER!
Order $100 or more from this catalog and receive a FREE copy of *RETIRE WORRY FREE!*

Please use this space if you wish to make address corrections.

NAME _____
COMPANY _____
STREET ADDRESS _____
CITY _____
STATE _____ ZIP _____
DAYTIME TELEPHONE _____

THE ENTERPRISE • DEARBORN GUARANTEE:
Your satisfaction in our products is very important to us. Therefore, if for any reason you are not delighted with your purchase, return it in good condition within 30 days of receipt for refund, credit or exchange. This applies to all books, publications and reports. Computer diskettes are covered by warranty.

TITLE	ORDER NUMBER	NO. OF UNITS	UNIT PRICE	TOTAL
Retire Worry Free	5608-10	\multicolumn{2}{l}{*Free with orders of $100 or more*}	

SHIPPING/HANDLING CHARGES:
$0-24.99 .... $ 4
$25-49.99 .... $ 5
$50-99.99 .... $ 6
$100-249.99 .... $ 8
$250.00 and over $11

Orders shipped to these states must include applicable sales tax: CA, FL, IL, NY

Minimum order is $20.00. Prices are subject to change without notice.

Subtotal ____
Less $1.00 if you FAX order ____
Tax ____
Shipping/Handling ____
TOTAL ____

E10500

PLEASE INDICATE FORM OF PAYMENT:

☐ CHECK; amount enclosed $ _____
☐ CREDIT CARD   ☐ VISA   ☐ MASTERCARD   ☐ AMERICAN EXPRESS

CARD NUMBER ☐☐☐☐ ☐☐☐☐ ☐☐☐☐ ☐☐☐☐

EXP. DATE ☐☐–☐☐   SIGNATURE _____
(All charge orders must be signed)

Sample Press Release

Dearborn Financial Publishing, Inc.

- *Commodity Trend Service, Inc.*
- *Dearborn R&R Newkirk*
- *Real Estate Education Company*
- *Upstart Publishing Company, Inc.*
- *Vernon Publishing, Inc.*

520 North Dearborn Street Chicago, Illinois 60610-4354 312/836-4400 Fax 312/836-1021

FOR IMMEDIATE RELEASE

CONTACT: Wendy Glait
312/836-4400 ext. 434
Or, Rick Frishman
Planned Television Arts
212/921-5111

HOW TO INCORPORATE WITHOUT LEGAL ASSISTANCE AND FEES IS FOCUS OF NEW BOOK

According to the *Wall Street Journal*, over 50,000 new corporations are formed each month in North America. In a recessionary period, that number is expected to increase greatly, as more and more individuals are seeking the stability and tax advantages of self-employment by forming their own businesses.

Thanks to recent tax changes, small business people are able to enjoy better tax rates, as well as fringe benefits, by incorporating. Yet many hesitate to do so, balking at the complex process and high legal fees often involved. According to business expert and entrepreneur Ted Nicholas, "Lawyer's fees for incorporating range from $300 to $3,000 or more. Yet a little known fact is that in many states an individual can legally incorporate without the services of a lawyer."

Nicholas has devised a system of self-incorporating that allows entrepreneurs to avoid the legal fees and confusion of incorporation. The book detailing this system, <u>How To Form Your Own Corporation Without A Lawyer For Under $75.00</u>, is now in its 20th anniversary edition, just released by Enterprise • Dearborn ($19.95). With over 900,000 copies in print, the bestseller has helped thousands learn how quick, easy and inexpensive the process can be.

.../

In clear language, the book details the many benefits to incorporating, including:
- Tax-deductible automobiles and meals
- Medical insurance
- Limited personal liability
- Improved access to raising capital
- Advantages of estate planning techniques

By following simple instructions, readers will learn how to incorporate without a lawyer at minimal cost. A complete set of forms is provided, along with a certificate of incorporation, minutes, by-laws and more. Once incorporated, business owners will be able to benefit from the many tax- and money-saving ideas Nicholas presents.

<u>How To Form Your Own Corporation Without A Lawyer For Under $75.00</u> ($19.95, 150 pages, 8 1/2 x 11, paperback, ISBN: 0-79310-419-X) is available at local bookstores or from Enterprise • Dearborn, 520 N. Dearborn St., Chicago, IL 60610-4354. Consumers can order the book by calling toll-free 1-800-322-8621. In Illinois, call 312-836-4400 ext. 650.

Dearborn Publishing Group, Inc., under the Enterprise • Dearborn and Upstart imprints, has become one of the nation's premier publishers of small business information resources.

###

Sample Option Notice

Dear Customer:

Thank you for your order. We are sorry to inform you that there will be a delay in shipping the merchandise you ordered. We shall make shipment by the revised shipping date of (   ). It is quite possible we could ship earlier.

You have the right to consent to this delay or to cancel your order and receive a prompt refund. Please return this letter in the enclosed postpaid envelope with your instructions indicated by checking the appropriate block below.

Unless we hear from you prior to shipment or prior to *the revised shipping date*, it will be assumed that you have consented to a delayed shipment on or before the definite revised shipping date stated above.

Sincerely yours,

Name & Title of Signer
Company Name
Address

Enclosure: Envelope

☐ Yes, I will accept a further delay in shipment of my order for this item until _____
(Insert date which is 30 days or less.)

☐ I cannot wait. Please cancel my order for this item and promptly refund my money.

_____
Please Sign Here

Sample Renewed Option Notice

Dear Customer:

We are sorry to inform you that there will be a further delay in shipping the merchandise you ordered. We shall make shipment by *(new definite revised shipping date)*. It is quite possible we could ship earlier.

You have the right to consent to a further delay or to cancel your order and receive a prompt refund. Please return this letter in the enclosed postpaid envelope with your instructions indicated by checking the appropriate block below.

Unless we hear from you prior to the old shipping date to which you previously agreed, it will be assumed that you have rejected any further shipping delay and your order will be canceled and a prompt refund made.

Sincerely yours,

Name & Title of Signer
Company Name
Address

Enclosure: Envelope

☐ Yes, I will accept a delay in shipment of my order for this item until _____
(Insert date which is 30 days or less.)

☐ I cannot wait. Please cancel my order for this item and promptly refund my money.

_____
Please Sign Here

Afterword

I hope you've both enjoyed and benefited from this book. I'd welcome comments from you at any time.

People often ask if I'm available for copywriting, marketing consulting or provision of advertising agency services through my company. Others ask if I am interested in marketing products and services for others or doing joint ventures.

There is no single answer to these questions. If I feel that there is a good *fit* between myself and another, philosophically and through their product or service, it is certainly possible.

I also do seminars and would be happy to provide you with a schedule.

You may write to me at:
Nicholas Direct
Dept. GM1
19918 Gulf Blvd. Unit 7
Indian Shores, FL 34635
Fax: (813) 596-6900

Index

A

account executive, 5
ad agency, xi
ad insert, 129
ad size, 77
ad, xii
add-on offers, 60
add-on products, 56
add-ons, 38
address changes, 5
Address Correction Requested, 5, 167
advertising, xi
Advertising Age, 69
advertising agency, xvii
age, 76
American Express, 18
anecdotes, 103
Anheuser-Busch, 68
appealing, 39
art, xiv, 122
artist, 39, 92
artwork, 146
associations, 75
attention, 62, 101
attention-getters, 132
audited circulation figures, 87
Austrian economics, 26
average family income, 3
Ayer Directory of Yearbooks, 48

B

back-end promotion, 62
bad debts, 97, 183
bait and switch, 180
Banana Republic, 66
banker's flap, 159
Bartko, Max, 92
base list, 4
benefits, xii, xvii, 21, 39
best customers, 5
Bewley, Stuart, 68
bill inserts, 83
bill-me-later option, 183
billboard, xvi
billing, 7
binding, 158
bleeds, 89
Bloomingdale's, 18, 26, 27, 54
Bloomingdale's by Mail, 27
bluelines, 159
Boardroom Reports, 10
boastful headline, 114
body copy, 121
Bon Appetit, 2
book clubs, 97
booklet envelopes, 159
bounce-back orders, 13
bouncebacks, 60, 134
brainstorming sessions, 15
break-even chart, 47
break-even point, 49
breakthrough concept, 15
broadsides, 3
brochure, xvii, 148
Brookstone, 18
Building a Mail Order Business, 30
bulk-rate, 69
business plan, 30
business reply envelope, 81
business segments, 60
Business Week, xvii
buy-outs, 54
buy-sell agreement, 182
buying behavior, 45
buying decisions, 26
buying habits, 12, 57

C

cable television, 71
California Cooler, 68
call to action, xiv

camera-ready art, 156
campaign, xii
Campbell's Soup, 71
capital assets, 84
capital risks, 50
Caples, John, 118
captions, 149
card decks, 56, 81
careers, xix
Carlson, Len, 69
cash discount, 38
cash flow, 162
catalog sales, 2
catalogs, 10, 81, 130
Census Bureau, 76
centers of influence, 67
character traits, xxi
cheshire labels, 87
circulars, 148
city dwellers, 76
classified ad, 5, 73
classified display ad, 73
clean lists, 166
cluster analysis, 78
Coca-Cola, 71
Coca-Cola Company, 12
coding, 5, 84
Cohen, William, 30
collating, 158
color, 89, 146, 149
color separations, 153
combination offer, 180
command headlines, 115
Commerce Clearing House, 10
commercial envelope, 159
commissions, 85
commitment, 5
common cost cutting mistakes, 128
company name, 8
comparisons, 80
competition, xii, xiii
compiled lists, 76
complaints, 164
compositor, 156
CompuServe, 91
computer, xii, 3, 166
computer databases, 30, 75
computer-generated letters, 70
computer service, 167
confidence, xv, 54
confidentiality contracts, 182
Constitutional Law, xix
consumer publications, 10
continuous free offer, 180
controls, xix
conversion, 56
copy testing, 37
Copyright Office, 30, 31
copyrighting, 30, 31
copywriter, xii
copywriter's questionnaire, 104
Cosmopolitan, 9
cost-cutting guidelines, 153
costs per thousand (CPM), 45
country dwellers, 76
coupon, 39, 89
coupon response, xiv
creativity, xii
credit policies, 183
Crete, Michael, 68
cross promotion, 66
curiosity headlines, 116
customer list, 84
customer rating grid, 85
customer's point of view, 7
customers, xix
cut and paste, 156
cyclical sales, 22

D

damaged goods, 54
decoy names, 86
demographic, 76
depreciate, 84
design, 146
detail, xxi
Direct Marketing News, 92
direct delivery, 68
direct impression, 70
direct mail, xii
direct mail campaigns, xii
direct mail letters, 81
direct mail package, xxi, 129
direct mail piece, 128
direct marketing, xi

direct response, 9
direct response advertising, xi
direct response copy, xii
discontinued products, 31
discounts, 38
dollar amount, 5, 85
dollar volume, 14
door-to-door, 70
door-to-door surveys, 11
double-your-money-back guarantee, 70
dreams, xxi
drop shipped, 161
Drucker, Peter, 20
dry testing, 181
dummy, 156
Dun's Review, xvii

E

economic forecasting, 25
economies of scale, 59
Edgar B Furniture Plantation, 28
800 number, 36
electronic catalog, 3, 83
electronic mail, 91
electronic media, 3, 89
emotional appeal, 132
emotional headlines, 115
emotional need, 17, 102
Enterprise • Dearborn, 88, 188, 191
Enterprise Publishing, xv, 50, 98, 100, 106, 122, 124, 169
entertaining style, 21
entrepreneur, 2
entrepreneurism, 25
envelope sizes, 8
excitement, xii
exclusive representative, 12
expenses, 41
expires, 76

F

factor analysis, 78
fair trade laws, 8
featured benefit headline, 114
features, xvii
Federal Communications Commission (FCC), 54
federal excise tax, 8
Federal Trade Commission (FTC), 1, 8
fidelity bonding coverage, 182
finishers, 159
first draft, 105
first-class mail, 69
flexography, 156
flyers, 148
focus group, 11
folding, 158
follow-up sales, 60
Food and Drug Administration, 8
Forbes, 80
forecasting, 41
foreign goods, 14
form letters, 163
Fortune, xvii
Franklin, Benjamin, xx
free gift, 38, 151
frequency, 5, 85
front-end promotion, 62
fulfilling orders, 12, 161
fulfillment, 162
fulfillment house, 167
full-page ads, xvii
fundraising, 3, 62

G

Gallo, 68
gathered, 157
GEICO Insurance, 106
General Motors, 84
gifts, 38
goal, xxi
Good Housekeeping, 3
good-better-best offer, 55
government publications, 30
graphic designer, 39
graphics, 122, 146
grid method, 149
guarantee, 38, 181
gutter, 152

H

habits, 75
halftones, 156

Halbert, Gary, 69
Hauptman, Don, 103
Haverhill's, 10, 41
headline, xiv
Headline and Teaser Technique Checklist, 112
Henniker's, 10, 41
Home Shopping Network, 71
How To Form Your Own Corporation Without a Lawyer For Under $75, xv, 100
Human Engineering Laboratories, xix
human interest, 103
humanistic forms of management, 26

I

IBM, 71
ideas, 29
illustration, 122
imagination, 4
improving the offer, 222
Inc. Magazine, 70
information headlines, 117
inner characteristics, 77
inner need, 17, 102
innovation, 17
Innovation and Entrepreneurship, 20
inquiries, 77
insert, 128
insertion cards, 89
Inside the Leading Mail Order Houses, 18
insurance, 3, 181
interest-creating devices, 123
introductory offer, 38, 57
inventory, 161
inventory control, xii
Ivory Soap, 71

J

J.C. Penney's, 3
J.E. Miller Nurseries, Inc., 61
job specifications, 159
Joffe, Gerardo, 41
JS & A, 20
just in time inventory, 162

K

K mart, 3, 54
key man policy, 182

L

labels, 70
Lands' End, 66
laser printer, 70
layouts, 146
lead, xiv, 121
leading, 156
learning, xix
LeBarron, Dennis S., 103
legal and ethical issues, 176
letter, xiv
letterpress, 155
license, 8
Life, 2
list broker, 75, 86
list compilers, 86
list management, xii
list managers, 57
list rental, 167
lithography, 155
L.L. Bean, 26, 27
local manufacturers, 31
logo, 122
logotype, 122
Look, 2
loss leaders, 13, 54
lost or damaged goods, 163
Lyndon Johnson, President, xv

M

Macy's-by-Mail, 3
Made in Europe, 14
magazines, xii, 75, 83
magnetic tape, 87
mail, 3
Mail Order Product Evaluation Form, 32
Mail Order Rule, 1
mailroom, 167
mail stuffer, 67
mailing lists, 75
managing production, 153
market, 1
market-driven, 1
marketing consultant, xiii
marketing costs, 54
marketing mix, 27
marketing questionnaire, xxi

Marketing to Win, 71
Marlboro Man, 53
Mars, Inc., 41
match code, 166
McCann-Erickson, xi
mechanical, 156
media, xiv, 81
medical goods, 31
Memo to Mailers, 168
merge and purge, 78
me-you statements, 124
milk, 55
milking, 55
Miller Lite, 44
money-back guarantees, 37
Montgomery Ward, 3
multiple choice society, 26

N

name identification, 83
narrative, 102
National Geographic, 2
National Geographic Society, The, 70
National Technical Information Service, 30
negative option, 179
Neiman-Marcus, 54, 71
new customers, 14
new markets, 59
new products, xii, 59
New York Times, The, xix, 100
news headline, 113
Newsletter Yearbook, 30
newsletters, 27
newspaper inserts, 74
newspapers, xix, 77, 83
niche, 52, 53
Nicholas's Copy Mistake Checklist, 105
no money down, xvi
no-pays, 54
no-risk trial, 38
nontraditional direct mailers, 27
Nth name, 97

O

objections, 33
offer, xii, xiv, 1, 9, 117
offer headlines, 117

Official Gazette, The, 17
offset paper, 158
Ogilvy & Mather, 155
Ogilvy on Advertising, 155
Ogilvy, David, 155
one-on-one selling, 75
operational costs, 36
order form, 39, 151, 158
order fulfillment, xii
order size, 59
orders, xxi
outer envelope, 158
outer need, 17
overhead, 47
overhead costs, 54
Oxbridge Directory of Newsletters, 30

P

packaging, 170
Pantone, 157
paper, 196
paper, bond, 157
    book, 158
    coated, 157
    cover, 158
    index, 158
    text, 158
paper overlay, 156
paper supplier, 158
Parade, 102
Passavant, Pierre, 98
Patent and Trademark Office, 30
patent, 17, 30
Pepsi, 125
permit, 8
personalized items, 36
Peterson's House of Fudge, xv
philosophy, xix
phone, 3
photo, 122
photostat, 156
picas, 156
Point of Difference, 102
point of purchase display, 170
point system, 57
positioning, 41, 44
positive skeptics, 25
postage-paid envelope, 39

Postal Bulletin, 8
postal regulations, 8
power of repetition, 126
practice, xix
prediction headlines, 119
premiums, 170
prep costs, 155
presort, 168
press release, 175
pressmen, 159
Pretty Neat Industries, Inc., 70
price, 9
pricing, 12
pricing strategies, 54
pricing theories, 34
print ads, 3
printers, 153
printing, 153
private delivery firms, 73
private sale, 27
Procter & Gamble, 74
product, 1, 9
product features, 59
product name, 122
production, xiv, 155
production cost, 152
professional association, 67
profit margin, 14
profit strategies, 55
profit worksheet, 79
profit, 12, 45, 53
profit-loss statement, 99
project fee, 7
promotion, 59, 60
promotional offers, 10
proofs, 159
prospect needs, 102
psychographics, 77
psychology, xvii
psychology of selling, xii
public relations, 169, 222
purchase order, 159

Q

Quaker Oats, 18
qualify, 101
quality, 10

quality guarantees, 12
questionnaire, 11

R

radio, 83, 91
radio and TV talk shows, 172
rate card, 87
RCA, 71
Reader's Digest, xix, 114
Reality in Advertising, 101
reason-why copy, 125
recency, 5, 85
Recency-Frequency-Dollar Amount Model, 84
records, 41
Reeves, Rosser, 101
refunds, 54, 96
register, 157
renting lists, 85
repeat business, 28
repeat customers, 3
reply device, 39
research, 10, 40, 103
response records, 1
retesting, 97
Return Postage Guaranteed, 5
returned goods, 163
returns, 31, 54
revenue, 41
revitalize, 55
rewriting, 105
Ries, Al, 71
roll out, 4
rotogravure, 156
Royal Silk, 9
Runner's World, 2

S

sales, xvii
sales angles, 107
sales cycle, 69
sales force, 3
sales instincts, 86
sales volume, 58
salespeople, xv
Saturday Evening Post, The, 2
screen printing, 156

Sears Roebuck & Co., 2, 44
second color, 158
second draft, 105
secondary market, 170
secondary sales, 60
segment, 76
segmented markets, 12
self-mailers, 56, 81, 129
self-sealing envelopes, 159
selling, xiii
seminars, 169, 170
service, 9
sheet-fed, 157
shippers, 159
signature, 157
skills, xx
skimming, 55
slogan headlines, 117
small business, xvi
Small Business Administration, xv
space ads, 76
specialized magazines, 72
specialized markets, 3
specialized products, 3
specialty catalog, 71
specific audiences, 7
speedreading, xix
split-run, 99
Standard Rate and Data Service, 75
state sales tax, 8
Stone and Adler, 69
Stone, Bob, 69
strategic planning, xii
strengths, xx
stuffers, 83, 128
subheads, 121
Successful Meetings, 29
suffering points, 102
Sugarman, Joseph, 20-22, 189, 190
Sunset House, 69
suppliers, 10, 161
surveys, 95, 179
Sussman, Chuck, 70
sweepstakes, 38

T

taxes, 181
teaser, 101
telemarketing, 3, 83, 175
television, 71, 83
test, 1, 4
test responses, xxi
testimonial ads, 118
testimonial letters, 150
testimonials, 103, 126
testing, xx, 92
theft, 182
third-class mailings, 5
third-party influence selling, 125
Thomas Register of American Manufacturers, 14
Time, xvii, 83
Time-Life, 70
Timex, 125
toll-free number, 21, 83
tracking system, 58
trade, 85
trade journals, 10
trade out, 89
Trade Shows and Professional Exhibits Directory, 30
Tradeshow/Convention Guide, 74
trade shows, 10, 68
trademarks, 30
traditional values, 26
trends, 25
trick headline, 116
trimming, 158
Trout, Jack, 72
trust, 39, 102
two-step mailings, 56
type, 146, 156
typefaces, 102
typestyle, 146
typos, 160

U

Ultimate Tax Shelter, The, xvii
uncollectible bills, 54
uncovering needs, 12
undeliverable addresses, 76
Unique Selling Proposition, 101
unique benefits, 7
Uniqueness Test, 51
United Parcel Service, 73
U.S. News & World Report, xvii
U.S. Patent Office, 17

U.S. Postal system, 3
urgency, 125
use taxes, 181

V

velox, 156
videotext, 83, 121
Viguerie Company, Inc., 62
Virginia Slims, 53

W

Wall Street Journal, The, xvii
wallet flap, 159
warranty, 181
Washington Post, The, xix

web-fed, 157
White House, xv
Who's Mailing What!, 103
Williams, Bill, 70
window envelopes, 159
worksheets, xiv
writer, xvii
writing style, 103
writing, xvii

XYZ

Xerox, 71
Yankee Trader, 66
You messages, 102
zip codes, 3, 76

About the Author

Ted Nicholas is a multifaceted business personality. In addition to being a well-known author and respected speaker, Mr. Nicholas remains an active participant in his own entrepreneurial ventures.

Without capital, Ted Nicholas started his first business at the age 21. Since then, he has started 22 companies of his own.

Author of the critically acclaimed *How To Form Your Own Corporation Without a Lawyer for Under $75,* Mr. Nicholas has written 13 books on business and finance since his writing career began in 1972. Mr. Nicholas's enterprises have included Peterson's House of Fudge—a candy and ice cream manufacturing business conducted through 30 retail stores—and other food, franchising, machinery and real estate businesses.

When only 29 years old, he was selected by a group of business leaders as one of the most outstanding businessmen in the nation and invited to the White House to meet the President.

Although Mr. Nicholas has founded many successful enterprises, he has experienced two major setbacks and many minor ones. He considers setbacks necessary to success because they are the only true way to learn anything in life. That's why he teaches entrepreneurs his philosophy of how to *fail forward*.

Mr. Nicholas has appeared on numerous television and radio shows and conducts business seminars in Florida and Switzerland. Presently, he owns and operates four corporations of his own and acts as a marketing consultant and copywriter to businesses of all sizes.

How Ted Can Help You Build Wealth With His Monthly Newsletter On Direct Marketing

Imagine getting the inside information on the very latest direct marketing breakthroughs each and every month!

Ted Nicholas writes a monthly newsletter, entitled *The Ted Nicholas Letter*, available exclusively to his subscribers. Here are a few of the areas he covers:

- **The hottest new product ideas and how they can be profitably marketed**
- **The latest trends and how to cash in on them in both new product development and copy**
- **The most productive new mailing lists**
- **The magazines that pay out best for your ads**
- **Places to get free advertising and publicity**
- **Invaluable contacts to help your direct marketing business grow**
- **New copywriting discoveries that work**

A yearly subscription to *The Ted Nicholas Letter* is only $195.00, tax deductible. And you have an unconditional money-back guarantee. If at any time you wish to cancel your subscription, you will receive a refund on all remaining issues. To place your credit card order, subscribe by calling (813) 596-4966. Or, send a check to Nicholas Direct, Inc., 19918 Gulf Blvd., Unit 7, Indian Shores FL 34635.